AN ILLUSTRATED WORLD HISTORY

I

PREHISTORY AND THE ANCIENT WORLD

Also available in this series:

II

The Middle Ages and the Renaissance

III

Revolution and Empire

IV

The Modern World

PREHISTORY AND THE ANCIENT WORLD
was created and produced by
McRae Publishing Ltd, London
www.mcraepublishing.co.uk

Publishers: Anne McRae, Marco Nardi
Series Editor: Anne McRae
Authors: Neil Morris, Neil Grant, Tony Allan, Sean Connolly
Art Director: Marco Nardi
Layouts: Rebecca Milner
Project Editor: Loredana Agosta
Research: Valerie Meek, Claire Moore, Loredana Agosta
Repro: Litocolor, Florence

The Publishers of *An Illustrated World History* would like to thank all the authors and consultants who have participated in the elaboration of the text and the supervision of the illustrations created for this work.

Chapter I - **Prehistory**
Author: NEIL MORRIS
Consultants: Dr. IAN TATTERSALL, Curator of the Department of Anthropology at the American Museum of Natural History and Adjunct Professor of Anthropology at Columbia University.
Dr. KEN MOWBRAY, Curatorial Associate of the Department of Anthropology at the American Museum of Natural History.

Chapter II - **Mesopotamia and the Bible Lands**
Author: NEIL MORRIS
Consultants: Dr. DOMINIQUE COLLON and DR. IRVING L. FINKEL, Assistant Keepers, Department of the Ancient Near East, British Museum.

Chapter III - **Ancient Egypt and Greece**
Author: NEIL GRANT
Consultants: DR. AIDAN M. DODSON, FSA, Research Fellow, Department of Archeology and Anthropology, University of Bristol.
DR. MONICA BERTI, Research Fellow, Department of History, University of Turin.

Chapter IV - **The Roman World**
Author: TONY ALLAN
Consultant: DR. SIMON JAMES, Senior Lecturer in Archeology at the School of Archeology and Ancient History, University of Leicester.

Chapter V - **Asian Civilizations**
Author: NEIL MORRIS
Consultants: DR. ALFREDO CADONNA, University of Ca' Foscari, Venice, Italy.
DR. GREGORY POSSEHL, Professor of Archeology, Department of Anthropology, University of Pennsylvania, and Curator of the Asian Section, University of Pennsylvania Museum of Archeology and Anthropology.

Chapter VI - **The Americas and the Pacific**
Author: SEAN CONNOLLY
Consultants: MICHAEL JOHNSON, leading expert on Native Americans.
DR. JEFFREY QUILTER, Deputy Director for Curatorial Affairs, Peabody Museum of Archeology and Ethnology, Harvard University.
DR. PETER BELLWOOD, Professor of Archeology, School of Archeology and Anthropology, Australian National University.

An Imprint of Sterling Publishing
387 Park Avenue South
New York, NY 10016

This 2014 edition published by Sandy Creek.

ISBN 978-1-4351-5435-3

Manufactured in Hong Kong
Lot #:
2 4 6 8 10 9 7 5 3 1
02/14

AN ILLUSTRATED WORLD
HISTORY

PREHISTORY AND THE ANCIENT WORLD

Sandy Creek
NEW YORK

Contents

The Roman World 122–157

Asian Civilizations 158–195

The Americas and the Pacific 196–233

Glossary & Index 234–240

The term "prehistory" refers to the history of the world from its very beginnings up until the time when our ancestors first started keeping written records. Life began in the warm waters of the Earth and followed a succession of different forms, from single-celled animals through dinosaurs to the first mammals. They were followed by the first human-like creatures, called hominids, who learned to use tools and control the use of fire. After modern humans first appeared more than 130,000 years ago, they gradually colonized the planet and dominated its resources.

Some hunter-gatherer groups eventually took up farming and began to settle in one place. As their numbers grew, these prehistoric people were able to devote some of their time to art, religion, and trade. Simple settlements grew into impressive cities, leading to the beginning of modern civilization. More than 5,000 years ago, people invented writing systems and started keeping records, marking the end of the prehistoric period.

The long journey toward the modern world began when the first farmers appeared in the Middle East about 10,000 years ago.

CHRONOLOGY

THIS BOOK SHOWS DATES AS RELATED TO THE CONVENTIONAL BEGINNING OF OUR ERA, OR THE YEAR 1, UNDERSTOOD AS THE YEAR OF THE BIRTH OF JESUS CHRIST. ALL EVENTS DATING BEFORE THIS YEAR ARE LISTED AS BCE (BEFORE CURRENT ERA). EVENTS DATING AFTER THE YEAR 1 ARE DEFINED AS CE (CURRENT ERA).

EARTH'S HISTORY

Era	Period	Events
Precambrian	Hadean 4.6–3.8 billion years ago	The Earth forms as a molten mass.
	Archean 3.8–2.6 billion years ago	The Earth cools and the first forms of life appear.
	Proterozoic 2.6 billion–590 million years ago	Multi-celled animals appear, including trilobites.
Palaeozoic	Cambrian 590–505 million years ago	Jellyfish, sponges and shelled animals live in shallow seas.
	Ordovician 505–434 million years ago	The Earth's land mass is made up of one supercontinent, Pangaea. Mollusks, starfish, and corals are abundant in the seas.
	Silurian 434–408 million years ago	The Earth's temperature stabilizes and plants appear on land. Fish develop jaws.
	Devonian 408–354 million years ago	Fish dominate sea life; amphibians and insects appear on land.
	Carboniferous 354–286 million years ago	Reptiles appear; large swampy forests cover the land; there are giant flying insects.
	Permian 286–248 mya	Mammal-like reptiles and seed plants appear, with conifers dominant. Mass extinction at the end of the Permian.

HUMAN HISTORY

	7 million years ago	**5 million years ago**	**3 million years ago**
EARLY HOMINIDS	*Sahelanthropus tchadensis*; *Orrorin tugenensis*	*Australopithecus anamensis*; *Australopithecus afarensis*	*Australopithecus africanus*; *Homo erectus*; *Homo habilis*; *Paranthropus aethiopicus*; *Homo ergaster*; *Homo rudolfensis*; *Paranthropus boisei*
MODERN HUMANS			

Prehistory

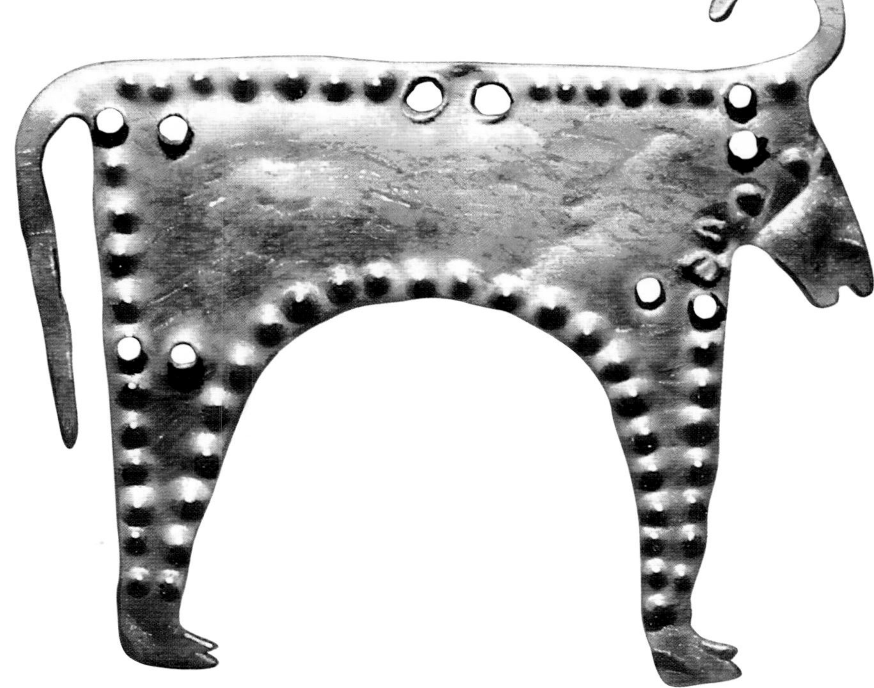

The earliest metal objects, dating from around 5000 BCE, were produced by hammering. These golden bull ornaments were found at a grave site in Bulgaria.

aeon	**Phanerozoic**									
era	Mesozoic			Cenozoic						
period	Triassic 248–213 million years ago	Jurassic 213–144 million years ago	Cretaceous 144–66.4 million years ago	Tertiary					Quaternary	
epoch	The first dinosaurs, flying reptiles and mammal-like tetrapods appear.	Dinosaurs flourish. The first birds and mammal-like creatures appear. Pangaea begins to break apart.	The first mammals and flowering plants appear. By the end of the Cretaceous the continents (except for Australia) are separate land masses.	Paleocene 66.4–58 million years ago	Eocene 58–36.7 million years ago	Oligocene 36.7–23.5 million years ago	Miocene 23.5–5.3 million years ago	Pliocene 5.3–1.8 million years ago	Pleistocene 1.8 million–10,000 years ago	Holocene 10,000 years ago–present
				Dinosaurs and other kinds of animals die out. First primates appear.	Early horses and camels appear.	Primates develop.	The earliest hominids, human-like creatures, develop.	Hominids make tools.	Spread of modern humans. Glaciers of the Great Ice Age cover much of the Earth's land mass.	

1 million years ago	**8000 BCE**	**6000 BCE**	**4000 BCE**	**2000 BCE**
Homo neanderthalensis				
Homo sapiens				
	Farming begins in Mesopotamia.	Farming begins in southern Europe and in the Indus Valley.	Farming begins in Central America.	Chinese use pictographs.
	Foundation of Çatal Hüyük.	Megalithic monuments are built in Europe.	Egyptians use hieroglyphics. Villages appear in South America.	Minoans begin to write.

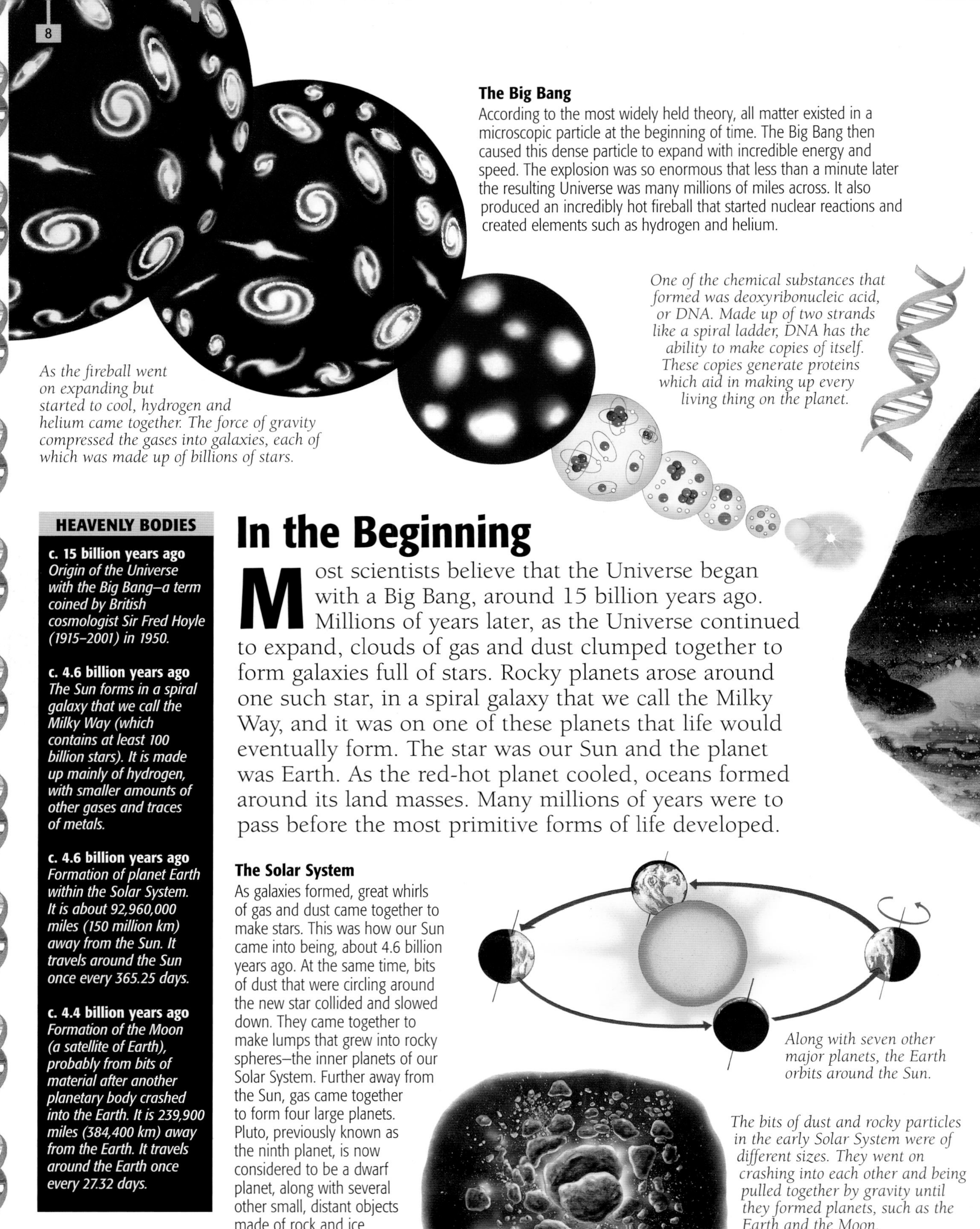

The Big Bang

According to the most widely held theory, all matter existed in a microscopic particle at the beginning of time. The Big Bang then caused this dense particle to expand with incredible energy and speed. The explosion was so enormous that less than a minute later the resulting Universe was many millions of miles across. It also produced an incredibly hot fireball that started nuclear reactions and created elements such as hydrogen and helium.

One of the chemical substances that formed was deoxyribonucleic acid, or DNA. Made up of two strands like a spiral ladder, DNA has the ability to make copies of itself. These copies generate proteins which aid in making up every living thing on the planet.

As the fireball went on expanding but started to cool, hydrogen and helium came together. The force of gravity compressed the gases into galaxies, each of which was made up of billions of stars.

In the Beginning

Most scientists believe that the Universe began with a Big Bang, around 15 billion years ago. Millions of years later, as the Universe continued to expand, clouds of gas and dust clumped together to form galaxies full of stars. Rocky planets arose around one such star, in a spiral galaxy that we call the Milky Way, and it was on one of these planets that life would eventually form. The star was our Sun and the planet was Earth. As the red-hot planet cooled, oceans formed around its land masses. Many millions of years were to pass before the most primitive forms of life developed.

HEAVENLY BODIES

c. 15 billion years ago
Origin of the Universe with the Big Bang—a term coined by British cosmologist Sir Fred Hoyle (1915–2001) in 1950.

c. 4.6 billion years ago
The Sun forms in a spiral galaxy that we call the Milky Way (which contains at least 100 billion stars). It is made up mainly of hydrogen, with smaller amounts of other gases and traces of metals.

c. 4.6 billion years ago
Formation of planet Earth within the Solar System. It is about 92,960,000 miles (150 million km) away from the Sun. It travels around the Sun once every 365.25 days.

c. 4.4 billion years ago
Formation of the Moon (a satellite of Earth), probably from bits of material after another planetary body crashed into the Earth. It is 239,900 miles (384,400 km) away from the Earth. It travels around the Earth once every 27.32 days.

The Solar System

As galaxies formed, great whirls of gas and dust came together to make stars. This was how our Sun came into being, about 4.6 billion years ago. At the same time, bits of dust that were circling around the new star collided and slowed down. They came together to make lumps that grew into rocky spheres—the inner planets of our Solar System. Further away from the Sun, gas came together to form four large planets. Pluto, previously known as the ninth planet, is now considered to be a dwarf planet, along with several other small, distant objects made of rock and ice.

Along with seven other major planets, the Earth orbits around the Sun.

The bits of dust and rocky particles in the early Solar System were of different sizes. They went on crashing into each other and being pulled together by gravity until they formed planets, such as the Earth and the Moon.

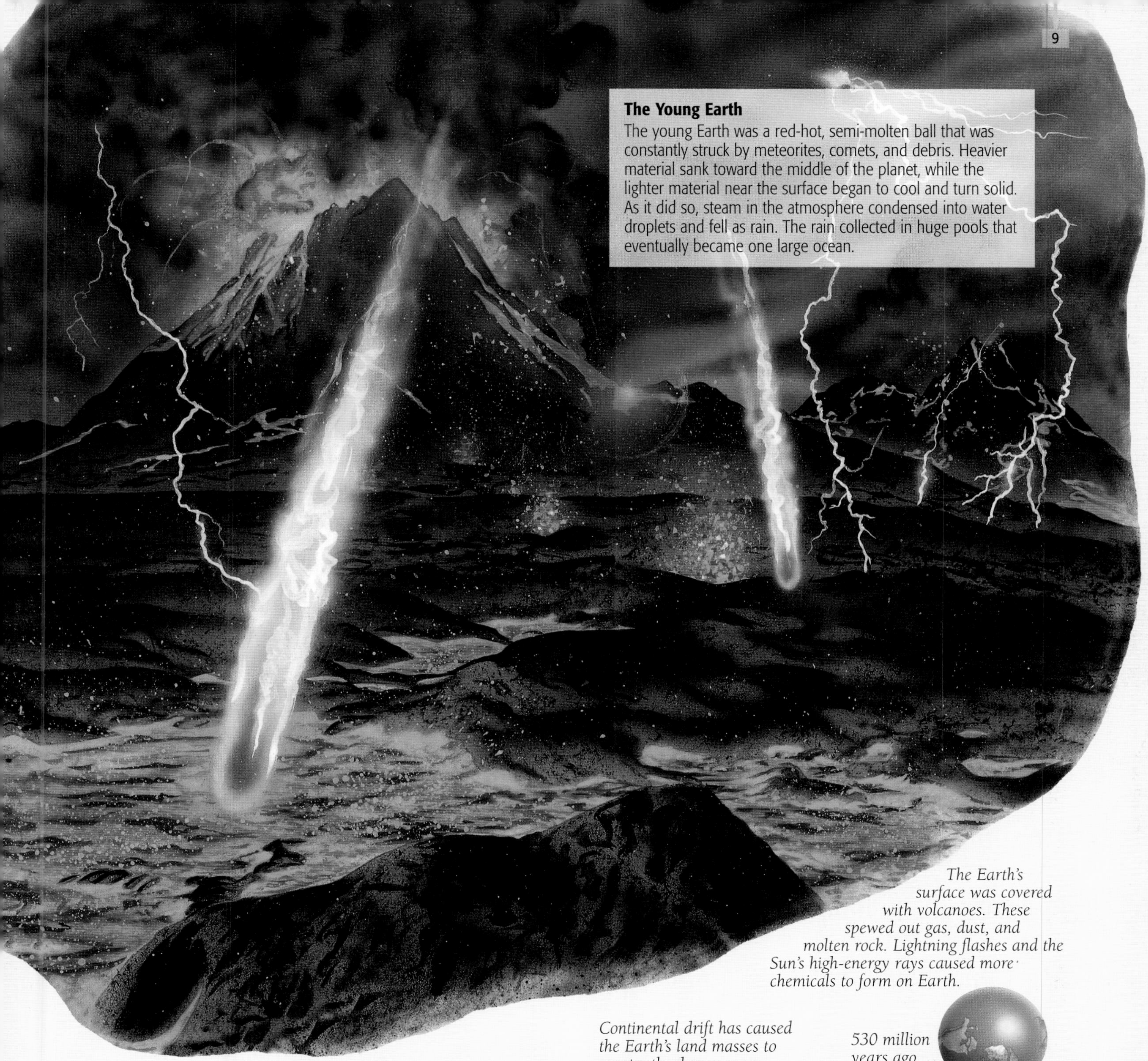

The Young Earth

The young Earth was a red-hot, semi-molten ball that was constantly struck by meteorites, comets, and debris. Heavier material sank toward the middle of the planet, while the lighter material near the surface began to cool and turn solid. As it did so, steam in the atmosphere condensed into water droplets and fell as rain. The rain collected in huge pools that eventually became one large ocean.

The Earth's surface was covered with volcanoes. These spewed out gas, dust, and molten rock. Lightning flashes and the Sun's high-energy rays caused more chemicals to form on Earth.

Continental drift has caused the Earth's land masses to constantly change over millions of years.

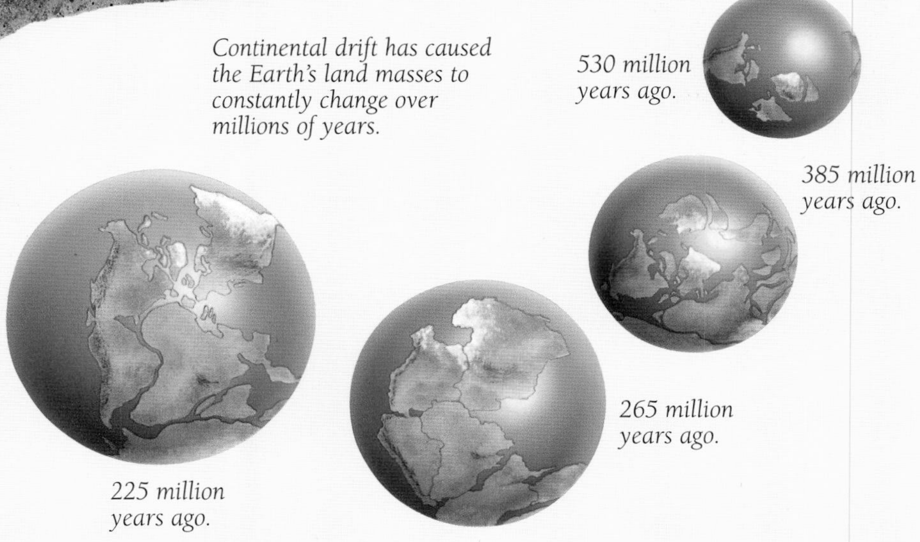

530 million years ago.

385 million years ago.

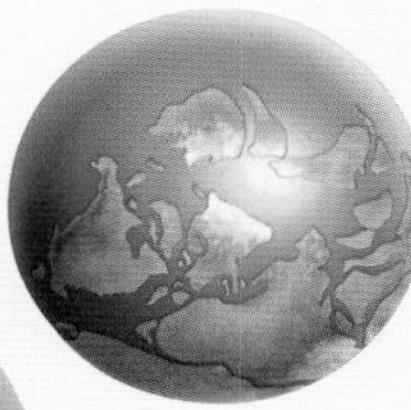

265 million years ago.

225 million years ago.

Continental Drift

The Earth's crust, or solid outer layer, is cracked into huge pieces, called plates. Hundreds of millions of years ago, the continental plates that made up the Earth's land began drifting together. By about 265 million years ago they had joined up to form a single supercontinent called Pangaea. Then, around 200–225 million years ago, the supercontinent began to break up and land masses slowly started moving apart. This slow movement, called continental drift, still continues today.

Early Forms of Life

The first long span of geological time, which we call the Precambrian eon, covers more than 4 billion years, or nearly nine-tenths of the whole history of the Earth. The planet's oceans, continents, and atmosphere changed considerably during that enormous time span. Simple, single-celled forms of life developed in the warm water and soft mud that were found at the edge of shallow seas. Later, more complex animals developed—also in the sea—until there was an explosion of life during the Cambrian period. By the end of this period, about 500 million years ago, the shallow seas were teeming with jellyfish, sponges, and the first shelled animals.

Precambrian Beginnings

Earth changed continually during the long Precambrian eon. The solid surface had cooled enough for ice to form, and there were at least three Precambrian ice ages. Nevertheless, a "soup" of chemicals continued to grow in warm shallow seas, leading eventually to the development of the first living cells. These were simple, single-celled organisms similar to the microscopic bacteria that are still alive today. Some forms, known as blue-green algae, gathered together to form mounds called stromatolites.

Stromatolites are created when the sticky mucus produced by blue-green algae traps sand, dust, and chemicals in seawater, forming rings of limestone in the shallow sea. Stromatolites continue to form today off the coast of Australia.

Early Life Forms

During the Precambrian eon, simple organisms such as blue-green algae started using the hydrogen in water and giving off oxygen. This enormous development was the beginning of photosynthesis, the process by which plants produce their own food today. During the last era of the Precambrian eon, the amount of oxygen in the atmosphere started to increase and a large number of different multi-celled, soft-bodied life forms developed.

Fossil of the Spriggina*, a Precambrian worm-like animal, named after the finder of its fossil, the geologist Sir Reginald Sprigg (1919–1994).*

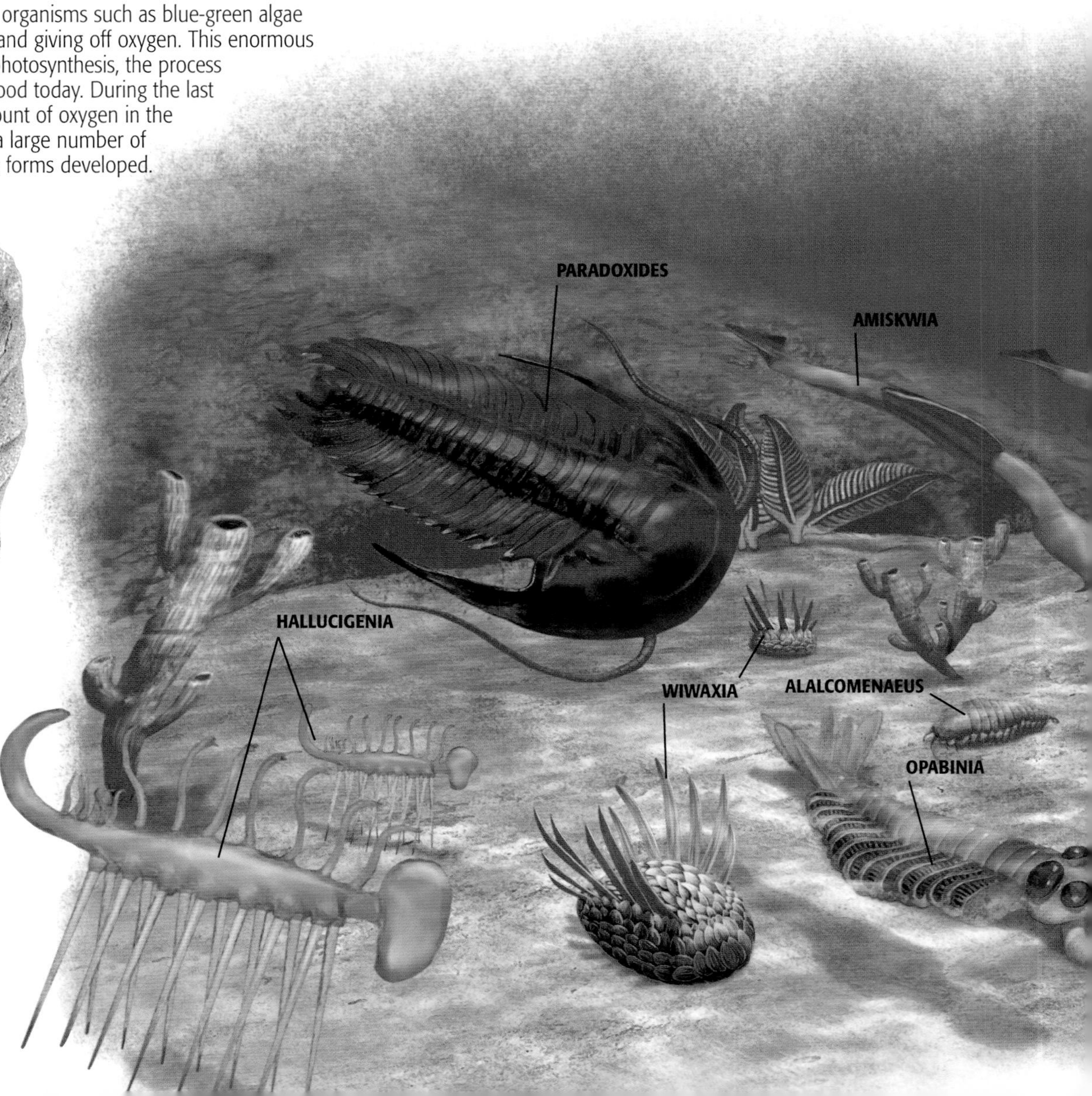

PARADOXIDES
AMISKWIA
HALLUCIGENIA
WIWAXIA
ALALCOMENAEUS
OPABINIA

The Cambrian Explosion

There was an explosion of new life forms early in the Cambrian period. Many of the major groups of animals that we know today appeared at that time. Some of the new life forms developed exoskeletons (shells) to protect their soft bodies. One of the most famous groups was made up of trilobites, which had a flat oval body divided into three sections and large curved eyes. Trilobites lived on the seabed, and some also swam in the waters above. They died out about 245 million years ago.

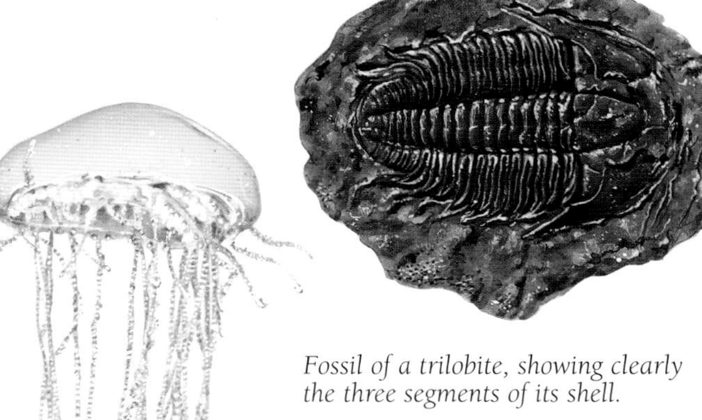

Fossil of a trilobite, showing clearly the three segments of its shell.

The earliest forms of fish, such as this Arandapis, *were covered in bony plates. They had no jaws, no body fins, and no internal bones.*

Different kinds of jellyfish developed in the late Precambrian.

An Extraordinary Discovery

In 1909, fossils of Cambrian life forms were found in a bed of shale (soft rock made of hardened mud) in the Rocky Mountains, in Canada. The fossils in this shale, known as the Burgess shale, revealed the forms of a large number of soft-bodied animals that lived in the warm, shallow, early Cambrian waters of what is now North America. The animals seem to have been buried by a mudslide. Then, over the course of many millions of years, their remains turned into fossils.

GEOLOGICAL TIME

Geological time, or Earth's history, is divided into two eons, the Precambrian and the Phanerozoic (see timeline on pages 4–5). The Phanerozoic eon is divided into three eras–Paleozoic, Mesozoic and Cenozoic–which are further divided into periods. The first period of the Paleozoic era is the Cambrian period. It was named in 1835 by Adam Sedgwick (1785–1873), a Cambridge professor of geology who studied a Welsh layer of shale and sandstone rocks. He referred to them by the Latin name for Wales, Cambria. Everything before that time was then called Precambrian. The Ordovician and Silurian periods were named after ancient Celtic tribes in Wales, because fossils from those times were found there. The Devonian refers to the English county of Devon. The name Carboniferous, given by two British scientists in 1822, refers to the carbon present in rocks of that period. Permian was named after the Perm region of the Ural Mountains in Russia.

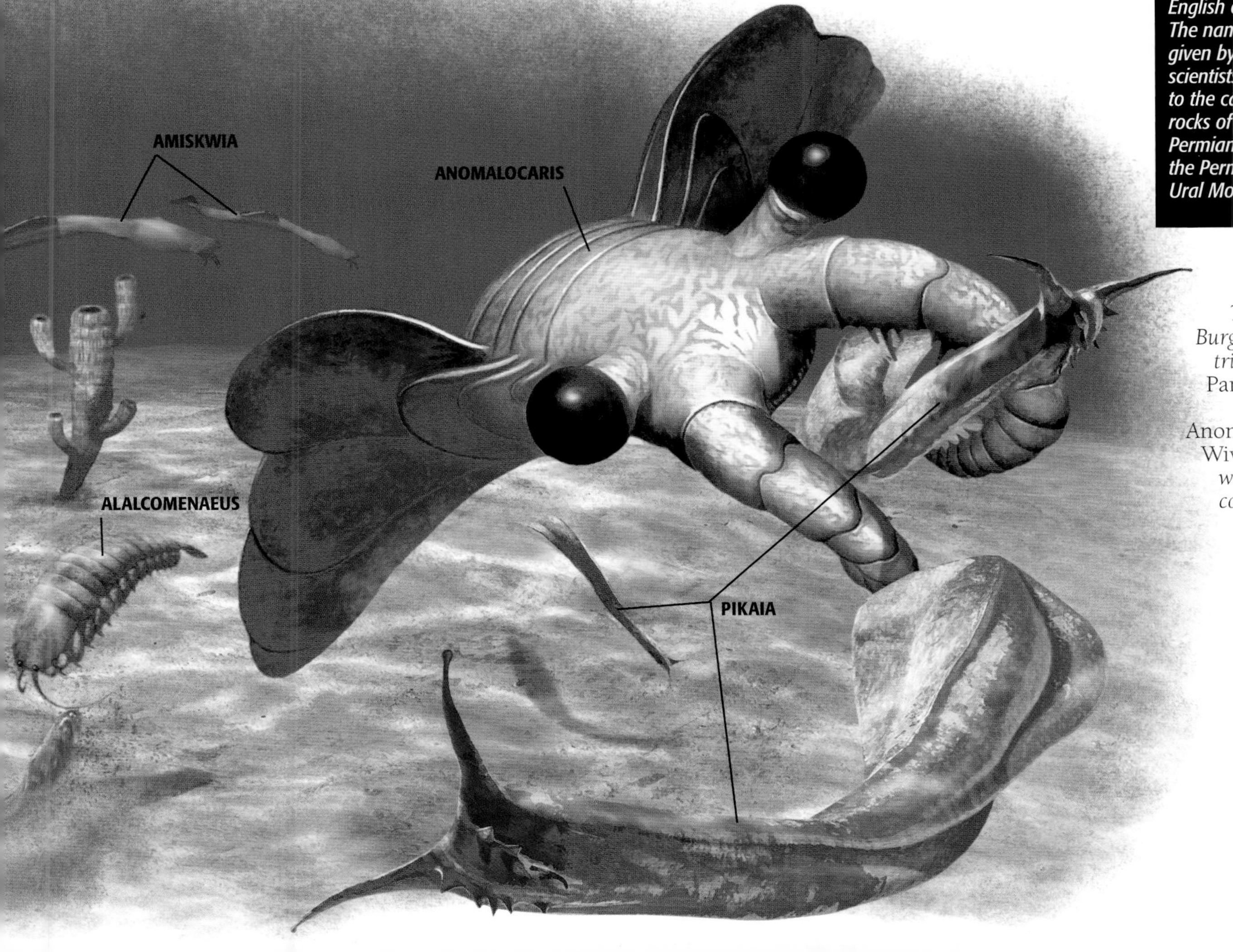

The animals of the Burgess shale included trilobites such as the Paradoxides, *a large predator called* Anomalocaris, *and the* Wiwaxia, *which were worm-like creatures covered with spines.*

Evolution of Species

Life on Earth went though tremendous change during the 250 million years following the Cambrian period. Fish and other marine creatures continued to develop, but the greatest change involved life moving on to land. The first amphibians appeared, to be followed by land-based reptiles, some of which developed features that were similar to the mammals that would follow later. Plants grew on land, and insects spread rapidly as large swampy forests appeared. But just as the number and variety of species increased, there were also great setbacks. These included three periods of mass extinction, the greatest of which occurred at the very end of the Permian period.

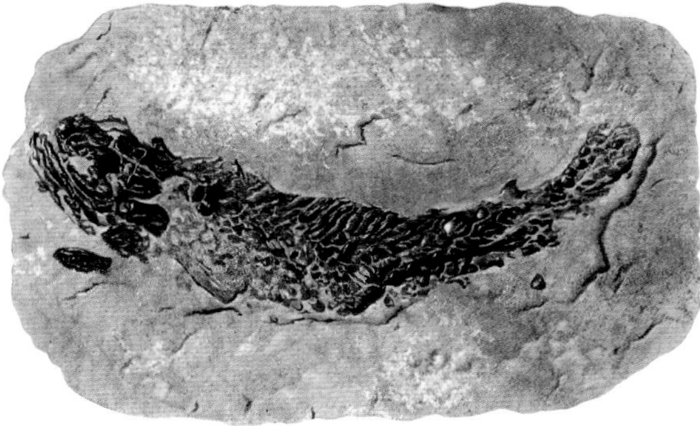

Devonian fossil of a small fish with muscular paired fins.

The Age of Fish

Fish developed jaws and became abundant in freshwater rivers and lakes. They dominated the oceans during the Devonian (408–354 million years ago), a period within the Paleozoic era which is often called the "age of fish." Some early bony fish had fleshy lobed fins, which they used to crawl along the seabed. Other species had rayed fins and were fast swimmers, and these included the first sharks.

Eusthenopteron *was a Devonian fish with paired, lobed fins. It could gulp air and may have pulled itself on to land to move between pools.*

Tree ferns became common during the Carboniferous period.

Early Reptiles

During the late Devonian period, some sea creatures crawled out on to land. These amphibians, like frogs and toads today, were able to lead a "double life" –on land and in water. They were followed by the first reptiles. These were small, lizard-like animals that laid their leathery-shelled eggs on land, whereas amphibians laid their soft eggs in water. The reptiles could spend all their time on land, where spreading forests were helping to increase the amount of oxygen in the atmosphere.

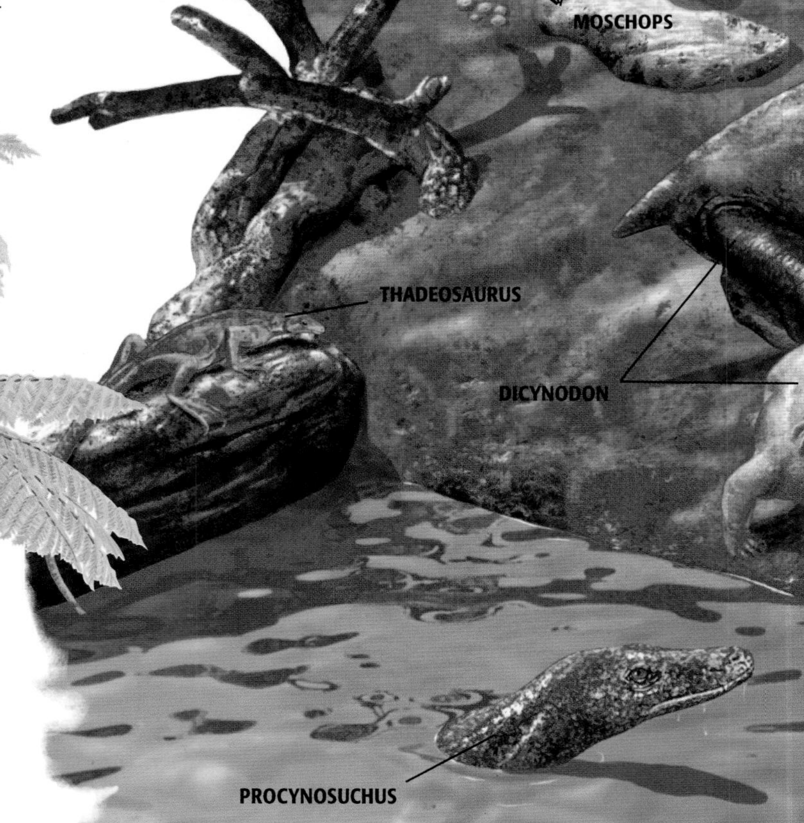

The Permian landscape was dominated by amphibians, reptiles, and mammal-like reptiles. Some were plant-eaters, and the earliest flying reptiles took to the air. Other reptiles, called mesosaurs, *went back to the water.*

Leading to Mammals

During the Permian period, amphibians and reptiles were joined on land by a group of animals that we call mammal-like reptiles. Some were quite small, but others grew as large as a modern rhinoceros. One group, the cynodonts, developed different kinds of teeth and a bony shelf in the roof of the mouth that allowed them to eat and breathe at the same time. Their limbs were more like later mammals, and they may even have had fur to keep them warm.

Forelimb and foot of a mammal-like reptile called a gorgonopsian. Along with many others, these creatures died out at the end of the Permian period.

Skeleton of an Eryops, an amphibian of the Permian period, measuring 6.5 feet (2 m) long. It probably fed mainly in the water, catching fish and smaller amphibians.

Mass Extinction

At the end of the Permian period an enormous number of animals died out –up to 95 percent of those that we know from the fossil record. There had been two earlier mass extinctions, but the Permian was the biggest the Earth has ever known. It almost wiped out the mammal-like reptiles, and more than three-quarters of land-based vertebrates were lost, along with half of all plant species. Even more species became extinct in the sea. Scientists believe a dramatic event caused the mass extinction, such as a gigantic asteroid or comet striking the Earth, or vast volcanic eruptions, which may have led to disastrous changes in global climate and sea levels.

Skeleton of a sail-backed reptile of Permian times. The large crest, or sail, on its back allowed it to heat up and cool down quickly. These animals belong to the group of mammal-like reptiles.

The Age of Dinosaurs

Scientists divide the Mesozoic era, which began about 248 million years ago, into three periods —the Triassic, the Jurassic, and the Cretaceous. Reptiles known as dinosaurs emerged during the first of these periods and dominated life on land for roughly 165 million years, before dying out completely at the end of the era. The dinosaurs were a wide-ranging group of animals. Some were gigantic, others quite small. Some plant-eaters moved around in herds, while most meat-eaters probably hunted alone. At the same time there were many other animals in the air and in the sea.

DINOSAURS IN THE MESOZOIC

Key: dinosaur name, time span, body length, diet, fossil location.

TRIASSIC AGE:
Eoraptor
228 million years ago, 3.3 feet (1 m), meat, Argentina.

Herrerasaurus
228 million years ago, 10 feet (3 m), meat, Argentina.

Coelophysis
225–220 million years ago, 10 feet (3 m), meat, USA.

Plateosaurus
210 million years ago, 23 feet (7 m), plants, Europe.

JURASSIC AGE:
Anchisaurus
190 million years ago, 6.5 feet (2 m), plants, USA.

Megalosaurus
170–155 million years ago, 30 feet (9 m), meat, England.

Apatosaurus
154–145 million years ago, 69 feet (21 m), plants, USA.

Archaeopteryx
147 million years ago, 1.5 feet (50 cm), meat, Germany.

CRETACEOUS AGE:
Iguanodon
140–110 million years ago, 33 feet (10 m), plants, Europe.

Oviraptor
85–75 million years ago, 6 feet (1.8 m), meat and plants, Mongolia.

Hadrosaurus
78–74 million years ago, 30 feet (9 m), plants, USA.

Triceratops
67–65 million years ago, 30 feet (9 m), plants, USA.

Fossilized dinosaur eggs. Female dinosaurs laid leathery, hard-shelled eggs, probably in mud nests or hollows.

What is a Dinosaur?

Though their name means "terrible lizard," dinosaurs were only distantly related to lizards (and many were not very terrible!). Scientists divide them into two groups, according to the structure of their hips. Saurischians, which had hips shaped like those of modern lizards, included herbivores and carnivores. The second and later group, called ornithischians, had hips like a bird's, and were all herbivores. Some dinosaurs walked on four legs, others on two.

Some reptiles took to the air during the late Triassic. The Eudimorphodon *(shown here), had a long tail and a short neck.*

Early Species

The first saurischian dinosaurs emerged during the Triassic period. The earliest were probably all carnivores, such as the bipedal *Coelophysis*. By the end of the period, there were also much larger herbivores, such as the *Riojasaurus*, and dinosaurs were spreading out as the Earth's land masses began drifting apart.

Supremacy on Land

During the Jurassic period dinosaurs flourished and took over the Earth's spreading continents. Ferns, mosses, cycads, and conifers thrived, providing food for the growing number of herbivores. Many herbivores, such as *Diplodocus*, grew very large, providing them with some protection against meat-eating species. Others developed bony plates and other armor. *Stegosaurus* and its cousins had pointed tail spikes, which could inflict damage on any attacking carnivore.

The Tuojiangosaurus, *a plant-eating* stegosaurus, *had a double row of bony plates, armor plating, and a spiked tail.*

The Cretaceous World

The range of dinosaurs continued to grow throughout the Cretaceous period, as the continents continued to drift apart. Great layers of chalk were laid down as the oceans advanced over shallow continental shelves. Marine reptiles, such as *Plesiosaurs*, thrived, and there were flowering plants on land. Some of the most famous dinosaurs came to prominence, such as the fierce carnivorous *Tyrannosaurs* and the duck-billed herbivorous *Hadrosaurs*.

Tyrannosaurus *("tyrant lizard") had a massive skull, immensely powerful jaws, and spiky teeth. It lived at the very end of the Cretaceous age.*

Skeleton of a sauropod's foot, which was wide and stout to carry the weight of such a large, heavy animal.

A giant meteorite or asteroid strike would cause devastation. A vast crater has been found in Mexico, which has been dated to the time of the dinosaurs' extinction.

The End of the Dinosaurs

Around 65 million years ago, at the end of the Mesozoic era, the dinosaurs died out, along with the flying reptiles and many other kinds of animals. This was the fifth mass extinction in Earth's history, following an earlier such event at the end of the Triassic period (and the Permian, see page 13). We can only guess at the cause, but many scientists believe that the planet was struck by a giant meteorite. This would have caused fires and a mass of dust that traveled around the globe, blocking out sunlight for months or even years.

This scene shows a large plant-eating sauropod being attacked by a group of much smaller carnivores. The powerful meat-eaters had very sharp teeth and claws.

MAMMAL FACTS

Mammal Birth
Three different kinds of mammals evolved: monotremes, which lay eggs (e.g. modern platypus); marsupials, which give birth to undeveloped young (e.g. koala); placentals, which give birth to more advanced young (and include most modern mammals).

Mammalian Characteristics
All mammals have a backbone and body hair or fur to keep warm; they are warm-blooded, so keep a constant body temperature; the lower jaw is a single bone, and there are three small bones in the middle ear; females feed young on their own milk; different teeth are shaped for different jobs.

A small Saltopus *dinosaur of the late Triassic has caught a* Morganucodon, *a tiny insect-eater that was one of the first true mammals.*

Skeleton of Mesohippus, *an early three-toed horse that lived during the Oligocene epoch.*

The Age of Mammals

Mammals first appeared during the Mesozoic era, having evolved from the so-called mammal-like reptiles. Their small size and burrowing habits may have helped them survive the events that caused the extinction of the dinosaurs. The mammals went on to thrive during the Tertiary period, which is often called the Age of Mammals. Carnivores, rodents, hoofed animals, elephants, and primates all emerged, adapting well to changing conditions on different continents. As in earlier periods, there was not a straight line of evolution that led from one species to another. Many of the early kinds of mammal died out, and we know of them only from fossil finds.

Early Species

The first, small mammal-like creatures of the late Triassic period (around 213 million years ago) probably lived in dense foliage or burrows and were active only at night. These tiny, shrew-like animals remained small during the rest of the Mesozoic era and fell prey to meat-eating dinosaurs. Nevertheless, more groups of mammals had developed by the time the dinosaurs died out. After their extinction, there was more food available and mammals started coming out in the day. Many groups were egg-laying monotremes, which are represented today by the spiny anteater and platypus of Australia.

This imaginary scene shows a timeline of mammal evolution.

PALEOCENE **EOCENE**

Marsupials

The group of mammals called marsupials give birth to less developed young, which spend their early life in a pouch of skin on their mother's abdomen. The early marsupials spread to most continents during the Eocene epoch, but today almost all of them live in Australia and South America.

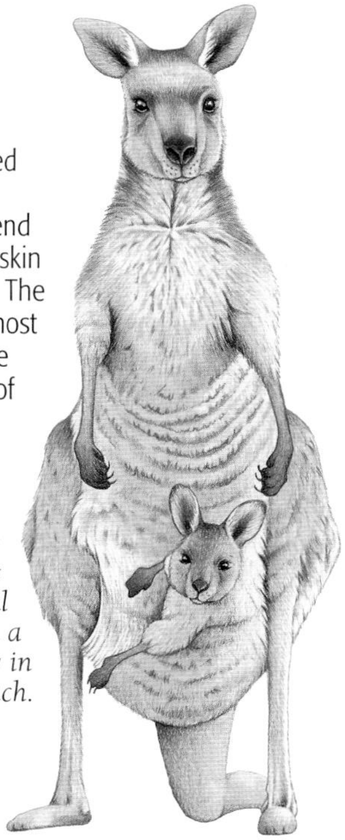

A female kangaroo, one of the marsupial mammals, with a young joey in her pouch.

Wide-Ranging Evolution

Soon after the start of the Tertiary period, mammals started evolving into different shapes and sizes. By the time of the Eocene epoch, the continents were moving to the positions they occupy today. At that time large herbivores emerged, including the ancestors of the camel, horse, and rhinoceros. Among smaller mammals, the first rodents appeared. Mammals even took to the water and the air, in the form of the first whales and bats.

Uintatherium *was an early large herbivore of the Eocene epoch. About the size of a modern rhinoceros, it ate leaves.*

Skeleton of Smilodectes, *a tree-climbing primate that lived about 50 million years ago.*

Primates

The primates (a word meaning "of the first rank") are considered to be the highest order of mammals. Today the group includes prosimians, monkeys, apes, and humans. The earliest primates appeared during the Paleocene epoch, and by about 50 million years ago they had the characteristic features of grasping hands, short snout, eyes at the front of the head, and an enlarged brain area.

Placentals

Placental mammals are much more developed when they are born than marsupials. They are nourished in their mother's uterus by an organ called the placenta. They evolved into the largest and most successful group of mammals, spreading to all parts of the world and adapting well to different climates and habitats. There are about 4,000 species alive today.

Fossil of a mouse-like creature, dated to 125 million years ago, which scientists think may have been the first placental mammal.

PLATYBELODON

INDRICOTHERIUM

NIMRAVUS

CLADOSICTIS

PACHYRUKHOS

OLIGOCENE

MIOCENE

HOMINID FAMILY TREE

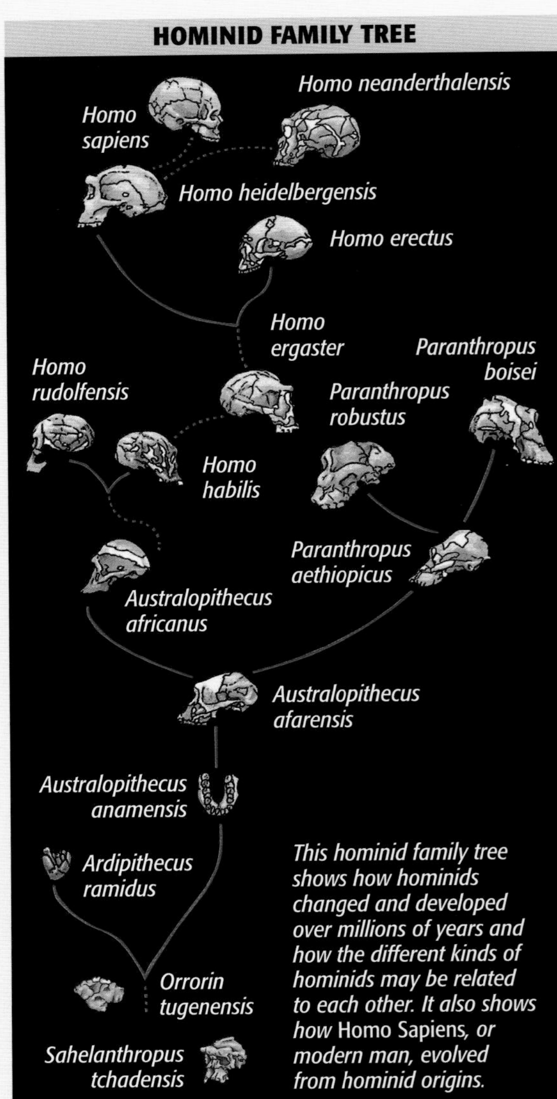

This hominid family tree shows how hominids changed and developed over millions of years and how the different kinds of hominids may be related to each other. It also shows how Homo Sapiens, *or modern man, evolved from hominid origins.*

Early Hominids

The first hominids, or human-like creatures, emerged some time between 10 and 5 million years ago. They shared a common ancestor with apes, but had different characteristics. Hominids developed a more upright posture, walked on two legs, and had more rounded skulls and eventually larger brains. Standing upright left their hands free to grasp food, carry it, and defend themselves, as well as allowing them to see further over tall grass and bushes. A group of hominids that we call *Australopithecus* (meaning "southern apes") appeared in Africa about 4 million years ago.

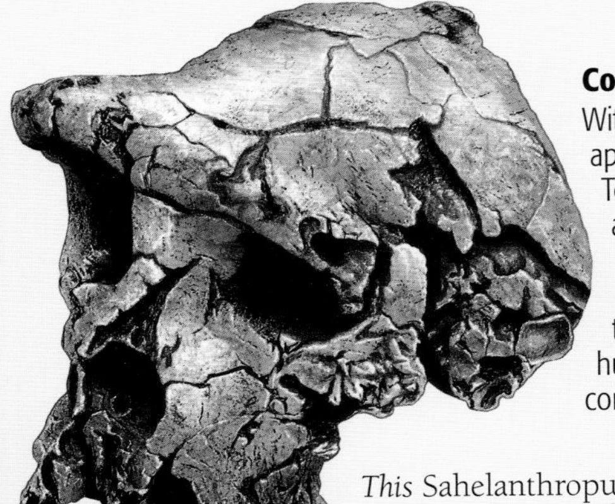

This Sahelanthropus tchadensis *skull was found in the African country of Chad and nicknamed Toumaï, meaning "hope of life."*

Common Ancestors

Within the order of primates, the first apes appeared about 25 million years ago. Today the family of so-called "great apes" (officially called *Pongidae*) includes chimpanzees, gorillas, and orangutans. At some distant point in the past, the great apes and the earliest human-like creatures, hominids, shared a common ancestor.

The First Hominids

In 2000, fossilized bone fragments of an early hominid were found in Kenya. It was given the species name *Orrorin tugenensis* and dated to 6 million years ago. Two years later, a French scientist announced the discovery of an even older hominid skull. It was given the species name *Sahelanthropus tchadensis* and found to be nearly 7 million years old. Its discoverer thinks that this hominid individual was about the size of a modern chimpanzee.

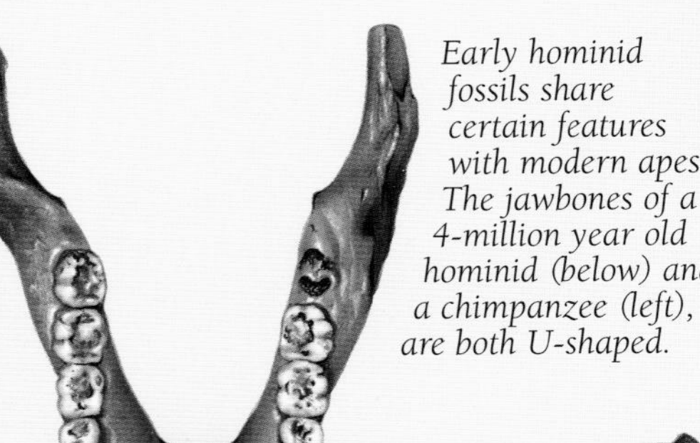

Early hominid fossils share certain features with modern apes. The jawbones of a 4-million year old hominid (below) and a chimpanzee (left), are both U-shaped.

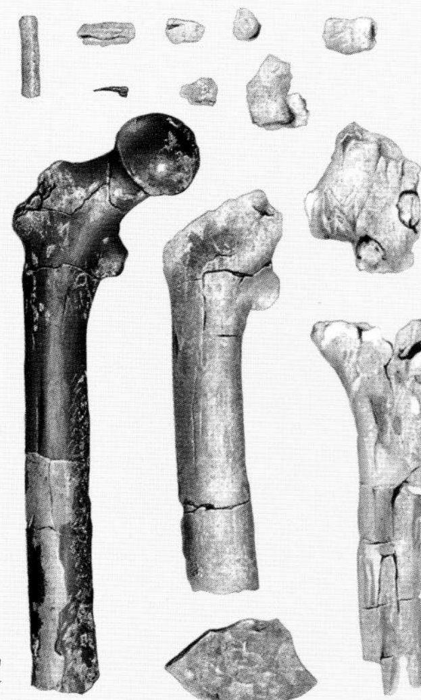

Bone fragments of Orrorin tugenensis*—the hominid also called "Millennium Man"—which were found in Kenya in 2000.*

Scientists believe that Australopithecus afarenis *lived in social groups led by the strongest male.*

Australopithecus anamensis lived about 4 million years ago. The fossils below show bone fragments of jaws (top), an arm (center), and a lower leg (bottom).

Many Species

Scientists have found several different *Australopithecus* species. Their craniums were small, about a third of the size of modern humans. The *Homo* group, to which modern humans belong, is believed to have evolved from an *Australopithecus* species (see hominid family tree on page 18).

Living Together

Before the discovery of fossil evidence, scientists thought that only one species of hominid lived at a time. Today we believe that different hominid species, such as *Paranthropus boisei*, *Homo rudolfensis*, *Homo habilis,* and *Homo ergaster* co-existed in what is now northern Kenya about 1.8 million years ago. *Homo habilis* and *Homo rudolfensis* were probably scavengers who may have competed for food.

A female Australopithecus afarensis nursing her young. A partial skeleton of this species, nicknamed "Lucy," was announced in 1974. She lived about 3.2 million years ago in what is now Ethiopia.

Out of Africa

Almost two million years ago the first hominids left Africa and migrated to other continents. The migration across the world was not achieved by individuals traveling great distances, but by groups gradually expanding and moving on in search of food. The initial migration, a journey of at least 6,200 miles (10,000 km), may have taken up to 100,000 years. Which of the hominid species was the first to migrate remains a question for modern research to answer.

This is how Homo erectus *("upright man") may have looked. Many "upright" fossils, similar to the African "workmen" have been found in Asia.*

Homo Species in Asia

One of the more developed species of the *Homo* group was *Homo erectus*. The first *Homo erectus* to have been discovered, the so-called "Java man," lived on an Indonesian island 1.8 million years ago. Similar fossils have also been found in China. The so-called "Peking man" was found near Beijing, in China, where hominid groups were living in caves. These fossil discoveries show how *Homo erectus* migrated and suggest that this species must have been able to adapt to different environments.

PEOPLING THE WORLD

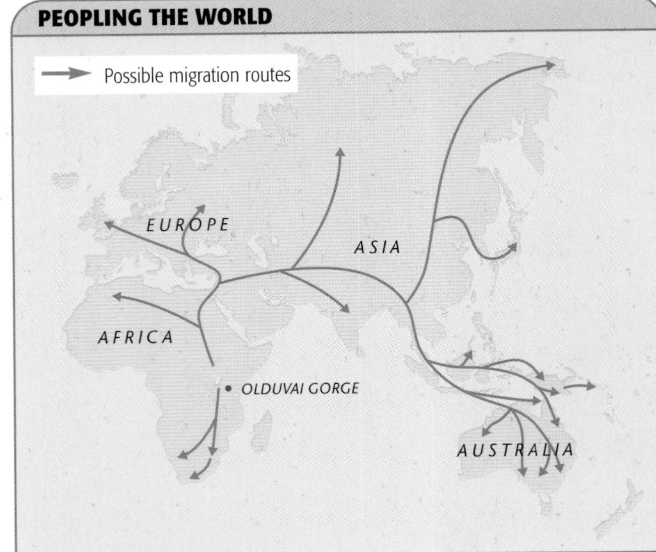

Migrating Species

Some experts believe that the first hominids to migrate were probably Homo ergaster *(or "workman"), a kind of hominid which appeared in the grasslands of east Africa around 1.9 million years ago. The* Homo ergaster *species was strong and athletic and may have been the earliest hunters.* Homo erectus*, or "upright man," was a descendant of the African "workman." This map above shows the routes that might have been taken by the migrating hominids as traced out by the various fossil finds.*

Fire

We know that Asian *Homo erectus* mastered the use of fire. This new skill brought enormous benefits. As well as being used for cooking and providing warmth and light, fire offered protection by frightening off animals. It could also be used for hardening stone and wooden tools. Smoke holes would have been built above the simple hearths in early shelters.

The skull of Java man, with a low forehead and thick brow-ridge, was found along the banks of the River Solo in Java.

Peopling the Rest of the Globe

Almost two million years after the first hominid migration, groups of modern humans migrated from Africa and gradually spread across the globe. They eventually reached Australia from Southeast Asia, arriving around 60,000 years ago. Other hunting groups migrated north and followed animal herds across what is now the Bering Strait into North America, about 18,000 years ago.

The first humans arrived in North America by crossing a land bridge from Asia. Hunter-gatherers followed ice-free corridors and river valleys (such as this one in present-day Alaska), as they slowly moved across the Arctic plain.

Homo erectus *people in China around a fire in their cave shelter. They gathered wild fruit and acquired meat, an important part of their diet, by scavenging and hunting.*

HOMINID FOSSIL FINDS AND DATES

7 million years ago
Sahelanthropus tchadensis *"Toumai" skull in Chad.*

6 million years ago
Orrorin tugenensis *in Kenya.*

4.4 million years ago
Ardipithecus ramidus *"ground ape" in Ethiopia.*

3.2 million years ago
Australopithecus afarensis *"Lucy" skeleton in Ethiopia.*

2.5 million years ago
Paranthropus robustus *hominids.*

2.4 million years ago
Homo rudolfensis*, the first Homo species.*

1.9 million years ago
Homo habilis *makes simple stone tools.*
Homo ergaster *"workman," probably the earliest hunters.*

1.8 million years ago
Homo erectus *"Java man" lives in Indonesia.*

1.75 million years ago
Paranthropus boisei*, nicknamed "Zinj" or "Nutcracker man," in Tanzania and Kenya.*

1.6 million years ago
Homo ergaster *"Nariokotome/Turkana boy" lives in Kenya.*

800,000 years ago
Homo antecessor *lives in Europe.*

500,000 years ago
Homo erectus *"Peking man" living in caves in China.*

400,000 years ago
Homo heidelbergensis *lives in Europe.*

18,000 years ago
Homo floresiensis *was still alive on the Indonesian island of Flores, according to findings announced in 2004.*

THE FIRST STONE TOOLS

The earliest stone tools are called "Oldowan," from the site at Olduvai Gorge, in Tanzania, where they were first found. They were made up to 1.9 million years ago by Homo habilis. *They included round hammerstones, which were used to strike sharp flakes from cobble cores. Some of the chipped cobbles may have been used as tools, but the most important parts were probably the stone flakes, which made hand-held knives and scrapers. Later "Acheulean" hand axes and other tools (made by* Homo ergaster *and* Homo erectus *from about 1.5 million years ago) were named after a prehistoric site at Saint-Acheul, in northern France.*

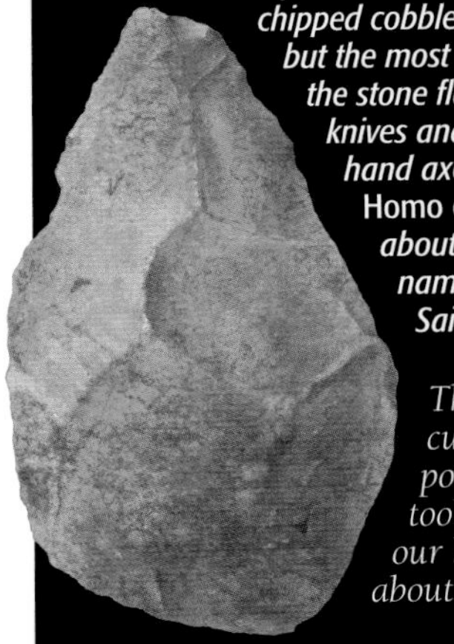

This hand axe has two cutting edges leading to a point. These teardrop-shaped tools were made by some of our human ancestors from about 1.5 million years ago.

Fossilized antelope bone found at Olduvai Gorge. The bones of zebras, pigs, monkeys, and many other animals have also been found there, along with the stone tools that were used to cut meat from them.

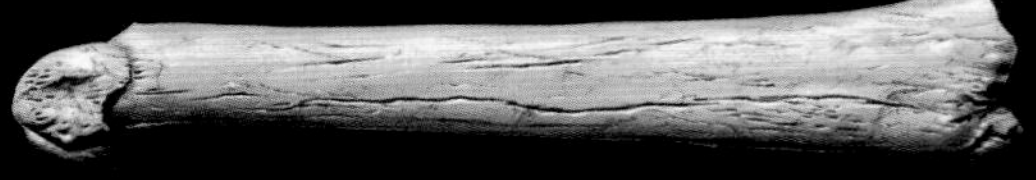

Tools and Shelter

Hominids made their first tools from stone, and the oldest examples found were made up to 2.5 million years ago. These were probably used to smash open bones and extract marrow, as well as to cut meat from scavenged animals. More sophisticated hand axes and blades were useful to later hunters. Cutting and scraping tools may also have been used to shape wood and to help construct the earliest shelters. These were simple structures, and the use of controlled fire made them warmer and safer. Tool-making, foraging, hunting, shelter-building, and fire-making must have helped bring groups of hominids closer together.

This is how a hut may have looked at Terra Amata, a prehistoric campsite in southern France. The bent wooden branches were held in place by rows of stones. Some huts were up to 24 feet (7.5 m) across.

Toolmakers

The early *Homo* species had larger brains than the earlier *Australopithecus* species. This enabled *Homo habilis, or* "handy man," to work out how to make effective tools. They could then butcher large carcasses; these early human-like creatures may have eaten meat regularly, scavenging rather than hunting. They probably made the tools on the spot. Later *Homo erectus* made more sophisticated tools, including hand axes with rounded grips, and may have taken them with them when they moved on.

Homo heidelbergensis *("Heidelberg man," named after a site in Germany), was an early European hominid. This skull found in Greece dates from about 450,000 years ago.*

Early Shelters

The first shelters were probably overhanging rocks and wide cave entrances. *Homo habilis* may have built camps of simple thorn-bush huts, and we know that *Homo erectus* were living in caves 500,000 years ago. About 100,000 years later, *Homo heidelbergensis* groups were building beach camps beside the Mediterranean Sea. We know this because of remains found at Terra Amata, near Nice, where large oval-shaped huts were built.

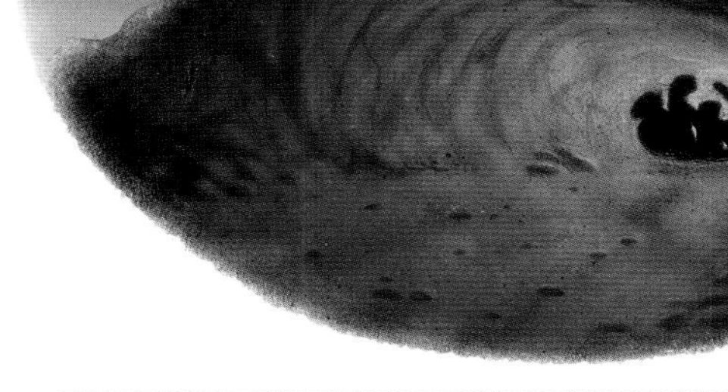

Small groups of early humans probably sheltered together in caves.

TOOL FINDS IN AFRICA, EUROPE, AND ASIA

Oldowan tools
Acheulean tools
Boundary line

ST. ACHEUL
EUROPE
ASIA
AFRICA
INDONESIA
OLDUVAI GORGE
AUSTRALIA

Spread of Tool Technology

Many scientists were surprised to discover more primitive Oldowan stone tools in China and Indonesia when more sophisticated Acheulean tools had already appeared in Africa. This evidence suggests that hominids began migrating to Asia, taking Oldowan tool technology with them, before the appearance of Acheulean tools in Africa. Also, the appearance of Acheulean tools in Europe and western Asia suggests that other migration waves took place after the appearance of Acheulean tools in Africa. However, the reason why Acheulean tools never reached east Asia (past the red boundary line shown on this map) is still a mystery.

Neanderthals and *Homo Sapiens*

The Neanderthals (or *Homo neanderthalensis*), emerged in Europe long before the modern humans who make up the species called *Homo sapiens* (meaning "wise man"). The two species were close relatives, though Neanderthals were shorter and stockier—well suited to a harsh ice-age existence. Nevertheless, around 27,000 years ago *Homo sapiens*—our direct ancestors—were left as the only hominid species on Earth. This probably happened as "wise" groups took over Neanderthal territories and competed with them for food and shelter. *Homo sapiens* numbers increased and *Homo neanderthalensis* became extinct.

Neanderthals

The Neanderthals were strong, stocky individuals. They had to be to survive the severely cold winters of ice-age Europe, which they did for more than 170,000 years. They hunted large animals, as well as scavenging meat and gathering plant foods. They were skillful makers of stone tools, which they used to scrape and prepare animal hides. They probably lived in small groups of up to 12 adults, moving around in search of food and sheltering in cave entrances and beneath overhanging rocks.

This bone tool, found in a French cave, was probably made and used by Neanderthals, who also appear to have made pendants and other ornaments.

Cro-Magnons

The early *Homo sapiens* who lived in Europe from about 40,000 years ago are known as Cro-Magnons, named after a site in France (see page 31). They were skilled hunters, tool-makers and artists, famous today for their cave paintings (see page 32). Cro-Magnons discovered how to start a fire by striking flint to produce sparks. They used bone needles to sew animal skins together for clothes and containers.

NEANDERTHAL AND *HOMO SAPIENS* SITES

Close Contact

Neanderthals and Homo sapiens *lived at the same time in Europe for a period of 16,000 years, and probably for longer in southwest Asia. Some groups probably occupied the same regions, in which case there would have been contact between the two species. Communication would have been difficult though, since experts believe that Cro-Magnons had a more evolved use of language than their Neanderthal neighbors.*

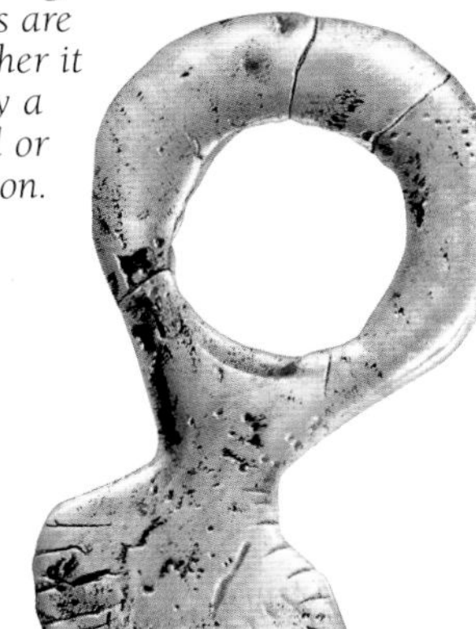

Bone pendant from a Neanderthal and Cro-Magnon site, made about 34,000 years ago. Archeologists are unsure whether it was made by a Neanderthal or a Cro-Magnon.

To withstand the cold, Neanderthals wore skins and furs. They put sharp stone points on their wooden spears.

This Cro-Magnon child's handprint was made by spraying pigment around the hand from the artist's mouth.

This child's skeleton, which is 24,500 years old, seems to have both Neanderthal and Homo sapiens *features. Some scientists believe this is evidence that the two species interbred.*

NEANDERTHALS VS. *HOMO SAPIENS*

The Neanderthals and early Homo sapiens, *or Cro-Magnon, appeared on Earth during the Pleistocene epoch of Earth's history (see page 7). During this epoch more than 30 percent of the Earth's surface was covered by ice.*

Dates:
Neanderthals inhabited much of Europe and the Mediterranean about 200,000–27,000 years ago. Homo sapiens *originated in Africa about 160,000–130,000 years ago.* Homo sapiens *migrated from Africa about 100,000 years ago and reached Australia about 60,000 years ago and North America about 18,000 years ago.*

Names:
The term "Neanderthalensis" comes from Neander Valley, near Düsseldorf, in Germany, where fossils of this hominid species were first found in 1856. The term "Cro-Magnon" comes from a rock shelter near Les Eyzies, in the Dordogne region of France, where skeletons of early modern Europeans (belonging to Homo sapiens*) were found in 1868.*

Characteristics:
Compared to Neanderthals, early Homo sapiens *were taller and more slender-boned and had a less sloping forehead, much less pronounced brow ridges, and a more pronounced chin.*

Barbed bone or antler hooks and harpoons made fishing more efficient.

Hunters and Gatherers

Prehistoric people lived as hunters and gatherers. The earliest hominids probably lived mainly on plant foods, adding meat to their diet when they happened to come across a dead animal. Later humans developed tools and worked together to improve their hunting skills. All hunter-gatherers were continually on the move, as they followed their prey and looked for new food sources. They generally stayed together in small groups, resting in rock overhangs, caves, or other simple shelters until it was time to move on again. Within each group, men were the hunters, while women concentrated on gathering plant foods.

This strange fish-like sculpture comes from a prehistoric site beside the River Danube in Serbia. Remains show that fish from the Danube played an important part in hunter-gatherers' diet.

Fishing

Early modern humans used spears and clubs to catch river fish which were a good source of high-protein food. Hunter-gatherers would have followed rivers and streams so as to be near a source of fresh water. Near the coast, they may have used the same approach and also collected shellfish. Around 25,000 years ago, fishermen were using the fish gorge, a baited toggle attached to a line that wedged in a fish's jaws. This was followed by the fish hook and barbed harpoon.

A Cro-Magnon man stands in a river and spears fish with a barbed harpoon. Later, fishermen learned to make wooden fences so that the trapped fish were easier to spear.

Cooking

Once humans had learned to control fire, they could cook meat and other foodstuffs. This not only made meat easier and more pleasant to eat, but also made it healthier. At first meat was roasted directly over the fire. The Cro-Magnons made skin-lined pits and dropped hot stones in to heat water for boiling food. In coastal regions, large shells were used as cooking containers.

Gathering

Among prehistoric peoples, women and children were mainly responsible for gathering roots, berries, seeds, fruits, nuts, grains, birds' eggs, and insects. These foods changed with the season, and women must have built up great knowledge of plants, which they passed on from generation to generation. The collected foodstuffs formed an important part of the diet, especially when hunting was poor.

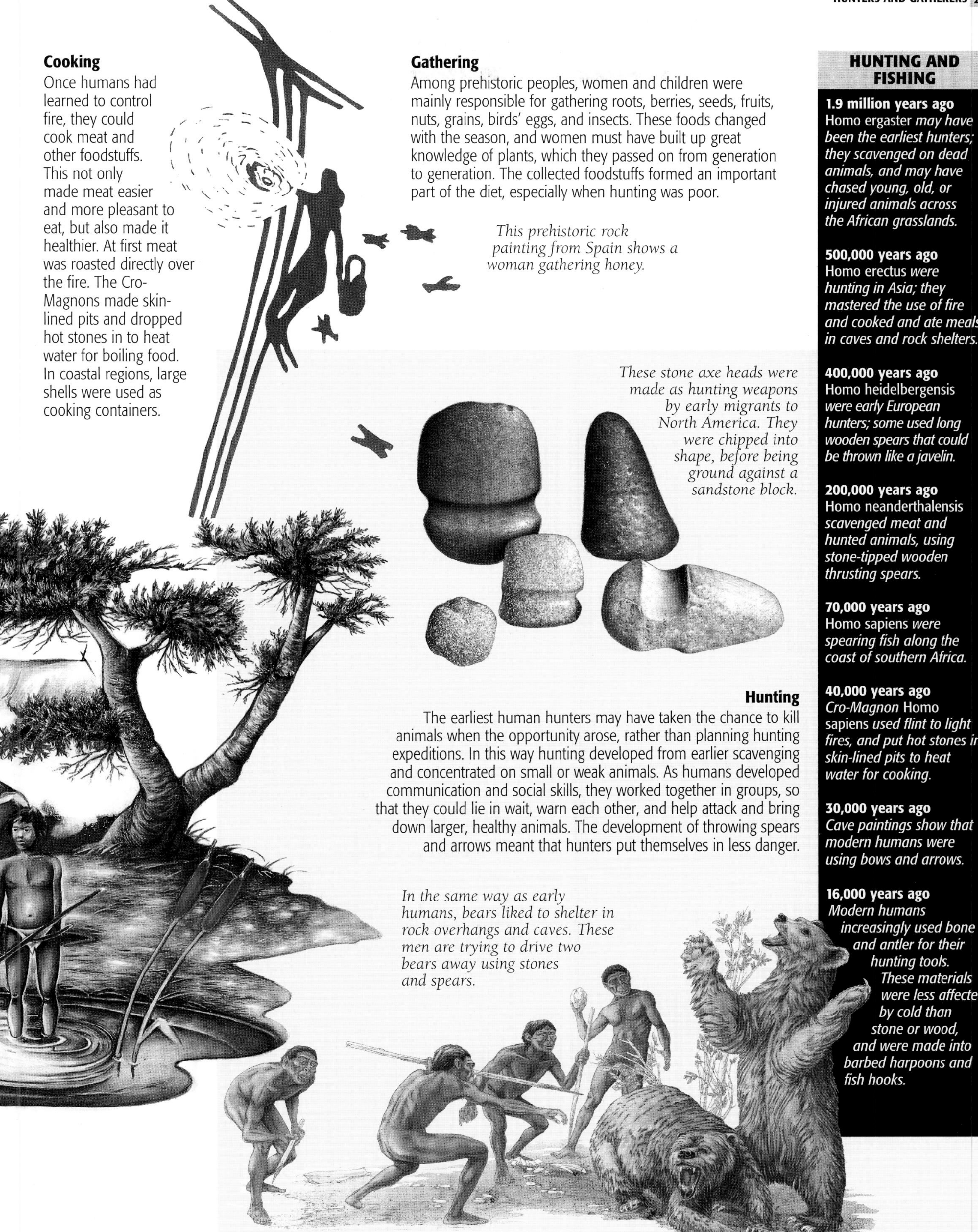

This prehistoric rock painting from Spain shows a woman gathering honey.

These stone axe heads were made as hunting weapons by early migrants to North America. They were chipped into shape, before being ground against a sandstone block.

Hunting

The earliest human hunters may have taken the chance to kill animals when the opportunity arose, rather than planning hunting expeditions. In this way hunting developed from earlier scavenging and concentrated on small or weak animals. As humans developed communication and social skills, they worked together in groups, so that they could lie in wait, warn each other, and help attack and bring down larger, healthy animals. The development of throwing spears and arrows meant that hunters put themselves in less danger.

In the same way as early humans, bears liked to shelter in rock overhangs and caves. These men are trying to drive two bears away using stones and spears.

HUNTING AND FISHING

1.9 million years ago
Homo ergaster *may have been the earliest hunters; they scavenged on dead animals, and may have chased young, old, or injured animals across the African grasslands.*

500,000 years ago
Homo erectus *were hunting in Asia; they mastered the use of fire and cooked and ate meals in caves and rock shelters.*

400,000 years ago
Homo heidelbergensis *were early European hunters; some used long wooden spears that could be thrown like a javelin.*

200,000 years ago
Homo neanderthalensis *scavenged meat and hunted animals, using stone-tipped wooden thrusting spears.*

70,000 years ago
Homo sapiens *were spearing fish along the coast of southern Africa.*

40,000 years ago
Cro-Magnon Homo sapiens *used flint to light fires, and put hot stones in skin-lined pits to heat water for cooking.*

30,000 years ago
Cave paintings show that modern humans were using bows and arrows.

16,000 years ago
Modern humans increasingly used bone and antler for their hunting tools. These materials were less affected by cold than stone or wood, and were made into barbed harpoons and fish hooks.

Religion and Rituals

Prehistoric people probably believed that spirits dwelled in the natural phenomena essential to life, such as sunshine and rain. Through magical rituals, prehistoric people thought that they could control natural events by pleasing these spirits. Some rituals, for example, would have been performed to ensure the fertility of the Earth, which was vital for a plentiful food supply. Although it is difficult to clearly define religion before the invention of writing, archeological finds, such as burial sites, representations of deities, and remains of temples or altars are evidence of early religious expression. We can only guess at the meaning and ritual use of these finds.

Figure of a shaman, perhaps performing a hunting dance, shown as a mix of different animals from a cave in France.

Ceremonial Sites
The world's earliest stone monuments, or megaliths, were probably raised for ritual function. Among the earliest examples are the great stone temples on the islands of Malta, situated south of Sicily in the Mediterranean Sea. It is believed that these temples were built for fertility rituals. Altars (possibly used for animal sacrifice), decorative reliefs, and statuettes of deities and "priests" have been found at these sites.

Hagar Qim, the best preserved of the Maltese temples, seen from above. The rounded divisions give the structure an organic form.

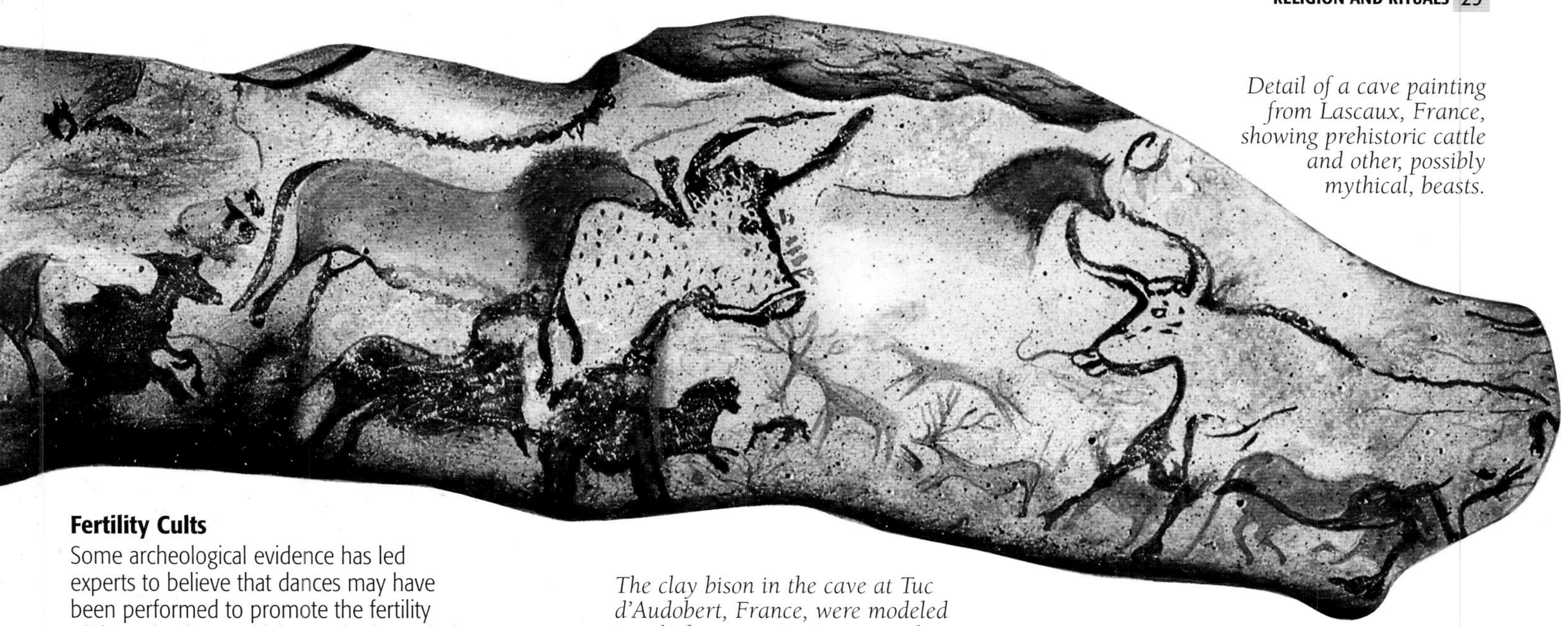

Detail of a cave painting from Lascaux, France, showing prehistoric cattle and other, possibly mythical, beasts.

Fertility Cults

Some archeological evidence has led experts to believe that dances may have been performed to promote the fertility of the animals on which people depended for their food supply. Footprints, thought to be of dancers, were found in a cave in France around a small mound decorated with male and female bison. The dancers may have thought that this ritual had a magical effect, increasing the number of bison available for the hunt.

The clay bison in the cave at Tuc d'Audobert, France, were modeled in relief on a projecting stone about 14,000 years ago.

Art and Ritual

Other possible evidence of the celebration of rituals and ceremonies is found in cave paintings (see page 32). Some caves were perhaps seen as sanctuaries, since they were not used as living quarters. Paintings of animals and hunting scenes may have been made to exert some kind of control, through ritual and magic, over the animals and the hunt. Magicians, or shamen, who were believed to be in touch with the spirits, may have led the rituals.

The famous 30,000 year-old Venus of Willendorf (below). *Many female figures were carved in limestone, showing exaggerated features.*

Mother Goddesses

This map shows sites in Europe where figurines commonly known as "Venuses" have been found. Some experts have suggested that these figurines represented the life-giving forces of nature, fertility, and growth. People may have believed that a kind of mother-goddess reigned over the fruitfulness of all life on Earth and that these figurines possessed magical fertility powers.

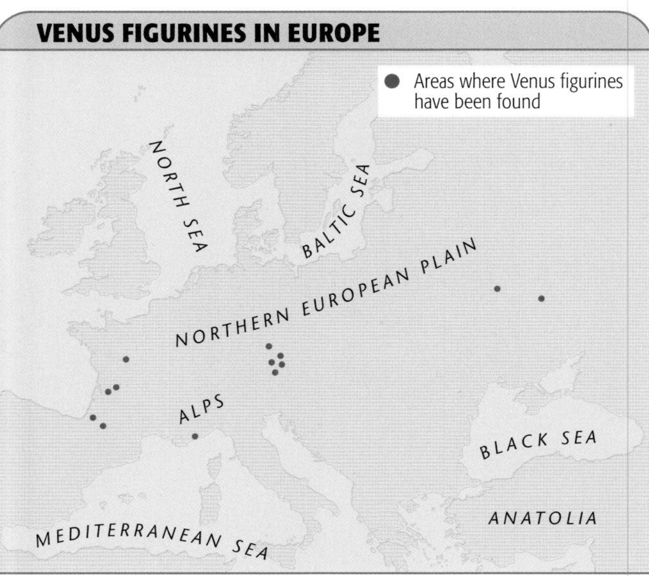

Burying the Dead

We know that the Neanderthals sometimes buried their dead. Their burials were probably occasional and certainly simple, though one site includes a ring of ibex horns and another may have contained flowers. Modern humans may have started practising burial up to 80,000 years ago. Later burials became more elaborate and included decorated clothing and grave goods. The bodies seem to have been simply laid in a shallow pit, but some graves were covered with rock slabs. The few very old sites that have been found have told us a great deal about prehistoric attitudes towards death.

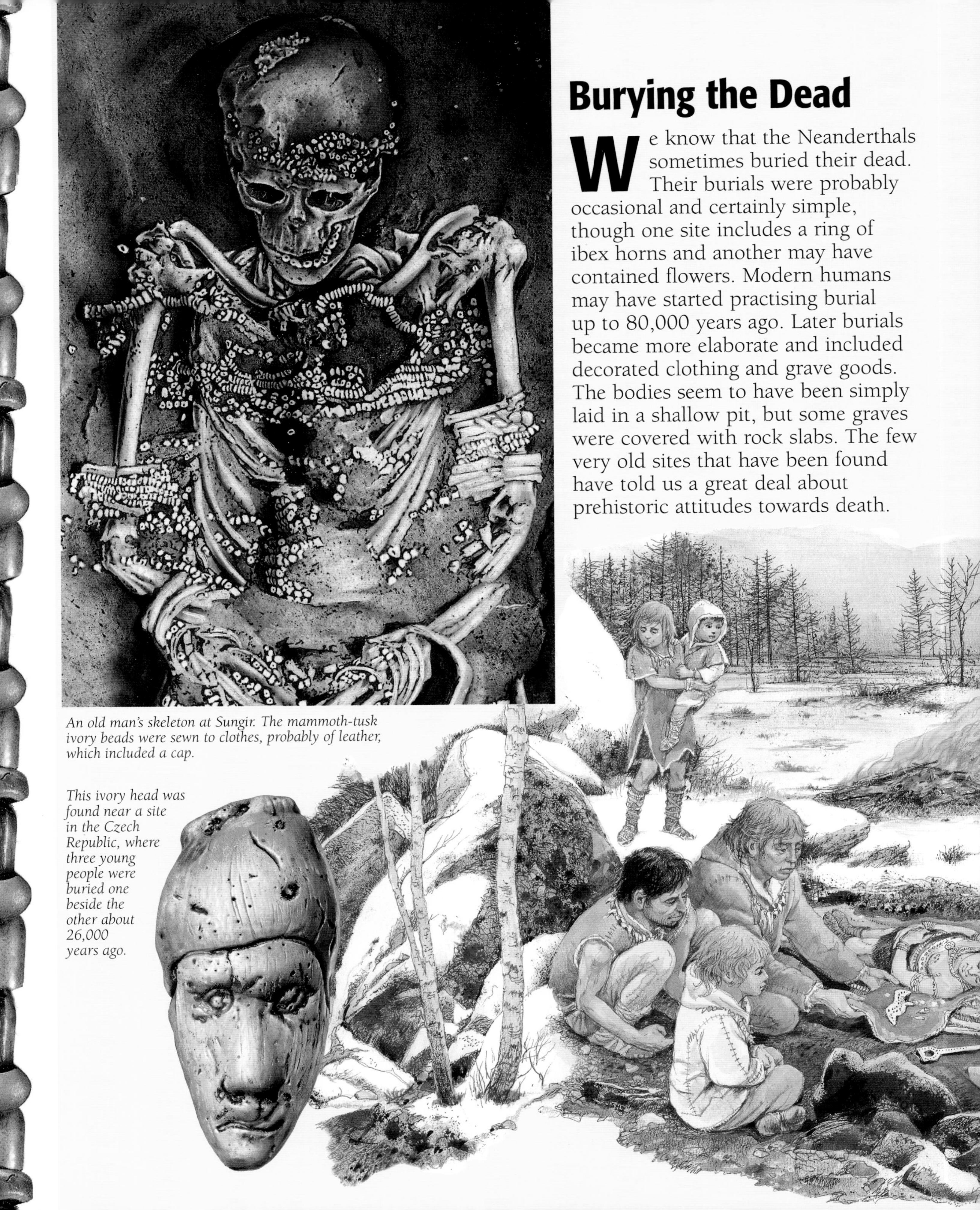

An old man's skeleton at Sungir. The mammoth-tusk ivory beads were sewn to clothes, probably of leather, which included a cap.

This ivory head was found near a site in the Czech Republic, where three young people were buried one beside the other about 26,000 years ago.

Burials

The little evidence that archeologists have found shows that more elaborate burial began about 35,000 years ago. A burial site discovered at Sungir, near the modern city of Vladimir in Russia, dates from 28,000 years ago. The bodies had been put in shallow graves that had been dug in the frozen earth. They were dressed in clothing sewn with thousands of ivory beads.

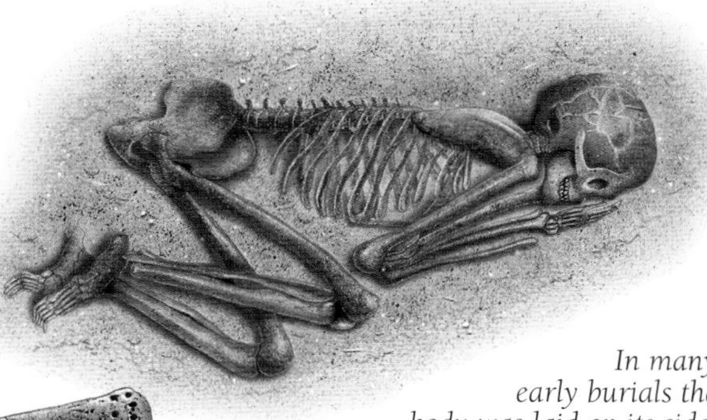

In many early burials the body was laid on its side, with the legs drawn up.

Grave Goods

The individuals found at Sungir were buried with different kinds of grave goods. These included carved pendants, bracelets, and shell necklaces. While ornaments, tools, and weapons have been found at some Cro-Magnon burial sites, such as this one, others are much simpler. This indicates a difference in importance and status between individuals, suggesting a social hierarchy of leaders and followers.

Ivory cloak pin, found on the remains of a Sungir boy.

SOME EARLY BURIAL SITES

c. 80,000–60,000 years ago:
Shanidar cave, Zagros Mountains, Iraq; discovered 1951; Neanderthal burial site with seven adults and one child. One grave was rich in pollen, suggesting that the burial may have been on a bed of flowers.

c. 70,000 years ago:
Teshik-Tash, Uzbekistan; discovered 1938; Neanderthal site, with an adolescent seemingly buried within a ring of ibex horns.

c. 32,000–30,000 years ago:
Cro-Magnon, Les Eyzies, France; discovered 1868; 5 modern human (since called Cro-Magnon) skeletons–three adult males, one adult female, and one infant; burial with body adornments.

c. 30,000–25,000 years ago:
Predmosti, Czech Republic; discovered 1894, destroyed 1945 (in World War II); remains of ten modern human children and eight adults in a large oval pit beneath stone slabs and mammoth bones with ornaments and grave goods.

c. 28,000 years ago:
Sungir, Russia; discovered 1956; remains of five modern humans, including a 60-year-old man, an 8-year-old girl, and a 13-year-old boy buried together in a head-to-head position; the man's body was adorned with 2,900 beads, as well as Arctic fox teeth; the boy was covered with 4,900 beads, and the girl had 5,200 (each single bead may have taken up to an hour to make!); next to the boy were two straightened mammoth tusks.

A small pendant of a horse found at Sungir. It was carved out of mammoth-tusk ivory, and its outline is considered unusual for such an early time.

Belief in an Afterlife

Experts believe that prehistoric people would only have buried their dead with grave goods if they thought the items would be useful to the deceased. This means that Cro-Magnons must have believed in some form of afterlife. Burying their dead must have made them think about a world beyond their everyday environment. Like a lot of prehistoric art, grave goods may be seen as evidence of early religious expression.

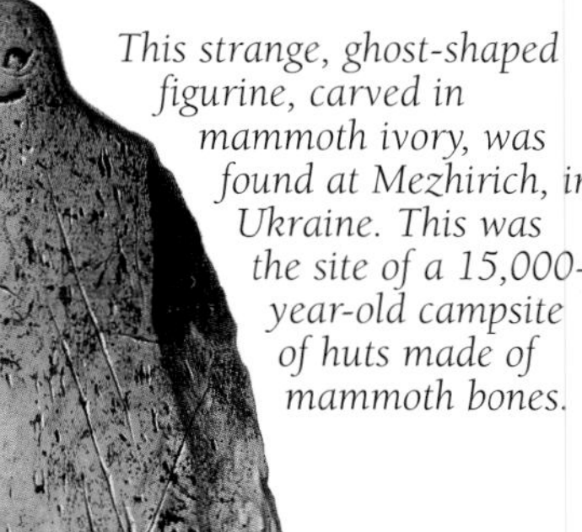

This strange, ghost-shaped figurine, carved in mammoth ivory, was found at Mezhirich, in Ukraine. This was the site of a 15,000-year-old campsite of huts made of mammoth bones.

The bodies at Sungir were laid on their backs, with their arms folded across their stomachs.

One of the many horses painted on the walls and ceilings at Lascaux. The artist succeeded in achieving a sense of depth and movement.

Prehistoric Art

Cave paintings are the most famous form of art created by prehistoric humans, and some date back more than 30,000 years. Sculptures and decorative items have been found that are even older, including a recent find that takes abstract art back 70,000 years. Many theories have been put forward as to the purpose of such works of art, including ideas about magic, religion, and hunting rituals. Experts agree that these works may have had a symbolic meaning for their creators, and they certainly represented a way for them to express their feelings and beliefs.

This delicate painting of reindeer was created in Font de Gaume cave, in southwest France, about 14,000 years ago.

Cave Painting

Using stone lamps filled with animal fat to light the pitch-dark caves, prehistoric artists depicted mainly animals—horses, bison, ibex, aurochs (long-horned wild oxen, now extinct), deer, and mammoths. At Lascaux there are also dots and geometric shapes, and one single representation of a person. The cave surfaces were easy to reach; the ceilings would have been just a few feet from the floor. Today most cave art sites have been dug out to create higher ceilings, making them more easily accessible to visitors.

Detail of the Carnarvon Gorge rock painting site in Australia, where stencil designs were made on sandstone cliffs.

Jewelry

Necklaces, bracelets, and other items were made from beads, animal teeth, and shells. Beads were made of ivory (mainly from mammoth tusks), bone, antler, and stone pebbles. The teeth were usually the canines of foxes, but wolf, bear, and lion teeth were also used. Seashells from the Atlantic and Mediterranean coasts have been found in French and Spanish caves. All these items were pierced with pointed tools, before being strung together and attached to clothing or worn separately.

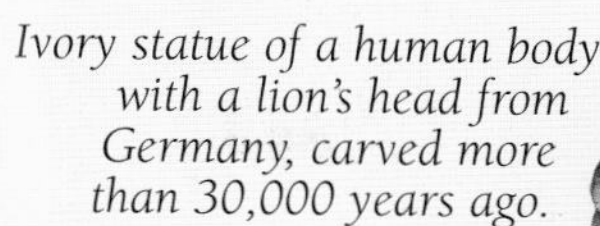

Ivory statue of a human body with a lion's head from Germany, carved more than 30,000 years ago.

Portable Art

Artists sculpted shapes and figurines from stone, and later from ivory, bone, and antler. The oldest examples of these include simple carvings of animals. Other, later, examples of portable art include the so-called Venus figurines (see page 29). As carving techniques became more sophisticated, simple incisions and dots gave way to more realistic representations. Artistic carvings were also added to some weapons and tools, such as spear-throwers.

Pierced animal teeth found in a grave in southern France.

This piece of iron ore was shaped and carved with geometric patterns more than 70,000 years ago. It was found in a cave in South Africa and may be the world's oldest example of abstract art.

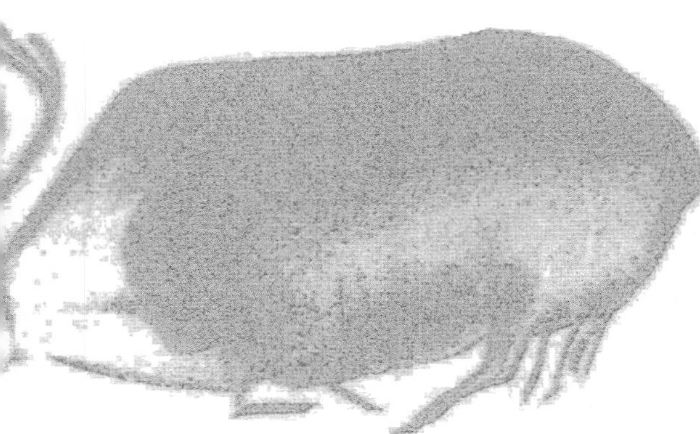

Use of Color

Artists worked with the surfaces as they found them. They chose smooth surfaces for painting, using contours to add depth. Their main colors were black, obtained from manganese or charcoal, and red, which came from ochre (a form of iron oxide mixed with clay and sand that produced a range of colors from deep red to light yellow). The minerals were scraped and crushed into powder form and then mixed with water.

PREHISTORIC PAINTING

Africa:
Twyfelfontein, Damaraland, Namibia; painted c. 25,000 years ago; images of animals painted in red and black pigment.

Australia:
Carnarvon Gorge, Queensland; 646 stencils of hands, forearms, boomerangs, and axes were created by blowing a spray of pigment mixed with water from the mouth over objects held up against the surface.

Europe:
Chauvet, France; decorated c. 32,000 years ago; mainly paintings of rhinoceroses, lions, mammoths, horses, bison, bears, reindeer, aurochs, ibex, stags, a red panther, and an engraved owl; no human images, but one composite being, half-man, half-bison.

Lascaux, France; decorated c. 17,000 years ago; seven chambers, with 600 paintings and 1500 engravings.

Altamira, Spain; decorated c. 14,000 years ago; S-shaped cave about 885 feet (270 m) long; main galleries decorated with engravings and black outline paintings of bison, horses, aurochs, ibex, deer, and boar; also geometric signs.

A selection of minerals used by prehistoric painters. White clay or chalk was added in later times. The pigments were applied with fingers, pads of vegetable fibers, or simple brushes made of twigs or fur.

HUMAN PREHISTORY

Human prehistory is divided by stages in development. Different parts of the world reached these stages at different times, so dates of these periods vary from region to region. The first stage is called the Paleolithic age. Experts divide the early Paleolithic age in Europe (40,000–10,000 years ago) into the following cultures or periods which are named after prehistoric sites in southern France:

Aurignacian
c. 40,000–28,000 years ago, named after Aurignac, a site discovered in 1860. During this time advanced tools and the first bone spear points were used, along with other tools made of stone.

Gravettian
c. 28,000–22,000 years ago, named after La Gravette cave. Neanderthals used backed blades, the first eyed bone needles, and ivory beads as ornaments. They also decorated spear-throwers and baked clay figurines.

Solutrean
c. 22,000–18,000 years ago, named after Solutré, a horse-hunting site discovered in 1867. Elegant tools, which were sometimes improved by heating and cooling flint, were used.

Magdalenian
c. 18,000–10,000 years ago, named after La Madeleine, a site discovered in 1863. During this time there was an increased use of very small flaked stones and barbed harpoon points made of bone and antler. Bows and arrows appeared. The Magdalenian is also known as the "golden age" of Ice Age art.

Composite tools: (left) a simple tool for digging up roots was made from a stick weighted with a smooth pierced pebble; (center) the stone head was fixed firmly into a shaped piece of horn, which was attached to a wooden handle with a leather strap; (right) this smaller tool has a sharp flint blade at the end of a wooden axehead.

This family of reindeer-hunters is busy making tools near their campfire. Generations of children learned tool-making skills by watching their parents.

Prehistoric Technology

Early technology revolved around the making of tools which made it possible for prehistoric people to hunt animals, dig up roots, and make shelters. During the last period of the Paleolithic, or Old Stone Age, the human hunter-gatherers' toolkit became more intricate, as individuals spent more time crafting a range of stone blades and points. These were used to carve bone and wood, which were used in large composite tools (see left), as well as for small, delicate needles. Towards the end of the period, new technologies were discovered, as people started to shape baked clay into pots and hammer copper into figurines.

Using Stone, Flint, and Wood

Many stone tools were fashioned from flint, a hard rock that ranges in color from brown to dark grey and black. Flint can be chipped into flakes more easily than other kinds of rock. As toolmakers became more skillful, they made smaller, more delicate tools from flakes of flint. These were very useful for shaping bone, antler, and wood. Points of bone or antler were used to produce even more razor-sharp slices of flint. Shaped wood was used to make handles for axes and spears. The handle gave the user a firmer grip and greater leverage.

Another late Paleolithic invention was the arrow. This painting from a rock shelter in Spain shows a group of archers shooting their arrows at a herd of deer.

Making Clothing

Neanderthals and early modern humans probably wore clothing made of animal hides tied together with thongs or leather strips. The introduction of sharper tools and needles with eyes made them easier to cut and shape. Plant fibers were used much later, and the earliest known textiles are the linens found at Çatal Hüyük (see page 38), dating from about 6500 BCE.

Sharper flint tools made the task of skinning animals easier.

The Invention of Pottery

The first pots were made in Japan about 12,500 years ago (see page 190). Potters pressed coils or lumps of wet clay together into the shape of a vessel, smoothed the sides, and then baked it in an open fire. This fired the clay so that it was hard and dry. The early Japanese pot-making culture is known as Jomon.

Cone-shaped Japanese cooking pot, with typical rope-pattern markings, from around 6000 BCE.

Early Use of Metal

The first metal to be used was copper, which was found as nuggets in rocks. A soft metal, it could be beaten into shape for use in tools and ornaments. Copper was probably first used in the Mesopotamia region about 10,000 years ago. Early metalworkers soon learned to heat the metal, so that it could be hammered without becoming brittle. Some time after 5000 BCE, people discovered how to extract metal from its ore by smelting.

These small copper models of long-horned oxen were made about 6,000 years ago in eastern Europe.

The First Farmers

At the end of the last ice age, about 10,000 years ago, the Earth generally became warmer and drier and the landscape changed. In some parts of the world hunter-gatherers began planting seeds in one place and settling there. They continued to hunt for meat, but also began to domesticate animals which could be kept near their settlements. In this way the early farmers of Mesopotamia and elsewhere controlled the supply of their food and completely changed their way of life. Since fresh water was essential to the well-being of their plants, animals, and themselves, the earliest farmers settled in great river valleys in different parts of the world.

Animals

Animals were domesticated by separating them from their wild herds. Farmers soon learned that these animals could provide milk, hides, and wool, as well as meat, and that they could also pull and carry heavy loads. Sheep and goats were herded in Mesopotamia, gazelle in the Middle East, pigs in Anatolia (present-day Turkey) and China, cattle in North Africa and around the Aegean region, and llamas and guinea pigs in South America.

This small figurine of a dog is more than 5,000 years old. It comes from Egypt, where dogs helped with hunting and later became domestic pets. Earlier hunter-gatherers probably used wolves, the ancestors of all dogs, in the hunt.

FARMING AROUND THE WORLD

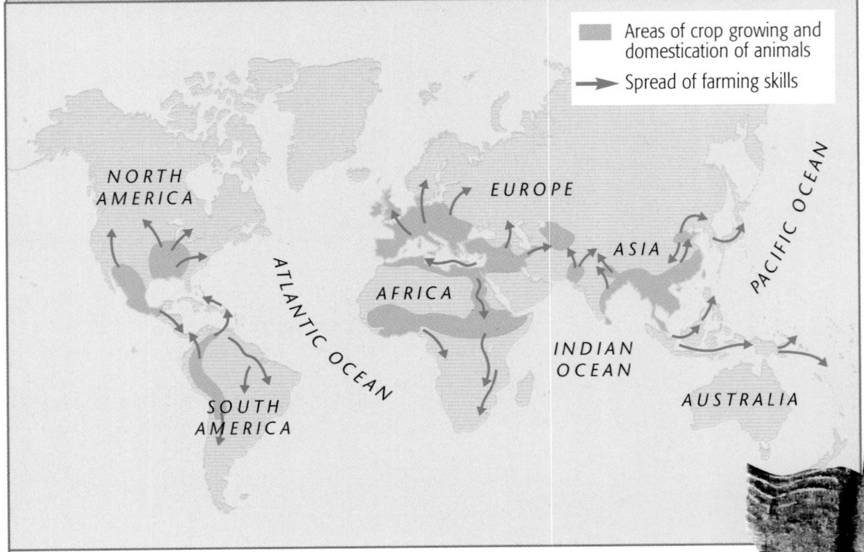

The Spread of Farming

By 6000 BCE, there were settled farmers in southwest and eastern Asia, northern Africa, and southern Europe. About 3,000 years later, farming had also developed in Central America and the Andes region of South America.

Irrigation

Early Mesopotamian farmers had to deal with floods in spring, when their fields were full of young crops, and drought conditions later in the growing season. Some time after 7000 BCE, they began building dykes and embankments to hold back the floodwaters of the Euphrates and Tigris rivers. They also dug irrigation canals and water-storage basins, so that they could use the rivers' water throughout the year.

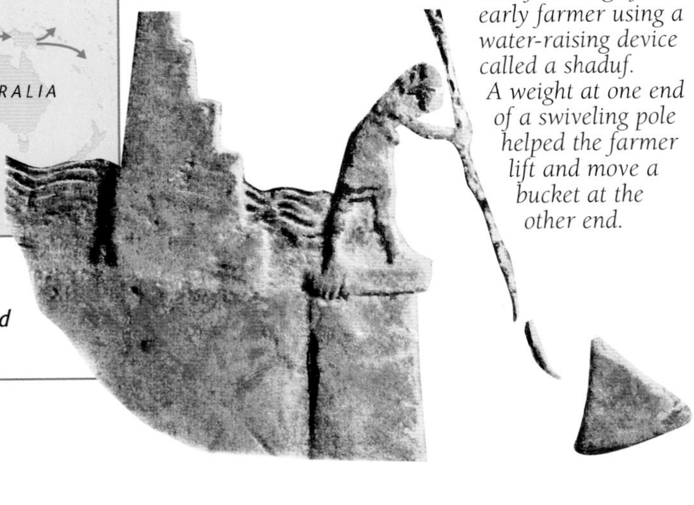

Relief carving of an early farmer using a water-raising device called a shaduf. A weight at one end of a swiveling pole helped the farmer lift and move a bucket at the other end.

Mesopotamian farmers harvesting wheat. At harvest time all members of the family were put to work.

DEVELOPMENT OF FARMING

c. 10,000 BCE
Hunter-gatherers harvest wild cereals in the Middle East.

c. 8000 BCE
The first farmers in Mesopotamia.

c. 7000 BCE
Settled farmers begin irrigating their fields in southern Mesopotamia (dry farming in the north), while millet farming is under way in Yellow River Valley, northern China.

c. 6500 BCE
Rice farming in Yangzi Valley, southern China.

c.6000 BCE
Cattle herding in northern Africa; first cattle domesticated in the Middle East; farming in the Indus Valley and southern Europe.

c. 5000 BCE
Farming spreads to central Europe.

c. 4500 BCE
Farming villages develop into small towns; earliest plows used; wheat and barley in the Nile Valley; farming on the River Ganges plain.

c. 3600 BCE
Farming of maize and beans in Central America.

c. 3500 BCE
Linen produced from flax in Egypt.

c. 3000 BCE
Potatoes and quinoa farmed in the Andes, on terraced fields.

Farming Tools

Early farmers used pointed digging sticks to prepare the ground for sowing their seeds. The first simple wooden plows were used to turn the soil in Mesopotamia around 4500 BCE, and by about 3000 BCE a bronze plowshare had been added. This made a much deeper furrow in hard ground further away from irrigated land. Wheeled carts were introduced at about the same time.

Terra-cotta model of a bullock cart, from the Indus Valley.

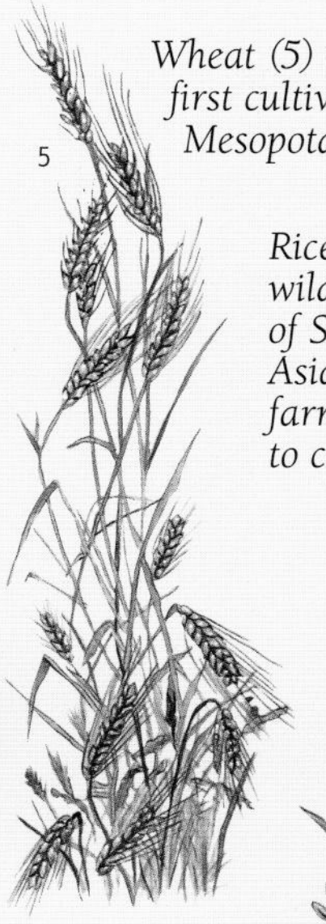

Wheat (5) was first cultivated in Mesopotamia.

Rice (6) grew wild in areas of Southeast Asia. Later farmers began to cultivate it.

Early Crops

In Mesopotamia, the first farmers collected and planted the seeds of wild cereals, such as wheat and barley (see page 49). At each harvest they kept the seeds of the best cereals and sowed them the following season. In this way the crops developed and improved. In northern China, around the valley of the Yellow River (Huang He), early farmers did the same with millet, and in the valley of the River Yangzi (Chang Jiang), they domesticated rice (see page 171). In Central America the main crop was another cereal—maize—along with beans and squash (see pages 208–9).

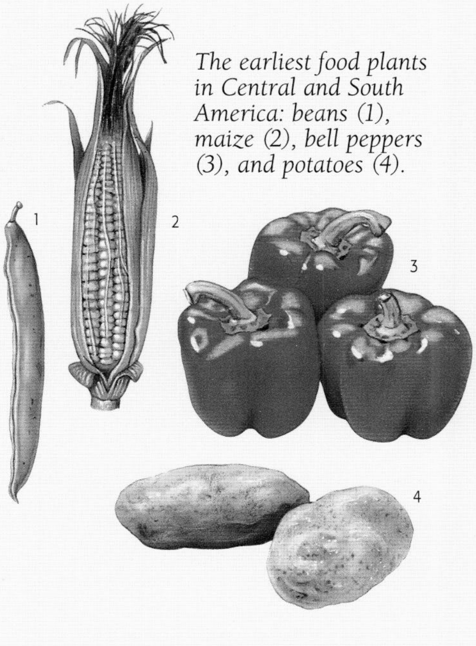

The earliest food plants in Central and South America: beans (1), maize (2), bell peppers (3), and potatoes (4).

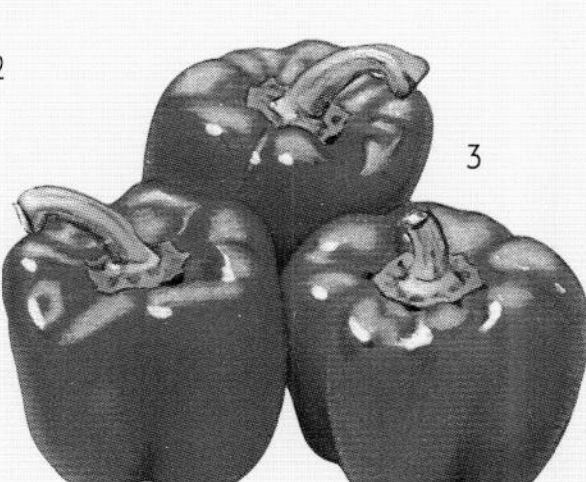

Settling Down

Villages grew up near settled farmers' fields, as people started building stronger, more permanent houses. Families often shared a single dwelling, and houses were built very close together. Structures varied according to the climate and availability of building materials, from mud bricks in warm river valleys to stone slabs near cooler coasts. Good harvests and the successful storage of food meant that some people had time to do other things, such as make jewelry and pottery. Settled people began making useful items that earlier hunter-gatherers would have found too heavy and breakable.

This carved bone necklace was found at Skara Brae.

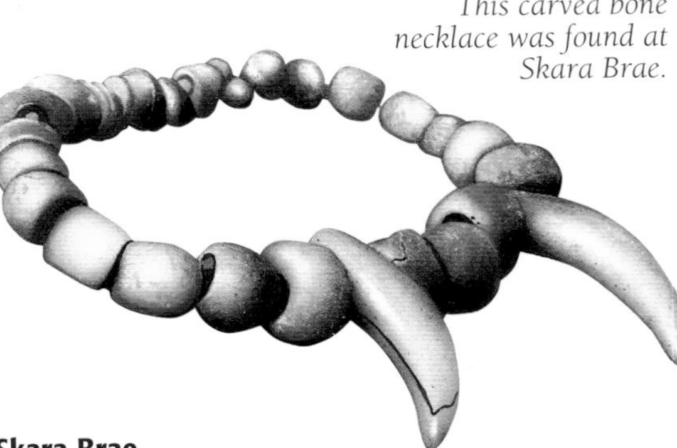

Skara Brae

The settlement of Skara Brae lay on Mainland, one of the Orkney Islands off the northeast coast of Scotland. There was good pastureland on the island but little wood, so the villagers built and furnished their houses with stone. These substantial structures kept out the cold and wet of a northern European winter, though the settlement may eventually have been abandoned because of severe storms.

A reconstruction of the village of Çatal Hüyük. Archeologists believe that more than 1,000 houses may have been built on the site.

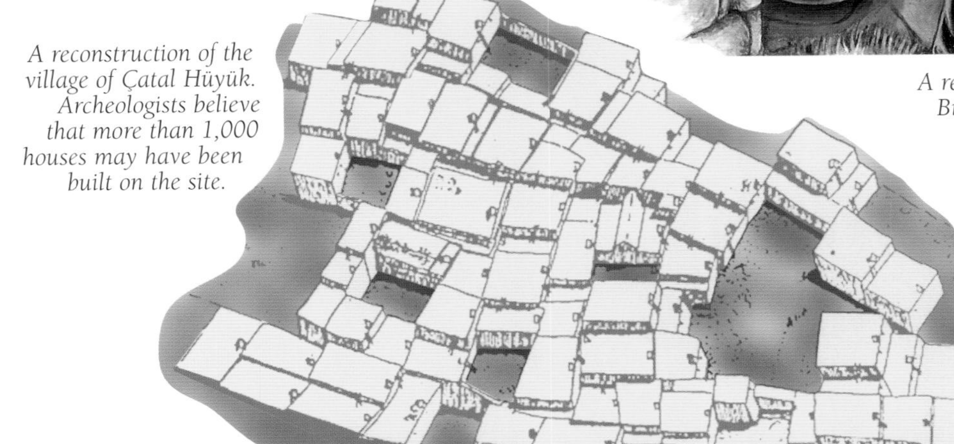

A reconstructed scene of everyday village life at Skara Brae. A cut-away section shows a woman tending to the hearth in a one-room stone dwelling.

Çatal Hüyük

People founded a farming village at Çatal Hüyük, in Anatolia, around 7000 BCE. They built rectangular mud-brick houses that adjoined each other. There were entrances on the flat roofs, and ladders were used to connect the different levels. All around the growing settlement, villagers grew crops of wheat, barley, lentils, and peas.

Mesopotamia

Some time after 7000 BCE, farming villages grew up beside the Euphrates and Tigris rivers. The villagers built their simple houses of sundried mud bricks, and villages began to appear further south as Mesopotamian techniques of irrigation improved. We know that some villages were surrounded by a mudbrick wall and a defensive ditch.

Villagers began to use clay pots as storage containers and cooking vessels. This Mesopotamian pottery beaker dates back to about 4000 BCE.

EARLY SETTLEMENTS AND VILLAGES

c. 8000 BCE
Settlement of Jericho near a spring, surrounded by cereal fields.

c.7000 BCE
Foundation of Çatal Hüyük, in Anatolia.

c. 6000 BCE
Farming villages established in the Mediterranean region; also in China, where pigs and dogs are kept.

c. 5500 BCE
Domed round houses of the Halaf culture, in northern Syria.

c. 5000 BCE
Ubaid culture of Mesopotamia based on irrigation farming.

c. 3400 BCE
Villages of round pit houses in the Tehuacán Valley, Mexico.

c. 3300 BCE
Walled towns appear in ancient Egypt.

c. 3100–2500 BCE
Farming and fishing village of Skara Brae in the Orkney Islands, Scotland.

c. 2800 BCE
Villages appear in the region of the River Amazon in South America.

c. 1150 BCE
Large villages in the Valley of Oaxaca, Mexico.

Africa

By about 6000 BCE nomadic peoples of the Sahara Desert were cultivating millet, and later sorghum and rice. Farming villages appeared in the Nile River valley in about 4000 BCE after wheat and barley were introduced from western Asia. Early Egyptian villages were made up of perhaps 50 people, but they soon grew to a population of around 1,000.

Cutaway illustration of a grass-covered dome-shaped hut from southern Africa, around 500 BCE.

Central and South America

Maize was probably being farmed in the Tehuacán Valley of Mexico by 5000 BCE, and villages of up to ten pit houses developed there. In South America, the first permanent villages grew up near the Pacific coast in present-day Peru, where cotton was being cultivated by 3500 BCE. About 1,000 years later, settlements were growing up in the river valleys leading down from the Andes Mountains to the coast.

Painted pottery figurine from the Tehuacán Valley.

Clay image of a goddess from the Hongshan culture, which developed in northern China around 4500 BCE.

South and East Asia

Early farming villages developed near the River Bolan on the Kacchi Plain, in modern Pakistan. From about 6000 BCE, villagers in this region were also building mudbrick storehouses. At around the same time, farming villages such as Banpo were appearing in northern China, near the Yellow River. Farming families lived there in round huts with walls made of a mixture of mud and straw supported by wooden posts.

The Growth of Towns

Cities developed in similar ways at different times in various parts of the world. The first large urban centers appeared in Mesopotamia. As farming populations increased, small villages grew into towns and some eventually became cities. In order to organize communities and control social living, hierarchies grew up in the cities and these led to the rule of kings. For defense against others, cities were generally walled. People living in well-organized communities were able to build temples and palaces and begin trading with other similar communities.

China

By about 3000 BCE Chinese villagers began to protect their small settlements with earth walls. Later, under the Shang dynasty of rulers (who began their reign soon after 1800 BCE), several cities developed and became successive capitals. Two of the most important were Zhengzhou and Anyang, which had palaces and temples surrounded by houses and workshops (see pages 171–3).

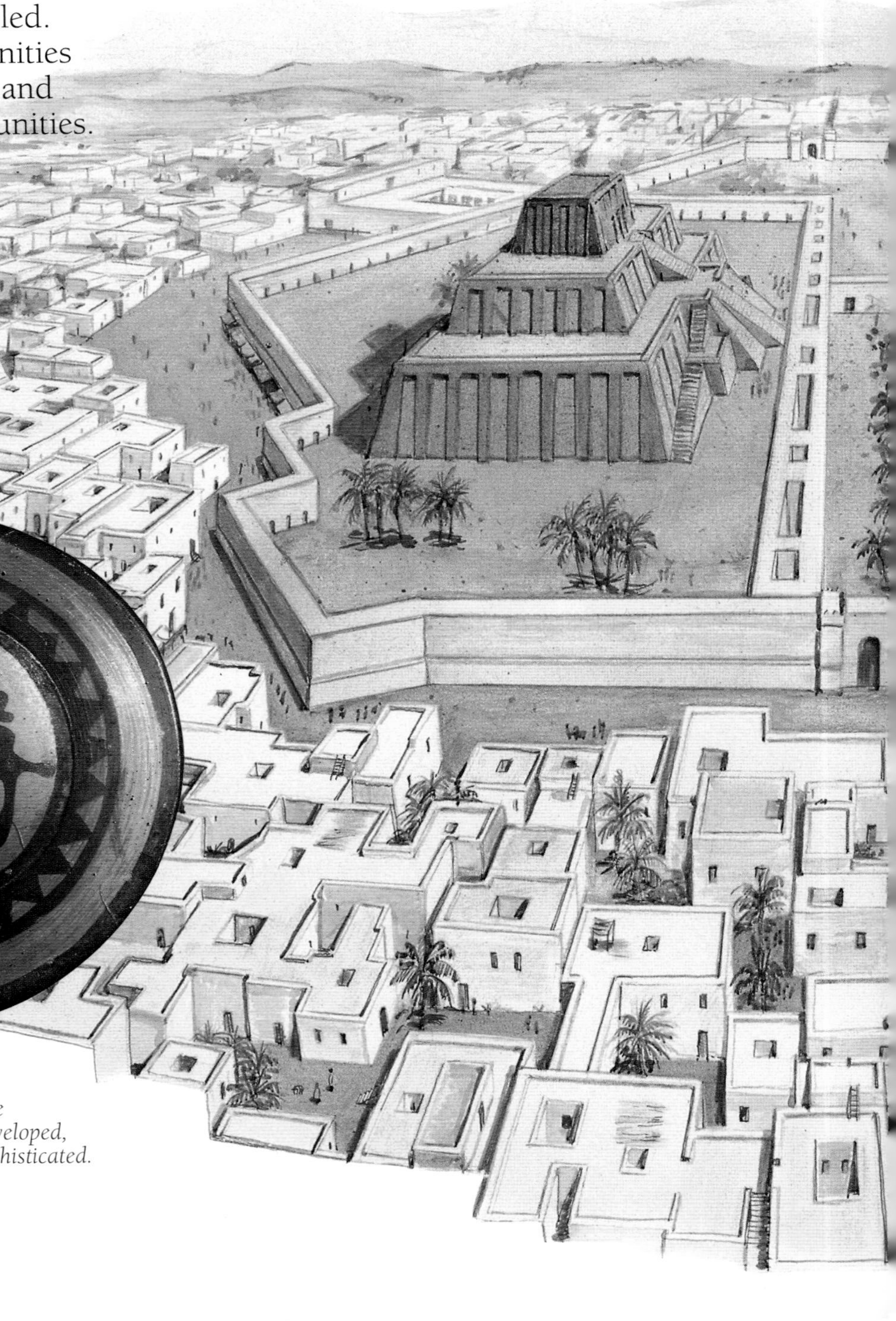

Developments in pottery making, such as the use of kilns, allowed Chinese potters to make beautiful red and black vases.

Mesopotamia and Egypt

The world's first cities developed in southern Mesopotamia around 3500 BCE. The city of Ur, which stood on the Euphrates River, grew into a thriving commercial center. As its power grew, the city took over neighboring villages and surrounding land, becoming a small kingdom. Neighboring Uruk was another important early city. Outside the walls, farmers grew barley, sesame, and onions, as well as raising sheep, goats, and cattle. In Egypt, fortified towns began to appear along the Nile. Later, they were unified by the first pharaoh in c. 3100 BCE. Giza, Memphis, and Saqqara were among the most important sites.

In the Indus Valley

Major farming settlements on the fertile land of the Indus floodplain (in present-day Pakistan) eventually grew into two great cities, Mohenjo-Daro and Harappa (see pages 160–3). They were well planned, with streets laid out in a grid pattern. Their mud-brick houses had washrooms and lavatories, and these were connected to drains that ran beneath the streets.

Painted terra-cotta pottery from Harappa. As village farming communities developed, pottery became more sophisticated.

FARMING COMMUNITIES AND URBAN AREAS IN 2500 BCE

- Areas in transition to farming
- Developed farming areas
- Urban areas
- Remote and under-developed area

Development of Urban Areas

As people began making the transition from hunting and gathering to agriculture, villages of settled farmers gradually developed into larger urban areas or cities. This map of the world shows how areas of North America, South America, Central America, Africa, and Asia were still in the early stages of farming development in 2500 BCE while urban areas had already formed in Mesopotamia, the Indus Valley, and Egypt.

The Americas

The city of Monte Alban, in modern-day Mexico, was founded by the Zapotecs in 500 BCE when they leveled off the top of a mountain. The founders must have had contact with the Olmecs, and by 200 BCE about 15,000 people were living around the ceremonial center of their city (see pages 208–9). In North America, the largest city grew at Cahokia around 800 CE, beside the Mississippi River in present-day Illinois. At its height, Cahokia had a population of up to 30,000.

A greenstone mask from the city of Teotihuacan, in the Valley of Mexico, which by 100 CE had a population of about 60,000.

Painted baked clay statuette of the Snake Goddess from Knossos.

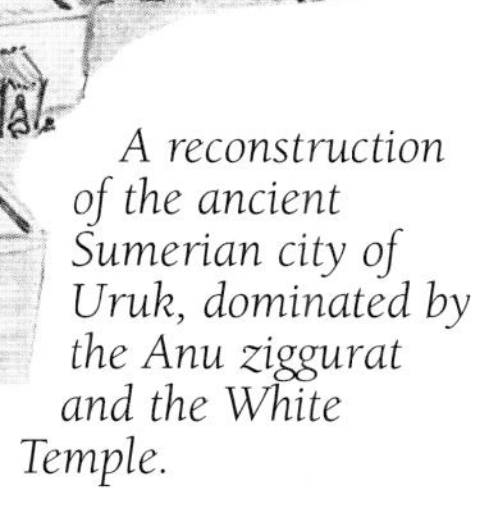

A reconstruction of the ancient Sumerian city of Uruk, dominated by the Anu ziggurat and the White Temple.

Europe

Europe's first cities developed on the Mediterranean island of Crete over 4,000 years ago (see pages 102–3). They were built by the Minoans, who were so called after their legendary King Minos. The Minoans built large palace cities. The great palace city at Knossos had as many as 1,500 rooms. By 2000 BCE there were many other palace cities on Crete, including Phaistos, Mallia, and Zakro.

Protecting Trade

The early city-states that controlled trade had great power and did everything they could to protect their position. Cities such as Troy (on the coast of modern Turkey), which watched over trade between the Mediterranean and Black seas, were heavily protected but constantly attacked. Trade routes also had to be defended, and since they often ran through rival territories, overzealous protection sometimes led to disagreements and warfare.

Copper axe from Ur, about 2500 BCE. Such weapons may have been carried by royal guards.

Trade and Warfare

By 2000 BCE a long-distance trading system was developing around Mesopotamia. Because cities developed in river valleys, much of the transport was by water—along rivers and following coastlines on the open sea. Long before the first coins were minted, trade was carried out by exchanging goods. These included valuable and luxury items, such as metals and gemstones. The new trade routes led to communication between growing cities and smaller settlements in neighboring regions. Before long a trading network covered an extensive region from the Mediterranean Sea to the Indus Valley.

Mesopotamian professional soldiers rode off to battle in chariots drawn by asses. The invention of these vehicles revolutionized warfare.

Armies

The kings or other rulers of city-states generally acted as supreme commanders of their armies, often leading their troops into battle. There was usually a permanent standing army, paid for by the king, though military campaigns were normally organized after the harvest had been safely gathered. Troops carried shields and most foot soldiers were armed with spears. Spearmen also rode in chariots, and were replaced by archers in later, more maneuvrable models.

This carving shows helmeted troops of the city-state of Lagash, in modern southern Iraq, moving against neighboring Umma about 2560 BCE. Both cities lay between trade routes that ran from the Persian Gulf.

TRADE AMONG THE FIRST CITIES

Trading Networks

The earliest cities and states set up trading networks. As well as trading with each other, Mesopotamian city-states engaged in trade with Indus Valley cities such as Mohenjo-Daro. An overland trade route passed through Susa, while a sea route passed through the Persian Gulf. Shipbuilding, the domestication of the horse and camel, and the development of wheeled vehicles, all helped to advance trade.

Valuable Goods

Much early trade between regions was in useful materials that were not available everywhere. A good example is obsidian, a black volcanic glass that was used for arrowheads and knives before the use of copper and bronze. Areas rich in minerals and metals were at a natural advantage. Gold and silver were valued for their beauty and rarity, and the Egyptians mined for gold in southern Nubia from early times. Hard green jade was used for making axes and musical instruments, as well as for beautiful jewelry and ornaments.

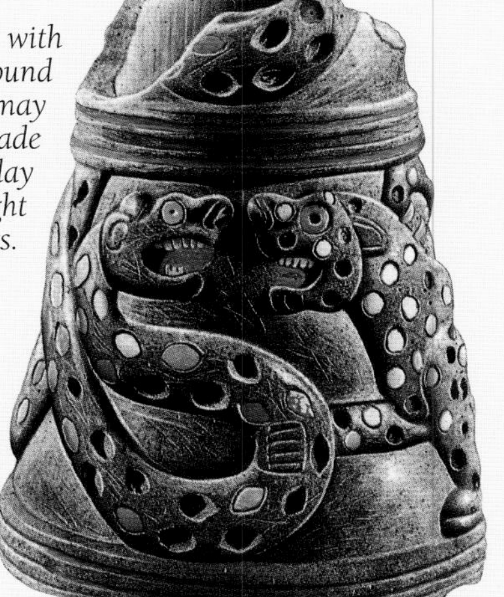

Chlorite vessel with stone inlay found in Nippur. It may have been made in modern-day Iran and brought over by traders.

Exchange of Ideas

Ideas were exchanged as well as materials and goods. The first wheeled vehicles probably appeared in Mesopotamia around 3600 BCE, and knowledge of this extraordinary invention soon spread far and wide. The same was true of advances in metalwork, especially smelting methods, though many developments seem to have appeared independently at different times in various places.

This jade mask made by Zapotecs, dating from about 200 BCE, is thought to represent a bat or a jaguar.

In Mesopotamia, writing was carved onto clay tablets. Important tablets were left to harden in the sun so they could be preserved and stored in libraries.

The Invention of Writing

People started writing about 5,500 years ago, when traders began using special marks to keep records and business accounts. The marks were made up of small pictures and symbols, and different writing systems arose in various cultures. The invention of writing, at a time when civilization was developing around the world, marked the end of prehistory. From that time on, people were able to record all their transactions, laws, and stories. This was the beginning of written history.

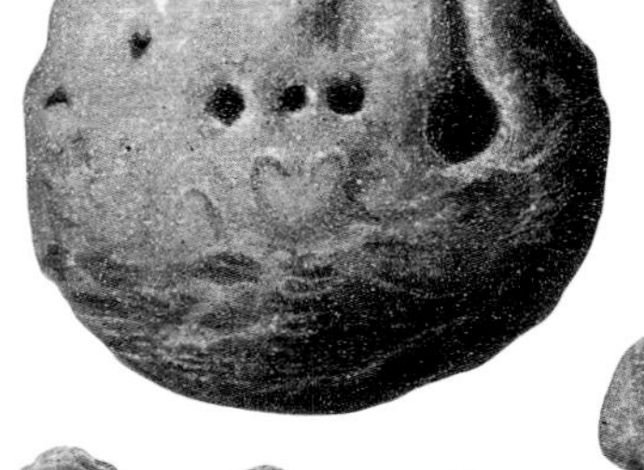

A hollow clay ball and tokens from Mesopotamia. The tokens were pressed on to the surface of the ball, recording trading items and amounts. Then they were sealed inside.

Cuneiform

The first writing system probably developed from clay tokens made by early Mesopotamian traders. By 3500 BCE the tokens were being kept in clay balls, and a few hundred years later the Mesopotamians began using reed stems to make wedge-shaped marks on wet clay tablets. The marks developed into a script called cuneiform (meaning "wedge-shaped"), which was used for about 3,000 years to record important events (see page 52).

Hieroglyphics

By about 3250 BCE the Egyptians were using a writing system that we call hieroglyphics (meaning "sacred carving"). This script used a mixture of picture symbols, sound signs (such as an owl for the letter "m"), and other symbols. It was used mainly for writing inscriptions in tombs and temples, and fewer than one in every hundred Egyptians could read or write the script. This meant that scribes played an important part in Egyptian life, working mainly for rulers and priests.

Oracle Bones

The earliest examples of Chinese writing are engraved on animal bones or pieces of tortoise shell. The bones and shells were heated until they cracked, and the pattern of cracks was seen as a message from ancestral spirits. The questions and answers were then inscribed on the bones with sharp metal pens.

Ancient oracle bones from Shang China, inscribed with pictographs.

This papyrus contains a hieroglyphic hymn to the hawk-headed sun-god Ra. Such writings were placed in coffins to help dead people on their way to the afterlife.

WRITING HISTORY

c. 3500 BCE
The earliest form of writing, which developed into cuneiform, is used in Mesopotamia.

c. 3250 BCE
The Egyptians use hieroglyphic script.

c. 2500 BCE
Pictographs, writing in the form of pictures and drawings, are used in the Indus Valley.

c. 2300 BCE
The Akkadian language is written in cuneiform.

c. 1700 BCE
The Minoans write in so-called Linear A, a script that we still cannot understand.

c. 1500 BCE
Chinese pictographic writing on bones and shells; though some characters have changed, the basic system is still the same, making Chinese the oldest writing system still in use.

c. 1200 BCE
The Phoenicians use a 22-letter alphabet to write their Semitic language; this is later adopted by the ancient Greeks and is the ancestor of all Western alphabets.

c. 800 BCE
Hieroglyphic script is developed in Central America.

WRITING AROUND THE WORLD

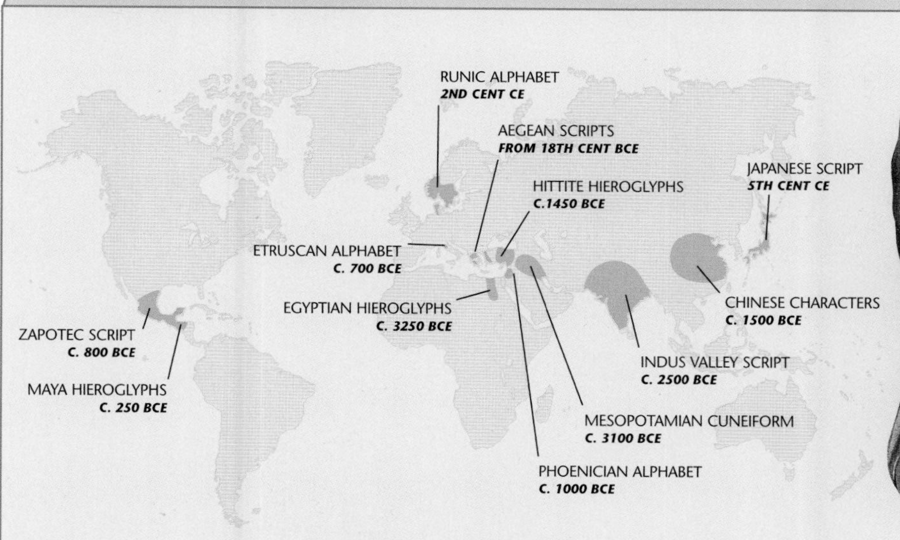

Writing Systems

We know that separate writing systems appeared at different times in various parts of the world, but we are not sure how much one system influenced another. It could be that the idea of writing spread from one culture to another, especially through trade, but that individual scripts arose independently.

This statuette shows a female Mayan scribe with a folded codex book.

Central America

In Central America the Zapotecs (see page 41) developed a hieroglyphic script around 800 BCE. All the later scripts of the region developed from this, including Mayan writing. The Maya wrote on thin strips of fig-tree bark, which they folded up like an accordion to make pages. We call these books codices.

It was in Mesopotamia—the land between and around the Euphrates and Tigris rivers—that farmers first started growing their own crops. Their simple settlements grew into the world's first cities, leading to many interrelated cultures, kingdoms, and empires.

The story of the region comprises the history of many peoples, including the Sumerians, Babylonians, Hittites, Assyrians, Phoenicians, and Persians. Together they were responsible for many amazing inventions, from the wheel to the written word. According to the Bible, Abraham's origins also lay in Mesopotamia, and we follow his migration to Canaan, the founding of the kingdom of Israel, and the years of exile and foreign occupation. In this chapter, our look at many thousands of years of this fascinating region's history ends with the birth of Christianity.

Jewelry in the form of gold beads from ancient Arabia. Archeologists have found evidence of gold mines and workshops in Yemen.

	8000 BCE	**4500 BCE**	**3500 BCE**	**1500 BCE**
EARLY MESOPOTAMIA AND THE SUMERIANS	First farmers in Mesopotamia. Hassuna culture and Samarra culture.	Farming villages develop into small towns; the earliest plows are used.	Development of the first cities in southern Mesopotamia.	The Akkad region, north of Sumer, is supreme. Third Dynasty of Ur, the city is capital of an important empire.
BABYLONIANS				Elamites sack Ur and capture the city's king. King Hammurabi rules Babylon.
HITTITES				The Hittites arrive in Anatolia Battle of Qadesh between the Hittites and Egyptians. Fall of the Hittite Empire.
ASSYRIANS			The city of Ashur is settled.	Hittites invade and sack Babylon. Assyrian trading colonies are founded in Anatolia.
PHOENICIANS				Phoenician city-states start to form a major trading empire.
PERSIANS				
ARABIAN NOMADS				
ISRAELITES				Abraham leads his people to Canaan. Hebrews migrate from Canaan to Egypt. Judges lead Israelites.

Mesopotamia and the Bible Lands

Silver statuette of a fertility goddess from Anatolia.

1000 BCE **800 BCE** **600 BCE** **400 BCE** **200 BCE**

Nabopolassar, first of the Chaldean dynasty, comes to rule Babylonia.

Nebuchadnezzar II rebuilds Babylon.

Babylon is captured by Cyrus II of Persia.

Nimrud is capital.

Assyrians occupy Babylon.

Babylon is sacked after rebelling against Assyria.

Nineveh is sacked by the Babylonians and Medes.

The first Phoenician colony is founded in Cyprus.

Colonists from Tyre found the city of Carthage.

Tyre allies itself with Egypt against Assyria.

Tyre is besieged by the Babylonians.

Tyre and other cities fall under Persian rule.

Tyre is captured by Alexander the Great after an eight-month siege.

Carthage is destroyed by the Romans.

Persian ruler Hakhamanish founds the Achaemenid dynasty.

Cyrus the Great becomes king of the Medes and Persians and rules Babylon.

Cambyses II conquers Egypt.

The Persians are defeated by the Athenians.

The Persians are defeated by Alexander the Great.

Traders travel the "Incense Road."

According to legend, the Queen of Sheba visits King Solomon in Jerusalem.

Rise of states in southern Arabia.

Minaeans trade successfully from Ma'in, southern Arabia.

The Nabataeans fight off an attack by Demetrius I Poliorcetes, king of Macedonia, at their capital city of Petra.

King David makes Jerusalem capital of Israel.

Reign of Solomon.

The kingdom is divided.

The Assyrians conquer Israel.

Judah is overrun by the Babylonians; Judaeans are exiled to Babylon.

Exiled people return to their homeland.

Macedonian king rules Palestine.

Roman rule.

Revolt of the Macabees.

Life Near the Rivers
Some time after 7000 BCE, the people of Mesopotamia began digging irrigation canals from the two rivers to water their fields. They also built dykes and embankments, as well as water-storage basins, so that they could use the rivers' water throughout the year. The system of canals, especially to the east of the Euphrates, was quite large by about 4000 BCE.

Mesopotamia: The Two Rivers

Mesopotamia is the name of an ancient region where the world's first civilization developed. The region stretched from the Taurus Mountains of present-day Turkey in the north to the Persian Gulf in the south, covering parts of present-day Syria and most of Iraq. It was called Mesopotamia, meaning "land between the rivers," by the ancient Greeks. They were referring to the two great rivers that flow through the region—the Euphrates and the Tigris. They made a fertile flood plain in the south, although the summers were long and hot with little rainfall. Early farmers had to learn to use their water wisely.

The two rivers were also used for transport. Boats carried food and building materials, especially downstream toward the south (upstream was more difficult).

EARLY MESOPOTAMIA

c. 8000 BCE
The first farmers appear in Mesopotamia.

c. 7000 BCE
The first pottery is made; the first villages in the north; settled farmers begin irrigating their fields in the south.

c. 6500 BCE
Hassuna culture in northern Mesopotamia and Samarra culture in central Mesopotamia, where farming is well established.

c. 5900–4300 BCE
Ubaid period, based around the site of Tell al-Ubaid, located west of Ur.

c. 4500 BCE
Farming villages develop into small towns; the earliest plows are used.

c. 4000 BCE
A complex system of irrigation canals beside the Euphrates and Tigris rivers is used.

c. 4000–3000 BCE
Uruk period, based around the city of Uruk (built c. 3500 BCE).

c. 3500–3000 BCE
Development of the first cities in southern Mesopotamia.

MESOPOTAMIA

The Euphrates and the Tigris Rivers
The two rivers begin close to each other, high in the mountains of present-day eastern Turkey. They flow in a south-easterly direction, through modern northern Syria and Iraq to the Persian Gulf. In ancient times, the rivers flooded the Mesopotamian plains every year during spring and early summer. The floods were so strong that early farmers had to build embankments to protect their crops.

Some early Mesopotamian boats were made of bundles of reeds tied together. Other boats were made from wooden planks while rafts were kept afloat with inflated animal skins. Reed houses were built, similar to those still used in the southern marshes.

The first plows were simple wooden devices. By 3000 BCE bronze blades had been added, and some plows had funnels for dropping seeds into the ground.

Goats were herded by early farmers, along with sheep. Pigs and cattle were domesticated later. These animals were kept for their milk, hides, and wool, as well as for meat.

Farming

About 10,000 years ago, groups of hunter-gatherers who settled in Mesopotamia began growing their own crops. They started by collecting the seeds of wild grains, such as einkorn and emmer wheat. Then they planted the seeds near the river and kept the growing plants well watered. Farming villages gradually grew up near the fields of crops.

Clay tablets such as this one, which dates from around 3000 BCE, were used by early traders to keep account of goods. The picture symbols represent the goods, and the deeper impressions show quantities.

Fragment of a pitcher, made about 5200 BCE, with a face painted on its neck. Early paint was usually made from iron oxide and other minerals.

Pottery

Settled villagers found that clay pots were ideal to use as storage containers and cooking vessels. Pots were shaped by hand and then fired in a simple kiln. They were painted in a variety of designs. By about 4000 BCE, potters were using a simple turntable that they rotated by hand. A more sophisticated potter's wheel was developed later.

THE SUMERIANS

c. 3000 BCE
Ur becomes an important city and then city-state.

c. 3000–2350 BCE
Early Dynastic period —independent city-states have their own rulers.

c. 2340–2200 BCE
Akkadian period, the Akkad region north of Sumer is supreme.

c. 2100–2004 BCE
Third Dynasty of Ur, the city is capital of an important Neo-Sumerian empire.

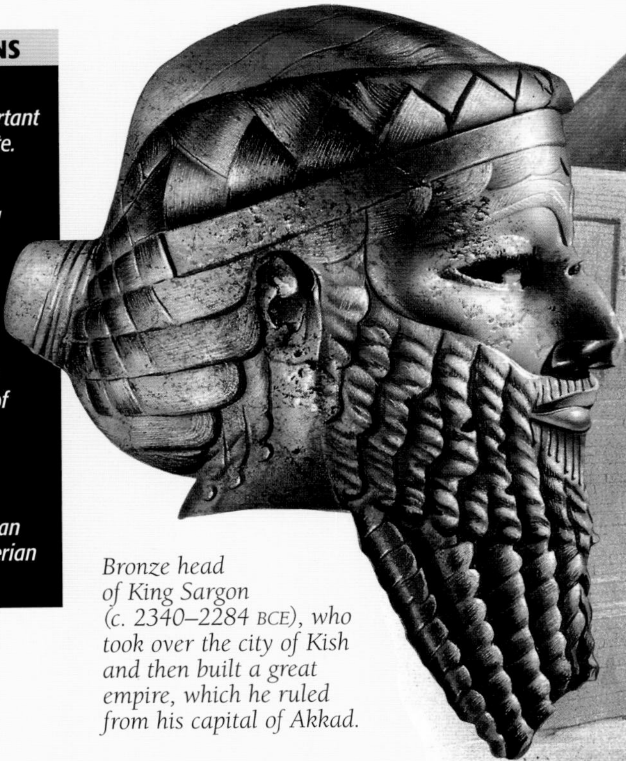

Bronze head of King Sargon (c. 2340–2284 BCE), who took over the city of Kish and then built a great empire, which he ruled from his capital of Akkad.

Sumer: Cities, Kings, and Gods

Cities developed in a region of southern Mesopotamia that we call Sumer (from the name of the region in the Akkadian language). The Sumerians themselves called the region Kalam, meaning "the Land." They lived in cities that were surrounded by small settlements and farmland. City-dwellers lived in mud-brick houses, and in time some became craftworkers and traders. Some cities took over the nearby area, becoming city-states, and then some even conquered their neighbors as their kingdoms grew. Each city was dedicated to a god and led by a king, who was thought to have been chosen by the gods.

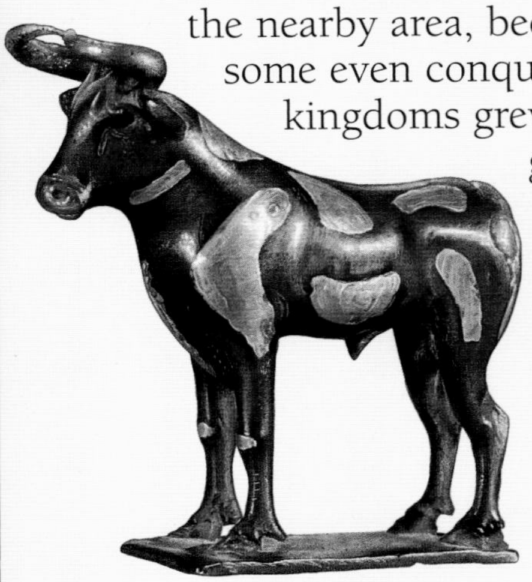

This bronze bull, inlaid with silver, was made some time after 2500 BCE. Bulls were seen as a symbol of strength and may have been used in religious sacrifices.

Early Cities

As the farming population grew, small settlements became towns and cities. Successful harvests and storing of food meant that some people had time to do other things, such as make jewelry or build temples. In order to control irrigation and organize people, a hierarchy grew up and led to the rule of kings. For defence against others, cities were walled. They were each dominated by a temple, which served as a house on Earth for the city's individual god.

In about 2100 BCE Ur-Nammu, a governor of the city of Ur who later became king, built a ziggurat dedicated to the moon-god Nanna. Forced donations of grain and other food to the temple's priests were carefully recorded by scribes on clay tablets.

Wooden board game dating from about 2500 BCE, found in the royal cemetery at Ur. The game probably involved moving around the board according to the throw of dice or dice-sticks.

A necklace made of beaten gold, c. 1800 BCE. The gold was probably obtained from eastern Anatolia (modern-day Turkey) or the Persian Gulf.

Trade

Early Sumerian cities exchanged goods with each other. Materials that could not be found in Mesopotamia were imported from elsewhere. From the earliest times, volcanic glass called obsidian—used to make cutting blades—was obtained from the mountains of the north and east. Before 3000 BCE the Sumerians traded with Egypt and from c. 2300 BCE with the cities of the Indus Valley. They created a network of trading routes.

Gods and Goddesses

The Sumerians worshiped many different gods and goddesses, and each city had its own special deity. One of the most important gods was Enlil, who was known as the supreme lord, father and creator. He was the brother of the mother goddess Aruru and husband to Ninlil. The Sumerians believed that it was important to perform the correct rituals when worshiping the gods, so that they would continue to favor their city.

Akkadian cylinder seal from about 2250 BCE. In the center, the sun god, Shamash, rises from the eastern mountains. To the right, the water god, Ea, surrounded by gushing water and fish, is attended by another god. To the left are the winged goddess of love and war, Ishtar, and a warrior-god.

Statue of a priestess wearing a ceremonial cloak dating from about 2400 BCE. Many priestesses served and worshiped goddesses.

Myths and Legends

Important Sumerian kings were treated as gods, and after their death legends were told of their great exploits. There were also creation myths and stories about the gods, which at the time were probably seen as historical truth. Fortunately for us, some of these were written down on clay tablets. Stories in *The Epic of Gilgamesh*, found on 12 tablets in the library of an Assyrian king, tell of how Gilgamesh showed great strength and bravery, but failed to find immortality. Only his fame lives on.

Knowledge and Invention

Some of the most important inventions in human history came from Mesopotamia. Most importantly, the Sumerians began recorded history by developing their own written language. This has helped modern historians understand more about ancient knowledge. Other developments, such as the invention of the wheel and the smelting and use of various metals, were to have a great effect well beyond the region of Mesopotamia.

The invention of wheeled carts also facilitated trade. Grain, which was traded for other valuable goods, was stored in granaries like the ones shown here in the distance.

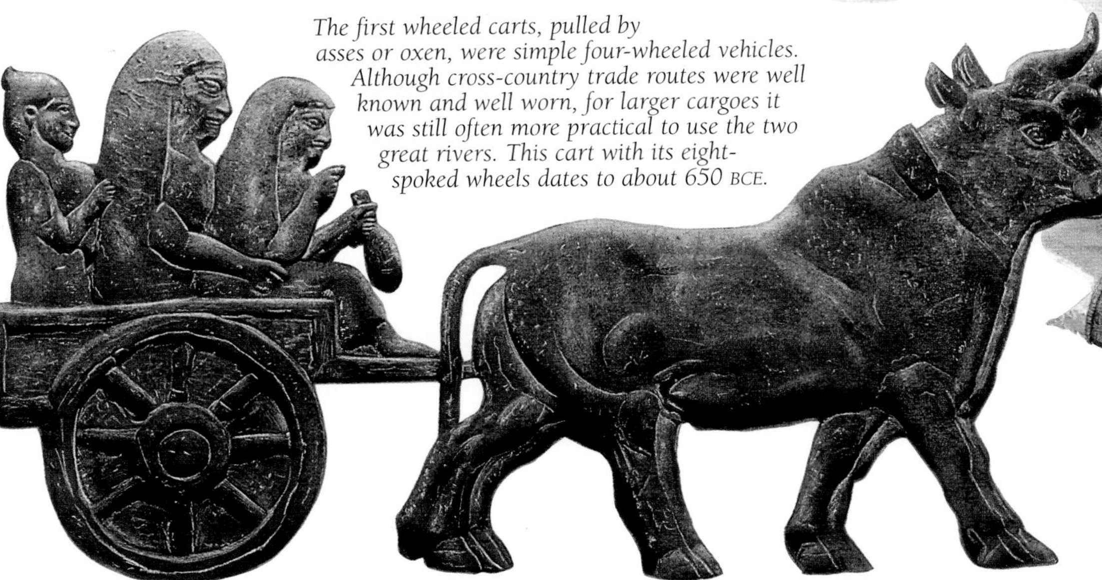

The first wheeled carts, pulled by asses or oxen, were simple four-wheeled vehicles. Although cross-country trade routes were well known and well worn, for larger cargoes it was still often more practical to use the two great rivers. This cart with its eight-spoked wheels dates to about 650 BCE.

The Wheel

The first wheels were probably turntables made by potters, who used them to turn the clay around as they built up and shaped their pots. Around 3250 BCE, the first wheeled vehicles came into use. Early solid wheels were made of pieces of wood, cut to form a disk shape and fastened together with wooden or copper brackets. Wheeled carts were first used to transport goods, replacing earlier sledges.

The Sumerian King List *was written in about 1820 BCE, making it one of the world's earliest historical records. The clay block lists kings of various Sumerian cities in chronological order.*

Writing

The first Mesopotamian writing system probably developed from the use of clay tokens by early Sumerian traders. By 3500 BCE the tokens were being enclosed in clay balls, and a few hundred years later, the Sumerians were writing on flat clay tablets with pointed reed pens. The original picture signs were simplified into symbols that made up a script called cuneiform, which means "wedge-shaped." Scribes used a wedge-shaped stylus to write quickly on wet clay.

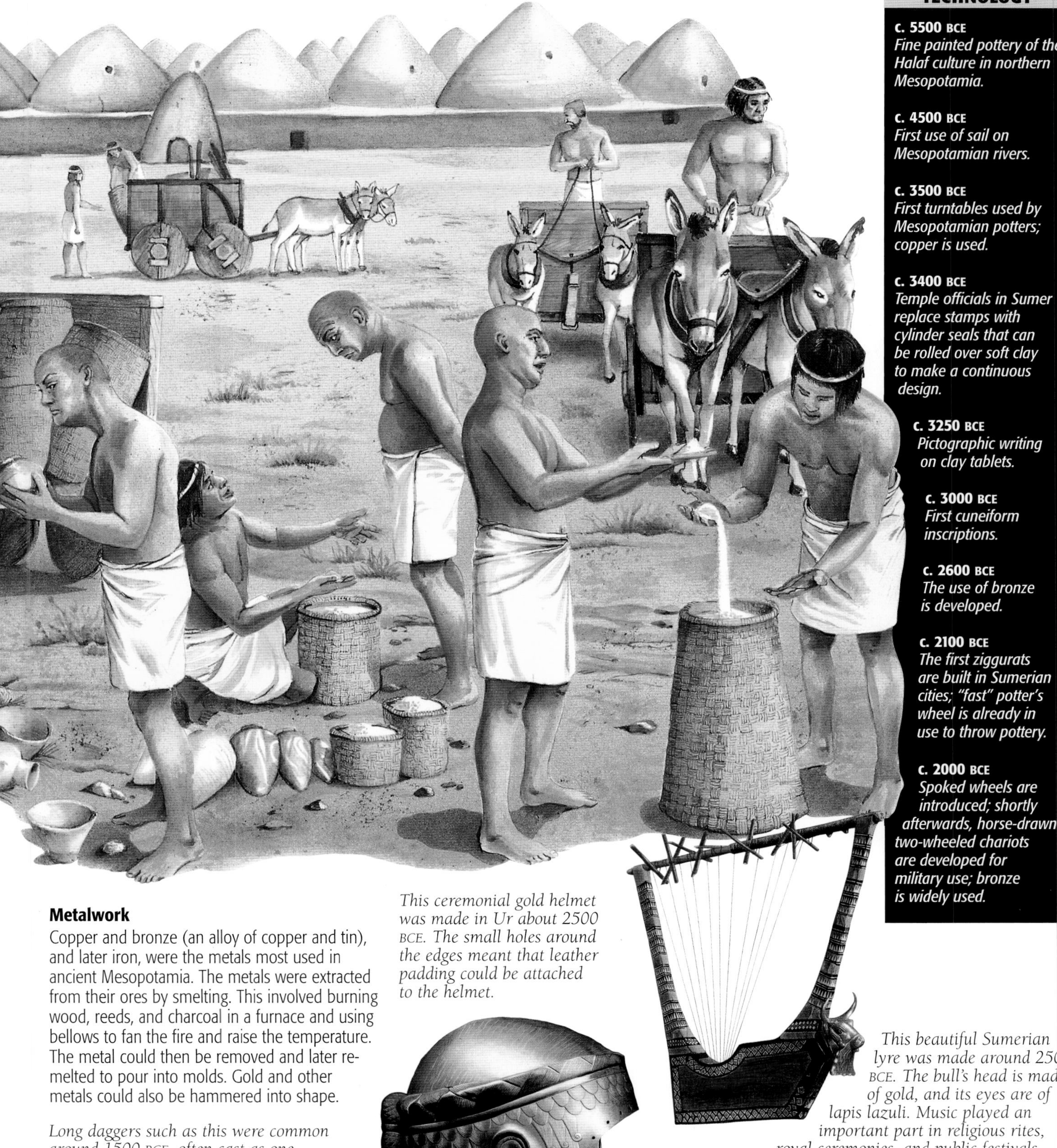

TECHNOLOGY

c. 5500 BCE
Fine painted pottery of the Halaf culture in northern Mesopotamia.

c. 4500 BCE
First use of sail on Mesopotamian rivers.

c. 3500 BCE
First turntables used by Mesopotamian potters; copper is used.

c. 3400 BCE
Temple officials in Sumer replace stamps with cylinder seals that can be rolled over soft clay to make a continuous design.

c. 3250 BCE
Pictographic writing on clay tablets.

c. 3000 BCE
First cuneiform inscriptions.

c. 2600 BCE
The use of bronze is developed.

c. 2100 BCE
The first ziggurats are built in Sumerian cities; "fast" potter's wheel is already in use to throw pottery.

c. 2000 BCE
Spoked wheels are introduced; shortly afterwards, horse-drawn two-wheeled chariots are developed for military use; bronze is widely used.

Metalwork

Copper and bronze (an alloy of copper and tin), and later iron, were the metals most used in ancient Mesopotamia. The metals were extracted from their ores by smelting. This involved burning wood, reeds, and charcoal in a furnace and using bellows to fan the fire and raise the temperature. The metal could then be removed and later re-melted to pour into molds. Gold and other metals could also be hammered into shape.

This ceremonial gold helmet was made in Ur about 2500 BCE. The small holes around the edges meant that leather padding could be attached to the helmet.

Long daggers such as this were common around 1500 BCE, often cast as one piece in bronze.

This beautiful Sumerian lyre was made around 2500 BCE. The bull's head is made of gold, and its eyes are of lapis lazuli. Music played an important part in religious rites, royal ceremonies, and public festivals. Harps, pipes, and percussion instruments were also common.

Early Babylonia: Rule of Law

Around 4,000 years ago the city of Ur lost its power in Mesopotamia. Other cities, such as Isin and Larsa, fought for supremacy, but it was Babylon that eventually came to rule over the whole region. The city's name came from an Akkadian word meaning "gateway of the god." It lay on the Euphrates, to the north of the other cities. Babylon had a dynasty of kings that grew in power, and they ruled for centuries over a region that came to be known as Babylonia. Historians call the four centuries between 2000 and 1600 BCE the Old Babylonian period. The greatest Babylonian ruler was Hammurabi, who introduced a system of laws throughout his kingdom.

EARLY BABYLONIA

2004 BCE
Elamites (from Elam, east of Mesopotamia, in modern Iran) sack Ur and capture the city's king.

c. 1894 BCE
Sumu-abum becomes the first Amorite ruler of Babylon; he reigns at the same time as the seventh king of Isin (Bur-Sin) and Larsa (Sumuel).

c. 1813–1781 BCE
Amorite king Shamshi-Adad rules Assyria, north of Babylonia in the Upper Tigris region.

1792–1750 BCE
King Hammurabi rules Babylon.

1787 BCE
Hammurabi captures Uruk and Isin.

1761 BCE
Hammurabi takes over the Kingdom of Larsa, bringing the whole of Babylonia under his rule.

1760 BCE
Hammurabi conquers the northern city of Mari.

1749–1712 BCE
Reign of Hammurabi's son Samsu-iluna, who loses most of Babylonia's southern lands.

1625–1595 BCE
Reign of Samsu-ditana, last of the kings of the First Dynasty of Babylon.

Kingdom of Babylon

Babylon, on the east bank of the Euphrates, was an unimportant town until about 1894 BCE. Then it was taken over by the first of a line of rulers from an Amorite tribe, a wandering people from Mesopotamia. Babylon was still quite a small kingdom when Hammurabi came to the throne, but by the end of his reign it controlled the whole of Mesopotamia.

Stone head of King Hammurabi. He undertook great building works in Babylon, as well as improving the defence of his kingdom and the irrigation of its lands.

Laying Down the Law

Hammurabi established a famous Code of Laws, which was made up of at least 280 "cases of justice." The laws were written on clay tablets and sent around Babylonia to serve as models of behavior. Though many of the suggested punishments were harsh, the king saw it as his duty to "protect the orphan and widow." Two of the laws read: "If a man has put out the eye of a free man, they shall put out his eye. … If a slave has struck the cheek of a free man, they shall cut off his ear."

This stele lists Hammurabi's laws. It was found at Susa, in Elam, where it had been taken as war booty. The carving on top shows the king standing before Shamash, the sun god and patron of justice.

Expanding Trade

In years of good harvests Babylonia had enough grain for merchants to export and exchange for timber, stone, and other goods. If there was no direct exchange, payment was usually in silver. Ur was still an important trading city, with boats coming up from the Persian Gulf, and it had its own merchants' organization. Some traders also acted as royal envoys, carrying valuable gifts between rulers.

This relief carving, dating to about 700 BCE, shows a merchant leading a camel loaded with goods. Camels were well suited to the harsh conditions of desert trade routes.

Babylonian Trade

Babylonia lay on the main trade routes between the Persian Gulf and the Mediterranean Sea. One of the main stops on the Euphrates to the north of Babylon was the city of Mari, which was known for its tin trade. Mari was finally conquered by Hammurabi.

Looking to the Heavens

The Babylonians greatly increased their knowledge of astronomy by keeping detailed records of their observations of the stars and planets. They likened the wandering planets to wild goats and the fixed stars to tame goats. Their greatest purpose in looking at the night sky was to predict future events. The Babylonians believed that what happened up in the heavens was mirrored down on Earth.

Astronomers study an eclipse of the Sun, which was generally seen as an omen of disaster. A scribe carefully records their findings.

A carving showing the sun god Shamash on his throne receiving a king and two other gods. The disk in the center symbolizes the Sun.

The Babylonian Way of Life

The Babylonians lived in a similar way to earlier peoples of Mesopotamia. They had mud-brick houses, and their successful farming methods meant that food was good and plentiful. Grains such as barley were ground into flour and used to make bread, beer, and porridge-like soups. Vegetables were grown, and fish, sheep, and goats were also eaten. The people's rulers and priests organized seasonal festivals, and everyone worshiped Marduk, the patron god of Babylon from early times. But after their great king Hammurabi died in about 1750 BCE, the Old Babylonian Empire gradually went into decline.

Sacred Sacrifice

Religious festivals were important in Babylonia, and many involved great processions. These gave ordinary people the opportunity to take part in religious events and communicate with the gods. There were festivals of thanksgiving, and many were associated with the phases of the Moon. Special events took place at New Year, which was celebrated in spring, at the beginning of the month of Nisannu (around mid-March by our calendar). During some sacred festivals, a bull was led outside the city before being sacrificed.

Statue of a goddess that acted as a fountain in the courtyard of the palace at Mari.

A king leads the procession of a bull sacrifice.

Interpreting Omens

The Babylonians believed that the gods sometimes allowed them to see into the future by interpreting omens. Diviners were specialists at prediction. They often examined the entrails of slaughtered animals, looking especially at the liver for any peculiarities. They sometimes poured drops of oil into a beaker of water and studied the shapes made, or they watched clouds of smoke rising from burning incense. In this way they gained insight into the will of the gods.

Clay model of a sheep's liver. The shape of the real liver was examined and omens written on the model. This one ominously forecasts the destruction of small towns.

This terra-cotta plaque showing a loving couple, dating from about 1900–1600 BCE, was found at Ur.

Marriage

By the laws of Hammurabi, a wife received a written contract of marriage from her husband. Men generally had only one wife, and her main duty was to produce children, especially sons. If she failed to do this, her husband could divorce her, but he had to return any money paid to him when they married. She also had the right to a divorce if her husband disgraced her and she could show that she was blameless. According to the law, a man could leave his property to his wife rather than to his sons.

Women's Roles

Wives and especially mothers of kings had great power and authority. Women could also be scribes in royal palaces. Priestesses had special roles, and some were allowed to buy and sell fields. Among ordinary people, both weaving and the brewing of beer were normally done by women, and each activity had its own goddess—Uttu for weaving and Ninkasi for beer-making.

This terra-cotta statue of a woman, dating to about 2000–1700 BCE, was probably placed in a temple.

Rise of the Hittites

The Hittites invaded Anatolia, to the northwest of Mesopotamia in present-day Turkey, around 2000 BCE. They built a kingdom, and about 400 years later the Hittite king went down the Euphrates to Babylon and defeated its Amorite ruler. The Hittites soon returned to their own capital of Hattusa, leaving a new dynasty of Kassite kings from the east to rule Babylon. The Hittites were a warrior people, and from 1400 BCE they built an empire by taking over Mesopotamian cities and small states. These territories were then ruled by locals under the authority of the Hittite king.

HITTITES

c. 2300 BCE
The Hittites arrive in Anatolia, probably from the central Asian region.

c. 1700–1400 BCE
Period of the Hittite Old Kingdom.

c. 1650 BCE
Hattusa is made capital of the Hittite kingdom.

c. 1595 BCE
Mursilis I (reigned c.1620–1590 BCE) invades and sacks Babylon.

c. 1550 BCE
The kingdom of Mitanni is founded.

c. 1400–1190 BCE
Period of the Hittite New Kingdom (or Hittite Empire).

c. 1370–1330 BCE
Reign of Suppililiumas I, one of the greatest Hittite kings.

1350 BCE
The Hittites destroy the kingdom of Mitanni.

c. 1340 BCE
The Hittites conquer western Mitanni.

c. 1275 BCE
Battle of Qadesh between the Hittites and Egyptians.

c. 1190 BCE
Fall of the Hittite Empire as Hattusa is destroyed.

Masters of Metal

The Hittites were great metalworkers, skilled at making objects in gold, silver, and other metals. They were probably the first people to smelt iron, and so helped bring in the true Iron Age. Certainly iron was in use as early as 2000 BCE in Anatolia, when it may have been considered more valuable than gold. By 1400 BCE it had become a very important metal, and the Hittites found it useful for making strong, dependable weapons.

Gold pendant figurine of a god wearing a typical Hittite conical hat, from about 1300 BCE.

Horsemen

Throughout ancient Mesopotamia the horse was known as the "donkey of the mountains." The Hittites became expert at breeding and training horses, mainly for pulling their war chariots (see page 60). Horses were also used by kings, princes, and important landowners.

Decorative part of a bronze standard, in the shape of a man and his horse, from Anatolia, about 2000 BCE.

The guardian warrior-god of the King's Gate at Hattusa is armed with a battleaxe and a curved dagger.

THE HITTITE EMPIRE

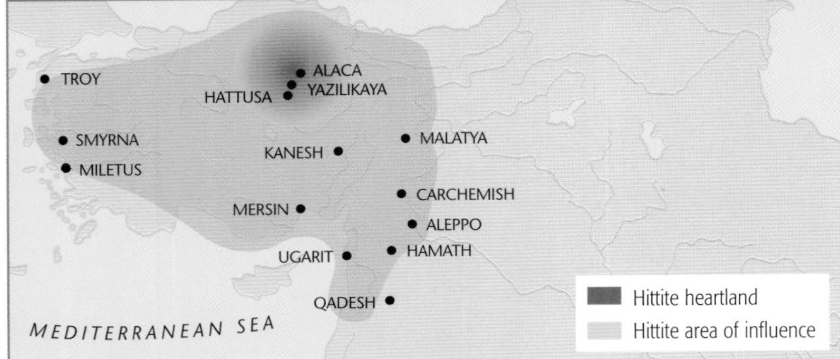

The Hittite Capital

In the middle of the 17th century BCE, the Hittite King Labarnas (reigned c. 1650–1620 BCE) made Hattusa, in Anatolia, his capital and took the name Hattusilis ("the one from Hattusa"). A later Hittite king fortified the city, rebuilding the walls around the original citadel and the whole city. A royal palace and several temples were added. In the southern section of the city there were three large gates in the double walls: one was flanked by guardian stone lions, another by sphinxes, and a third by a warrior-god.

Hittite Culture

After the fall of the Hittite Empire, some city-states survived in south-eastern Turkey and northern Syria under their own dynasties. Arameans also established principalities alongside the Neo-Hittite ones. They adopted aspects of Hittite culture, particularly in architecture and the way they decorated their buildings with relief sculpture, guardian sphinxes, and lions. As a result, Neo-Hittite culture survived until these small kingdoms were taken over by Assyria in 710 BCE.

Detail of a stone relief showing scenes of everyday life of a Neo-Hittite king of Carchemish (northern Syria) and his family. Here two young princes play a game of knucklebones.

Range of Gods

The Hittites believed in many different gods and goddesses. As their empire grew, they adopted the gods of the peoples they conquered, so the range became even larger. One of the main Hittite deities was the storm-god of Hatti who was often shown carrying a trident or a bolt of lightning as he drove his chariot drawn by two sacred bulls. Teshup was the companion of the sun-goddess Arinna.

This pitcher from about 1550 BCE was used for pouring wine, oil, or honey for the gods.

A golden disk surrounds the head of the protective sun-goddess Arinna, who was seen as the queen of heaven. The Hittite king and queen were her high priest and priestess.

A Clash of Empires

As the Hittites moved south along trade routes beside the Syrian Desert, they clashed with the Egyptian Empire as it spread north from Africa. The meetings of the two empires were not always hostile. In the 14th century BCE the widow of an Egyptian pharaoh asked the Hittite king to send one of his sons to become her husband. But the young king was killed before this could happen. Then, around 1275 BCE, Hittite king Muwatallis II fought the Egyptian pharaoh Ramesses II at Qadesh, in modern Syria. Less than a century later, the Hittite Empire and its capital were destroyed, probably by the Kashka people from the Black Sea area.

Fragments of a Hittite clay tablet outlining the peace treaty. It says that the treaty was also inscribed on a silver tablet that was sent to Egypt, but this has never been found.

Battle of Qadesh

The great battle began when Ramesses II (reigned 1279–1213 BCE) fell into a trap. He believed false reports that the Hittite army was still further north, at Aleppo. When the Hittites forded the Orontes River and suddenly attacked, the Egyptians were unprepared. Their first division was destroyed, but they fought back with the help of an auxiliary force. After two days the battle ended in stalemate, and the Egyptians moved back to the south. Later, both sides claimed a great victory.

War Chariots

The Hittite chariot was much lighter and faster than earlier Mesopotamian models. It was pulled by two specially trained horses, and the army kept other horses in reserve as replacements. The wooden chariot was wide enough to carry three men. The driver stood in the middle, and he was flanked on one side by an attacking spearman and on the other side by a defensive shield-bearer.

With its spoked wheels and axle set well back, the Hittite chariot was balanced and highly maneuverable.

The Peace Treaty

Sixteen years after the Battle of Qadesh, Muwatallis's brother Hattusilis III (reigned 1275–1245 BCE) signed a historic peace treaty with Ramesses II. The two rulers agreed not to attack each other and to help the other if there were a threat from elsewhere, such as Assyria. The treaty was further sealed in 1246 BCE, when Hattusilis sent his eldest daughter to become a wife to Ramesses II.

During the battle, the Hittites and the Egyptians used similar weapons. Both sides had many thousands of foot soldiers and charioteers. Ramesses II's four divisions contained 5,000 men each, but the Hittite army might still have outnumbered them. Both armies suffered great casualties.

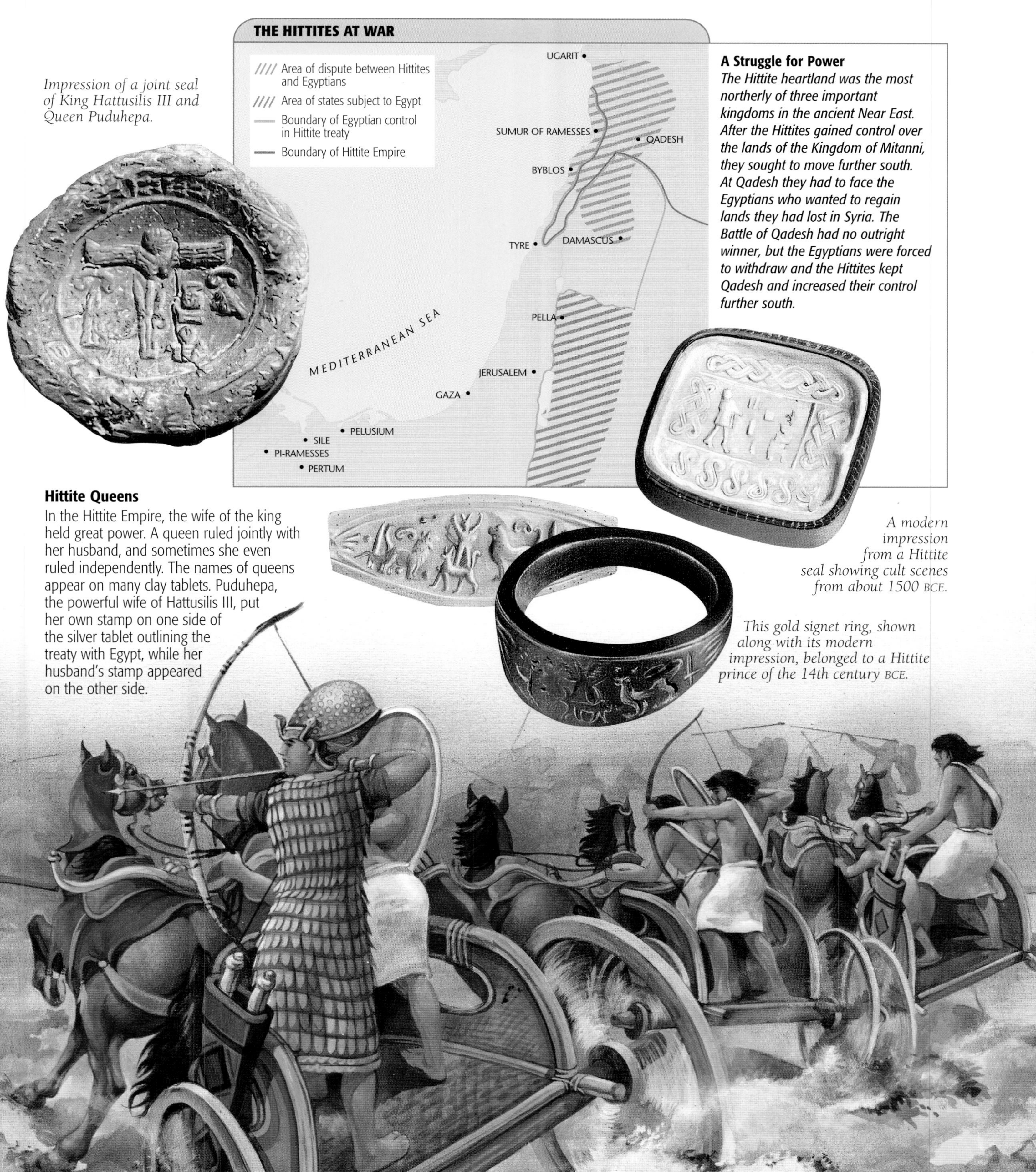

Impression of a joint seal of King Hattusilis III and Queen Puduhepa.

A Struggle for Power

The Hittite heartland was the most northerly of three important kingdoms in the ancient Near East. After the Hittites gained control over the lands of the Kingdom of Mitanni, they sought to move further south. At Qadesh they had to face the Egyptians who wanted to regain lands they had lost in Syria. The Battle of Qadesh had no outright winner, but the Egyptians were forced to withdraw and the Hittites kept Qadesh and increased their control further south.

Hittite Queens

In the Hittite Empire, the wife of the king held great power. A queen ruled jointly with her husband, and sometimes she even ruled independently. The names of queens appear on many clay tablets. Puduhepa, the powerful wife of Hattusilis III, put her own stamp on one side of the silver tablet outlining the treaty with Egypt, while her husband's stamp appeared on the other side.

A modern impression from a Hittite seal showing cult scenes from about 1500 BCE.

This gold signet ring, shown along with its modern impression, belonged to a Hittite prince of the 14th century BCE.

War Machine

The Assyrians had a powerful army. In the 8th century BCE, military reforms created an efficient war machine that included foot soldiers armed with bows and arrows, others with swords, spears, and battleaxes, as well as archers on horseback. The cavalrymen gradually replaced charioteers. The army also used wooden siege engines and heavy battering rams. Assyrian conquerors butchered and terrorized their opponents, which discouraged others from resisting them.

In 701 BCE King Sennacherib besieged and then destroyed the city of Lachish, in Palestine. This relief carving shows a family being taken into exile in Assyria.

This Assyrian foot soldier of about 740 BCE carries a spear and a painted shield. He wears a coat of bronze or iron scale armor.

Ashurnasirpal's Palace

Around 878 BCE King Ashurnasirpal II used workmen from conquered lands to build an enormous palace in the new capital of Nimrud, beside the Tigris. Sculptors and artists carved reliefs and painted murals on the walls of the palace, which also contained great stone statues of mythical animals. When it was finished, the king held a huge banquet and the festivities went on for ten days.

The Assyrians

The homeland of the Assyrians centered on the hills and fertile plains of northern Mesopotamia, beside the River Tigris. From about the 14th century BCE, the small kingdom began to grow. The Assyrians were surrounded by many other states, and they fought their way to an empire. They became famous for their military strength and brutal treatment of their victims. They were happy with this, because their reputation made it easier for them to conquer others. Many of those they defeated were captured and made to work as slaves on huge building projects. This helped the mighty empire grow.

King Ashurnasirpal II receives Phoenician guests in a palace courtyard beside his throne room. The guests bring valuable gifts as tribute to the king.

Gods and Demons

The chief god of Assyria was Ashur, who may originally have been the local god of the ancient city of the same name. Ninurta was the all-important god of war and had his own temple at Nimrud. Most of the Assyrian gods and goddesses were similar to those of Sumer and Babylon. The Assyrians also believed in demons and evil spirits.

An Assyrian queen's crown. Made of gold and semiprecious stones, it was beautifully worked into flowers, vines, and guardian spirits.

THE NEO-ASSYRIAN EMPIRE

A Growing Empire

During the 11th century BCE, nomadic invaders from the north, east, and west squeezed the Assyrians back into their heartland. Toward the end of the following century, however, the Assyrians used their great military skills to start rebuilding a large empire. In the 7th century BCE the Assyrian empire stretched from the Persian Gulf to the eastern Mediterranean and the Nile Valley. When Ashurbanipal's army sacked the Egyptian city of Thebes in 663 BCE, the empire's power and culture were at their height.

THE ASSYRIANS

c. 2500 BCE
The ancient city of Ashur is settled, probably by local peoples.

c. 1950 BCE
Assyrian trading colonies are founded in Anatolia.

c. 1307–1275 BCE
Reign of King Adad-nirari, who expands Assyria's frontiers.

c. 934–911 BCE
Reign of Ashur-dan II, who re-conquers lands previously held by the Assyrians.

883–859 BCE
Reign of Ashurnasirpal II.

c. 878–707 BCE
Nimrud is capital.

744–727 BCE
Reign of Tiglath-pileser III.

729 BCE
Assyrians occupy Babylon.

721–705 BCE
Reign of Sargon II.

c. 707–705 BCE
Khorsabad is capital.

c. 704 BCE
Nineveh becomes capital under Sennacherib (reigned 704–681 BCE).

689 BCE
Babylon is sacked after rebelling against Assyria.

668–627 BCE
Reign of Ashurbanipal.

652–648 BCE
Civil war ends with Assyrian victory.

612 BCE
Nineveh is sacked by the Babylonians and Medes.

Assyrian Society

Assyria's rulers were powerful men who put great emphasis on authority and discipline. In Assyrian society, women had little say in important matters, and artists and craftsmen used their skills to portray their state's strength. Nevertheless, under King Ashurbanipal a huge library of Sumerian, Babylonian, and Assyrian clay tablets was put together at Nineveh. By then there was growing unrest among Assyria's enemies, and at the end of the 7th century BCE Nineveh fell to a group of subject states led by Babylon. This brought an end to the Assyrian Empire.

Women in Assyria

It seems that women had a lower social position and less authority than they did in Babylonia or among the Hittites. A man could send his wife away without any divorce settlement. If she committed adultery, he was allowed to beat her severely or even kill her. Outside the house, a woman had to wear a veil and observe many other restrictions. Royal women held more power, but they exercised it behind the scenes.

Smiling female face carved in ivory in the 8th century BCE.

Stone carving from about 860 BCE showing the preparation of food. Clockwise from top left: ingredients are collected from a storeroom; whisks are used to keep flies away; a baker checks his oven; butchering and carving meat.

These bracelets of gold and semiprecious stones were found in a queen's tomb beneath the palace at Nimrud.

Fashion and Style

Men and women wore long woolen tunics with narrow short sleeves. Male officials and military officers wore a shawl over the tunic. Linen was also used for clothing, and cotton was introduced around 700 BCE. The Assyrians often went barefoot, but leather sandals were sometimes worn. Both men and women wore jewelry, such as earrings and amulets. Women also had ankle bracelets.

Assyrian noblemen had square-cut beards and wore their hair long. Both hair and beard were waved and curled at the ends.

The Royal Hunt

It was the king's duty to protect his people from danger. This included the threat from lions, which were seen as a symbol of brutal strength. Mesopotamian kings had hunted lions since the earliest times, and the Assyrians continued this tradition. In later times, the royal hunt took place in a specially enclosed park. After killing a lion, the king poured oil or wine over the dead animal and offered it to the gods.

In this carved relief, the king thrusts his spear into a leaping lion. Showing how ferocious the animals were, another lion attacks the king's spare horse.

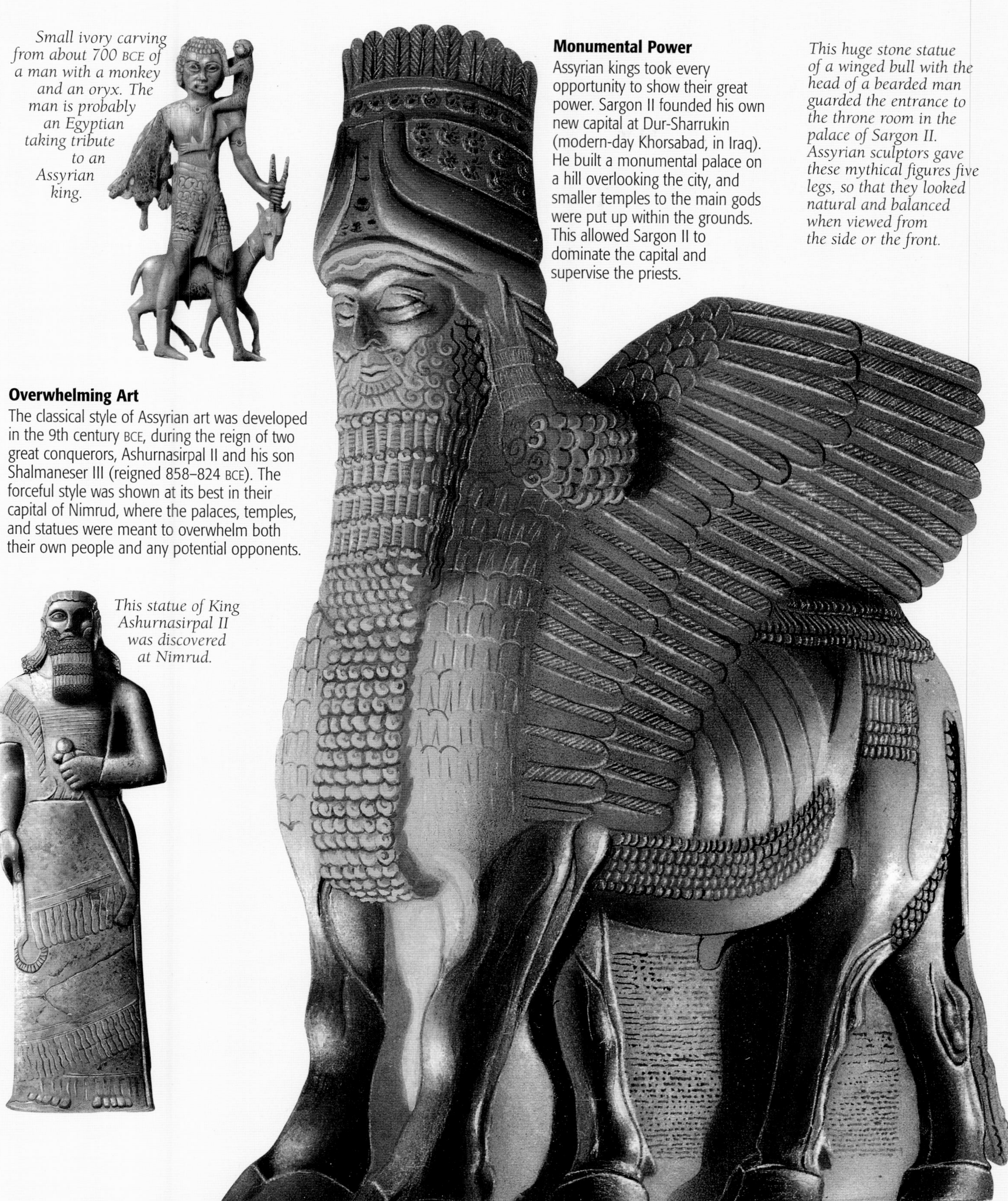

Small ivory carving from about 700 BCE of a man with a monkey and an oryx. The man is probably an Egyptian taking tribute to an Assyrian king.

Monumental Power

Assyrian kings took every opportunity to show their great power. Sargon II founded his own new capital at Dur-Sharrukin (modern-day Khorsabad, in Iraq). He built a monumental palace on a hill overlooking the city, and smaller temples to the main gods were put up within the grounds. This allowed Sargon II to dominate the capital and supervise the priests.

This huge stone statue of a winged bull with the head of a bearded man guarded the entrance to the throne room in the palace of Sargon II. Assyrian sculptors gave these mythical figures five legs, so that they looked natural and balanced when viewed from the side or the front.

Overwhelming Art

The classical style of Assyrian art was developed in the 9th century BCE, during the reign of two great conquerors, Ashurnasirpal II and his son Shalmaneser III (reigned 858–824 BCE). The forceful style was shown at its best in their capital of Nimrud, where the palaces, temples, and statues were meant to overwhelm both their own people and any potential opponents.

This statue of King Ashurnasirpal II was discovered at Nimrud.

NEO-BABYLONIAN EMPIRE

626 BCE
Nabopolassar (reigned 626–605 BCE), first of the Chaldean dynasty from southern Babylonia takes the throne.

c. 613 BCE
Nabopolassar's son, Nebuchadnezzar II, marries the daughter of Cyaxares, the king of the Medes.

605 BCE
Nebuchadnezzar II leads the Babylonian army and defeats the Egyptians at Carchemish.

c. 605–561 BCE
Major rebuilding of Babylon in imperial splendor.

597 and 586 BCE
Attacks on Jerusalem and deportation of Judaeans to Babylon.

571 BCE
Babylonians take Tyre, on the Mediterranean coast, after a long siege.

555 BCE
Nabonidus (reigned 556–539 BCE), son of a Babylonian nobleman, comes to the throne after a palace conspiracy.

554 BCE
Nabonidus's daughter becomes high priestess at Ur.

550–c. 540 BCE
Nabonidus goes to Arabia, leaving his son Belshazzar (died c. 529 BCE) in charge.

539 BCE
Cyrus II (c. 580–c. 529) of Persia, also known as Cyrus the Great, captures Babylon and ends the Neo-Babylonian Empire.

The Last Babylonian Empire

In 626 BCE, the first of a new dynasty of kings came to rule Babylonia. The new king belonged to a people known as Chaldeans, who lived in southern Iraq and the region near the Persian Gulf. The greatest ruler of this period of the Neo-Babylonian Empire was Nebuchadnezzar II (reigned c. 605–561 BCE). He rebuilt the capital of Babylon in magnificent style, adding fortified walls, a new palace, temples, and other impressive buildings. He also expanded and strengthened his empire. After Nebuchadnezzar II's death, the Empire soon began to lose power. It had lasted for less than a century when the Persians invaded and made Babylonia part of their own empire.

Terracotta figure from about 600 BCE. The animal may be a dog and represent Gula, the goddess of healing. Dogs were also thought to offer magic protection.

Historians believe that the legendary Hanging Gardens of Babylon may have been located to the west of the Ishtar Gate, between the royal palace and the Euphrates. Perhaps Nebuchadnezzar II and his homesick wife went to the uppermost level to enjoy the wonderful views over the city.

The magnificent Ishtar Gate, which formed the northern entrance to the city and led to the great Processional Way. This double gateway was covered with blue-glazed bricks and decorated with serpent-headed dragons and bulls.

Walls and Gates

The city of Babylon was protected by strong double walls, with nine gates, all named after deities. The main gate was dedicated to the Babylonian goddess of love and war, Ishtar. The walls had towers at regular intervals and were surrounded by a moat filled from the Euphrates. The walls were up to 82 feet (25 m) high and wide enough for four-horsed chariots to turn around.

The City

There was a large temple precinct dedicated to the god Marduk. It included a tall, six-level ziggurat, with a shrine to Marduk on top. This was reached by a monumental stairway, and the ziggurat included two further sets of steps. The ziggurat was about 295 feet (90 m) square. This ziggurat was probably the inspiration for the biblical Tower of Babel.

Stele depicting King Nabonidus, the last king of the Neo-Babylonian Empire, with the divine symbols of the moon-god Sin, the winged disk of the sun-god Shamash, and the star of Ishtar.

This 5th-century BCE tablet is one of a series that lists the main events of Babylonian history from 747 BCE, including Nebuchadnezzar II's conquests.

Imperial Conquest

As well as rebuilding Babylon, Nebuchadnezzar II extended and strengthened the Empire. Before he became king, he marched the Babylonian army up the Euphrates to Carchemish (in modern Turkey), where he defeated the Egyptians. Then, as king, Nebuchadnezzar II secured Damascus and twice attacked Jerusalem. This led to many Judaeans being deported (see page 81).

The Phoenicians: Masters of the Sea

The Phoenicians lived along a narrow coastal strip of northern Canaan. There they built important city-states, such as Byblos, Sidon, and Tyre. They were successful traders and skillful craftworkers, and above all they were adventurous seafarers. By the 8th century they had settled faraway colonies and their strong merchant ships were carrying cedar wood and oil, purple-dyed cloth, and many other goods all around the Mediterranean. After their homeland came under Assyrian control, the Phoenician settlements gained independence under the most important colony, Carthage.

Phoenician Origins

The Phoenicians probably called themselves *Kenaani*, or Canaanites. They occupied the coastal strip of ancient northern Canaan that forms present-day Lebanon. They became known to the Greeks as *Phoinikoi*, from their word for "reddish purple." This probably referred to the dye for which the Phoenicians became famous.

This black stone coffin was made for King Eshmunazar II of Sidon (reigned 475–461 BCE), in the 5th century BCE. It bears an inscription in praise of the king and his family in Phoenician script.

Trade Goods

The Phoenicians' greatest natural resource was wood, from their forests of cedar and pine. The fertile land away from the coast also produced grapes, olives, dates, and figs. As traders, they imported linen from Egypt, grain from southern Canaan, wool from Syria, silver and iron from the western Mediterranean, semiprecious stones from Arabia, and gold and ivory from Africa.

A clay vessel from the 7th century BCE. It was probably used for carrying wine or oil. It is decorated with dancers in a sacred garden.

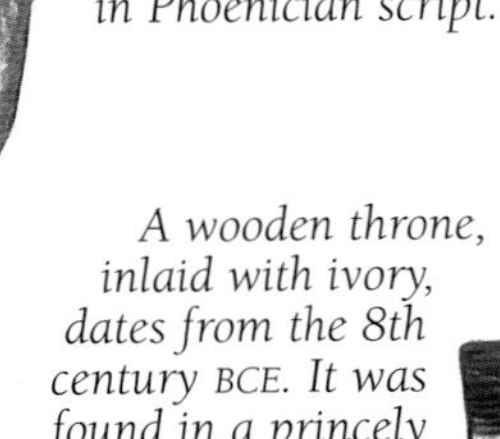

A wooden throne, inlaid with ivory, dates from the 8th century BCE. It was found in a princely grave at Salamis, on the island of Cyprus, a city that traded with Phoenicia.

This Canaanite, from an Egyptian mosaic of the 12th century BCE, is shown wearing a striking dyed tunic.

Carthage

After being colonized in the 8th century BCE, Carthage (meaning "New Town") soon became the most important settlement. The colonists were independent from about 600 BCE and acted as leaders of the other Phoenician settlements. Their interests in Sicily troubled first the Greeks and then the Romans. The Carthaginians fought three unsuccessful wars (called the Punic Wars) against the Romans, who eventually destroyed Carthage (see page 137).

Purple Dye

The famous purple dye was obtained from murex shellfish. These spiny-shelled sea snails were collected just off the Phoenician coast. Workers smashed the shells and put the snails in vats. As they decayed, the dead creatures produced a colored liquid that was then boiled to give the dye. Many thousands of shellfish were needed to produce just a small quantity of dye, which came to be known as "Tyrian" or "royal" purple. It was worth more than its weight in gold.

Carthaginian breastplate made of gilded bronze, worn as ceremonial armor around 250 BCE.

PHOENICIAN COLONIES

Phoenician homeland
Phoenician colonies
Phoenician trade route

IBERIA
GADES
LIXUS
MEDITERRANEAN
ITALY
THARRUS
SULCIS
NORA
HIPPO REGIUS
HIPPO DIARRHYTUS
UTICA
CARTHAGE
MOTYA
PANORMUS
LILYBAEUM
HADRUMETUM
THAPSUS
THENAE
SABRATA
OEA
LEPTIS
MACEDONIA
PERSIAN EMPIRE
ARADUS
IDALIUM
CITIUM
BYBLOS
SIDON
TYRE
AFRICA

The Phoenician Mediterranean
The Phoenicians founded trading cities and established colonies all along the North African coast, including Carthage (in modern-day Tunisia) and Tingis (modern Tangier, in Morocco). In the western Mediterranean, they colonized many islands, including Sicily, Sardinia, and the Balearic Islands.

Sailing the Mediterranean

The Phoenicians developed trading colonies throughout the Mediterranean. At first they sailed their strong trading ships along the coast, within sight of land, using a single square sail and a pair of steering oars. When they needed to sail on the open sea, they traveled at night and steered by the stars. Eventually, the Phoenicians sailed through the Straits of Gibraltar to Gadir (Cadiz, in present-day Spain), West Africa, and possibly Britain.

A Phoenician port was a place of great activity, where raw materials and finished goods were loaded onto and unloaded from trading vessels. The Phoenician coast had many fine harbors.

THE PHOENICIANS

c. 1200 BCE
Phoenician city-states start to form a major trading empire.

c. 1000 BCE
The first Phoenician colony is founded at Kition, Cyprus.

969–936 BCE
Hiram I rules Tyre.

868 BCE
Assyrian king Ashurnasirpal II collects tribute from Phoenician cities.

c. 814 BCE
Colonists from Tyre found the city of Carthage.

701 BCE
Assyrian king Sennacherib (reigned 705–681 BCE) drives out the king of Sidon and Tyre.

c. 680 BCE
Colonies on the Balearic Islands are established.

672 BCE
Tyre allies with Egypt against Assyria.

c. 600 BCE
Carthage becomes leader of the western Phoenician colonies.

586–573 BCE
Babylonians besiege Tyre.

538 BCE
Tyre and other cities fall under Persian rule.

c. 425 BCE
Carthaginian captain Hanno (active 5th century BCE) colonizes the west coast of Africa.

332 BCE
Tyre is captured by Alexander the Great after an eight-month siege.

264–241, 218–201 and 149–146 BCE
Punic Wars between Carthage and Rome.

146 BCE
Carthage is destroyed by the Romans.

PERSIA

A baked clay cylinder recording how Cyrus the Great conquered Babylon at the wish of the city's patron god, Marduk.

c. 700 BCE
Persian ruler Hakhamanish (active 7th century BCE), called Achaemenes by the Greeks, founds the Achaemenid dynasty.

c. 660–630 BCE
Reign of Cyrus I (active 7th century BCE), king of Anshan (part of ancient Elam).

550 BCE
Cyrus the Great deposes the Median king Astyages (reigned 585–550 BCE) and becomes King of the Medes and Persians.

525 BCE
Cambyses II conquers Egypt.

490 BCE
The Athenians defeat the Persians at the Battle of Marathon (in present-day Greece).

486–465 BCE
Reign of Xerxes I (son of Darius I).

480 BCE
The Persian fleet loses to the Greeks in the Bay of Salamis.

331 BCE
Alexander the Great defeats the Persian army of Darius III (reigned 336–330 BCE) at the Battle of Gaugamela (in present-day Iraq).

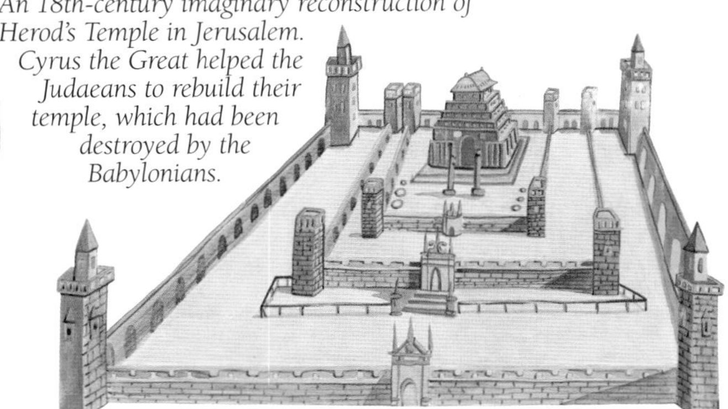

An 18th-century imaginary reconstruction of Herod's Temple in Jerusalem. Cyrus the Great helped the Judaeans to rebuild their temple, which had been destroyed by the Babylonians.

The tomb of Cyrus the Great at Pasargadae, the first royal capital of the Achaemenid kings. After the king's burial in a gold sarcophagus, priests sacrificed a horse at the spot every month.

Tolerance and Order

As their empire expanded, the Persians demanded loyalty and tribute from conquered lands. Once these conditions were met, provinces were allowed to continue with their local ways and customs. After capturing Babylon in 539 BCE, Cyrus the Great decreed that the exiled people of Judah could go back to their homeland. He even returned the gold and silver that had been looted from their temple in Jerusalem.

Who were the Persians?

The Persians were descended from nomadic Indo-European tribes from northeast of the Caspian Sea. They moved south to the Zagros Mountains, where some groups—known to us as the Medes—settled the uplands around 1000 BCE. Others moved on to a region that came to be known as Parsa (the modern Iranian region of Fars), and these people were the first Persians.

Double-headed griffin capital from the city of Persepolis.

Persepolis

Around 515 BCE, Darius I chose Persepolis (the "Persian City") as the site for his new royal capital. He built a palace on a raised terrace, which was reached by a monumental double stairway. The main buildings were columned halls, and these were added to by later Persian kings. The royal court stayed at Persepolis for part of the year, and it acted as a ceremonial symbol of the Persian Empire's power.

Running the Regions

Darius I divided his empire into 20 large provinces, each of which was ruled by a satrap, or provincial governor. The satraps were noblemen who lived in regal style and had great power, but they were always subject to the "King of Kings," who could send orders quickly by royal messenger. The Persian cities were connected by good roads, the most famous of which was the Royal Road from Sardis, in Lydia, to Susa, the administrative capital. The road was more than 1,491 miles (2,400 km) long.

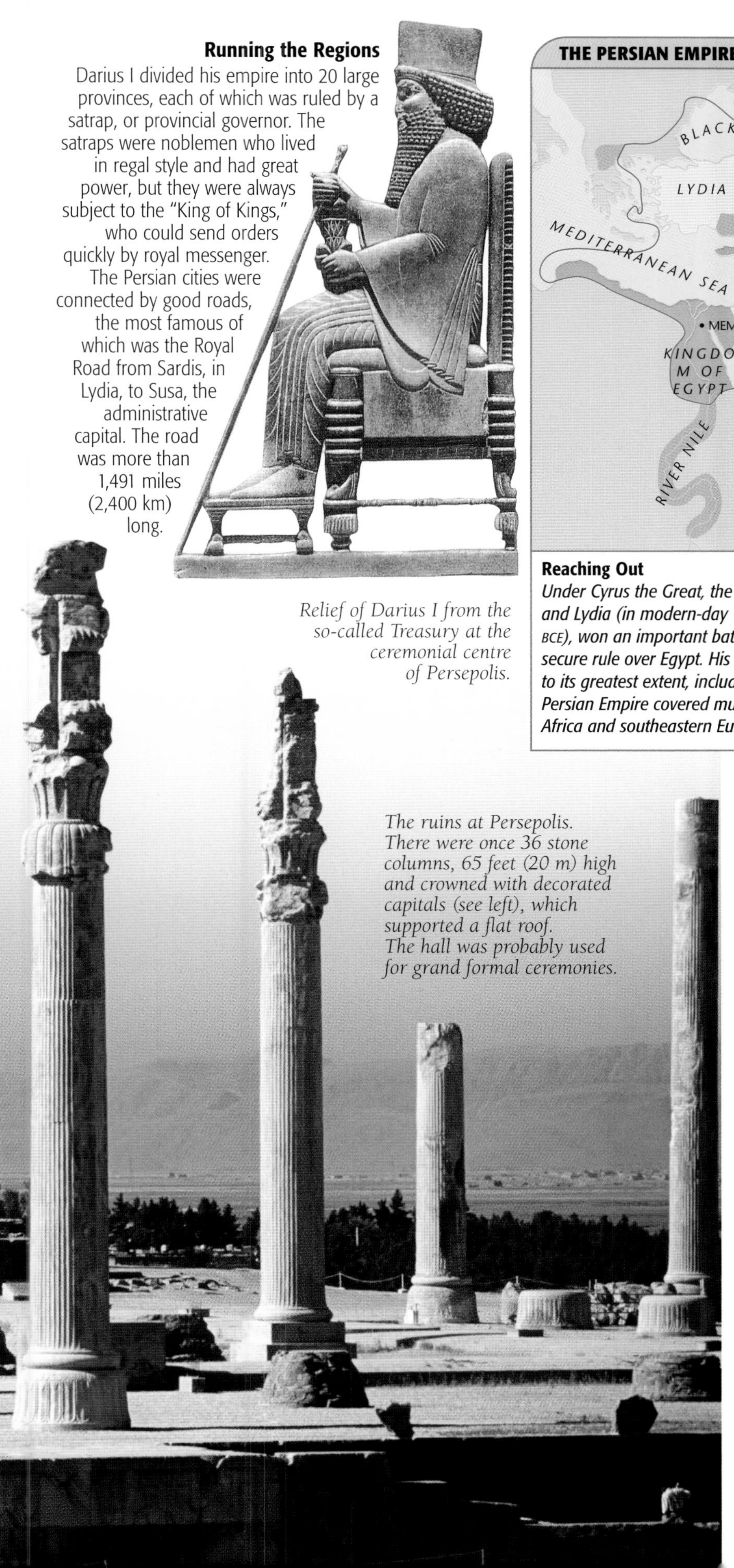

Relief of Darius I from the so-called Treasury at the ceremonial centre of Persepolis.

The ruins at Persepolis. There were once 36 stone columns, 65 feet (20 m) high and crowned with decorated capitals (see left), which supported a flat roof. The hall was probably used for grand formal ceremonies.

THE PERSIAN EMPIRE

Reaching Out

Under Cyrus the Great, the Persian Empire stretched all the way to the Mediterranean coast and Lydia (in modern-day Turkey) in the west. Cyrus's son, Cambyses II (reigned 529–522 BCE), won an important battle near the Nile River and went on to capture Memphis and secure rule over Egypt. His successor, Darius I (reigned 522–486 BCE), expanded the empire to its greatest extent, including control of the Indus Valley in the east. At its greatest, the Persian Empire covered much of southwest Asia. The Persians were also pushing into North Africa and southeastern Europe. But Darius I's planned conquest of Greece ultimately failed.

The Persian Empire

Around 550 BCE, Cyrus II, known as Cyrus the Great (c. 590–c. 522 BCE), defeated the king of Media and founded the Persian Empire. Less than 30 years later, it had grown to become the largest empire there had ever been. It was different in style from previous states, too. Persian rulers respected the ways of their new subjects, showing understanding and inspiring loyalty. Their laws were fair. The Persians were also highly organized, dividing their huge territory into provinces that were linked by good roads. This helped with administration, including the collection of taxes from their most distant lands.

Last Great Eastern Empire

The great extent and wealth of the Persian Empire meant that its art and culture were influenced by many different traditions. Persian religious customs had been based on sacrifice and centered on fire, and these developed into a belief in Zoroastrianism. This included belief in an afterlife, where those who had followed the cause of good would be rewarded. This faith was to have a great influence on many later religions. After the failure to include Greece in the empire, Persian rule went into decline. The end of the Achaemenid dynasty and the empire came with a decisive defeat by Alexander the Great, in 331 BCE.

This winged figure represents Ahura Mazda. Zoroastrians believed that their supreme god was in a constant struggle with Ahriman, the destructive force of greed and anger.

A Supreme God

The ancient Persians believed in many gods of nature, including Mithra, the god of light. A prophet named Zoroaster (believed to have lived during the 12th century BCE) began teaching that there was one single god of goodness, truth, and light, called Ahura Mazda, meaning "Wise Lord." Followers of the prophet and worshipers of the single god, called Zoroastrians, spread these beliefs throughout the empire.

A gold daric coin showing an archer representing the Persian king. The coin was named after Darius I, who introduced a standard currency throughout the empire. Only the royal mint was allowed to produce gold coins.

NEW YEAR CEREMONY

At New Year, which was celebrated at the time of the spring equinox, officials from all over the empire made their way to the ceremonial center at Persepolis. They brought gifts for the king, which represented the tribute for the year that had been demanded by the imperial government. The tributes were presented to the king in his great audience hall.

Conflict with the West

By 500 BCE small Greek island-states along the Anatolian coast had been conquered by the Persians, but the Greeks then rose up against the invaders. Darius I was defeated by the weather in 492 BCE, when his fleet was destroyed in a storm. After the disastrous defeat at Marathon two years later, it was left to Xerxes I to try and conquer Greece. But at the naval Battle of Salamis, in 480 BCE, his 800 galleys were crammed into a narrow strait and outflanked by the smaller Greek fleet.

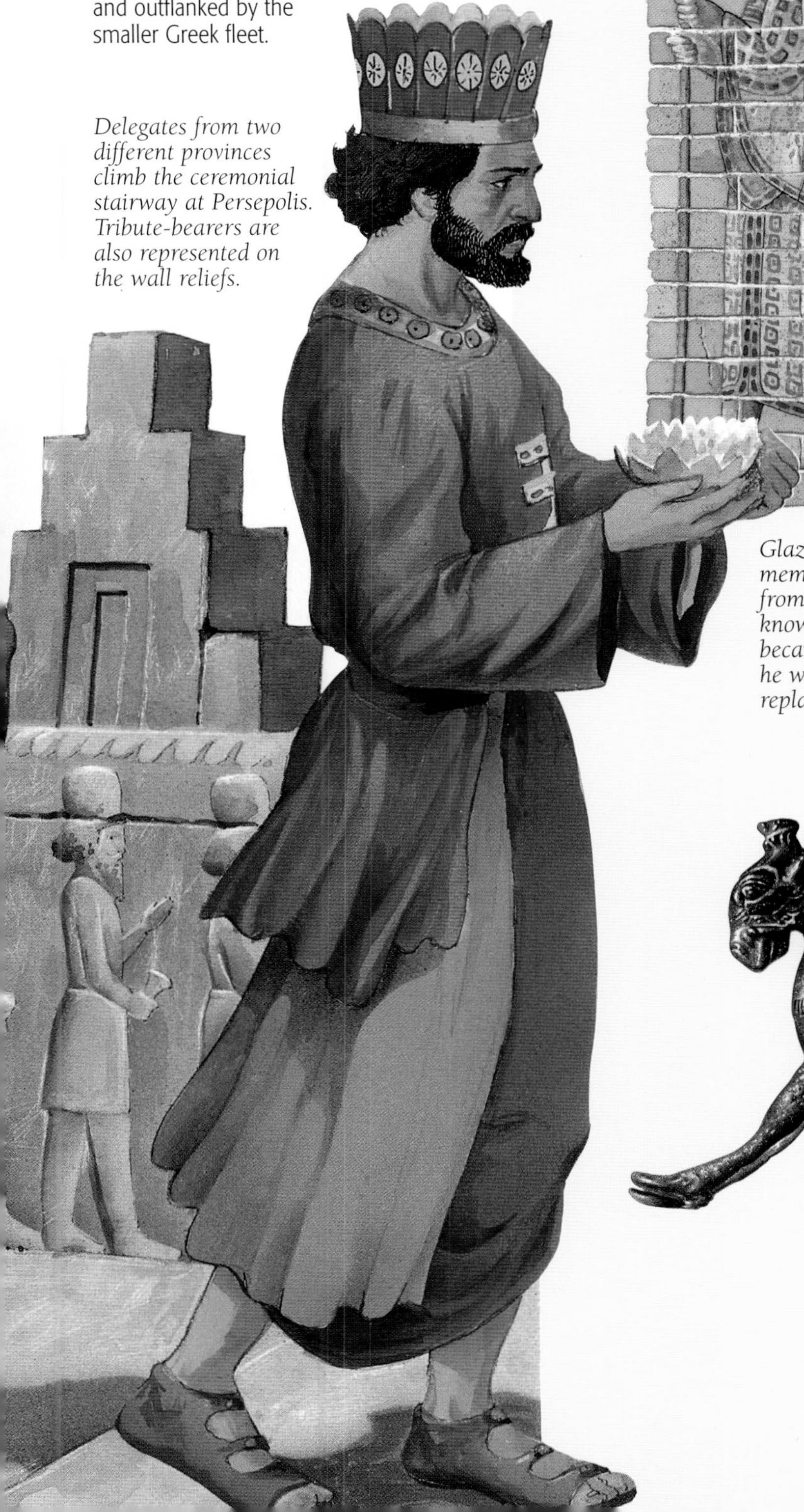

Delegates from two different provinces climb the ceremonial stairway at Persepolis. Tribute-bearers are also represented on the wall reliefs.

Glazed-brick relief of members of the royal guard, from Susa. The guards were known as the "Immortals," because if one was killed, he was immediately replaced by another.

Art of Many Lands

Just as ambassadors and merchants moved between the different provinces of the empire, so too did artists and craftworkers. This meant that different artistic traditions could continue to flourish. The glazed bricks at Susa and elsewhere were reminiscent of Babylon. Metalwork was also important, and beautiful objects were made in gold and silver.

A Persian horseman. The Persian cavalry were greatly feared by the Greeks and other opponents.

A 5th-century silver deer.

Traders of the Desert

The Arabian Peninsula lies to the south of Mesopotamia and the Mediterranean coast, across the Red Sea from Egypt. It is separated from Persia (modern-day Iran) by the Persian Gulf. In ancient times Arabia was inhabited by nomadic tribes of herders. After some groups began to settle, towns grew into city-states and kingdoms, especially in the south. They all thrived by trading incense and spices, which were popular in Egypt and Mesopotamia, and later in the Greek and Roman empires. The difficult journey across the desert became a way of life that created wealth for Arabian traders.

This Roman ivory plaque shows a priestess sprinkling incense on an altar to Jupiter, king of the gods.

A bronze incense burner decorated with an ibex, about 3rd century BCE, from Marib in Saba (modern-day Yemen).

The Power of Incense

The fragrance of frankincense resin was used for several purposes. The main use was in religious ceremonies, when the resin was burned as incense. Frankincense gives off a strong, sweet smell, which was thought to be divine and pure. The ancient Egyptians used incense in religious rituals and embalming, and the Babylonians also burned it to work out omens from its smoke. Myrrh, the gum of a similar plant, was also used in medicine and perfumes.

A branch of the myrrh tree. Its resin is used to make incense.

The so-called Monastery at Petra, which was probably a royal tomb.

Ships of the Desert

The one-humped dromedary, or Arabian camel, was domesticated by nomadic Arabs by 1500 BCE or perhaps earlier. Camels are the ideal beasts of burden in the desert because they can withstand severe heat and go for many days without water. They can also carry heavy loads.

The Arabian camel stores fat in its single hump, which provides it with energy over a long period.

Arabian Cities

There were several small, independent kingdoms in southern Arabia, including Hadhramaut, Ma'in, Qataban, and Saba. Each of the kingdoms' capitals—Shabwa, Qarnaw, Timna and Marib—was a thriving walled city that controlled overland trade. At the northern end of the caravan routes, the city of Petra (in modern-day Jordan) was the capital of the Nabataeans. Petra was hewn out of rock and could only be entered through a narrow gorge. Like the southern cities' walls, this offered the city protection against attack.

People of the ancient oasis city of Palmyra (modern-day Tadmor, in Syria) grew rich from their services to traders. Camels and camel-drivers could refresh themselves before carrying on across the desert with their goods. Palmyra came under Roman control around 20 CE.

ARABIA

c. 1000 BCE
Traders travel the "Incense Road," carrying spices from southern Arabia.

c. 950 BCE
According to legend, the Queen of Sheba visits King Solomon in Jerusalem.

c. 700 BCE
A dam is built at Marib, in the kingdom of Saba.

c. 550 BCE
Rise of states in southern Arabia.

c. 400 BCE
The Nabataean rulers of Petra become rich from the spice trade.

c. 350–150 BCE
The Minaeans trade successfully from Ma'in, southern Arabia (modern-day Yemen).

312 BCE
The Nabataeans fight off an attack by Demetrius I Poliorcetes (c. 337–283 BCE), king of Macedonia, at their capital city of Petra.

c. 250 BCE
Palmyra (in modern-day Syria) becomes an important trading city.

SEA ROUTES IN THE MIDDLE EAST

Arabian Ports
Sea routes led to major Arabian ports, such as Qani and those of the ancient region of Dhofar (centered on Salalah, in present-day Oman). Spice cargoes were taken north through the Red Sea and the Persian Gulf.

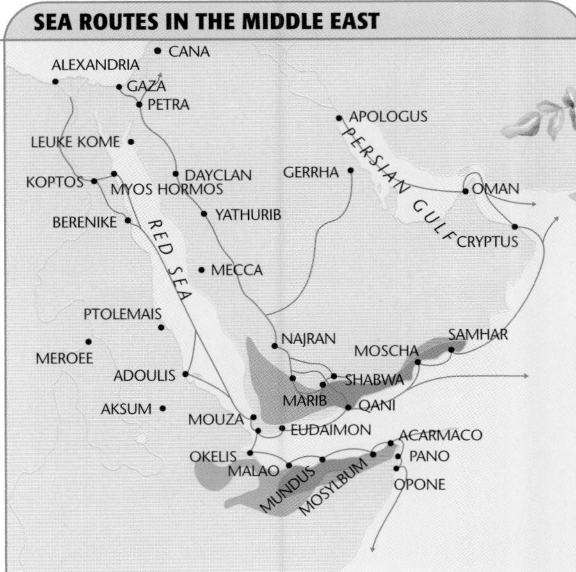

— Incense trade routes
Area of pyrrh production
Area of frankincense production
Area of both myrrh and frankincense production

A branch of the Boswellia franca *tree, from which frankincense (meaning "high-quality incense") is obtained. Harvesters cut into the tree's bark and collect the colorless or pale yellow resin, or gum, which has a spicy fragrance.*

The Spice Route

Frankincense and myrrh were produced in great quantity in the southern region of the Arabian Peninsula. Trade routes ran through the desert along the west of the peninsula, past the oasis settlement of Mecca, all the way to Petra and further north. The main land route is sometimes called the "Incense Road." Perfumed oils were also shipped from the west-coast ports of India, and Arabia acted as a stopping and collection point for Egypt and Mesopotamia.

This Egyptian wall painting from about 1900 BCE shows a nomadic group, possibly Hebrews from Canaan, trading with Egypt. The presence of women and children suggests that they were hoping to settle in Egypt.

The Promised Land

About 2000 BCE nomadic Semitic peoples came from the east to the land of Canaan, which included most of modern-day Israel, Jordan, and Syria. Among them, according to the Bible, were the Hebrews. They believed that Canaan had been promised to them by God. After migrating to Egypt, the Hebrews returned to their Promised Land and formed the kingdom of Israel. Throughout their history, the Hebrews were influenced by the great civilizations on their borders—Mesopotamia and Egypt.

THE HEBREWS

c. 2000–1750 BCE
Abraham is born in Ur and leads his people to Canaan.

c. 1700 BCE
Hebrews migrate from Canaan to Egypt.

c. 1650–1550 BCE
The Hyksos ("rulers of foreign lands") govern Egypt.

c. 1300 BCE
Hebrews are led out of Egypt by Moses.

c. 1200–1020 BCE
The Israelites are led by "judges."

c. 1100–1020 BCE
The Israelites come into conflict with the Philistines.

Hebrew Origins

According to biblical tradition, the patriarch Abraham lived in the southern Mesopotamian city of Ur some time after 2000 BCE. This was during the Old Babylonian period (see pages 54–55). Abraham's father took his family north to the trading city of Haran (in modern-day Turkey). The Bible says that God then told Abraham to travel on to a new land–Canaan.

Exodus

Famine in Canaan may have driven the Hebrews to Egypt, where they lived peaceably. According to the Bible, an Egyptian pharaoh forced the Hebrews to work as slaves and killed their babies. Moses, a Hebrew boy who was saved by the pharaoh's daughter, led his people out of slavery. He took them back to Canaan, the land that had been promised to Abraham. There is no historical evidence for the Exodus, but it may be that Hebrew groups migrated between Canaan and Egypt.

The route from Egypt to Canaan took Moses and his people across the Sinai Desert. According to the Bible, the journey took 40 years. It was a long, hazardous journey to the Promised Land.

THE TERRITORIES OF THE TWELVE TRIBES

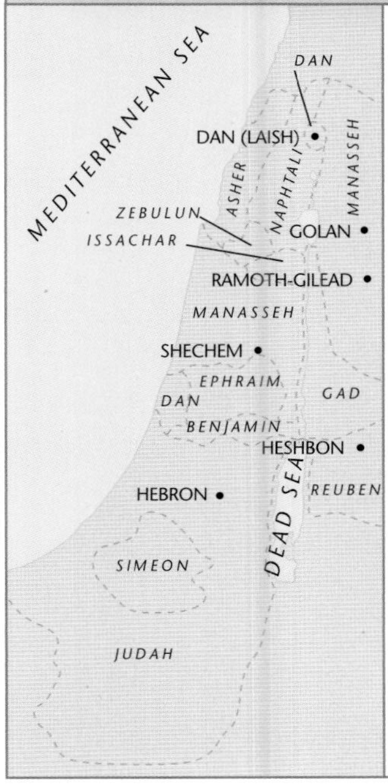

MEDITERRANEAN SEA
DAN
DAN (LAISH)
ASHER
NAPHTALI
MANASSEH
ZEBULUN
ISSACHAR
GOLAN
RAMOTH-GILEAD
MANASSEH
SHECHEM
EPHRAIM
DAN
GAD
BENJAMIN
HESHBON
HEBRON
DEAD SEA
REUBEN
SIMEON
JUDAH

The Twelve Tribes of Israel

Abraham's grandson Jacob, who was also named Israel, had 12 sons. The Hebrews organized themselves into groups that traced their descent to the sons and became the Twelve Tribes of Israel. Two of Jacob's sons–Joseph and Levi–did not have territories. They were replaced by Joseph's sons Ephraim and Manasseh. The Israelites divided the land up between the tribes and were ruled by leaders called "judges." Toward the end of the 11th century BCE, the threat of invasion by the Philistines led the Israelites to choose their first king, Saul.

The Israelites were forbidden to worship idols like the golden calf shown here, which Moses destroyed.

Canaanite Religion

The Canaanites worshiped a range of gods. Their chief deity was the creator El (a Semitic word for "god"), who ruled the sky and lived on a sacred mountain. His son Baal (Semitic for "lord" or "owner") was a popular weather god who brought powerful thunderstorms and welcome rain. Canaanites worshiped at hilltop sites known as "high places."

One God

While leading his people to the Promised Land, Moses received the Ten Commandments from God. These began: "I am the Lord, your God, and you must not worship any other god." The Israelites were also told not to make or worship any images or idols. The belief in a single god was quite different from the tradition in ancient Canaan. Moses is considered the founder of the Jewish faith, or Judaism, the religion of the Hebrews.

Stele showing Baal, the weather god.

Molded gold figurine of a Canaanite goddess, dating from the 16th century BCE.

The Kingdom of Israel

Under its first three rulers—Saul, David, and Solomon—the Kingdom of Israel grew in size and power. This was also the case for the new walled capital, Jerusalem, which King David captured from the Jebusites. David succeeded in uniting the Twelve Tribes, and was able to pass on a stable kingdom to his son, Solomon. This allowed the third ruler to devote more energy to enlarging his cities, especially Jerusalem, as well as improving the state's administration. After King Solomon's death, however, the kingdom split in two when the northern region, Israel, refused to recognize Solomon's son Rehoboam as king. The smaller southern region, Judah, became a separate kingdom.

The Hebrew Kings

Though Saul was the first king of Israel, it was his successor, David, who united the people. David expanded the kingdom's territory through successful wars against neighboring peoples, such as the Moabites. His troops also defeated the Philistines. David made Jerusalem his capital, which was accepted by all the tribes, and had the Ark of the Covenant moved to the city. As well as being an able ruler, David was an excellent musician and poet. According to tradition, he wrote many psalms in the Old Testament.

THE KINGDOM OF ISRAEL

Territory of Judah and Israel
Conquered territory

These stele fragments, inscribed in Aramaic in the 9th century BCE*, refer to the King of Israel and the House of David.*

ISRAEL

c. 1020–1006 BCE
Reign of Saul, the first king of the Israelites.

c. 1006–965 BCE
Reign of David, who makes Jerusalem the capital.

c. 965–928 BCE
Reign of Solomon, David's wise son.

928 BCE
The kingdom is divided ito Israel (ruled by Jeroboam I) and southern Judah (ruled by Rehoboam, son of Solomon).

The Ark of the Covenant, which was covered with gold and had two cherubs on top. It disappeared before Jerusalem was destroyed by the Babylonians and has never been found.

Ark of the Covenant

The Ark was a sacred wooden chest that held the tablets inscribed with the Ten Commandments. The "covenant" referred to the agreement between God and the Israelites based on the commandments. The Israelites carried the chest through the desert on their exodus from Egypt and kept it in a sacred tent called the Tabernacle. After David recaptured the Ark from the Philistines, Solomon eventually placed it in the Temple of Jerusalem.

The Philistines

The Philistines were one of a number of migrating groups known as the Sea Peoples. They came to Canaan from the Aegean region early in the 12th century BCE. The name Palestine, which was later used for their new lands, comes from a word meaning "land of the Philistines." They developed five city-states near the Mediterranean Sea, including Gaza. The Philistines fought many battles with the Israelites, until David finally subdued them.

A Phoenician ship. Solomon recognized the Phoenicians as great sailors and craftsmen. He made an alliance with Hiram I and invited the Phoenicians to help build the Temple.

Wisdom of Solomon

King Solomon is best known for his great wisdom, his reorganization of the state's administration (including the appointment of local governors), and his building works. His most famous achievement was the Temple of Jerusalem, later called the First Temple. Solomon's reputation for wisdom was based on his skill in dealing sensibly with difficult situations. He also encouraged writers and thinkers, and according to tradition composed many proverbs and songs.

Women prepared food and cooked in the busy courtyard, where there was a mill for grinding grain and a clay oven for baking bread. Sheep and goats were raised for meat, milk, and wool.

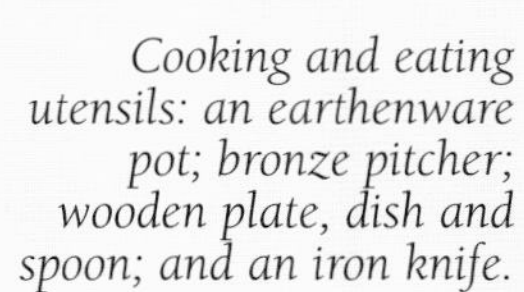

Cooking and eating utensils: an earthenware pot; bronze pitcher; wooden plate, dish and spoon; and an iron knife.

Hebrew Homes

Houses were usually built around a central open courtyard. The walls were made of mud bricks and stones coated with mud plaster. There were often four rooms, including a large living room where the family also slept. On warm nights people used an outside staircase or a wooden ladder to go up to the flat roof to sleep, where there might be a welcome breeze.

Exile and Occupation

The divided kingdoms of Israel and Judah fought each other, which weakened both. Nevertheless, Israel existed independently for 200 years, until it was conquered by the Assyrians. Judah remained independent for longer, until it too was taken, by the Babylonians. More invaders followed—Persians, Macedonians under Alexander the Great, and the Greek descendants of Alexander's generals. As well as having their lands occupied, Israelites and Judaeans were sent away to other parts of the conquering empires. Toward the end of this period, Jewish beliefs were coming into conflict with Greek customs.

To break through at Lachish, the Assyrians built a large ramp made of stones and wood at the city's main gateway. They then moved siege engines with metal-tipped battering rams up the slope. The defenders did their best to set fire to the wooden rams and covers, but eventually their walls were breached.

Assyrian Sieges

The mighty Assyrians invaded Israel, and in 721 BCE their forces captured the capital of Samaria, after a siege lasting two or three years. Samaria became the capital of an Assyrian province, and many important and wealthy Israelites were sent into exile to various parts of the Assyrian Empire. In 701 BCE, the Assyrians moved south and attacked many of the towns of Judah, laying siege to the walled city of Lachish. The city finally fell, but the walls outside Jerusalem had been poisoned, so the Assyrian army had to withdraw.

Babylonian Exile

After Jerusalem surrendered to the Babylonians in 597 BCE, the city's leading citizens were exiled to Babylon. Following a later rebellion and a long siege, the capital of Judah fell again ten years later. This time many more inhabitants were deported to Babylonia. The exile lasted for almost 50 years, during which time the Judaeans were allowed to live by their own customs. At last they were allowed back to rebuild Jerusalem after the Persians captured Babylon (see page 70).

THE RETURN FROM EXILE

Clay figures of warriors on horseback, from the borders of northern Israel and Phoenicia.

This small terra-cotta sculpture, dating from about 300 BCE, shows two women playing the Greek game of knucklebones. This was similar to modern jacks.

Greek Influence

Alexander the Great, who had conquered the Persian Empire, died in Babylon. His generals Ptolemy and Seleucus divided the Middle East between them and founded dynasties: the Ptolemies captured Egypt and the Seleucids ruled Syria and Mesopotamia. Both dynasties of rulers brought Greek culture to Palestine, where rich city-dwellers and others adopted many Greek customs. Nevertheless, the Jews of Palestine were allowed to follow their own religion.

THE HEBREWS

721 BCE
The Assyrians conquer Israel.

587 BCE
Judah is overrun by the Babylonians; deportation of Judaeans to Babylon.

539 BCE
The Persian king, Cyrus the Great (Cyrus II), allows the exiled people of Judah to return to their homeland after he conquers Babylon.

c. 304 BCE
Macedonian king, Ptolemy I (died c. 284 BCE) rules Palestine.

c. 200 BCE
Seleucid king, Antiochus III (reigned 223–187 BCE), gains control of much of the region.

164 BCE
The people of Judah revolt against the Greek-Syrian king, Antiochis IV (reigned 175–163 BCE), who tried to impose Greek culture. During this revolt, known as the Revolt of the Maccabees, Jerusalem was recaptured by the Judaeans.

The original menorah *was a seven-branched* candelabrum *that stood in the Temple of Jerusalem. Many later examples have eight branches that are lit during the eight-day festival of Hanukkah.*

The Synagogue

The synagogue, or Jewish place of worship, developed as a house of assembly, prayer, and study. The first synagogues may have existed as early as the 3rd century BCE, and they became places where the Torah, or Hebrew Bible, was read and taught. Synagogues became more important as places of worship after the destruction of Herod's Temple of Jerusalem in 70 CE.

Hanukkah

In 168 BCE the Seleucid king, Antiochus IV (reigned 175–163 BCE), tried to force the Jews to adopt Greek beliefs. He had an altar to Zeus set up in the Temple of Jerusalem. This caused a revolt, led by Judah Maccabee (died c. 161 BCE), who with his followers created a Jewish state in Judaea. In 164 BCE they relit the Temple lights, and the Jewish festival of Hanukkah (meaning "dedication") celebrates this event.

Roman Judaea

Rome took control of Palestine in 63 BCE. The new rulers saw many Jewish people as a threat, especially as they refused to adopt Roman religion. After the execution of Jesus, who was born in Judaea and whose followers believed he had been sent by God as their savior, Christianity spread. The Romans then governed a land with two religions, Judaism and Christianity, which were themselves in conflict.

ROMAN RULE

63 BCE
Roman general Pompey (106–48 BCE) enters Jerusalem. Romans take control and call their province Judaea.

c. 37–4 BCE
Reign of Herod the Great as King of Judaea.

27 BCE–14 CE
Reign of Roman emperor Augustus.

c. 6 BCE–33 CE
Life of Jesus Christ.

c. 10–64 CE
Life of Saint Paul, who founds Christian colonies on his missionary journeys.

14–37 CE
Reign of Roman emperor Tiberius.

26–36 CE
Pontius Pilate is Roman provincial prefect of Judaea.

49 CE
At the Council of Jerusalem it is agreed that gentiles do not have to follow strict Jewish law to become Christians.

66 CE
Beginning of the first Jewish revolt against Roman rule.

73 CE
The fall of Masada marks the end of the first revolt.

70 CE
Jerusalem and Herod's Temple are destroyed.

132–135 CE
Second Jewish revolt is led by Simeon bar Kochba, who dies in the final struggle.

Roman Religion

The Romans believed in a wide range of gods and goddesses, headed by Jupiter. Roman religion included ceremonies in which offerings were made and animals were sacrificed. Most Roman families had a shrine to their own household gods. Emperors also encouraged the idea that they themselves were divine, and this became a strong cult, along with those of Isis and Mithras. Jews and Christians had no belief in the Roman gods.

Bronze statue of Fortuna, the Roman goddess of good luck and fertility.

King Herod the Great

Herod the Great (reigned 37–4 BCE) became governor of Galilee in 47 BCE, and ten years later the Romans made him King of Judaea. He was a loyal supporter and representative of Rome. During his reign he made Jerusalem a great city in the Roman style, rebuilding the Temple and adding palaces, a theater, and an aqueduct. He also built the port of Caesarea and the fortress of Herodium. Herod's parents were both Arabs, which meant he was considered an outsider by many Jews.

Cutaway reconstruction of the Herodium. The circular fortress stood on top of a man-made hill in the desert south of Jerusalem. It had comfortable living quarters around a courtyard, as well as a bathhouse and a garden.

The Founding of Christianity

After being tried by the Romans, Jesus Christ (c. 6 BCE–c. 30 CE), a prophet from Galilee, was judged to be a revolutionary and sentenced to death by crucifixion. According to the Bible, his followers, known as Christians, numbered only about 120 people at the time of his death. These first Christians followed Jewish law as well as the teachings of Jesus Christ, and at first they tried to convert only other Jews rather than gentiles. As this situation gradually changed, however, Christianity became the religion of gentiles and orthodox Jews rejected it.

Two followers of Jesus Christ, Peter (died c. 64 CE) and Paul (c. 10–c. 67 CE), began preaching and spreading Christianity. Paul traveled to many parts of the Mediterranean.

The cross and the fish, two ancient Christian symbols. Since the early Christians refused to worship Roman gods, they were persecuted and often arrested and executed.

The Jewish Revolts

A group of Jews rebelled in 66 CE, after the Roman governor of Judaea tried to rob the Temple treasury. The rebels were led by high-ranking priests, but the revolt was brutally put down by the future emperor Titus, after a long siege of Jerusalem. A second revolt, started in 132 CE, was also defeated by the powerful Roman military machine. According to a 3rd-century historian, it resulted in the deaths of more than half a million Jews.

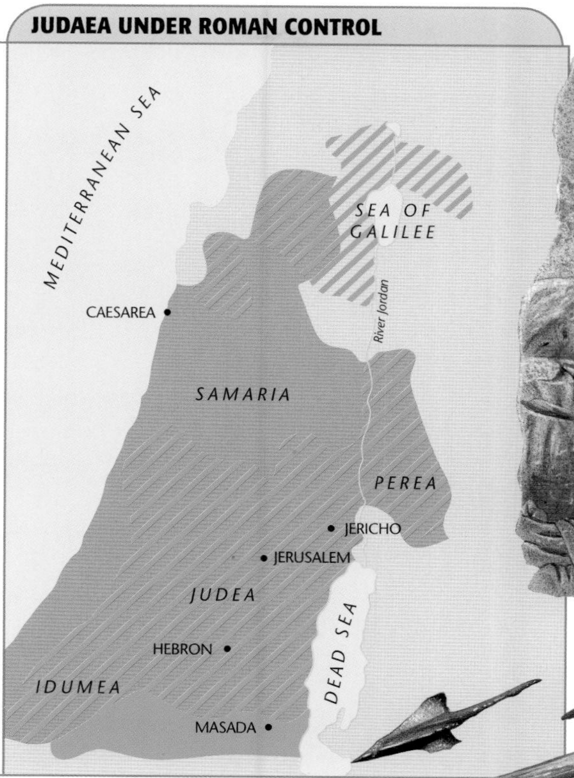

JUDAEA UNDER ROMAN CONTROL

This relief carving from the Arch of Titus in Rome shows Roman soldiers leading Jewish captives and parading war booty as they return from Jerusalem. The arch was built in 81 CE.

Arrowheads found at Masada.

A view of Masada, an ancient desert mountaintop fortress in Israel, renovated by Herod the Great. It was captured in 66 CE by the Jews in their revolt against Rome. Before the Romans could reach the top, the Jews committed suicide to avoid being taken alive in 73 CE.

Ancient Egypt, founded about 5,000 years ago, was the world's first nation-state. It was also the longest-lived, lasting about 2,500 years, far longer than any European state. Ancient Greece reached a peak as Egypt was declining. It marks the beginning of European civilization.

Democratic government began in the Greek city-states, and Greek culture was to be a powerful influence on Europe until modern times. The Ancient Greeks admired the skills and understanding of the Egyptians (the Egyptian calendar, for example, was more scientific than the Greek). As early as the 7th century BCE, Greek merchants set up a settlement in Egypt, the source of much trade. Egypt influenced the Greeks in other ways, possibly in religion, certainly in art. Greek sculpture of the Archaic Period is clearly based on Egyptian style, although the Greeks soon developed new ideas. After the invasion of Alexander the Great in 332 BCE, Egypt itself became part of the Hellenistic (Greek) world. Alexandria succeeded Athens as the center of Hellenistic learning, and the last pharaohs, of the Ptolemiac Dynasty, were Greek-speaking descendants of one of Alexander's generals.

Minoan bronze sculpture of a bull-jumper. As the subject appears so often in art, bull-jumping must have been important.

	4000 BCE	3000 BCE	2000 BCE	1000 BCE
ANCIENT EGYPTIANS	The city of Hierakonpolis develops in Lower Egypt.	Menes, the first pharaoh, unites Upper and Lower Egypt. The first Dynasty is founded. The Great Pyramid at Giza is built.	Pharaoh Ahmose I reunites the divided kingdoms of Egypt.	Pharaoh Ramesses III defends Egypt from foreign invaders. Egypt is divided.
AFRICAN KINGDOMS		Egyptians send military expeditions into Nubia to mine gold.	The Kingdom of Kush is founded in Nubia. Kush becomes an Egyptian province. Queen Hatshepsut sends an expedition to Punt.	
THE MINOANS		The Bronze Age begins in the Aegean.	Rise of Minoan civilization on island of Crete. The Minoans rebuild Crete after widespread destruction. Mycenaeans take over Crete.	
THE MYCENAEANS		Mycenaean ancestors settle in Greece.	Rise of Mycenaean civilization. Mycenaeans capture Troy.	End of Mycenaean civilization.
ANCIENT GREEKS				Period of migrations in the Aegean. The city-state of Sparta is founded.
THE MACEDONIANS				

Ancient Egypt and Greece

A gold figure of an Egyptian pharaoh with the symbols of kingship —a crown, with the protective cobra and vulture, and a crook and flail.

800 BCE	600 BCE	400 BCE	200 BCE	1 CE

Nubian kings undertake building work at Thebes, Memphis, and other religious centers.

Egypt is taken over by the Persians.

Alexander the Great conquers Egypt.

Egypt becomes a Roman province.

Ptolemy I, general of Alexander the Great, rules Egypt.

Nubians rule Egypt as the 25th Dynasty.

The Kushite capital is established at Meroe.

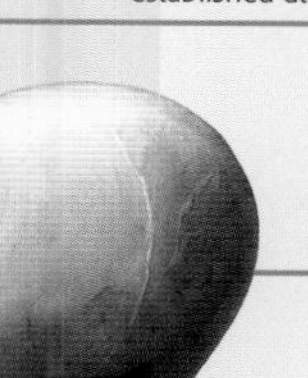

The first Olympic Games are held.

Athens and Sparta battle in the Peloponnesian War.

Greece is taken over by the Romans.

The Archaic period.

Beginning of democracy in Athens.

Philip II, King of Macedonia conquers Greece.

The Macedonian kingdom is founded.

Alexander the Great invades Persia.

Macedonians are defeated by the Romans.

Macedonia becomes a Roman province.

Early Egyptian Civilization

In the third century BCE, an Egyptian priest named Manetho (active c. 300 BCE) made a record of the 31 Egyptian dynasties covering 2,800 years. We still follow his system, but we also divide Egyptian history into periods, as shown in the box (left). Ancient writers often described Egypt and its great buildings, but most of what we know today was discovered in the last 200 years, especially since Egyptian writing, called hieroglyphs, was first deciphered in 1822. Thanks to the work of archeologists, and the evidence of tombs and temples, we know more about the Egyptians than any other ancient society.

PERIODS OF EGYPTIAN HISTORY

Predynastic Period
c. 5000–3150 BCE

Early Dynasties
3150–2686 BCE
1st and 2nd Dynasties

Old Kingdom
2686–2181 BCE
3rd to 6th Dynasties

First Intermediate Period
2181–2040 BCE
7th and 10th Dynasties

Middle Kingdom
2040–1782 BCE
11th to 12th Dynasties

Second Intermediate Period
1782–1570 BCE
13th and 17th Dynasties

New Kingdom
1570–1070 BCE
18th to 20th Dynasties

Third Intermediate Period
1070–525 BCE
21st to 26th Dynasties

The Late Period
525–332 BCE
27th to 31st Dynasties

The Greek and Roman Period
332 BCE–641 CE

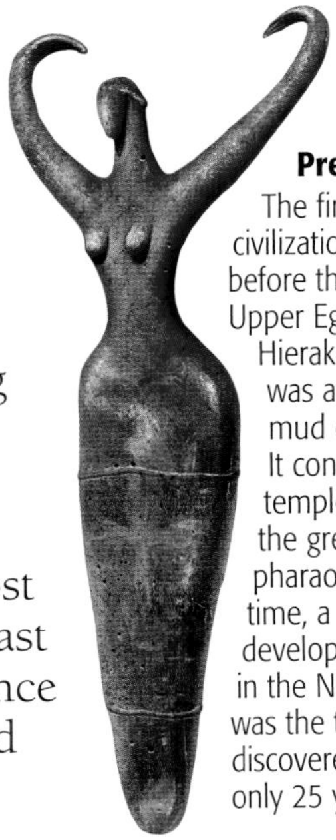

The Narmer Palette. Slate palettes were made for grinding minerals to powder, perhaps for cosmetics.

Predynastic Egypt

The first signs of Egyptian civilization appeared, long before the pharaohs, in Upper Egypt. By 3500 BCE, Hierakonpolis, the capital, was a large, lively city of mud or stone houses. It contained the first temple, the model for the great temples of the pharaohs. At the same time, a different society developed in Lower Egypt, in the Nile Delta. Its center was the town of Buto, first discovered by archeologists only 25 years ago.

A female figure from the Predynastic, or prehistoric, age.

United Egypt

The first pharaoh was Menes (or Narmer), King of Upper Egypt. He conquered Lower Egypt and united the Two Lands in about 3150 BCE. Legend says he ruled for 60 years, until he was killed by a hippopotamus. He may be the king shown on the carved slate known as the Narmer Palette. On the side shown above he is wearing the "White Crown" of Upper Egypt (his prisoner may represent the north of Egypt). On the other side, which has more scenes of conquest, he wears the "Red Crown" of Lower Egypt.

Foreigners thought the Egyptians were lucky: the Nile gave them plenty of food without too much hard work.

The River Nile

Egypt would not have existed without the Nile River. The longest river in the world, it ran for over 3,728 miles (6,000 km) through dry, barren desert, creating a strip of fertile land along its banks. About 93 miles (150 km) from the coast, it spread out into a delta, watering the broad plain of Lower Egypt. The Nile was a mystery. Unlike other rivers, it flooded in the summer and no one knew where the water came from. Explorers discovered the sources of the Nile in East Africa just 150 years ago. We now know that the summer monsoon caused the flood.

Cattle being carried across the River Nile by boat. The ancient Egyptians may have been the first people to keep cattle.

The Waters of the Nile

The Egyptians divided the year into three seasons, based on the behavior of the river. Summer was the time of the flood, when the Nile overflowed and deposited rich black silt. In fall, the flood went down and farmers planted their seeds. Spring was the "Dry Time," when they harvested the crops. But nature is unreliable. If the flood was too low, there was not enough fertile soil. If it was too high, it flooded the villages.

The throne of the pharaoh Tutankhamun, found in his tomb. Made of gold-plated wood, it has a scene of the young king and his wife on the back.

The Divine Pharaoh

The pharaoh was not only the ruler, he was also a god. He was seen as a form of the falcon-headed Horus, the royal god, and sometimes as the sun god, Ra. He had no private life; everything he did was a ceremony, every incident had some meaning. Even washing his hands was a religious act and, if he caught a cold, it was a bad omen for the kingdom.

The king was also head of the Egyptian army, and his power over foreign enemies is shown by the bound images of enemies on the side of his throne (above).

Royal Women

The title of the pharaoh's senior partner, who was sometimes of royal birth, but was usually the daughter of a non-royal official, was the "Great Royal Wife." Her main task was to produce an heir to continue the dynasty. But some, like Nefertiti (whose husband reigned 1350–1334 BCE), were powerful figures, who shared the royal power (see page 101). There were even three female pharaohs, of whom the greatest was Hatshepsut (reigned 1498–1483 BCE).

A painted stone head of the beautiful Nefertiti, wife of Akhenaten (Amenhotep IV), who acted as ruler herself.

The Rulers of Egypt

The supreme ruler of Egypt was the king, also called "pharaoh" and other titles. He was also the chief priest. As the all-powerful ruler of the country with a horde of officials and servants, he was able to carry out huge projects, such as building a pyramid, or digging a canal to the Red Sea. Pharaoh could do no wrong, but he was no selfish dictator. He was protector of the people, the representative of good order, and the enemy of chaos.

Statue of a vizier. He looks well fed.

Government

The pharaoh owned the country; in a sense he was the country. In practice he was served by hundreds of officials, headed by the vizier. Some viziers, even if non-royal, were very grand, as their fine tombs suggest. Imhotep, chancellor of Djoser (reigned 2630–2611 BCE) and architect of the step pyramid at Saqqara, later became a god. Women sometimes served in official posts: we know of two female viziers.

FAMOUS PHARAOHS

Khufu
(reigned 2589–2566 BCE)
Also known as Cheops, he ordered the building of the Great Pyramid at Giza, his own tomb, in 2500 BCE.

Mentuhotep II
(reigned 2010–1998 BCE)
During the Middle Kingdom he restored the unity of Egypt.

Kamose
(reigned 1573–1570 BCE)
Began to expel the 15th Dynasty, a line of foreign rulers from Lower Egypt.

Queen Hatshepsut
(reigned 1498–1483 BCE)
She sought to assert her power through propaganda reliefs. She was depicted as a man with a king's regalia, complete with the official false beard.

Akhenaten
(reigned 1350–1334 BCE)
Known at the beginning of his reign as Amenhotep IV. He changed his name when he revolutionized Egyptian religion and art, also moving his capital to a brand-new city, Akhenaten (known today as Amarna).

Ramesses II
(reigned 1304–1237 BCE)
Warrior king who expanded the Egyptian empire, built vast temples, and fathered 100 children.

Symbols of Kingship

Representations of a pharaoh can be recognized by the symbols of royalty. He often wears one of several crowns or a striped head cloth, with a cobra and vulture, his protectors, above the forehead. He carries one or more scepters, often a crook and flail (symbols of the god Osiris), and sometimes wears a neat false beard, attached by a cord.

The mummified remains of Tutankhamun were placed inside a solid-gold coffin, the inner coffin of three. The one shown here is the second coffin.

The Pharaoh Tutankhamun

The tombs of the Egyptian kings were all raided by robbers with one exception. The entrance to the tomb of Tutankhamun (reigned 1334–1325 BCE), a ruler of the New Kingdom, was concealed and only discovered, after ten years searching, by an archeologist in 1922. It contained four chambers, each full of amazing objects of priceless materials and beautiful workmanship. It was the greatest and most valuable find ever made by archeologists.

The giant sphinx guarding the three pyramids of Giza (the Second Pyramid behind it). The face is generally thought to represent the pharaoh Khaefre (Chephren) son of Khufu.

Egyptian Tombs

Tombs full of valuable objects attracted thieves. Pyramids were obvious targets, so the New Kingdom royal tombs were hidden deep in the rocks of a remote valley. High-born people and officials had similar, smaller tombs. A false door painted on the wall helped the dead person's spirit go in and out.

The walls of tombs were decorated with pictures and texts. This scene, in the Valley of the Kings, shows the pharaoh Horemheb (reigned 1321–1292 BCE) standing in front of the goddess Hathor.

PYRAMID SITES IN EGYPT

MEDITERRANEAN SEA
ATHRIBIS
ABU RAWASH
GIZA
ZAWYET EL-ARYAN
ABUSIR
SAQQARA
DAHSHUR
MAZGHUNA
EL-LISHT
MEIDUM
SEILA
HAWARA
EL-LAHUN
ZAWYET SULTAN
DARA
RED SEA
ABYDOS
NAQADA
TARIF
EDFU
EL-KULA
ELEPHANTINE
GEBEL BARKUL
NURI
EL-KURRU
MEROE
Pyramid site

The Pyramids

The biggest (and oldest) buildings were the pyramids, built as tombs for the early pharaohs. The first stone pyramid (Third Dynasty), at Saqqara, had sides that rose like steps in six stages. The smooth-sided pyramids of Giza (about 2500 BCE) belong to the 4th Dynasty. The largest, the Great Pyramid of Khufu (or Cheops), is 482 feet (147 m) high, with sides 755 feet (230 m) long at the base. It contained about 2,300,000 blocks of stone, weighing nearly 6,000,000 tons. Now 4,500 years old, it has lost its smooth, glittering surface layer and about 39 feet (12 m) of its height.

The workers moved huge stones (one piece weighed over 1,000 tons) with ramps, poles, and ropes from the quarry to the river. Stones were then transported to the building site by boat.

Temples

Most of the huge temples that still stand date from the New Kingdom. They all followed the same basic plan—long and rectangular, with vast columns—and, like the pyramids, they were built on a massive scale. In area, the Great Temple of Amun at Karnak was (and is) the world's largest religious building. Temples were the houses of the gods, and only priests could go inside. Anyone wishing to consult the god had to wait until a festival, when the priests paraded his or her image outside.

The Temple at Luxor, completed under Ramesses II, has colossal statues of him on the front and two rows of human-headed sphinxes lining the approach.

Building Egypt

The greatness of ancient Egypt is still to be seen in its monumental buildings. The Egyptians had only simple methods and feeble tools, yet these buildings would be astonishing in any age. The great temples and tombs are not especially beautiful, but they give a sense of terrific strength and power. They were built to impress people, and they were built to last for ever. Ordinary houses were made of mud bricks, a good material in a dry climate, but monumental buildings were of stone. Limestone and sandstone quarries were nearby, and granite was available, although hard to cut with copper chisels and wooden mallets.

Construction Workers

With no machines, the Egyptians raised their great buildings by human muscle alone. Labor on public works was a kind of tax—all the peasants had to do it. Most of the work took place in the flood season, when they had no other tasks. The workers lived in specially built "towns." They received their pay in the form of food, drink, clothes, and other supplies.

Part of a wall painting from a tomb showing workers making bricks from Nile mud hardened in the Sun.

Egyptian Society

Ancient Egypt was a society of order, where everyone belonged to a particular class. A person's place in society depended on their birth, and they followed the same occupation as their parents. Boys were taught their father's trade, and only a few learned to read and write. They were mostly the sons of scribes, who would become scribes in their turn. For pharaoh or carpenter, occupations were hereditary. People believed that life was balanced between the forces of order and justice, which they called Maat, and the forces of chaos, represented by Seth, the wild god of the desert. The duty of their god-king was to uphold this balance.

Scribes and Officials

The scribes, or writers, were the managers, bookkeepers, and clerks of Egypt. They kept careful records of farm production, trade, taxes, and legal judgements. Training was hard, as students had to learn the great number of hieroglyphic signs. But they had important, well-paid jobs, with no hard physical work, and others envied them. "Be a scribe," said a teacher, "so your limbs may grow smooth and your hands soft."

Scribes, with their scrolls of papyrus, appear often in Egyptian art. This ivory figure comes from the Middle Kingdom.

Priests

Along with the courtiers and chief officials, the high priests ranked highest outside the royal family. Priests belonged to a separate class. They were divided into many ranks, from high to low. The chief priest and his assistants performed the complicated daily rituals of the temple and organized religious festivals and processions, where the image of the god was shown to the people. Others looked after temple business, studied and taught.

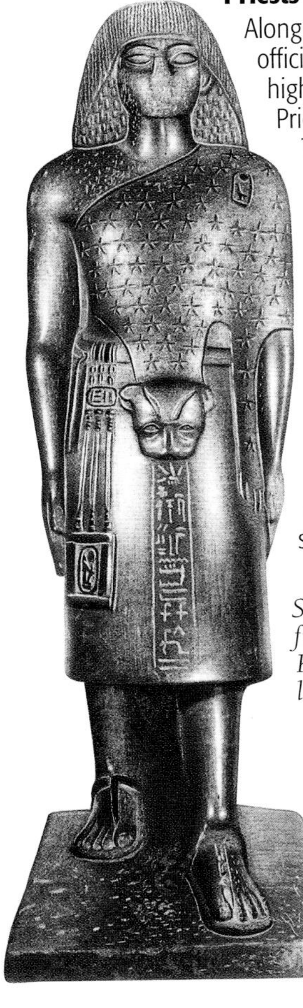

Statue of a priest from the New Kingdom wearing a leopard skin garment.

A faience tablet used as a label to identify a batch of scrolls.

Taxes

Egypt was a rich country and much of its wealth went as taxes to the central government. As the Egyptians did not use money, taxes were paid in the form of produce, such as corn, and the rate of tax depended on whether the harvest was good or bad. Government inspectors went round at harvest time to calculate the tax due from each district, or nome. They were not popular!

Herdsmen driving cattle past a kiosk where the tax collectors count them to calculate how much is due in tax.

Justice

The law was based on the idea of Maat—what was right and orderly. The supreme judge was the pharaoh, but as in government, high officials, including priests, actually directed the justice system. Local governors, or nomarchs, judged disputes about property, contracts, wills, and such matters. Punishments could be harsh, with the death penalty for serious crimes. Minor crimes were punished by a fine or a beating.

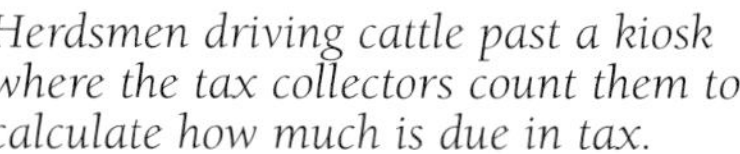

The idea of Maat was represented by a goddess, who often wore a headdress of ostrich feathers and was sometimes indicated in paintings by a single feather.

Gods and Goddesses

There were about 700 gods and goddesses, many only worshiped locally. Among the best known were Osiris, god of the Underworld, his wife Isis, and brother, the sinister Seth, who was defeated by falcon-headed Horus, ruler of Earth. Others widely respected were Ptah, god of craftsmen; Hathor, cow-goddess of music and pleasure; Thoth, ibis-headed god of wisdom; and Anubis, jackal-headed god of death.

Gold figure of Amun, state god of the New Kingdom and a version of the sun god. His chief temple was at Karnak, where his festival lasted a month.

A royal funeral procession led by the chief priest (in leopard skin). The body is carried on a papyrus boat. Funerals often had to cross the Nile River, and model boats were often placed in tombs.

The Creation

The world began when Atum-Ra (the sun god), who personified life, goodness, light, and energy, arose on the "mound of creation." He created the Earth (Geb) and the Sky (Nut), and the rest of creation followed. For the Egyptians, creation was a daily happening, repeated with every rising and setting of the Sun.

Instructed by Atum-Ra, who created him, Shu, god of the air, holds up the Sky (Nut), separating her from her husband the Earth (Geb).

Religion in Ancient Egypt

The purpose of religion is to explain life, and in an unscientific age religion had a lot to explain. In Egypt, religion was a part of everyday life. Temples stood at the center of society. Besides being homes for gods, they had schools, libraries, warehouses, and workshops. Priests made offerings to the gods so that they would maintain peace and security. The gods were thought to be responsible for everything that happened. Yet they were often treated as if human. A god who was thought to have failed in his duty might be "punished" by receiving no offerings for a month.

Death and Burial

The Egyptians believed that when people died they went to a heavenly Egypt in the West. First, many ceremonies were required, supervised by Anubis (in fact by his priests). The dead person's heart was weighed against a feather, representing Maat (goddess of law, truth, and justice), to see if he were worthy. His new home was his tomb which was looked after by priests who said prayers daily, brought food, and guarded the possessions buried with him in case needed in the other world.

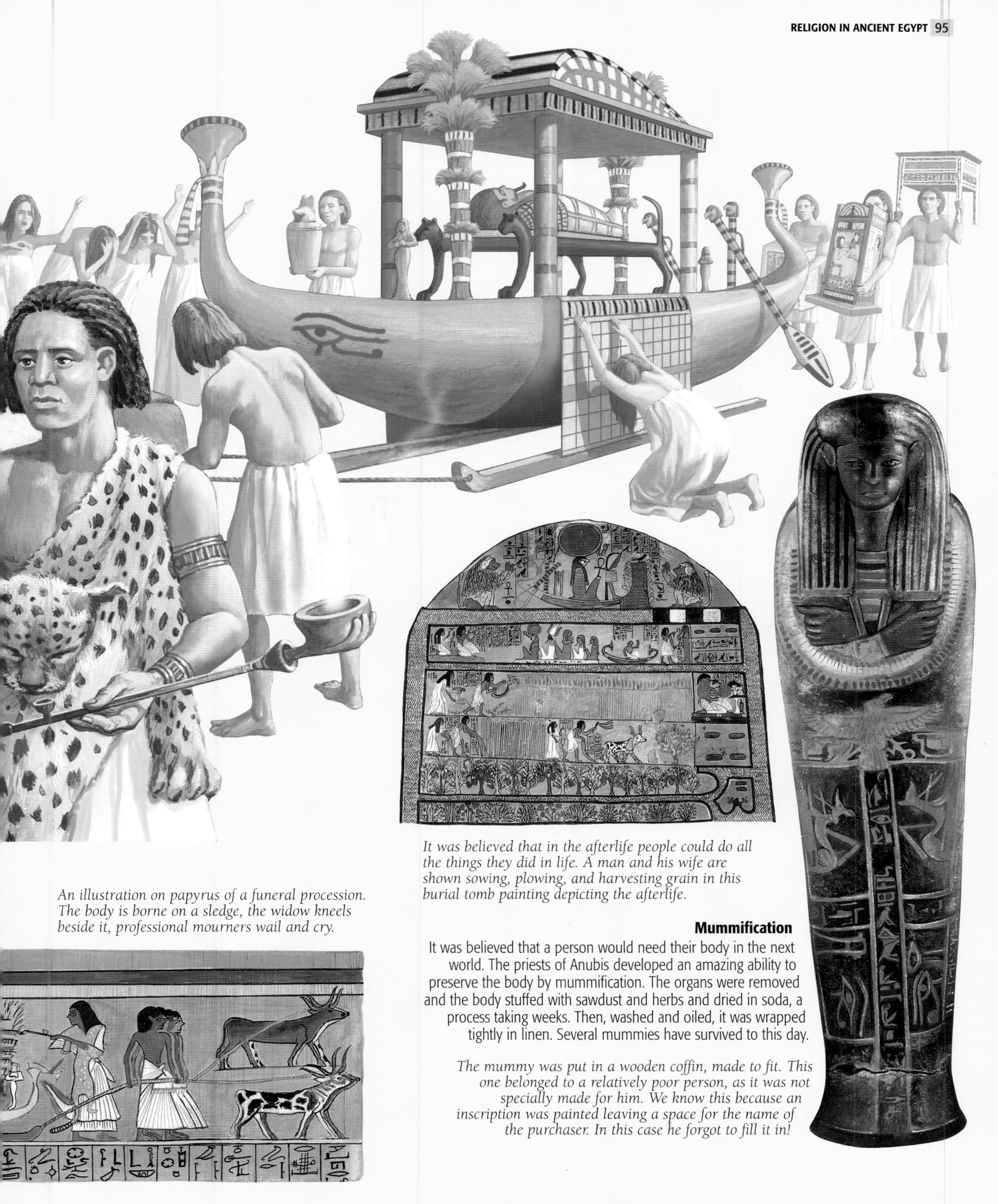

An illustration on papyrus of a funeral procession. The body is borne on a sledge, the widow kneels beside it, professional mourners wail and cry.

It was believed that in the afterlife people could do all the things they did in life. A man and his wife are shown sowing, plowing, and harvesting grain in this burial tomb painting depicting the afterlife.

Mummification

It was believed that a person would need their body in the next world. The priests of Anubis developed an amazing ability to preserve the body by mummification. The organs were removed and the body stuffed with sawdust and herbs and dried in soda, a process taking weeks. Then, washed and oiled, it was wrapped tightly in linen. Several mummies have survived to this day.

The mummy was put in a wooden coffin, made to fit. This one belonged to a relatively poor person, as it was not specially made for him. We know this because an inscription was painted leaving a space for the name of the purchaser. In this case he forgot to fill it in!

Egypt and Its Neighbors

Protected by sea and desert, Egypt had developed with little foreign influence. Egyptian culture passed into Africa through Kush in Nubia. Eventually the Kushites formed their own kingdom, bringing Egypt's control over their precious resources, namely gold, to an end. Meanwhile Hyksos settlers from western Asia established their own ruling dynasty, with its capital at Avaris in the Nile Delta.

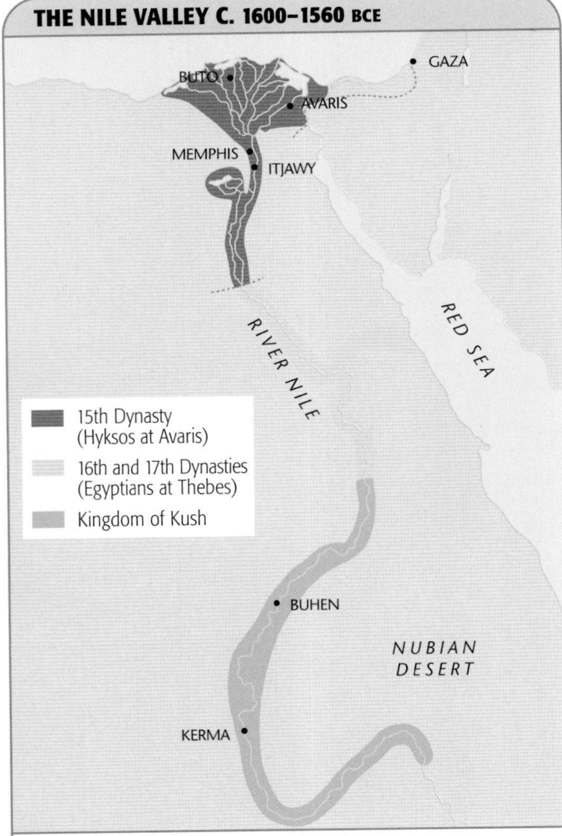

Divided Kingship

At the end of the Middle Kingdom Egypt lost power and the Nile Valley was divided into several kingdoms. The kingdom of Kush lay to the south, in Nubia, while the Hyksos ruled from Avaris (14th and 15th Dynasties) in the Delta. Central Egypt was ruled by Egyptians, from Thebes (16th and 17th Dynasties).

The Kingdom of Kush

The gold of Nubia, and its trade routes to the luxuries of tropical Africa attracted armed Egyptian expeditions. In defence, the Nubians formed the kingdom of Kush, based on the Egyptian state, about 1560 BCE. The kingdom competed with Egypt for control over the Nile.

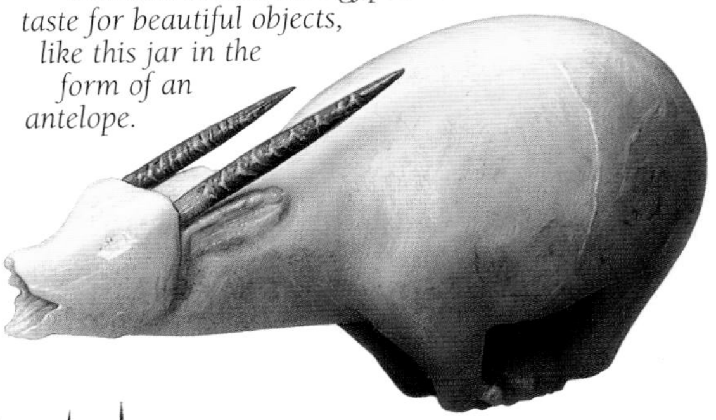

Nubians shared the Egyptians' taste for beautiful objects, like this jar in the form of an antelope.

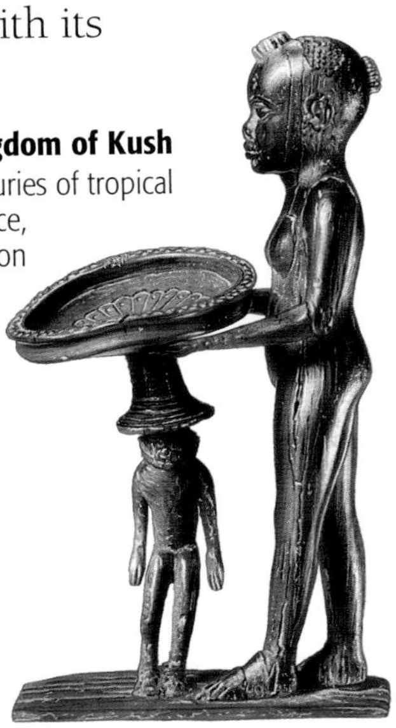

Ebony figure of a Nubian girl with a dish and pet monkey, from Egypt, 18th Dynasty.

Nubian archers on the march, from a wooden model found in a tomb.

Trade with Kush

Nubian gold and slaves, as well as the luxury goods that came from further south passed through Kerma, the first Kushite capital. Kerma was a center for trade over a wide region. The Egyptians levied taxes, or tributes, in gold and slaves, from the Nubian chiefs whom they controlled, or paid for them in grain.

A wall painting from Thebes showing a Nubian princess bringing gifts to pharaoh.

Pyramids at Meroe, an example of the Kushites' adoption of Egyptian customs.

The Hyksos

During the Second Intermediate Period (1782–1570 BCE) foreigners from western Asia who had settled in Egypt gained power and ruled part of Egypt. Manetho called these rulers of the 15th Dynasty "Hyksos," but the Egyptians called them "Rulers of the Foreign Lands." The Hyksos established their capital at Avaris (Tell el-Dab'a) and eventually took control of Memphis. They had superior military technology and it is believed that they introduced the use of horse-drawn chariots.

Reverse sides of two scarabs, ornamental beetle-shaped stones, of Hyksos rulers.

Neighbors and Enemies

Pharaohs of the 18th Dynasty, after driving out the foreign Hyksos rulers, conquered nearby lands for greater protection. They had contacts, some friendly some hostile, with Assyrians, Babylonians, Hittites (powerful enemies), Libyans, and Mycenaeans. Queen Hatshepsut traded with the kingdom of Punt in East Africa, which was reached by ships sailing down the Red Sea. From Punt the Egyptians obtained slaves, gold, and incense.

Detail of a painted stone relief showing men from Punt bringing goods to Egypt.

COMPETING DYNASTIES

c. 1700 BCE
During the last years of the 13th Dynasty, rulers of the 14th Dynasty rule at the same time from the eastern Delta.
The kingdom of Kush is founded in Nubia.

c. 1669 BCE
The kingdom of the Hyksos at Avaris is founded (15th Dynasty).

1663 BCE
The 17th Dynasty is founded at Thebes.

1573–1570 BCE
Reign of the pharaoh Kamose, who attacks the Hyksos rulers at Avaris.

1520 BCE
Pharaoh Ahmose I (reigned 1570–1546) of the 18th Dynasty (New Kingdom) defeats the Hyksos Kingdom at Avaris.

c. 1500–1000 BCE
Kush becomes an Egyptian province.

c. 1460 BCE
Queen Hatshepsut sends an expedition to Punt.

c. 715–663 BCE
Kushites rule Egypt as 25th Dynasty.

c. 592 BCE
New Kushite capital is established at Meroe.

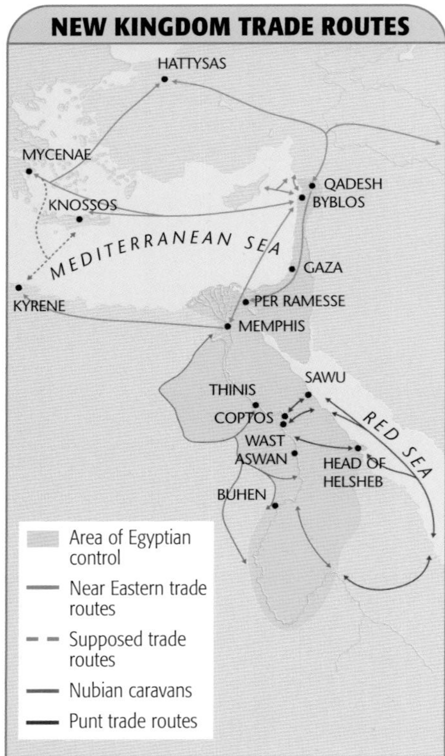

Trade Routes
The Nile River carried internal trade, and led to the Mediterranean and foreign trade routes. The desert roads, west and south, were older. During the Middle Kingdom, the Egyptians traveled from Aswan on the Nile to Darfur, bringing back ebony, ivory, and a "dancing dwarf."

Traders on the way to market with wild fowl, hunted in the delta, and wine.

Means of Exchange
As money did not exist, most trade was barter, or exchange of goods. However, traders could calculate the relative value of goods by known units, such as bags of grain of a standard size, or copper (or gold) of a certain weight. If someone bought a dried fish for a deben of copper, payment was not made in copper, but something of equivalent value.

Imports and Exports
Thanks to the fertility of the land, the Egyptians produced enough grain to feed themselves and sell to others. Another export was papyrus, an early form of paper made from reeds. Imports included cedarwood, which came from Lebanon. Metals and precious stones came from the desert. One favorite, lapis lazuli, originated in Afghanistan.

Trading on the Nile

The rich country of Egypt provided most of the products ordinary people needed, but some goods had to be imported from other lands. For example, wood was scarce (few trees grew in Egypt) and was brought from Lebanon. The Egyptians obtained valuable minerals, including gold, from the desert oases and from Nubia in the south (see page 97). In a time when iron was not to be had, all the Egyptians' copper, the metal from which tools and weapons were made, came from Sinai.

A spoon for cosmetic powder, carved in elephant ivory from East Africa.

A treasury official weighs gold rings. Cheating was not easy, and scales like these were very accurate.

Quaysides

As everyone lived near the river, which was also the highway for trade, markets grew up on the quaysides. Pictures in tombs show that these markets were visited by foreign merchants, but they were mostly for local trade and were Egypt's only "shopping centers." Besides regular traders, craftsmen, local fishermen, and farmers' wives would come to buy and sell surplus products.

People of many sorts mingled at the quayside market.

TRADE

c. 3800 BCE
Early trade contacts between Egypt and Mesopotamia and Syria.

c. 3200 BCE
Earliest record of Egyptian sea voyages; copper brought from Sinai.

c. 3100 BCE
Military expeditions to Nubia to mine gold.

c. 2300 BCE
Harkhuf (active c. 2290–2270 BCE), governor of Upper Egypt, leads expedition to southern Nubia with 300 donkeys: 100 carried water, the rest brought back incense, ebony, "panthers," ivory, and other goods.

c. 1500 BCE
Increasing trade with countries throughout the eastern Mediterranean region.

c. 1492 BCE
First voyage to "Punt" (probably Somalia) via the Nile and the Red Sea, where the ships were built. They brought back myrrh (incense) trees, ivory, ebony, and other rare woods, and live baboons, in exchange for jewelry and weapons.

c. 500 BCE
An 53-mile 85-km canal was built between the Nile and the Red Sea.

Nile Boats

Small boats for short journeys were made of bundles of papyrus reeds. Larger vessels were made of cedarwood, joined by wooden pegs and ropes of tough grass. Seagoing ships had a mast and single sail, plus 12 or more oars each side and steering oars at the stern.

Sailors carry grain (their wages) off the ship at Thebes. They will exchange some at the market.

The New Kingdom

After 200 years of disunity and foreign invasion, the kingdom of Egypt was restored in about 1550 BCE by Ahmose I. Under the 18th and early 19th Dynasties, Egypt reached its greatest glory. It became the chief commercial and military power in the Near East. Thanks to gold from conquered Nubia in the south, tribute paid by lesser rulers, and the profits of trade, the state grew immensely rich. The pharaoh was exalted as the personification of the sun god, and the wealth and influence of the priesthood increased.

Statue of Tuthmosis III. His successful military campaigns in Syria and Palestine extended Egypt's control in the Middle East.

THE EGYPTIAN EMPIRE

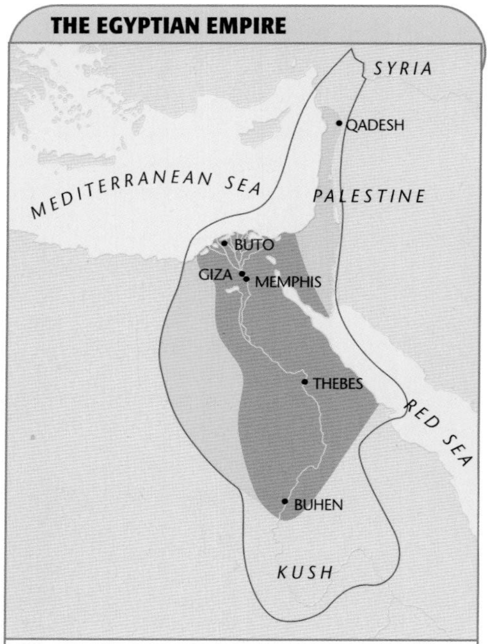

Area under direct Egyptian control, Middle Kingdom

Area under Egyptian dominance, Middle Kingdom

Maximum extent of the New Kingdom during reign of Tuthmosis III

Egypt's Conquests

The growth of an empire brought great wealth to Egypt. Besides regaining control of Nubia, Tuthmosis III (reigned 1504–1450 BCE) conquered Palestine, where the Hyksos had come from (see page 97) and much of Syria. The empire was never so large again, but serious decline only began after the death of Ramesses II. This map shows the expansion of the Egyptian Empire in the New Kingdom.

The Army

In the New Kingdom, Egypt had a regular army for the first time. Some soldiers were mercenaries, Nubians, Libyans, and others who fought for money, and some were specialist charioteers or bowmen. Soldiers had a shield but no armor, and the main weapons were mace, spear, and bow. Ramesses II challenged the Hittites at Qadesh (1275 BCE) with 5,000 men and 50 chariots.

The ceremonial axe of Ahmose I, founder of the 18th Dynasty.

The army of Ramesses III (reigned 1182–1151 BCE) resists attack by "Sea Peoples," one of the enemies who weakened the New Kingdom.

Akhenaten

One of the more famous New Kingdom pharaohs was Amenhotep IV (reigned 1350–1334 BCE). At the beginning of his reign he changed his name to Akhenaten and dedicated a temple near Karnak to Aten, the Sun disk, instead of Amun (the supreme god). He also closed the temple dedicated to Amun. This shocked everyone, in fact, after his death he was labelled a heretic.

This gold amulet, representing Maat, was found with the mummy of Tutankhamun.

Relief showing Akhenaten and Queen Nefertiti with three of their children.

Gold

The Egyptians wanted to control Nubia for its luxury trade, above all its gold. Gold came from dry river beds, where it was easily collected, and rocky hills east of the Nile River. It reached Egypt as gold dust or nuggets. Nubian gold paid for the expansion of the empire.

THE DECLINE

1570 BCE
Beginning of the New Kingdom. Ahmose I consolidates the empire's borders.

1483 BCE
Death of Queen Hatshepsut. Tuthmosis III, Hatshepsut's co-regent and step-son, assumes full power.

1386 BCE
Amenhotep III (reigned 1386–1349 BCE) brings prosperity and stability to the empire.

1324 BCE
Tutankhamun dies and is replaced by Ay (reigned 1324–1319 BCE), the first of the three non-royal army generals to become pharaoh.

1279 BCE
Ramesses II takes the throne. He orders the building of the great temple at Abu Simbel in Nubia.

c. 1177 BCE
Invading "Sea Peoples" are driven back by Ramesses III.

1069 BCE
Beginning of the Third Intermediate Period, with Smendes I (reigned 1069–1043 BCE) of the 21st Dynasty. Tanis, in Lower Egypt, is the new capital.

525 BCE
Egyptians are defeated by the Persians who take charge of Egypt, founding the 27th Dynasty and marking the beginning of the Late Period.

332 BCE
Alexander the Great, king of Macedonia (see page 119), invades Egypt.

The Minoans

The first European civilization arose on the island of Crete over 4,000 years ago and lasted about 600 years. It was a complex society of great palaces and cities, with high living standards based on farming, but gaining its wealth from trade. The people are called Minoans after a legendary king, Minos, who kept a bull-like monster, the Minotaur, in a labyrinth (underground maze). Minoan civilization was entirely unknown until its remains were discovered by archeologists about 100 years ago. As we cannot read the Minoan language, our knowledge comes mainly from their finds.

Religion

Minoan religion was closely related to nature. The chief deity was a goddess, whose sign was the double-headed axe of King Minos. The male god, a junior figure, was linked with the bull, a sacred animal. He "died" each fall and was "reborn" in spring. Complicated rituals may have taken place in temples, but most worship was at small household shrines, in the open, or in sacred caves.

THE MINOANS

c. 2900–2000 BCE
Beginning of early Bronze Age cultures in the Aegean. Inhabitants of the Cyclades, a group of small islands north of Crete, develop their own distinct culture.

c. 2100 BCE
Rise of Minoan civilization; palaces are built in Crete.

c. 1700 BCE
Widespread destruction, followed by rebuilding.

c. 1600 BCE
Rise of Mycenaeans in Greece.

c. 1500 BCE
Minoan society and art at its peak.

c. 1450 BCE
Major disaster (earthquake?), followed by Mycenaean takeover.

This fine ewer or pitcher, with a pattern based on leaves of grass, comes from the palace of Phaistos.

A scene from a Minoan tomb with priestesses taking part in a religious ceremony.

Minoan ships were up to 30 m (98 ft) long, with oars and a sail. They also shipped goods for other peoples.

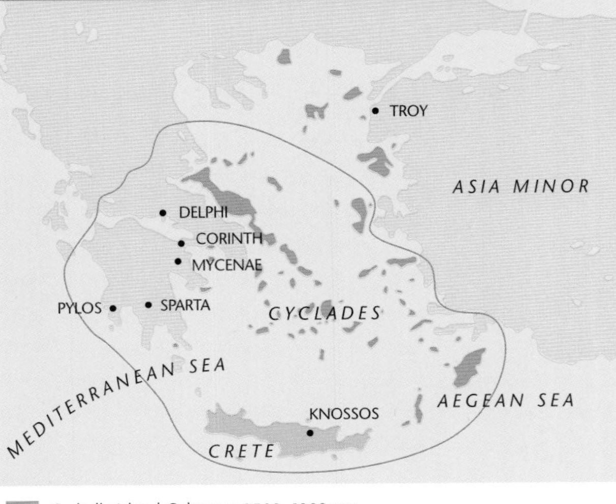

Crete

Although Crete was said to contain 100 towns, the island is only about 155 miles (250 km) long, east to west, and 34 miles (55 km) across at the widest. It has many good harbors, where sailors took refuge from the earliest times. It is very mountainous, and only about one-quarter was farmed, but the land was so fertile it supported a large population.

Trade and the Sea

Minoan Crete was a sea power. Its navy kept the island safe from attack, its trade made it wealthy, and its colonies provided agents and bases abroad. The Minoans' finest manufactures—pottery, jewelry, metal wares—have been found throughout the eastern Mediterranean. They also exported food, olive oil, and cloth. Egypt was their biggest customer. The Minoans imported gold and other metals, along with ivory and fine stone.

Architecture

The most remarkable buildings of ancient Crete were the Minoan palaces, which were like small towns and the centers of economic life, religion, and government. They had no defensive walls, as the Minoans did not fear attack. City streets were paved, with a piped water supply and sewage system.

Images of Minoan houses, which were square, flat-roofed, and sometimes with several floors.

The Queen's Hall at Knossos was decorated with a painting of dolphins.

Knossos

The palace of Knossos was up to five floors high and covered the area of two football fields. The buildings, around a courtyard, housed thousands of people. Living quarters were on the light and airy upper floors. Besides elegant court chambers, beautifully decorated with frescoes (wall paintings), the palace contained shrines, workshops, storerooms, and offices.

THE MYCENAEANS

The Mycenaeans were strongly influenced by the Minoans. This Mycenaean krater shows an octopus: a Minoan favorite.

c. 3000–2000 BCE
Ancestors of the Mycenaeans settle in Greece.

c. 1600 BCE
Mycenaeans begin to trade with Minoans.

c. 1500 BCE
Mycenaeans begin to use chariots.

c. 1400 BCE
Mycenaeans control Crete.

c. 1250 BCE
The city of Troy is captured.

c. 1150 BCE
Collapse of Mycenaean civilization, cities deserted.

The Mycenaeans

Soon after 1450 BCE Crete was taken over by the Mycenaeans, the dominant people of mainland Greece from before 1600 BCE, who are named after their largest city. A stronger, more warlike people than the Minoans, they inherited the Minoan trading empire and enlarged it, with bases throughout the eastern Mediterranean. They lived in independent cities, which sometimes acted together but sometimes fought each other. In each city, the king was supported by landowning warriors, who ruled over craftsmen, peasants, and slaves.

Fortified Cities

Built on hilltops, Mycenaean cities (unlike Minoan) were strongly fortified, with stone walls up to 20 feet (6 m) thick. At the center was the citadel, containing the royal palace. The city was the center of government and the economy, controlling a large area of farm land.

The entrance, known as the Lion Gate, to the citadel at Mycenae.

Writing

We cannot read the Minoan script, called Linear A. But about 1400 BCE another system, Linear B, appeared in Crete. This was famously deciphered in the 1950s, when the language turned out to be an early form of Greek, which was used by the Mycenaeans.

Written records were made on clay tablets. Thousands have survived thanks to their being fired, which hardened the clay.

A bronze suit of armor that must have belonged to a king or great warrior.

Warfare

The Mycenaeans were warriors. Shaft graves contained many weapons, and walls were decorated with battle scenes. They learned chariot warfare from Egypt, and fought with spear and sword. They wore helmets and leather or bronze armor, with huge, body-length shields. The northerners who finally overcame them probably had iron weapons, superior to bronze.

Gold death mask from Mycenae: its discoverer thought it was Agamemnon, a leader in the Trojan War.

Troy fell when the "Greeks" smuggled in a raiding party concealed in a huge wooden horse.

The Trojan War

The first great work of European literature is *The Iliad*, composed by the poet Homer (active 9th or 8th century BCE). It tells the story of the ten-year siege of Troy (in Asia Minor) by "Greeks," led by Agamemnon. Archeologists have proved the story is based on fact, and Homer's "Greeks" were actually Mycenaeans. The war was probably not fought over a woman, as the poet says, but was more likely a trade dispute.

Incidents in the final capture of the royal palace of Troy, painted on a Greek vase.

Lefkandi
At Lefkandi, on the island of Euboea, archeologists recently found evidence of great prosperity during the Dark Age. About 1000 BCE, Lefkandi had overseas trade, a metalworking industry, and a large building that resembled the future Greek temples. Graves contained valuable and beautiful objects, some imported. There may be other such places, still undiscovered.

Greece: The Dark Age

Mycenaean civilization disappeared quickly and almost completely. Within 100 years, trade ceased, cities fell into ruins, population dropped sharply, and people were much poorer. There were no more clay tablets—no written records—for the art of writing was forgotten. Darkness fell on Greece. For over three centuries, so far as we can tell, life seems to have been grim. But there were bright spots. A few Mycenaeans settled successfully in Cyprus and some places, such as Lefkandi, recovered much sooner.

Clay model of a centaur (half man, half horse), found in a tomb at Lefkandi.

Bards played a vital part in spreading and strengthening the Greeks' idea of themselves as a special people.

Archaic Pottery

In art, the later centuries of the Dark Age are called the Archaic period. Its chief product is pottery, painted in abstract, geometric designs associated especially with Athens. Stylized human figures and animals appear in the 8th century BCE, when bronze sculptures in similar, geometric style were also made.

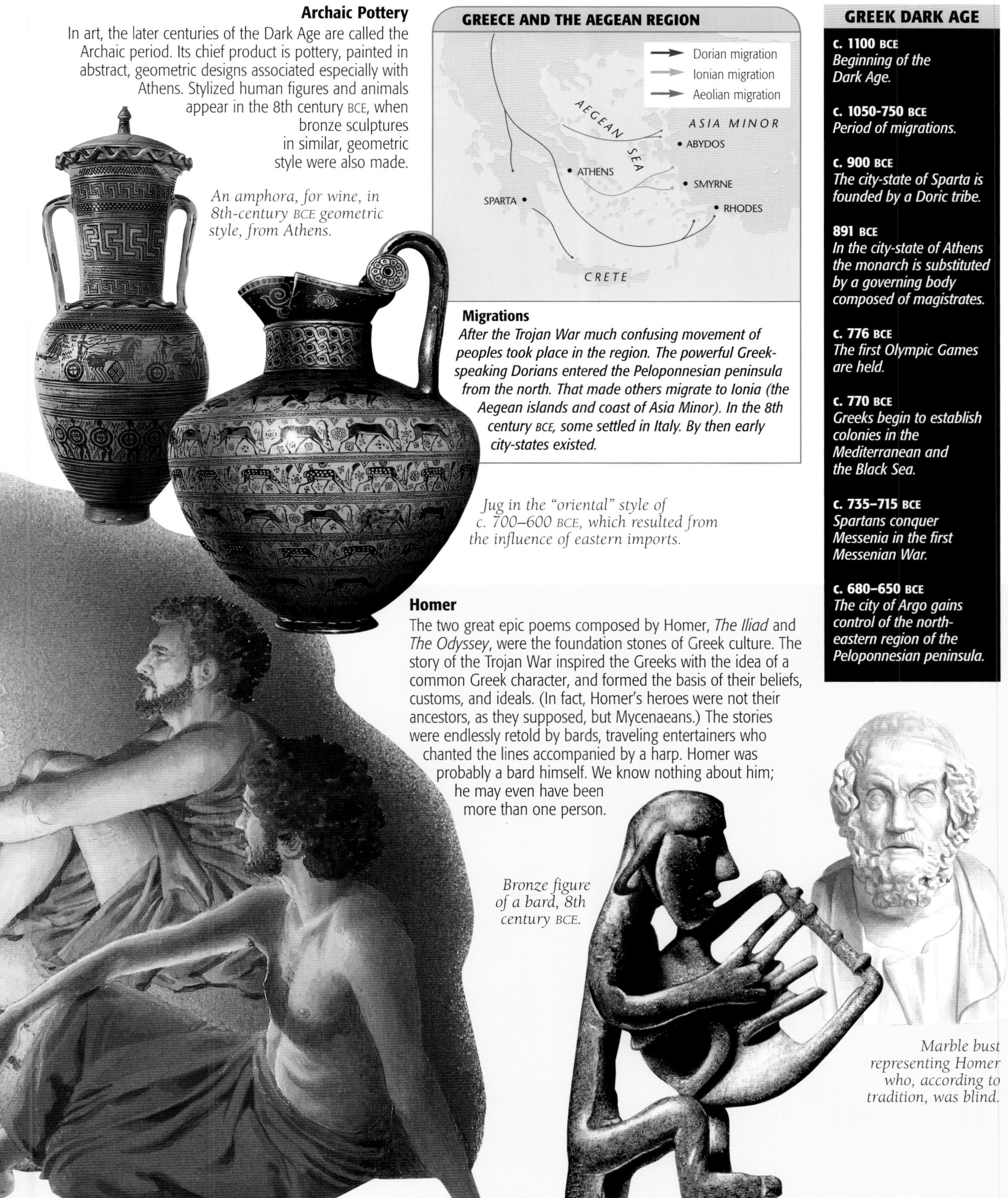

An amphora, for wine, in 8th-century BCE geometric style, from Athens.

Migrations

After the Trojan War much confusing movement of peoples took place in the region. The powerful Greek-speaking Dorians entered the Peloponnesian peninsula from the north. That made others migrate to Ionia (the Aegean islands and coast of Asia Minor). In the 8th century BCE, some settled in Italy. By then early city-states existed.

Jug in the "oriental" style of c. 700–600 BCE, which resulted from the influence of eastern imports.

GREEK DARK AGE

c. 1100 BCE
Beginning of the Dark Age.

c. 1050-750 BCE
Period of migrations.

c. 900 BCE
The city-state of Sparta is founded by a Doric tribe.

891 BCE
In the city-state of Athens the monarch is substituted by a governing body composed of magistrates.

c. 776 BCE
The first Olympic Games are held.

c. 770 BCE
Greeks begin to establish colonies in the Mediterranean and the Black Sea.

c. 735–715 BCE
Spartans conquer Messenia in the first Messenian War.

c. 680–650 BCE
The city of Argo gains control of the north-eastern region of the Peloponnesian peninsula.

Homer

The two great epic poems composed by Homer, *The Iliad* and *The Odyssey*, were the foundation stones of Greek culture. The story of the Trojan War inspired the Greeks with the idea of a common Greek character, and formed the basis of their beliefs, customs, and ideals. (In fact, Homer's heroes were not their ancestors, as they supposed, but Mycenaeans.) The stories were endlessly retold by bards, traveling entertainers who chanted the lines accompanied by a harp. Homer was probably a bard himself. We know nothing about him; he may even have been more than one person.

Bronze figure of a bard, 8th century BCE.

Marble bust representing Homer who, according to tradition, was blind.

THE CLASSICAL AGE

508 BCE
Beginning of democracy in Athens.

c. 500 BCE
Beginning of the Classical age.

478 BCE
Formation of the Delian League, dominated by Athens, which profits from tribute-paying members.

432 BCE
Spartans establish a military alliance with other city-states, called the Peloponnesian League, in order to resist Persian invasions and to ally against Athens.

431–404 BCE
The Peloponnesian War (Athens vs. Sparta).

Classical Greece

During the Classical age in Greece, c. 500–300 BCE, a combination of individuals of huge ability, living in a society that encouraged thought and the arts, lifted human society to new levels. The warring city-states of Athens and Sparta gained control of large areas beyond their city walls. The Spartans became a great military power while the Athenians flourished in the arts and learning. Like every society, the Greeks learned from earlier civilizations, yet they more or less invented democracy.

The City-State

The Greeks, with the same language, religion, and customs, shared an idea of "Greekness," but lived in independent city-states, and their first loyalty was to their state, or *polis*. The *polis* was more than a state, it was a kind of living body of the citizens, almost a club—but for men only. Women, slaves, and foreigners were excluded. Many of these communities were small enough for the citizens to all know each other.

Athens and Sparta

Although they might combine against a common enemy, the two greatest Greek cities were intense rivals. Athens was the cultural heart of the Greek world; it was democratic, tolerant, and intellectually curious. Sparta, in contrast, belonged to an older tradition, and was authoritarian and militaristic, with a huge underclass of helots, who were really the slaves of the state. Sparta had the most formidable army, Athens the best navy.

A Spartan hoplite (soldier). All male Spartan citizens were trained soldiers.

A herdsman tends his goats outside Athens, with the Acropolis, or citadel, in the distance.

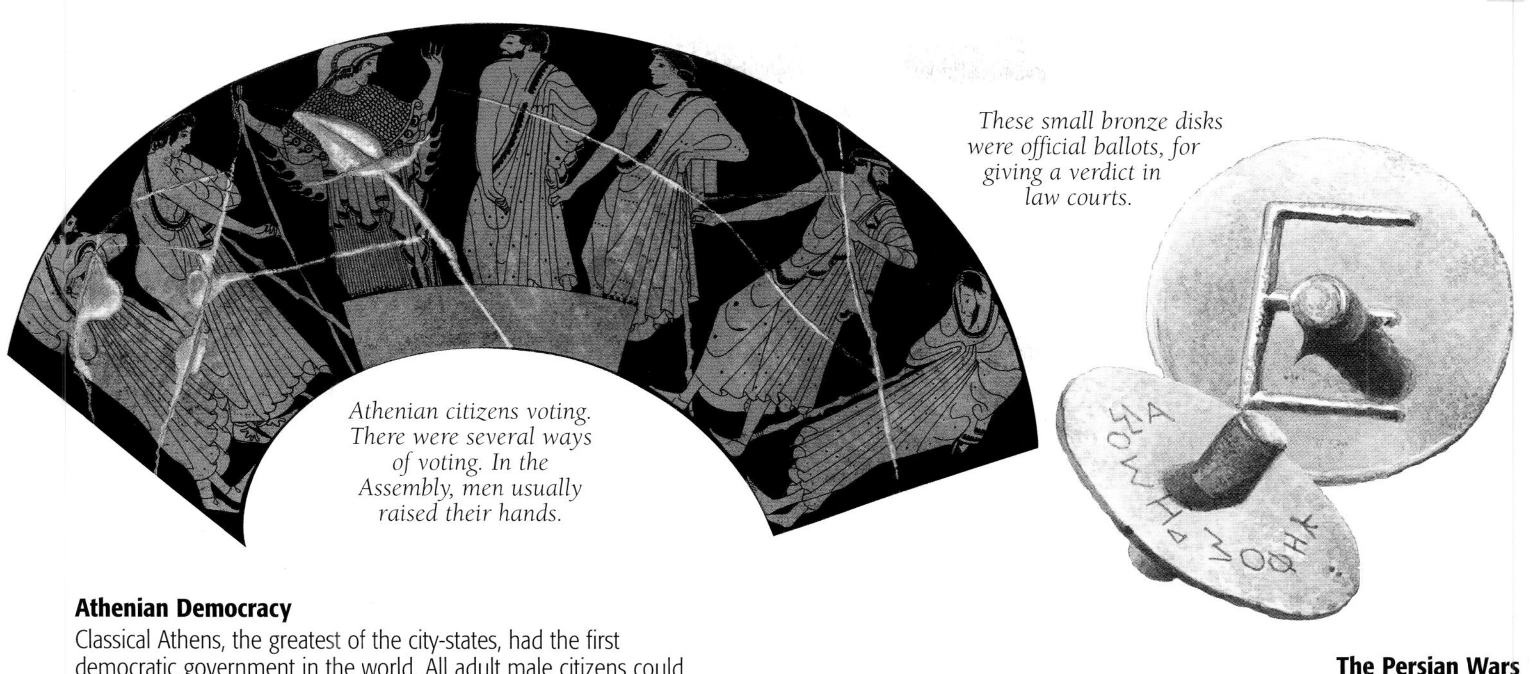

Athenian citizens voting. There were several ways of voting. In the Assembly, men usually raised their hands.

These small bronze disks were official ballots, for giving a verdict in law courts.

Athenian Democracy

Classical Athens, the greatest of the city-states, had the first democratic government in the world. All adult male citizens could vote, speak in the Assembly, elect ministers, and take part in government. The example of Athenian democracy was followed by many other city-states within Athens' area of influence. Others looked to Sparta, still ruled by a king and nobles.

The Persian Wars

In 490 BCE Athens defeated a Persian invasion at Marathon, 23 miles (37 km) from Athens. Ten years later the Persians returned in greater strength. Athens and Sparta put differences aside to lead a coalition of Greek states. They defeated the Persian fleet at Salamis in 480 BCE and the Persian army at Plataea in 479 BCE. Their success stimulated Greek confidence and the rise of Athens.

The feats of the mighty Greek army were also celebrated in art. This late classical wine jar from Athens shows a Greek soldier (right) taking on three Persian soldiers.

ALLIES OF ATHENS AND SPARTA

Warring City-States

After the Persian Wars Athens became the leader of a confederation of states, with headquarters on the island of Delos, known as the Delian League. Members of the league followed the same military strategy and all contributed to a common fund. Athens soon took control of the funds and dominated the member states, creating an Athenian Empire. In response, Sparta formed allies of her own. Conflict soon erupted and the Peloponnesian War began (see page 118).

- Sparta and allies
- Athenian Empire
- Athenian allies

Trade and Colonies

In Greece, as in other ancient societies, the most important business was farming, and farming employed the largest number of people. But the mountainous countryside and hot, dry climate made good farming land scarce. Few crops except olives and grapes grew well. The Greeks therefore had to import much of their food, especially grain, from other countries. From the 8th century BCE onward, the shortage of good land, and the growing population, drove many Greeks to settle abroad. These colonies became useful centers of trade.

Trade

Overland travel was slow, difficult, and dangerous, and all trade went by sea. The largest import was grain. Athens imported two-thirds of the grain it needed. In exchange it traded manufactures such as painted pottery and olive oil. Traders were usually independent merchants with their own ship. One typical trader's cargo included scent bottles from Corinth, hides from Euboea, salt fish from the Black Sea, and wine from Chios.

The Greek cities issued their own coins, which were based on weight (the drachma). The variety of coins made exchange complicated.

GREEKS AT SEA

c. 1050 BCE
First Greek migrations to Asia Minor.

c. 750 BCE
The Italian colony of Tarentum (Taranto) is founded by Spartan settlers.

c. 730 BCE
The colony of Syracuse is founded by Corinthians in Sicily.

c. 630 BCE
Ionians from Thera settle at Cyrene.

c. 600 BCE
Ionians settle at Massalia (modern Marseilles). Development of sail-powered, specialist merchant ships.

c. 500 BCE
Ionian revolt against Persian rule.

c. 483 BCE
The great politician and naval strategist Themistocles (c. 524–c. 460 BCE) makes Athens a sea power.

c. 450 BCE
Piraeus, Athens' port, becomes the chief trading port. Athenian navy crushes pirates.

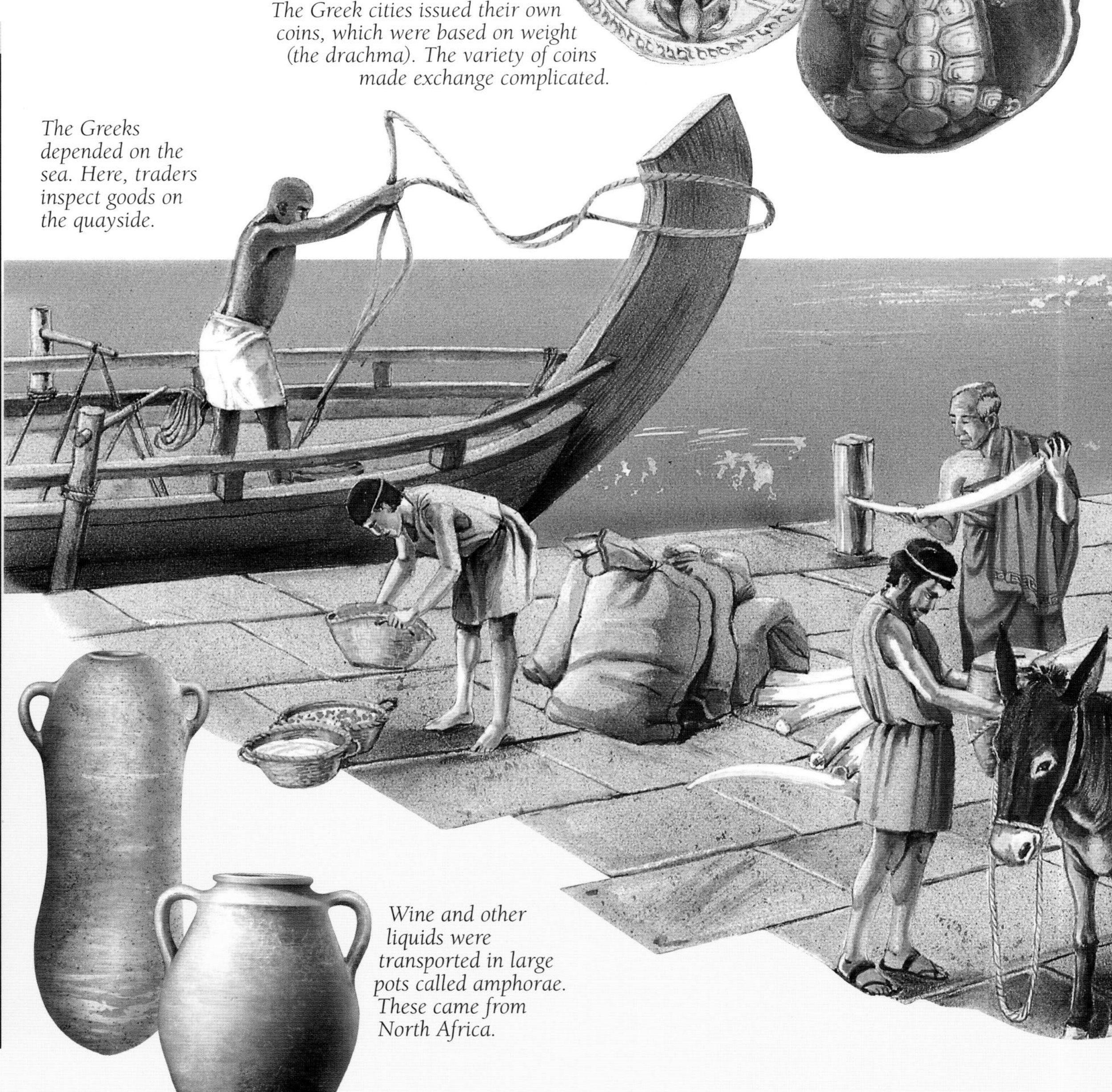

The Greeks depended on the sea. Here, traders inspect goods on the quayside.

Wine and other liquids were transported in large pots called amphorae. These came from North Africa.

Farming

Although some wheat was grown, the main cereal was barley. Farmers raised peas, beans, onions, and cabbages in small plots. They kept goats mainly for milk, sheep mainly for wool, and mules and donkeys for work. Meat, a luxury, came from goats and pigs. Having no sugar, the Greeks kept bees for honey.

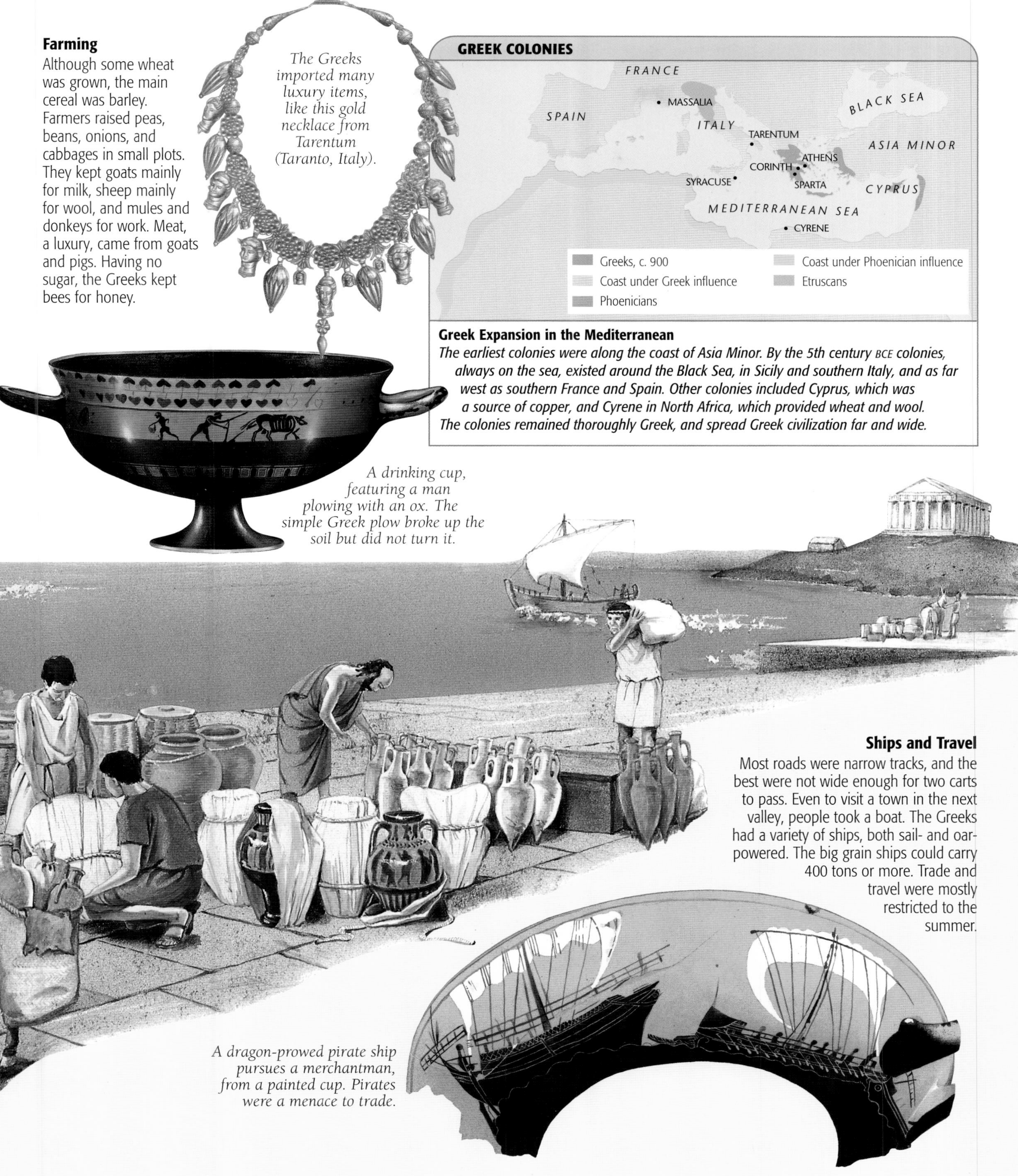

The Greeks imported many luxury items, like this gold necklace from Tarentum (Taranto, Italy).

Greek Expansion in the Mediterranean

The earliest colonies were along the coast of Asia Minor. By the 5th century BCE colonies, always on the sea, existed around the Black Sea, in Sicily and southern Italy, and as far west as southern France and Spain. Other colonies included Cyprus, which was a source of copper, and Cyrene in North Africa, which provided wheat and wool. The colonies remained thoroughly Greek, and spread Greek civilization far and wide.

A drinking cup, featuring a man plowing with an ox. The simple Greek plow broke up the soil but did not turn it.

Ships and Travel

Most roads were narrow tracks, and the best were not wide enough for two carts to pass. Even to visit a town in the next valley, people took a boat. The Greeks had a variety of ships, both sail- and oar-powered. The big grain ships could carry 400 tons or more. Trade and travel were mostly restricted to the summer.

A dragon-prowed pirate ship pursues a merchantman, from a painted cup. Pirates were a menace to trade.

LITERATURE AND DRAMA

c. 800 BCE
Homer composes The Iliad *and* The Odyssey.

c. 750 BCE
Greeks adopt the alphabet.

c. 581 BCE
Birth of Pythagoras.

c. 550 BCE
Beginning of Greek theater.

c. 534 BCE
Beginning of main drama festival at Athens.

c. 525 BCE
Birth of Aeschylus.

496 BCE
Birth of Sophocles.

484 BCE
Birth of Euripides.

470 BCE
Birth of Socrates.

387 BCE
Plato founds his Academy.

c. 385 BCE
Plato writes The Republic.

377 BCE
Death of Hippocrates.

367 BCE
Aristotle joins Plato's Academy.

322 BCE
Death of Aristotle.

Learning and Theater

In intellectual and artistic achievement, the Greeks, a uniquely creative people, were pioneers. Although they owed some ideas to other peoples, such as the Egyptians and the Phoenicians (who devised the alphabet), they practically invented epic poetry, drama, history, and philosophy, and they achieved a degree of excellence in those and other fields which no later age has surpassed. In spite of their limited information about the world and nature, they made such progress in science (or natural history) and medicine that no further great advance was made for about 1,500 years.

Statue of Chrysippus (c. 280– c. 206 BCE), a leader of the school of philosophers known as the Stoics.

Science

Greek thinkers were always seeking the causes of things. Their lively minds created wonderful theories, usually logical though often wrong, like the beautiful idea of the Universe as a series of spheres. Aristotle, who taught that collecting facts must come before forming theories, founded biology. Mathematicians included Pythagoras (active 6th century BCE) and Euclid (active c. 300 BCE). Hippocrates (c. 460–c. 377 BCE) was the father of medicine.

Literature

The love of knowledge and the freedom to seek it produced several "schools" of philosophy and some of the greatest thinkers who ever lived. Among them were Socrates (c. 470–399 BCE); his pupil Plato (c. 428–c. 348 BCE), who wrote *The Republic*, the first account of a state organized on sound principles; and the great Aristotle (384–322 BCE). The Greeks also produced fiction, such as *Aesop's Fables*, and the first true history.

A reading lesson. Boys might go on to specialist studies with a noted teacher.

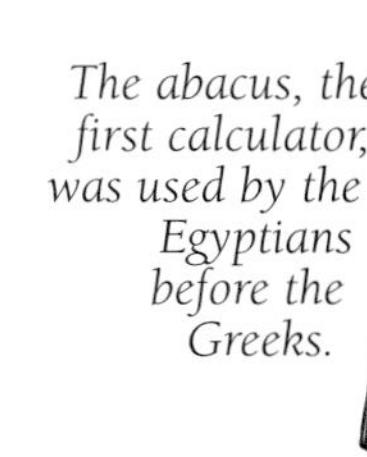

The abacus, the first calculator, was used by the Egyptians before the Greeks.

A doctor with his assistant and patient. This carving was a "thank-you" to Asclepius, god of medicine.

Education

Sons of citizens (adult males) went to school where they learned to read and write and also studied arithmetic, poetry, music, and gymnastics. School lasted from age 7 to about 15. It was not free, but fees were low. Probably, many girls learned to read at home. Education varied. In Sparta it was hard, even brutal, as the purpose was to breed toughness.

Theater

Greek drama grew from religious ritual. The greatest dramas were the tragedies of Aeschylus (c. 525–c. 456 BCE), Sophocles (c. 496–406 BCE), and Euripides (c. 484–406 BCE). The Greeks liked comedies too, and audiences in the open-air theaters watched several plays in a day. They sat on benches cut into a hill in a semicircle around the stage. Actors (men only) wore masks; little action happened on stage; a chorus provided a commentary; there was no scenery, but music was important.

Dancing and music filled interludes at the theater, as in this Archaic carving.

An acrobat in a comedy, on a 4th-century BCE Athenian red-figure vase.

It was a citizen's duty to attend the theater, and a man could reclaim any lost wages.

Art and Architecture

In art, the Greeks pursued an ideal, a perfection based on unchanging mathematical standards that govern shape and proportion. The artists' chief subject was mankind—the human form—which was also the form of the gods. Classical art strove for utter realism, reaching a peak in sculptures of the human (chiefly male) nude, and it set the standard for Western art for over 2,000 years. Few sculptures have survived, but we know others from later copies. Less durable art, such as paintings, has long vanished.

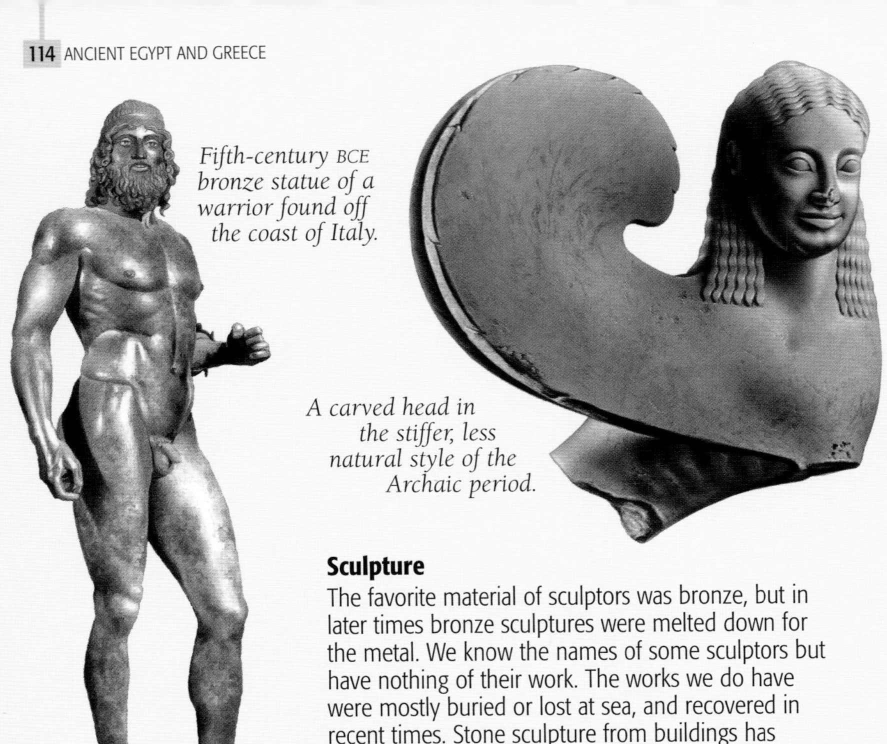

Fifth-century BCE bronze statue of a warrior found off the coast of Italy.

A carved head in the stiffer, less natural style of the Archaic period.

Sculpture

The favorite material of sculptors was bronze, but in later times bronze sculptures were melted down for the metal. We know the names of some sculptors but have nothing of their work. The works we do have were mostly buried or lost at sea, and recovered in recent times. Stone sculpture from buildings has survived better, especially in the decorative friezes running around temples, such as the Parthenon.

Figures from the Parthenon. The folds of cloth indicate the sculptor's skill and keen observation.

The Parthenon in Athens is made of marble, but most temples were built of limestone (which is easier to work).

Architecture

The features of Classical Greek architecture were boldness and simplicity. Although limited in technique and materials (no mortar, for example), the Greeks had plenty of building stone for their great temples. The design was one of straight lines, developed from wooden buildings and based on the column. The colonnaded buildings were built in the three Classical Orders, fundamental to most Western architecture.

THE CLASSICAL ORDERS

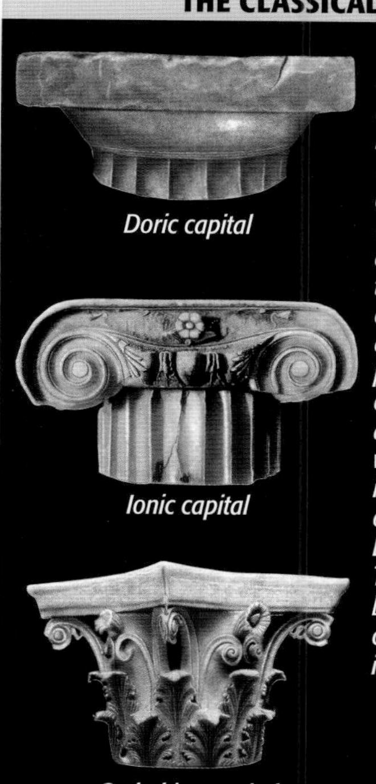

Doric capital

Ionic capital

Corinthian capital

The three orders of architecture are named after the people said to have invented them, Doric (Dorians), Ionic (Ionians) and Corinthian (Corinthians). They are defined by the design of the capitals that top the columns. Doric, with plain capitals, is the earliest and purest. Ionic, with scrolled capitals, is more slender and elegant. Corinthian, with a design of leaves, is the last and most elaborate. Athens had both Doric and Ionian orders. The Parthenon is Doric, but the slimness of the columns shows Ionic influence.

Vase Painting

Practically no painting has survived, with one important exception: painted pottery. Pottery was illustrated with scenes from mythology and everyday life—providing valuable information. There were two main types: black-figure pottery, with figures painted black against the lighter background of the clay (7th to 6th centuries BCE), and red-figure, with the background painted black and figures in the natural, reddish color of the clay.

A 7th-century black-figure vase depicting two legendary figures, Achilles and Ajax, playing a board game.

Minor Arts

A painter called Zeuxis (active second half of the 5th century BCE) painted grapes so realistic that birds pecked at them, but paintings, on walls or wood panels, have not survived. By 400 BCE the Greeks had developed the art of mosaics, for floors. They were also expert metal-workers, using most of the techniques of later goldsmiths. They made ornamental bronzes and carved gems, stones, and cameos. Even their coins seem to us works of art.

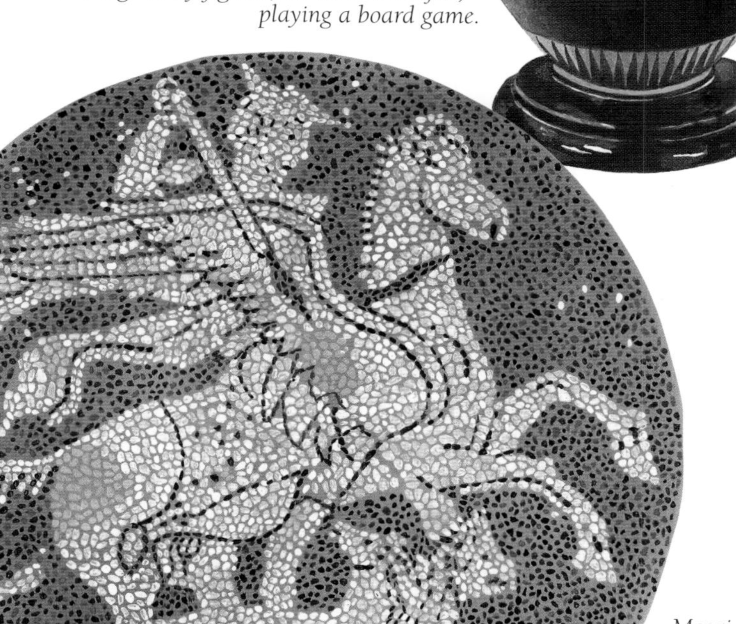

Mosaics were made of tiny colored pebbles or cubes of stone.

CHIEF GODS AND GODDESSES

Zeus
Father of the gods and head of the Olympian family, god of sky and Earth.

Hera
Wife of Zeus, jealous of his many love affairs.

Poseidon
Brother of Zeus, unruly god of the sea.

Hades
Brother of Zeus, harsh god of the Underworld, where he lived.

Demeter
Sister of Zeus, goddess of corn.

Hestia
Sister of Zeus, goddess of the home.

Athena
Powerful goddess of wisdom, born from Zeus' head shouting a war-cry.

Aphrodite
Goddess of love, born from the sea but perhaps Zeus' daughter

Ares
God of war, son of Zeus and Hera, lover of Aphrodite.

Hephaestus
Lame blacksmith-god of fire, son of Zeus and Hera, married to Aphrodite.

Apollo
Young and handsome god of music and poetry, son of Zeus and Leto.

Artemis
Goddess of hunting, Apollo's twin sister.

Hermes
Boyish, wing-footed messenger god and god of shepherds, son of Zeus and Maia.

Model of the gold and ivory statue of Athena in the Parthenon, which was 40 feet (12 m) high.

Religion in Ancient Greece

The Greeks loved order and unity, yet their religion seems very disorderly, with a bewildering number of gods and goddesses. They believed in honor and morality, yet the gods were often silly, cruel, or unjust. However, many of such stories were written later, when gods and religion were less important. In earlier times, religion was everywhere, in every place and event. As we have seen, the great festivals of drama and athletics began as religious ceremonies.

Gods and Goddesses

The gods of the ancient Greeks had superhuman powers, but they behaved like humans. They had the same pleasures, the same vices, and the same family quarrels in their home on Mount Olympus. They were often associated with a particular state. Athena, for instance, was the patron goddess of Athens, but she was also worshiped, under a different guise, in rival Sparta.

Detail of a painted vase showing a scene from Homer's The Odyssey.

A religious procession with a lamb to be sacrificed on an altar near the temple.

Myths

The Greeks told many stories about gods and superhuman heroes (such as Perseus or Herakles). These stories, which have never lost their fascination, began with Homer (in *The Iliad*, gods and goddesses support both sides in the Trojan War). They are the subject-matter of much Greek art, including sculpture, painted pottery, and the plays of the great 5th-century BCE tragedians.

Festivals

Religious festivals were held to honor the gods. They were times of celebration and included processions, sacrifices, and competitions (athletics, music, drama, etc.). In Athens, festivals occupied 60 days a year. The great summer festival was the Panathenaea (All-Athens Festival), when a new robe woven by the women of Athens was paraded through the city streets to the statue of Athena which stood in the Parthenon.

Worship and Sacrifice

Worship took place at open-air shrines. Temples were the homes of the gods, and people also provided them with food. They often sacrificed animals—white animals for the Olympians, darker ones for Underworld gods—but ate the best meat themselves. Many priests were part-time, and other leading citizens could act as priests.

A sacrificial cow: cattle, sheep, goats, and pigs were the usual animals for sacrifice.

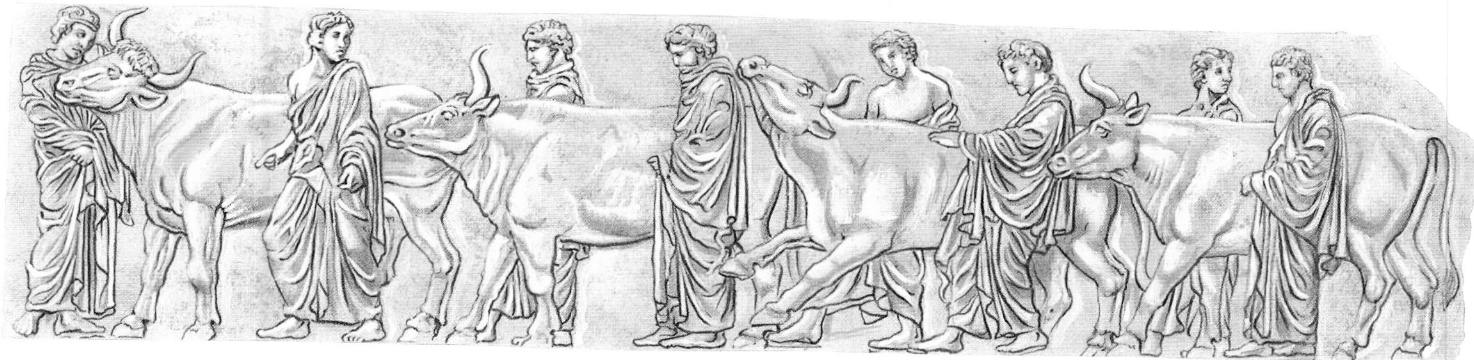

Part of a procession at the Panathenaea, from a sculpture on the Parthenon.

Oracles and Omens

The ancient Greeks believed that it was possible to predict the future, or learn the will of the gods, from omens, like a dream, an eclipse, or any unusual happening. Another way was to examine the liver of a slaughtered animal. These omens were interpreted by professionals. Or you could, for a fee, consult an oracle, notably Apollo's Oracle at Delphi, whose answer was delivered by his priestesses.

The meaning of the Oracle's answer was often unclear. If it proved wrong, you had misunderstood!

War and Conquest

The Classical age in Greece began and ended with wars—the Persian Wars and the Peloponnesian War. The Greeks were fine soldiers but not great tacticians. They depended on the formidable phalanx, a tight block of heavy infantry. Alexander the Great introduced new tactics in Asia—lighter, faster infantry, powerful cavalry, and artillery. At sea, warships had a ram to smash the enemy's oars and carried soldiers, who fought hand to hand much like a battle on land.

GREEKS AT WAR

479 BCE
Greeks repel Persian invasion.

490 BCE
Persians defeated at Marathon.

480–479 BCE
Second Persian invasion defeated.

477 BCE
Beginning of Delian League and the Athenian Empire.

431 BCE
Outbreak of Peloponnesian War.

415 BCE
Athenian expedition to Sicily.

404 BCE
End of Peloponnesian War, Athens surrenders.

395–386 BCE
Sparta victorious in Corinthian War.

371 BCE
Sparta defeated by Thebes.

339 BCE
Greek states conquered and controlled by King Philip II of Macedonia.

336 BCE
Alexander the Great becomes king of Macedonia.

334 BCE
Alexander the Great invades Persian Empire.

333 BCE
At the Battle of Issus Alexander the Great defeats King Darius III of Persia.

Armies and Soldiers

Greek hoplites, who fought in the phalanx, were mostly farmers, not professional soldiers, although the Spartans were highly trained. Men bought their own armor, handing it down to their sons. By the time of the Peloponnesian War, some states, including Athens, also employed mercenaries (hired soldiers), especially lighter-armed foot soldiers from Thrace, in the north.

Bronze figure of a mounted soldier, 6th century BCE. He would probably have fought on foot.

Weapons and Armor

Hoplites carried a shield and wore bronze armor–a helmet covering head and face, a cuirass protecting the body and greaves on the lower legs. The phalanx, which aimed to win by sheer force, by breaking the enemy's formation, fought with spears and short swords. Archers and sometimes chariots gave support, but the Greek landscape did not suit cavalry.

A bronze cuirass or breastplate, made roughly to measure for someone well off.

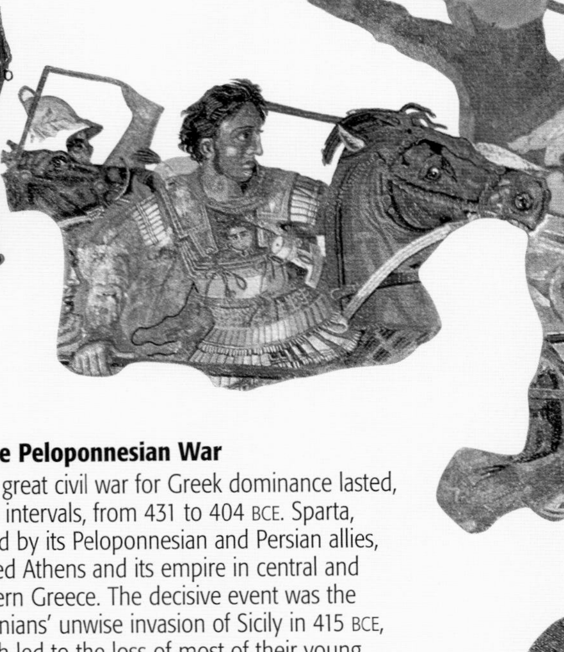

Relief representing the terrifying Medusa from the Greek colony of Syracuse in Sicily. Anyone who looked at her was turned into stone.

The Peloponnesian War

The great civil war for Greek dominance lasted, with intervals, from 431 to 404 BCE. Sparta, aided by its Peloponnesian and Persian allies, feared Athens and its empire in central and eastern Greece. The decisive event was the Athenians' unwise invasion of Sicily in 415 BCE, which led to the loss of most of their young men and eventual surrender. Athens never recovered, and Sparta became the leading state.

The King of Macedonia

The 18th king of Macedonia, Philip II (382–336 BCE), turned Macedonia into a dominating power thanks to the development of new weapons and clever military tactics and training. The Macedonian army became the world's most powerful military force. Philip II came to the throne in 359 BCE and by 339 BCE he had conquered all of Greece. He was assassinated before he could carry out his plans to invade the Persian Empire in Asia.

Detail of an ivory statue of King Philip II of Macedonia.

Alexander the Great

Philip II was succeeded by his son, Alexander III (356–323 BCE), known as Alexander the Great. As a young man Alexander was taught by the great philosopher Aristotle (see page 112) and by the time he became king, in 336 BCE, he had developed into a unique military genius. His victory over Darius III of Persia (reigned 336–330 BCE) at the Battle of Issus in 333 BCE marked the beginning of his conquest of the Persian Empire.

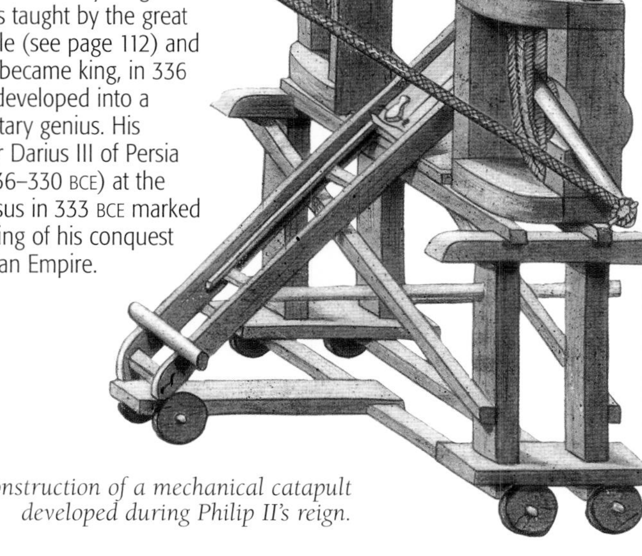

Reconstruction of a mechanical catapult developed during Philip II's reign.

Alexander the Great (far left) portrayed battling King Darius III (center) in a mosaic copy of a painting of the 4th century BCE.

The Hellenistic Age

Taking up his father's plans, Alexander the Great attacked the vast Persian Empire in 334 BCE and conquered it, from Egypt to Afghanistan, in just five years. Dreaming of a single, peaceful world empire, he pressed on eastward to the Indus River. Though his empire later broke up, Alexander's conquests spread the influence of Greek civilization over a huge area. The time that followed is known as the Hellenistic age (from the Greek word *hellenizein,* meaning "to act like a Greek"), because it was based on Greek culture but included many non-Greeks.

Alexandria

Among Alexander's many new cities was Alexandria in Egypt, which became the greatest city of the ancient world and the chief center of Hellenistic learning. After Alexander's death, a large library was established in Alexandria. Scholars were invited to live and study there.

The great lighthouse of Alexandria, one of the Seven Wonders of the ancient world.

Alexander the Great and his Hellenes (Greeks). After eight years abroad, his men insisted on going home. Alexander died on the way in 323 BCE, aged 33.

Hellenistic Art

The age of Greek culture following the Classical age, from the time of Alexander the Great's death to around the time of the first Roman emperor in 27 BCE, is known as the Hellenistic age. During this time Greek culture spread from the eastern Mediterranean to the Middle East. Hellenistic art flourished in Pella, Rhodes and Athens as well as in Alexandria, Pergamum, and Syracuse.

THE HELLENISTIC WORLD 240 BCE

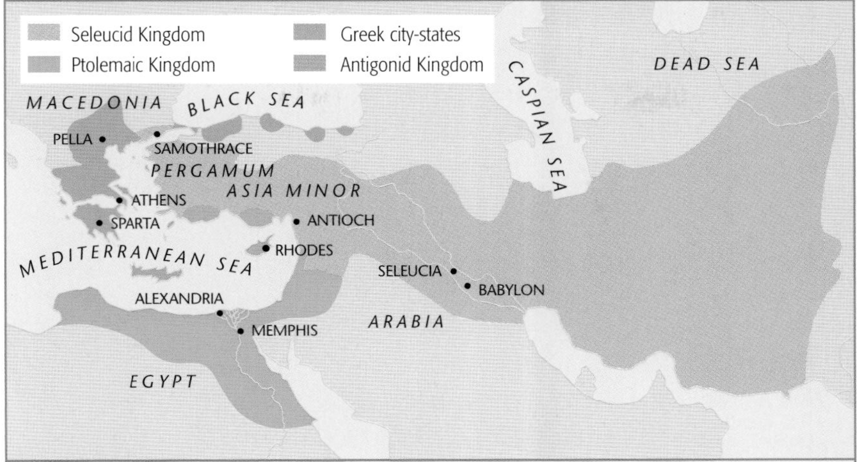

Divided Kingdoms

After the death of Alexander the Great, his Macedonian generals vied with each other for power. As a result Alexander's empire was divided into three main kingdoms. The Antigonid Kingdom, founded by the general Antigonus I (382–301 BCE), ruled Macedonia and re-established its supremacy over the Greek city-states. The vast Seleucid Empire, which was founded in 312 BCE by Seleucus (c. 358–281 BCE), one of Alexander's most able generals, stretched from Asia Minor to the Indus River. The Ptolemaic Kingdom in Egypt, with its capital at Alexandria, was founded by Ptolemy I (c. 367–c. 283 BCE), another of Alexander's generals. The Ptolemaic Dynasty's reign lasted the longest, falling to the Romans in 30 BCE.

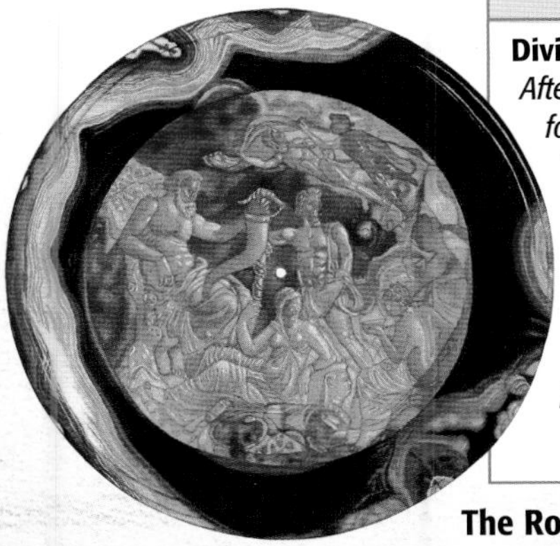

A cameo carved inside a cup. Hellenistic art was freer and more expressive, than Classical art.

The Roman Conquest

The city-state of Rome was established on the Italian peninsula in the mid 8th century BCE. Thanks to its strong army, the Romans had gained control of much of the Mediterranean by the 3rd century BCE. In 168 BCE the Romans won a decisive victory at the Battle of Pydna in which Macedonian forces were crushed. The Romans went on the conquer Greece and the rest of the Hellenistic world.

This Hellenistic sculpture of Nike, the winged goddess of victory, comes from Samothrace.

THE HELLENISTIC AGE

332 BCE
Alexander the Great invades Egypt, the city of Alexandria is founded.

330 BCE
Fall of the Persian Empire.

327 BCE
Alexander the Great defeats Prince Porus (active 4th century BCE) in India.

323 BCE
Death of Alexander in Babylon.

322 BCE
End of Athenian democracy.

287 BCE
King Antigonus II of Macedonia rules Greece.

230 BCE
Pergamum emerges as an independent kingdom.

200 BCE
During the second Macedonian War the Greeks, with support of the Romans, rebel against Macedonian rule. King Philip V (reigned 221–179 BCE) is forced to surrender Greece.

168 BCE
Macedonia becomes a Roman province.

146 BCE
Greece falls under Roman rule after the city of Corinth is captured.

A Roman cavalry soldier.

As farming made its way westward from Greece to the rest of Europe, permanent settlements began to appear across the continent. During the Metal Ages technological innovations affected settlement organization and ritual life, but also triggered drastic changes in the relations between different societies, giving a boost to trade and warfare.

The most powerful society of early Europe was that of the Romans. Through their expansion, the Romans came into conflict with the Etruscans and Greeks on the Italian peninsula and other peoples of Europe, such as the Celts, the Germanic tribes, and the nomads from the steppes of eastern Europe and Asia. By the 2nd century CE the Romans had reached the height of their power, dominating most of Europe, North Africa, and the Middle East. When their empire became too large to manage it was divided. The Empire in the West, however, was too weak to withstand foreign attacks and fell in 476, as centers of power moved to northern Europe. The Roman Empire in the East, on the other hand, continued for almost another thousand years.

The Celts were skillful metalworkers. This helmet, topped with a bronze hawk with flapping wings, would have been used for ceremonial purposes only.

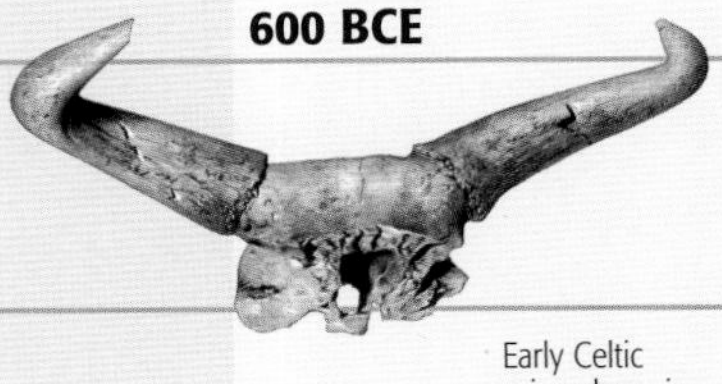

	9000 BCE	1000 BCE	800 BCE	600 BCE
Neolithic Europe	The Ice Age comes to an end. Hunter-gatherers move into northern Europe. Farming reaches Europe from the Middle East.			
Celts		Hallstatt Culture emerges north of the Alps. The Celts use iron to make tools and weapons.		Early Celtic princedoms in central Europe.
Steppe Peoples		The Cimmerians, Iranian nomadic steppe people, occupy areas of present-day Russia.	Scythians, steppe horsemen, drive the Cimmerians from the Russian Steppes.	
Etruscans		Villanovan Culture emerges in northern Italy.	Etruscan civilization develops on the Italian peninsula. Greeks establish colonies in the Mediterranean.	Etruscan monarchy is established. Romans drive out Etruscan monarchs.
Romans		First archeological evidence of settlement at Rome.	Legendary date of the founding of Rome.	The Roman Republic begins.
Germanic Peoples				

The Roman World

Steppe horseman, shown in a detail from a felt wallhanging found in a tomb in the Altai Mountains (in Russia).

400 BCE	200 BCE	1 CE	200 CE	400 CE
La Tène Culture starts replacing Hallstatt Culture. Celts sack Rome.	Romans defeat the Celts settled in northern Italy.	Julius Caesar invades and conquers northern Gaul. Celts are Romanized.		
The Mediterranean world comes into contact with the Scythians.	The Sarmatians, nomadic horsemen and warriors, conquer the Scythians.			Huns invade Germanic lands. The Huns attack the Eastern Empire.
The Etruscan city of Veii is conquered by the Romans after a ten-year siege.				
	The Punic Wars begin.	Julius Caesar is assassinated. Octavian defeats Mark Antony and becomes Rome's first emperor.	The Empire is at its fullest extent during Emperor Trajan's reign. The Roman Empire is divided.	Emperor Constantine makes Christianity official state religion. Emperor Theodosius I bans all pagan worship. Collapse of the Roman Empire in the West.
	The Germanic Cimbri tribe defeats Romans at Arausio.	The Romans occupy Germanic territory between the Rhine and Elbe rivers for a brief period. Germanic forces destroy three Roman legions in the Teutoburg Forest.	The Germanic Alamanni tribe invades Italy.	Visigoths settle within the borders of the Roman Empire. Vandals sack Rome.

Neolithic Europe

The Neolithic, or New Stone Age, was the time in which early Europeans stopped living as hunters and gathers and became farmers. Where they had once traveled constantly in search of game, they now settled down in villages. Regular harvests meant that there was more food to eat, and people had time to develop new skills, such as making pottery.

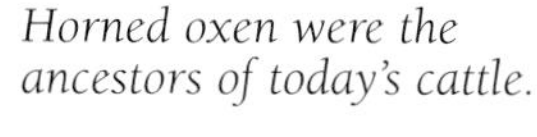

Horned oxen were the ancestors of today's cattle.

THE NEOLITHIC AGE

c. 9000 BCE
The Ice Age comes to an end. Hunter-gatherers move into northern Europe.

c. 7000 BCE
Farming, which began in the Middle East, gets under way in Greece and spreads westward.

c. 6000 BCE
The first pottery is produced in Europe.

c. 5000 BCE
Farming begins in southern France.

c. 5000 BCE
The earliest known ships appear in the Mediterranean Sea.

c. 4500 BCE
Megalith building starts in western Europe.

c. 4500 BCE
The plow is first used in southeast Europe.

c. 4400 BCE
Horses are domesticated in eastern Europe.

c. 4200 BCE
Crops and domesticated animals are introduced into northern Germany, Poland, and southern Scandinavia.

c. 4000 BCE
By this date farming is widespread in Europe.

c. 2800 BCE
Construction begins at Stonehenge.

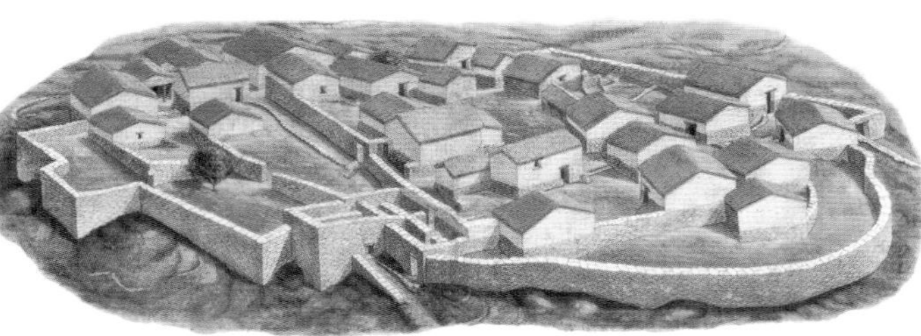

A reconstruction of Sesklo, a Neolithic faming village in Greece. Early villages were walled for defence against enemies and wild beasts.

Villages

Hunters had to keep on the move, often shifting camp to go in search of new herds to hunt and wild foods to gather. But farmers needed to stay put to tend the crops they had planted. So they started building permanent settlements–the first villages. In southern Europe they built huts of dried mud, roofing them with reeds or straw. In the colder, wetter northern lands, they used wood or else wattle and daub–a lattice of twigs plastered with clay.

The First Farmers

Farming spread gradually across Europe from the Middle East. The first farmers continued to hunt and gather wild food as their ancestors had done, but also started to plant crops as a sideline. In time they found the harvest was a more reliable source of food than wild game. The next step was to settle down on the lands they had planted.

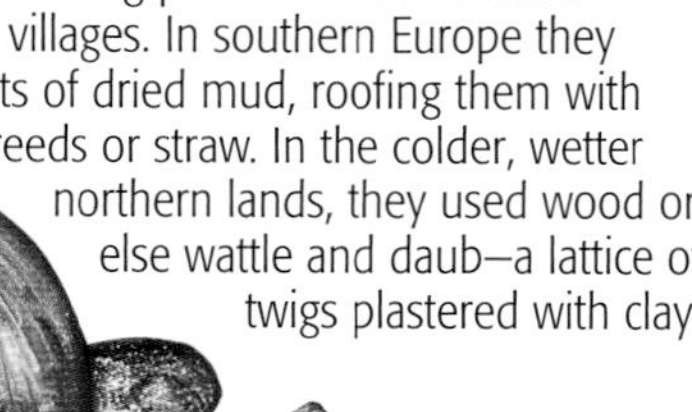

Picks and digging sticks made from deers' antlers were used to turn soil.

Monument Builders

From about 4500 BCE on, people in western Europe started building large monuments made of earth or stone. Sometimes they put up standing stones called megaliths. Elsewhere they constructed burial chambers topped with flat stones that were originally covered with barrows. Some people built stone circles that were probably used for religious rituals; the best known is England's Stonehenge, which was begun as an earthen monument.

Domestication of Animals

Besides growing crops, farmers learned to keep cattle, sheep, pigs, and goats. They chose gentle animals, driving away or killing the fiercer ones, so gradually tame breeds developed. The animals provided not just milk and meat but also wool and hides for making clothing.

Pottery pig from Turkey. Pigs were kept for meat.

A rock painting showing people driving a herd of sheep into an enclosed area.

MEGALITHIC MONUMENTS

Standing Stones

Europe's megalithic monuments are concentrated in the western part of the continent. The upsurge in stone construction seems to have been linked to the spread of farming. It is still unclear, though, whether the monuments were put up by the farming peoples themselves or by the hunter-gatherers they were replacing. One theory is that they were constructed partly as a way of showing ownership of the land, discouraging newcomers from moving into an area.

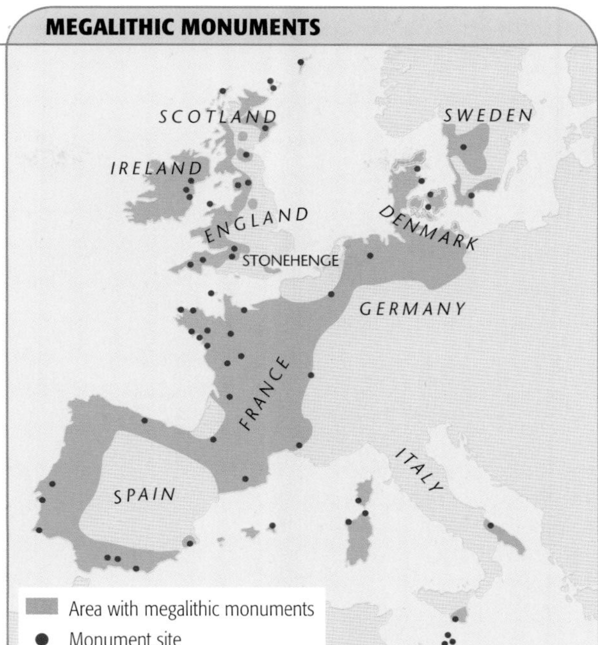

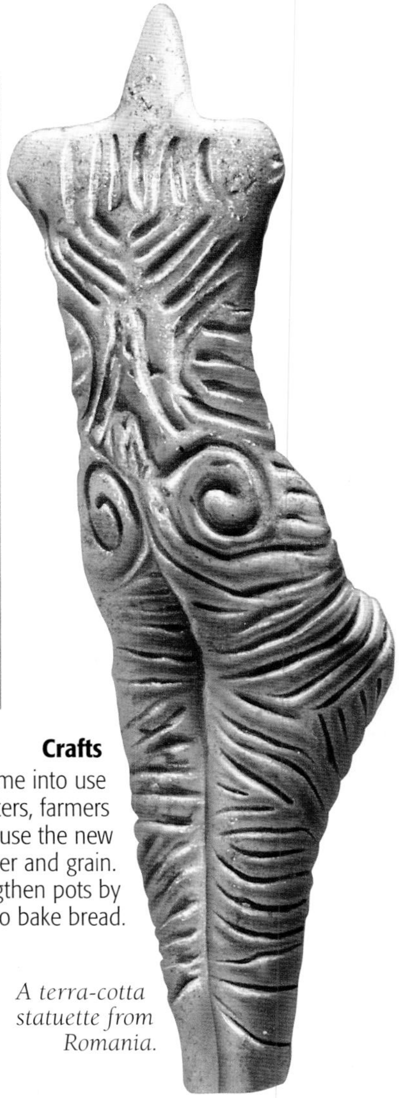

Crafts

It was not just chance that pottery came into use soon after farming began. Unlike hunters, farmers had permanent homes in which to house the new vessels, which they needed to store water and grain. Potters soon learned how to strengthen pots by firing them in the clay ovens used to bake bread.

A terra-cotta statuette from Romania.

The inner circle of standing stones at Stonehenge.

EARLY TRADE ROUTES IN EUROPE

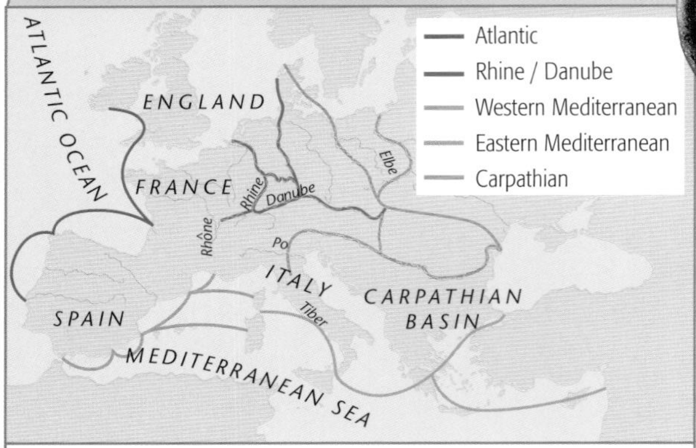

In Search of Bronze

Since the production of bronze required both copper and tin, trade networks developed to supply the ores to regions that had one metal but not the other. Tin was especially hard to come by: the main sources were in western England and France, northern Italy, and northwest Spain. The traders who carried the ores also brought finished goods. Soon there was a flourishing luxury trade for bronze ornaments, weapons, and tools.

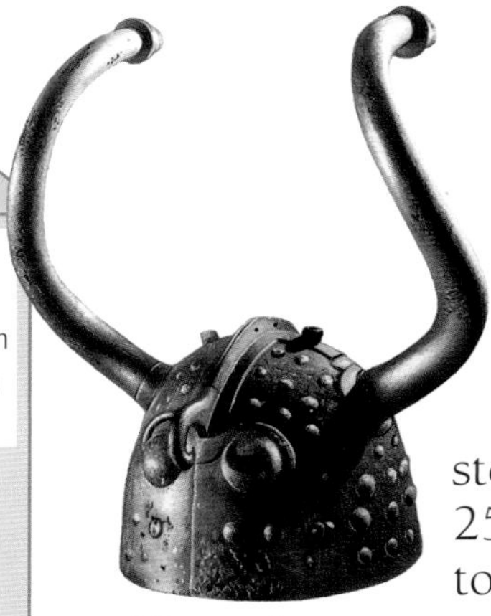

A Bronze Age horned helmet from Zealand, Denmark.

The Bronze Age

For thousands of years early humans survived in Europe using tools made only of stone and wood. Then, from about 2500 BCE on, people started to turn to metals, first used in the Near East several centuries earlier. At first they used copper, but it was soft and easily blunted. Then they learned how to mix copper with tin to make bronze—a much harder metal.

While a village smith mixes bronze, other workers shape the hot metal into weapons and polish them ready for use.

Metallurgy

To make bronze, metalsmiths had to melt copper over a high heat and then mix it with molten tin. Most bronze was made of about one part tin to nine parts copper. In Britain and France lead was also sometimes added, making the resulting metal easier to pour and to cast into the required shape.

Arms and Armor

Warriors wielding bronze swords and protected by metal body armor were more than a match for opponents who only had stone weapons. But bronze was scarce and expensive. The result was the development of warrior aristocracies who lorded it over the rest of society by force of arms.

This late Bronze Age cuirass, an upper body armor covering the chest and back, is from the Haute Marne region of France.

A relief showing a warrior and his arms—a lance, a sword, a flask, and a helmet at the top; a shield in the center; and part of a wagon at the bottom.

Burial

Archeologists investigating Bronze Age burial sites have noted a change in funerary customs from burying to cremating the dead. The new fashion started in eastern Europe in about 1400 BCE and spread across the continent over the following centuries. After cremation the ashes of the dead were buried in urns, so the culture associated with the change has become known as the Urnfield Culture.

Funerary urn with a chariot decoration dating back to c. 1300 BCE, found at a burial ground in Slovakia.

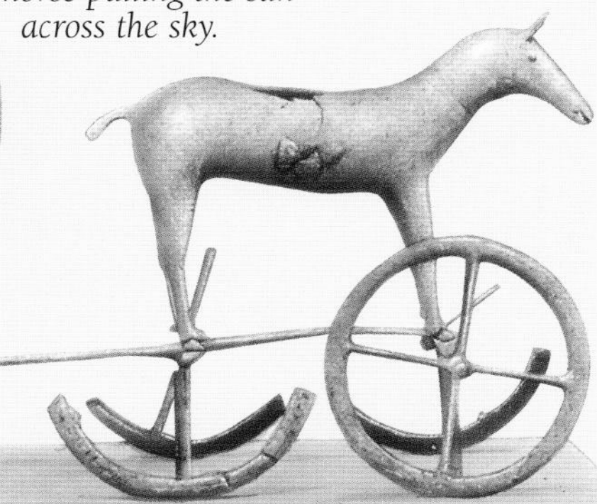

Found in Zealand in Denmark, the Trundholm Chariot is thought to represent a horse pulling the sun across the sky.

Salt Mines

One commodity that people could not do without was salt, which was used to preserve meat and fish, stopping them from going rotten. Salt mines in eastern Germany and Poland became important centers of trade, while mines at Hallstatt in Austria were to give their name to a whole culture of the ensuing Iron Age.

Cults and Beliefs

Little is known of Bronze Age religious beliefs, but archeologists have discovered that people in northern Europe threw objects including bronze ornaments and weapons into bogs as offerings to the gods. They also worshiped the Sun, to judge from the evidence of rock carvings and objects like the Trundholm Chariot (above).

Miner's pick axe and shovel of maple wood, discovered in the Hallstatt salt mines.

THE BRONZE AGE

c. 2500 BCE
Unetice Culture of central Europe is the first in Europe to make use of bronze.

c. 2300 BCE
Bronze casting reaches the Balkans, Greece and Italy.

c. 2000 BCE
Trade routes carry amber and metals across Europe.

c. 1800 BCE
Bronze working first appears in Britain.

c. 1650 BCE
Greece's Bronze Age Mycenaean civilization gets under way.

c. 1400 BCE
Walls are built around Mycenaean cities.

c. 1350 BCE
Urnfield Culture appears in central Europe.

c. 1250 BCE
Traditional date of Trojan War.

c. 1200 BCE
First iron objects appear in Europe.

c. 1200 BCE
Time of troubles, marked by large population movements, brings a dark age to the eastern Mediterranean.

c. 1000 BCE
Iron comes into widespread use in eastern Europe.

Iron Age Peoples

Bronze had made people's lives easier, but it was expensive and hard to obtain. From about 1000 BCE on, a new metal that was comparatively cheap and plentiful began to spread across Europe. This was iron, and knowledge of its use was carried by Celtic metalsmiths. Iron did not need to be mixed in an alloy as bronze did, and there were deposits on hand in many lands. It could be used to make arms that were sharper and tougher than ones made of bronze. In the Bronze Age only rich warlords could afford swords and spears; now whole tribes could be armed with the new weapons.

Hallstatt Culture

The Hallstatt Culture is named after Hallstatt in Austria, where archeologists in the 19th century found an Iron Age cemetery near ancient salt mines. It gave its name to the Celtic culture of the late Bronze Age and Iron Age, a time of hillforts and rich princely burials often featuring horse-riding equipment and iron swords. Foreign goods found in Hallstatt graves show that trade was widespread.

Iron sword with a bronze hilt decorated with a human figure, found in eastern France.

La Tène Culture

Named for an archeological site near Lake Neuchatel in Switzerland, La Tène Culture gradually replaced Hallstatt Culture from about 450 BCE on. Metalwork became more elaborate from this date, perhaps because Celtic smiths had become aware of the magnificent products of Etruscan Italy to the south (see pages 132–133).

For security, Celtic peoples across Europe built hillforts that could be defended against raiders.

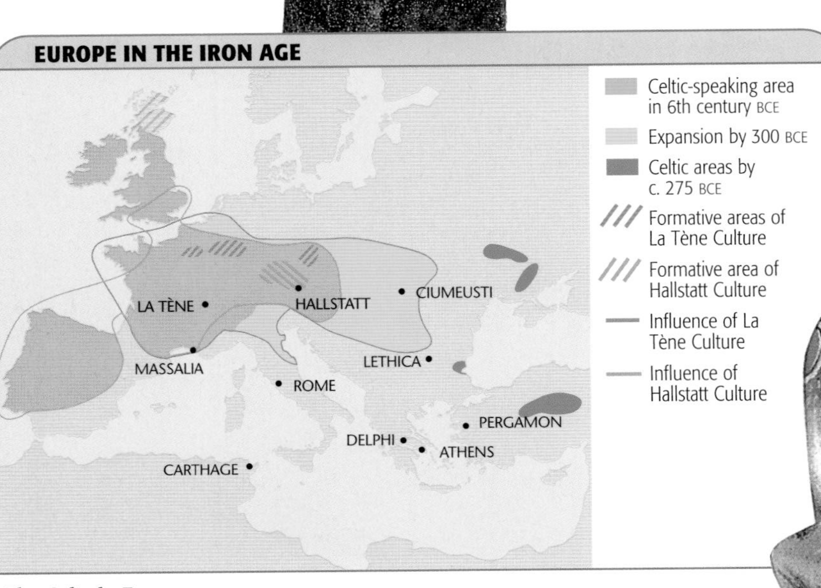

The Celts in Europe

There was never a Celtic empire in Europe, because the Celtic peoples were not united. Instead they lived in different groups, each with similar habits and beliefs and speaking similar languages—forerunners of modern Welsh, Gaelic, and Breton. The first traces of Celtic occupation have been dated back to 1200 BCE, but it was only after 800 BCE that they spread out widely on the European continent.

La Tène Culture bronze wine flagon with enamel and coral decorations.

A carving possibly representing a Celtic deity.

Horse and Chariot

Celtic war chariots were the first to have metal-rimmed wheels. Metalsmiths learned to make the metal rims slightly smaller than the wooden wheels, then heated them so that they expanded before fitting them into place. As the metal cooled the rims shrank, fitting snugly into position.

Celtic warriors rode into battle on two-horse war chariots like this one. Side screens prevented the rider from getting caught in the wheels.

Burials

Iron Age Celts buried their dead with goods that they thought would be useful to them in the afterlife. Thinking that life after death would be much like life before it, they provided them with pots, bowls, and cooking utensils as well as jewelry, tools, and clothing. Chiefs and princes were sometimes buried under large earth mounds in richly-furnished burial chambers.

CELTS IN EUROPE

c. 1200–800 BCE
Late Bronze Age; early phase of Hallstatt culture.

c. 800–600 BCE
Early Iron Age Hallstatt Culture gets under way. The first Celtic hillforts are built. Richly-furnished burial chambers appear.

c. 600–475 BCE
Last phase of Hallstatt culture.

c. 600 BCE
Celts begin trading with Greeks at Massalia.

c. 550 BCE
Hallstatt Culture reaches Britain and Ireland.

c. 410 BCE
Celts from northern Europe cross the Alps into northern Italy.

Inside a Celtic burial mound. A chief's body was laid out on a bronze couch amid rich burial goods.

STEPPE NOMADS

c. 900 BCE
The Cimmerians of southern Russia become the first mounted nomads.

c. 710 BCE
Scythians migrating from Central Asia drive Cimmerians from the Russian steppes.

c. 705 BCE
Displaced Cimmerians invade Asia Minor (modern Turkey), destroying the Parthian Kingdom previously established there.

c. 650 BCE
Scythians raid Syria and Assyria.

626 BCE
Scythians raid Palaestina (present-day Palestine).

c. 425 BCE
Herodotus' work, History *is published.*

c. 300 BCE
Sarmatian nomads conquer the Scythians.

c. 370 CE
The Huns, nomadic pastoralists, migrate into southern Russia, crushing the Sarmatians.

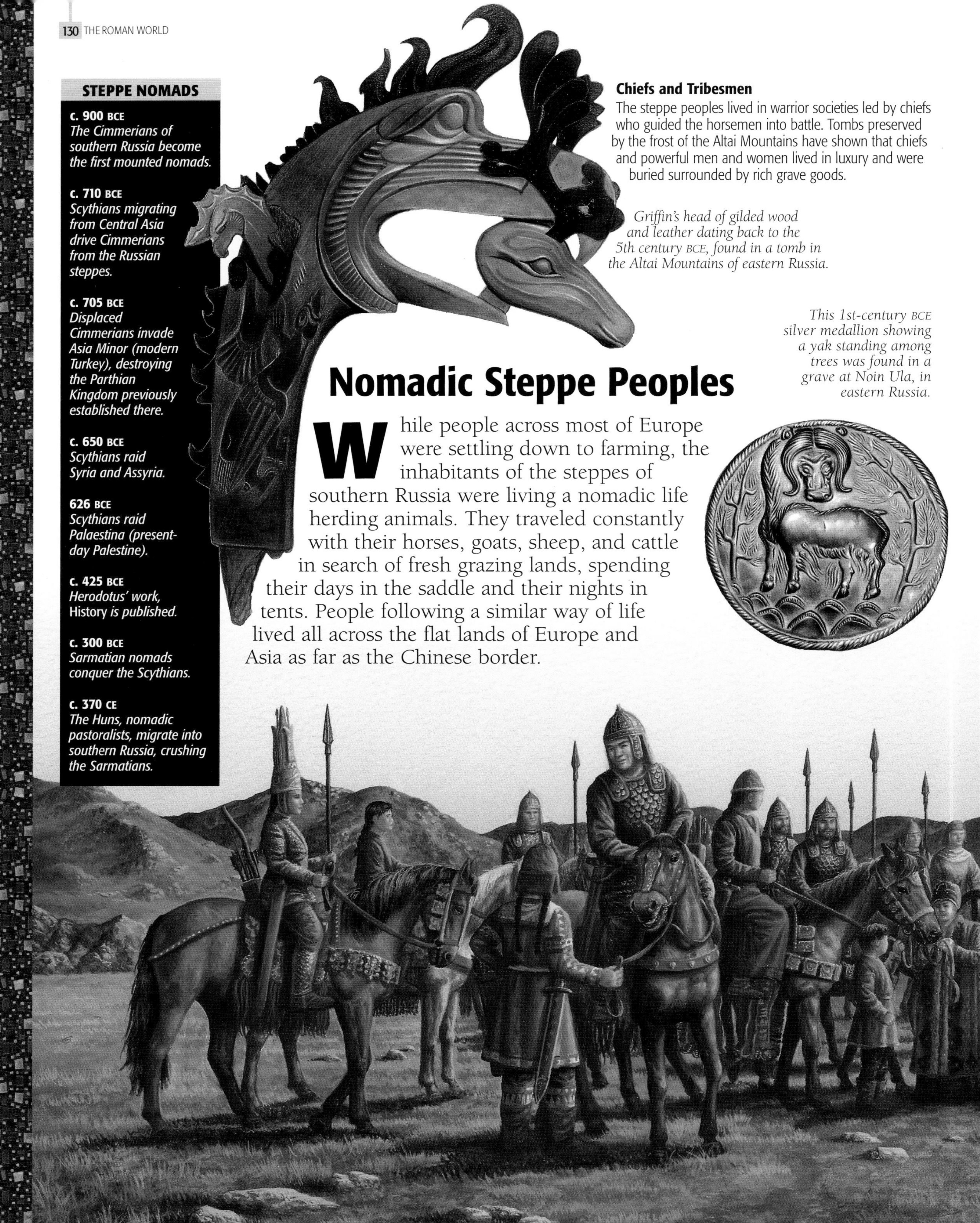

Griffin's head of gilded wood and leather dating back to the 5th century BCE, found in a tomb in the Altai Mountains of eastern Russia.

This 1st-century BCE silver medallion showing a yak standing among trees was found in a grave at Noin Ula, in eastern Russia.

Nomadic Steppe Peoples

While people across most of Europe were settling down to farming, the inhabitants of the steppes of southern Russia were living a nomadic life herding animals. They traveled constantly with their horses, goats, sheep, and cattle in search of fresh grazing lands, spending their days in the saddle and their nights in tents. People following a similar way of life lived all across the flat lands of Europe and Asia as far as the Chinese border.

Chiefs and Tribesmen

The steppe peoples lived in warrior societies led by chiefs who guided the horsemen into battle. Tombs preserved by the frost of the Altai Mountains have shown that chiefs and powerful men and women lived in luxury and were buried surrounded by rich grave goods.

MIGRATIONS OF THE STEPPE PEOPLES

Scythians c. 750 BCE
Cimmerians 705–695 BCE
Sarmatians c. 300 BCE
Huns c. 370 CE
Steppe and semi-desert area

GAUL
NORTHERN EUROPEAN PLAIN
GREAT HUNGARIAN PLAIN
GRECO-ROMAN CIVILISATION
WESTERN SIBERIAN PLAIN

Horsemen from the East

The steppe horsemen inhabited a huge band of mostly flat land stretching from the Great Wall of China in the east to the Danube River in Europe—a distance of over 4,350 miles (7,000 km). The Scythians of eastern Europe shared the same culture and lifestyle as tribes whose graves have been excavated in the Altai Mountains of eastern Russia more than 2,500 miles (4,000 km) away, and may in fact have originally come from that region.

The Sarmatians

Between the 6th and 4th century BCE another nomadic people, the Sarmatians, made their way to the Ural Mountains from Central Asia. Like the Scythians, the Sarmatians were accomplished horsemen and warriors. They eventually conquered the Scythians and by the 2nd century BCE controlled most of southern Russia. During the 1st century CE the Sarmatians were strong enough to cause trouble even for the powerful Romans. The decline of the Sarmatians began with their defeat by the Goths in the 3rd century. They were finally crushed by the Huns (see page 157) in the late 4th century.

Unmarried Sarmatian women were skilled hunters and warriors who rode alongside men in battle. According to Herodotus, no Sarmatian girl could marry unless she had killed an enemy in battle.

A golden comb found in the Ukraine. The decorative crest shows a horseman about to finish off a fallen enemy.

The Scythians

The ancient Greeks came into contact with steppe horsemen living in the lands north of the Black Sea. They called them Scythians. The Greek historian Herodotus (484?–430? BCE) visited them and wrote of their warlike customs. He claimed they often scalped their enemies and used their skulls for drinking vessels.

Scythian Art

Despite their wandering lifestyles, Scythian craftspeople became skilled artists, working in gold, bronze, wood, and textiles. They developed a distinctive style featuring stylized real and imaginary animals. They mostly produced practical objects—tools, weapons, harnesses—that could easily be carried on horseback.

An electrum (gold and silver alloy) vase, made by a Greek craftsman for a Scythian nobleman in the 4th century BCE shows a man pulling out a tooth.

The Italian Peninsula

Iron Age Italy was divided up among many peoples. Most were farmers living in villages, but two groups had towns and a rich culture. In the north were the Etruscans, who grew rich through mining and trade. In the south, Greek settlers founded cities on the shores of mainland Italy and Sicily, bringing with them the knowledge of writing.

EARLY ITALY

c. 900 BCE
Villanovan Culture emerges in northern Italy.

c. 800 BCE
Beginnings of Etruscan civilization.

753 BCE
Traditional date for the foundation of Rome by Romulus.

c. 745 BCE
Greeks found a colony at Cumae, near today's Naples.

733 BCE
Greeks found Syracuse in Sicily.

720 BCE
Greeks found Sybaris on the south coast.

c. 616 BCE
Etruscan monarchy is set up in Rome.

c. 600 BCE
Formation of the Etruscan League.

550 BCE
Etruscans win control of the Po Valley in northern Italy.

537 BCE
The Etruscans, allied with the Carthaginians, defeat the Greeks in modern-day Corsica.

524 BCE
Sybarites build temples at Paestum in southern Italy.

Some early Italians lived in houses of thatch built on piles over lakes.

Bronze figurine of a couple made by the Siculi, who lived in eastern Sicily.

Contacts in the Mediterranean

Early Italian peoples had contact by sea with two great civilizations: the Greeks of the Aegean and the Carthaginians of the North African coast. Both founded settlements in Italy—the Carthaginians in western Sicily, and the Greeks in eastern Sicily and on the mainland. Both groups traded with their neighbors and also maintained close trade links with the Etruscans, who even learned the use of the alphabet from the Greeks.

A Diversity of Peoples

The early inhabitants of the Italian peninsula formed a patchwork of peoples of different races, languages, and cultures. Most lived in small villages or isolated farmsteads and supported themselves by farming and keeping livestock. Like Iron Age peoples in the rest of Europe, many built fortified settlements on high ground that could be easily defended against attack.

POPULATING THE ITALIAN PENINSULA

Veneti
Po
CORSICA
Umbri
Latins
Tiber
ROME
CUMAE
NAPLES
Apulians
SICILY
CARTHAGE

Etruscan city
Greek city
Other city
Etruria, c. 600 BCE
Area under Etruscan domination, c. 500 BCE
Carthaginian Empire, c. 500 BCE
Area settled and controlled by Greeks, c. 500 BCE
Italic peoples
Illyrian peoples
Celtic and related peoples

Peoples of the Italian Peninsula
Many of the peoples who lived in Italy before Roman times left little behind except for the names of regions: the Umbri in Umbria, the Apulians in the south-eastern region of Apulia, and the Veneti where Venice now lies. The Latin people lived in the area south of Rome. Celts invaded northern Italy in 410 BCE and established themselves in the lands north of the Po River. The Greeks controlled much of the south coast.

This krater, found in the Etruscan city of Caere (modern-day Cerveteri), was made by a Greek artist in the mid-7th century. It shows a battle at sea.

The Etruscans

The Etruscans had the most advanced culture in Italy before Roman times. Their homeland, Etruria, occupied present-day Tuscany and reached down to the Tiber River in the south. By the 6th century their territory stretched further south and also included the Po Valley in the north and part of Corsica. Yet much about them remains mysterious. Scholars still argue over their origins; some claim that the Etruscans migrated to the Italian peninsula from Asia.

This detail from an Etruscan urn, which was used to store ashes of a cremated body, is decorated with a carving showing a banquet scene.

A 6th-century BCE Etruscan sarcophagus, bearing terracotta images of a dead couple from Caere.

Etruscan Practices

When Romans consulted soothsayers for advice about the future, they often used Etruscan techniques of divination. Etruscan diviners claimed to be able to discover the will of the gods by examining the livers of animals that had been sacrificed to them. Other methods included studying prodigies—unusual events like the birth of a two-headed calf—or watching out for flashes of lightning in the sky.

While citizens look on, an Etruscan soothsayer examines a sheep's liver for special marks, lumps, or discoloration that might help him discover the will of the gods.

Bronze model of a sheep's liver, used as a guide for Etruscan diviners.

The Origins of Rome

Rome started out as just one of dozens of small, fortified settlements along the length of the Italian peninsula. Although it had grown to be a city by 600 BCE, it fell under the control of the Etruscans, its powerful northern neighbors. For about a century it was ruled by a line of Etruscan kings. Eventually the Romans rebelled, throwing out the kings and establishing a republic in their place.

The Foundation Myth

According to legend, Rome was founded by Romulus in 753 BCE. Romulus and his twin Remus were abandoned babies who were found by a nurturing she-wolf on Palatine Hill. Later they fell out; Romulus killed Remus in a dispute over the future of the city.

Detail of an Etruscan bronze statue of the legendary she-wolf.

EARLY ROME

QUIRINAL HILL
VIMINAL HILL
TEMPLE OF JUPITER CAPITOLINUS
CAPITOLINE HILL
River Tiber
ROMAN FORUM
ESQUILINE HILL
Via Sacra
TEMPLE OF FORTUM AND MATER MATUTA
PALATINE HILL
FIRST BRIDGE OF ROME
CAELIAN HILL
AVENTINE HILL
SERVIAN CITY WALL 4TH CENTURY BCE

The Seven Hills

Like many Iron Age settlements across Europe, Rome was originally built on a hilltop for protection, and also to avoid the marshy ground around the nearby Tiber River. The Palatine Hill, where it began, was in fact one of a group of seven hills which would all eventually be occupied. As the city grew, houses were also built in the boggy valleys that lay between the hills. In time the marshes were drained, and the great city of Rome spread out on both banks of the river.

Early Inhabitants

Rome's first inhabitants were Latin-speakers related to other peoples who lived in the region of Latium, on the west coast of central Italy. The Palatine was the first of Rome's seven hills to be settled, in about 1000 BCE. Over the next two centuries villages were built on the neighboring hills. Rome grew into a powerful city-state and gradually came to dominate all the other surrounding city-states, some by conquest and others by alliance. Mastery of Latium was the first step in the process that saw Rome go on to rule much of the known world.

This 5th-century BCE stela bears the earliest known Latin inscription.

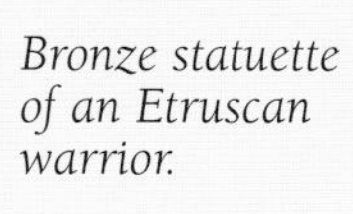

Bronze statuette of an Etruscan warrior.

The Etruscan Monarchy

In about 600 BCE, Rome and all of Latium came under the rule of a line of Etruscan kings. The last Etruscan dynasty, the Tarquin dynasty, is credited with the institution of Roman games (chariot races and gladiatorial fights) and the building of great public structures such as the Roman city walls, aqueducts, and temples.

Rebellion

Although the Etruscans contributed much to Rome, their kings eventually became hated as tyrants. In 509 BCE the Romans rebelled against the Etruscans who had already been weakened by attacks from Celts and other rivals. The last Etruscan king, Tarquinius Superbus (reigned 534–509 BCE) was forced into exile. Rome became a republic, governed by a law-making Senate and two elected consuls, who took the place of the kings, holding office for only a year at a time (see page 137).

Bronze bust of Lucius Junius Brutus (active late 6th century BCE), legendary founder of the Republic. Brutus played a leading role in overthrowing the Etruscan monarchy.

Rome's first settlers were sheep-herders who built a village of thatched mud huts on Palatine Hill.

THE RISE OF ROME

c. 1000 BCE
First archaeological evidence of settlement at Rome.

753 BCE
Traditional date for the foundation of Rome.

c. 600 BCE
The Etruscan monarchy is established.

509 BCE
The last Etruscan king is expelled from Rome. The Republic begins.

496 BCE
Romans defeat Latins at Lake Regillus.

396 BCE
Rome conquers its Etruscan neighbor Veii after a ten-year siege.

338 BCE
Rome completes the conquest of Latium.

Romanization

Rome spread its power by offering Roman citizenship to many of the peoples it conquered, giving them the same rights as the Romans themselves—a process called Romanization. When the Romans overcame their former Etruscan masters they extended citizenship rights to them. The Etruscans ended up being absorbed by Rome and losing their own identity.

Etruscan model of the Temple of Vulci. The Romans copied Etruscan designs for their own temples.

THE REPUBLICAN ERA

509 BCE
The Roman Republic is established.

c. 494 BCE
The plebeian revolt leads to creation of tribunes of the people.

390 BCE
Celtic Gauls sack Rome.

264 BCE
Outbreak of First Punic War against Carthage.

218 BCE
Hannibal invades Italy, starting Second Punic War.

202 BCE
The Carthaginians are defeated at Zama.

168 BCE
Victory at Pydna begins Roman conquest of Greece.

146 BCE
Carthage is destroyed.

60 BCE
First Triumvirate of Pompey, Caesar, and Crassus is established.

49 BCE
Civil war between Caesar and Pompey breaks out.

44 BCE
Caesar is assassinated.

31 BCE
Octavian defeats Mark Antony and Cleopatra at Actium.

27 BCE
Octavian takes supreme power under the name of Augustus ("Revered One").

The Roman Republic

Republican Rome lasted for almost 500 years, a time that saw Rome grow from a small city-state to the dominant power in the Mediterranean world. In these years Rome was constantly at war—first with its Italian neighbors, then with Carthage, Greece, and Celtic Gaul. At home, republican government broke down in the 1st century BCE into dictatorship and civil war.

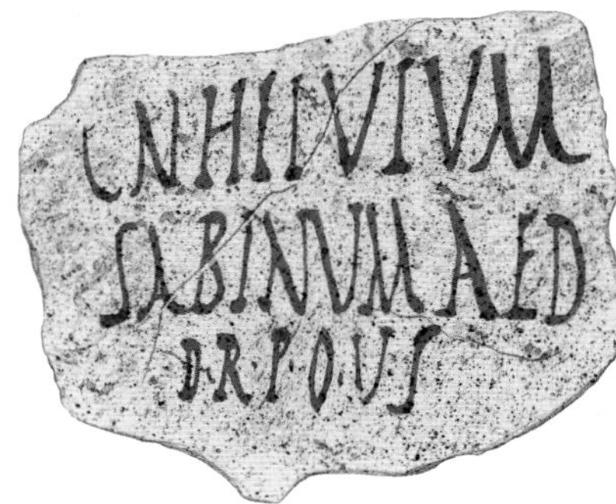

Roman politicians had their names written on city walls during election time as part of their campaigning.

Patricians and Plebeians

When Rome became a republic, its government passed to its aristocrats, the patricians. The rest of the population—the plebeians—resented their powers. In the struggle of the orders that followed, the plebeians soon won concessions—first officials called tribunes to represent their interests, then a People's Assembly.

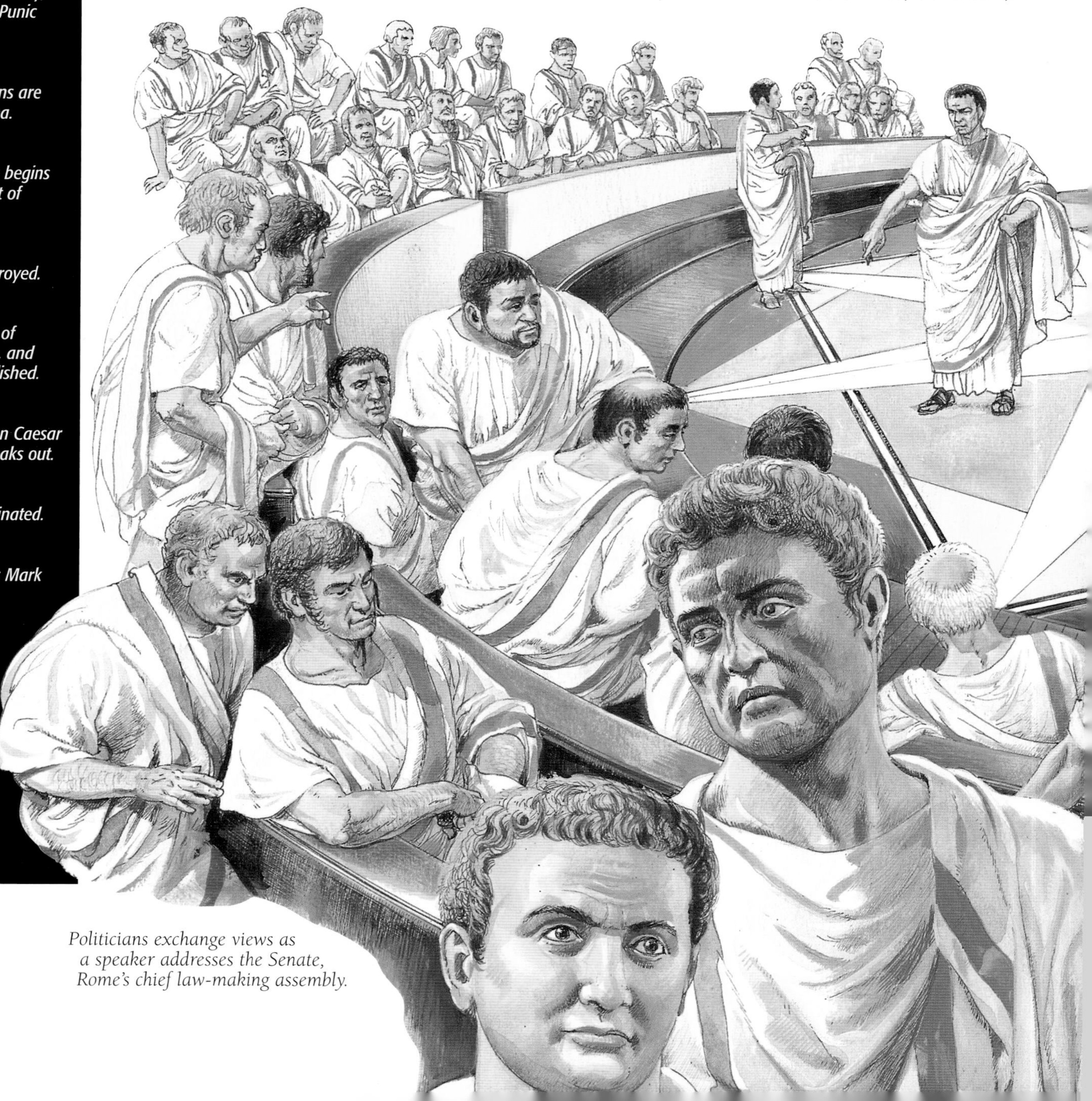

Politicians exchange views as a speaker addresses the Senate, Rome's chief law-making assembly.

The Punic Wars

Rome's chief rivals for control of the Mediterranean were the Carthaginians of North Africa (called *Punici* in Latin). Carthage was a great trading power whose interests inevitably clashed with Rome's when Rome began to expand overseas. The two powers fought three wars between 264 and 146 BCE. At the end of the third, the city of Carthage was razed to the ground.

CONTROL OF THE MEDITERRANEAN C. 500–201 BCE

A war elephant as used by the Carthaginians, shown on a 3rd-century BCE plate from southern Italy.

Victories in the Punic Wars

The First Punic War (264–241 BCE) was fought largely at sea, and ended with Rome taking control of Sicily. In the Second Punic War (218–201 BCE), the Romans gained control of southern Iberia, forcing out the Carthaginians. Eventually, Roman forces also invaded Carthaginian territory in Africa and defeated Hannibal at Zama. After the brief third war (149–146 BCE), the Romans gained control over the western Mediterranean.

- Roman territory c. 500 BCE
- Roman territory by 290 BCE
- Roman territory by 272 BCE
- Roman territory by 218 BCE
- Roman territory by 201 BCE
- Carthaginian territory c. 264 BCE
- Carthaginian territory c. 218 BCE
- Carthaginian territory c. 201 BCE

The Senate

The Senate was the body that proposed new laws for Rome and made vital decisions about war and peace. At first all its members were patricians, but plebeians who had held important offices soon won the right to a seat. The Senate usually met in a building called the *Curia* in the Roman Forum. The number of senators varied over the years from 300 to 900; votes were held to decide what action to take.

Crisis in the Republic

In the 1st century BCE constitutional government broke down as rival generals competed for power. First Caesar and Pompey fought a civil war that ended in victory for Caesar. When he was assassinated, his adopted son Octavian (63 BCE–14 CE) battled with Mark Antony (c. 83–30 BCE) for supreme power. Peace was restored only after Octavian's navy defeated Antony and his ally, Queen Cleopatra of Egypt (c. 70–30 BCE), at Actium in 31 BCE.

Julius Caesar

Julius Caesar (100–44 BCE) was one of Rome's greatest talents—an outstanding politician and general who also won fame as a writer. Having brought Celtic Gaul under Roman control, he fought a civil war against his rival Pompey (106–48 BCE) before establishing himself as dictator at Rome. But his rise attracted enemies, who feared his ambition. In 44 BCE he was assassinated as he went to address the Senate.

Portrait bust of Julius Caesar, conqueror of Gaul and dictator of Rome from 48–44 BCE.

Painting from the Golden House of Nero, built on land razed by the Great Fire of Rome of 64 CE (see page 153).

The Age of Emperors

Once Octavian, Julius Caesar's adoptive son, took power as the first emperor, Rome never returned to republican rule. For the first three centuries of the Empire—a period known as the Principate—the emperors continued to respect republican traditions, seeking the Senate's advice before taking action. Later that pretense was dropped and the emperors ruled supreme and alone.

Onyx cameo of an eagle, the emblem of imperial power. The bird holds a victor's laurel wreath in its claws.

The Emperor

The imperial title was kept in the family. For a time in the 2nd century CE–the age of the "five good emperors"–reigning emperors adopted suitable heirs. In the 3rd century emperors were mostly made and unmade by the legions. From 286 CE on, there were usually at least two emperors ruling at once, one in the East and one in the West (see page 154).

The title Augustus was conferred upon Octavian when he became emperor. This statue of Augustus (reigned 31 BCE–14 CE) shows him as a military leader. Scenes of victory decorate his ceremonial breastplate.

Coin bearing a portrait of Emperor Hadrian. The emperor's face was everywhere in imperial Rome.

IMPERIAL RULE

27 BCE
Octavian conquers Egypt and assumes power as Emperor Augustus.

43 CE
Emperor Claudius' (reigned 41 BCE –54 CE) engineering projects improve water supply and alleviate food shortages.

80 CE
The Colosseum is completed under the Emperor Titus.

106 CE
Emperor Trajan conquers Dacia.

180 CE
Emperor Marcus Aurelius dies leaving behind his philosophical writings, The Meditations.

235 CE
Time of troubles begins: 31 emperors hold power over the next 50 years.

284 CE
Emperor Diocletian (reigned 284–305 CE) restores imperial authority.

286 CE
Emperor Maximian (reigned 286–305, 307–308 CE) is appointed co-emperor in the west by Emperor Diocletian.

313 CE
Emperor Constantine (reigned 307–337 CE) makes Christianity the state religion.

476 CE
The last Western emperor is deposed.

Imperial Residences

The Palatine Hill had a special significance for the Romans since the very beginning of their history (see page 134). Emperor Augustus was born and lived on the Palatine, and his successors went on to build luxurious residences which dominated the hill. The Palatine became the official residence of the Roman emperors. Some emperors, like Hadrian, (reigned 117–138 CE) also built other residences outside Rome.

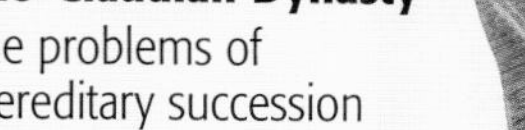

Bronze equestrian statue of Emperor Marcus Aurelius (reigned 161–180 CE), last of the so-called "five good emperors" who gave Romans a period of stable government between 96 and 180 CE.

Julio-Claudian Dynasty

The problems of hereditary succession soon showed up in Rome's first dynasty, which ruled from 27 BCE. Emperor Augustus, its founder, was a brilliant leader, but two of his successors, Caligula (reigned 37–41 CE) and Nero (reigned 54–68 CE), were possibly mad. The dynasty ended in chaos and civil war in 69 CE, a year in which four men claimed the title of emperor: three of them met violent deaths.

Emperor Hadrian's summer retreat, located near Tivoli, about 24 miles (37 km) northeast of Rome, was a huge complex with houses, baths, theaters, libraries, and hippodromes.

Flavian Dynasty

This short-lived dynasty was founded by the soldier-emperor Vespasian (reigned 69–79 CE), who restored order after the disastrous year of 69 CE. The Flavians came from country gentry and owed their rise to the army. Emperor Vespasian himself and his son Emperor Titus (reigned 79–81 CE) were both successful generals, but the last Flavian, Emperor Domitian (reigned 81–96 CE), was a tyrant whose rule ended in a reign of terror. He was assassinated in 96 CE.

Bust of Emperor Caracalla, who granted Roman citizenship to all freeborn inhabitants of the empire in 212 CE.

Severan Dynasty

The Severan Dynasty was founded in 193 CE by Emperor Septimius Severus (reigned 193–211 CE), an army leader who defeated three rivals to claim the throne. His successors all came to violent ends: one of his sons, Emperor Geta (reigned 211 CE), was killed on the orders of the other, Emperor Caracalla (reigned 211–217 CE), who himself was later assassinated. The last of the Severans, Emperor Alexander Severus (reigned 222–238 CE), was killed by his own soldiers.

Bust of Trajan (reigned 98–117 CE), the emperor who enlarged the empire to its greatest extent early in the 2nd century CE.

Literature and the Arts

Rome owed a huge debt to Greece in the arts. In its early years it had few artistic traditions of its own, but the conquest of Greece in the 2nd century BCE brought it into contact with the greatest artworks of the ancient world. The result was a vogue for all things Greek that triggered a creative upsurge among the Romans themselves, especially in literature. Great Roman authors like Virgil and Ovid are still read today.

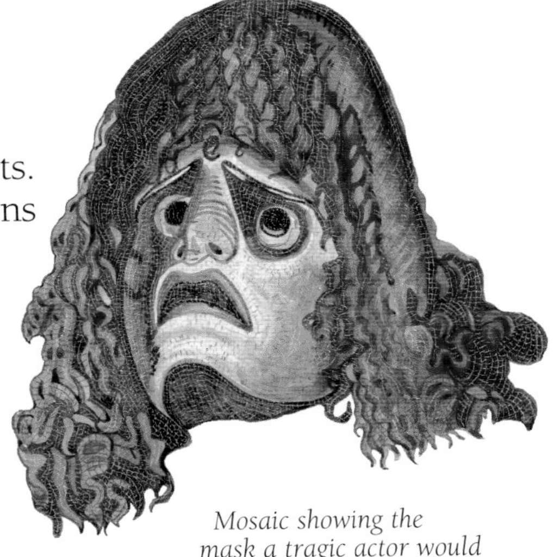

Mosaic showing the mask a tragic actor would have worn on stage.

Education

Rome had no state schools. Children of the wealthy were taught at home by tutors or by self-employed schoolmasters. The school day started early, at dawn, and ended early in the afternoon. Students learned reading, writing, and arithmetic. At age 11, boys could go on to secondary schools to learn Latin and Greek literature and public speaking. Girls over 11 were usually taught at home.

Bust of Cicero, a leading politician and lawyer famed now for his writings.

Literature

The golden age of Latin literature lasted about a century, between 80 BCE and 17 CE. Cicero (106–43 BCE), Lucretius (active 1st century BCE), Catullus (c. 84–54 BCE), Virgil (70–19 BCE), Horace (65–8 BCE), and Ovid (43 BCE –17 CE) are some of the greatest names of the period. Every schoolchild knew Virgil's *Aeneid*, Rome's national epic, telling the story of how the Romans first came to the Italian peninsula.

Mosaic from North Africa showing the poet Virgil seated between the muses of history and tragedy.

The Theater

Rome only got its first permanent theater in 55 BCE, but the art form was soon well-established. The actors were slaves or freedmen, and men played women's parts. In the early days, the actors wore masks—sad for tragedy, caricatured for comedy. Mime shows were popular.

Mosaic from Pompeii showing a scene from a comic play featuring musicians.

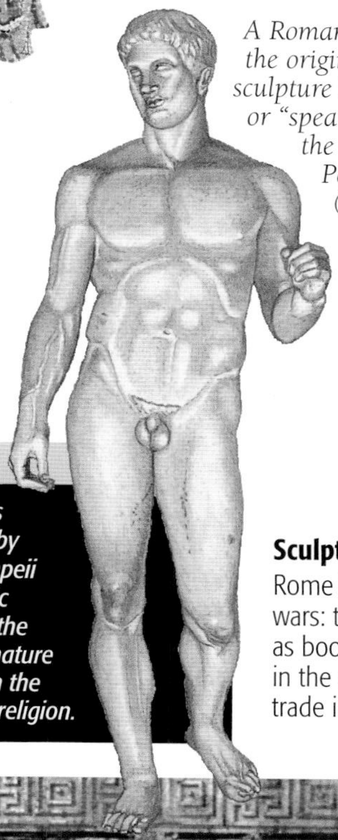

A Roman copy of the original bronze sculpture Doryphours, or "spear-bearer," by the Greek artist Polyclitus (active 5th century BCE).

Artists of the Roman era mastered the art of portraiture. This portrait of a boy from Egypt was painted on a piece of wood which was placed over the face of his mummy.

Mosaics

Works of art called mosaics, made up of tiny brightly-colored stones known as *tesserae*, imitated paintings, achieving both abstract and representational effects. Because the stones were hard-wearing, mosaics were often used to decorate floors.

DECORATED INTERIORS

Most of the surviving paintings of the Roman era come from the towns in the Bay of Naples which were buried, and consequently preserved, by the eruption of Mount Vesuvius in 79 CE. Works from the towns of Pompeii and Herculaneum reveal the Romans' love for bold colors and fantastic decoration. Whole rooms were decorated; some with paintings giving the illusion of three-dimensional space. The most common subjects were nature and mythological scenes. This 1st-century BCE wall painting below from the Villa of the Mysteries in Pompeii, shows rites of the Dionysiac mystery religion.

Sculpture

Rome literally brought a taste for sculpture back from the wars: thousands of Greek statues were carried off to Italy as booty. Romans never lost their taste for the Greek style in the centuries that followed, and there was a flourishing trade in copies, often made by Greek artists living in Italy.

Gaul

The Rhône Valley was occupied by Gaulish lords who controlled important trade routes in the area. In the 2nd century BCE the Romans were drawn to the area after their Greek ally, Massalia (present-day Marseilles), asked for help against the threatening Gauls. Roman forces consequently established military strongholds, marking the beginning of Roman dominance in Gaul.

Trading at a port on the River Rhône. Trade was controlled and taxed by Gaulish noblemen.

TRADE ROUTES

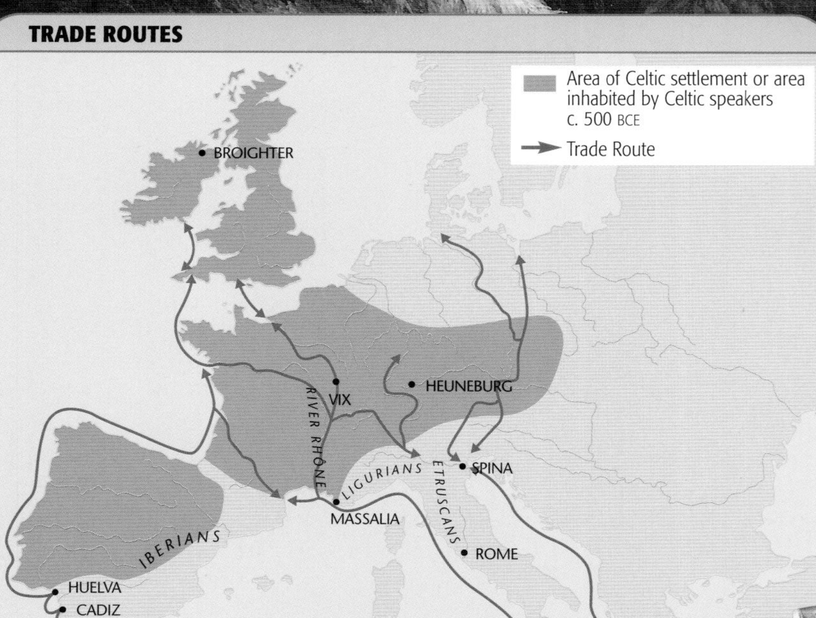

Trade of Luxury Goods and Raw Materials

The Rhône Valley provided an early channel for trade with the Greek city-state of Massalia (Marseilles) near the river's mouth. The Celts provided leather, textiles, salted meat, and slaves—usually prisoners of war—in return for pottery, metalwork, and wine. After the Roman conquest, the entire Celtic world was criss-crossed by traders bringing goods from the empire's most distant lands.

Celtic Europe

By the 3rd century BCE Celtic territory reached its greatest extent, stretching from Spain and Ireland to parts of modern-day Turkey. Though the Celtics worshiped similar gods and spoke related languages, they never came together to form one nation. Their loyalties were to the tribe, and different tribes were often at war. Ultimately, this led to their decline and Celtic tribes fell to Roman forces. Many tribes however maintained their identity under Roman rule.

The boar, Celtic symbol of power and strength, was considered a sacred animal. This 4th-century BCE bronze boar was found in France.

Celtic Language

The various Celtic languages all descended from a single tongue, referred to as Common Celtic. As the tribes split apart, different languages appeared. A marked division grew up between the Celtic spoken in Britain and Ireland and that in continental Europe. Celts in Gaul learned to use Greek letters to write down census records.

Celtic inscription carved on a 2nd-century BCE stone tablet from Italy. Celtic language was used in Italy as early as the 6th century BCE.

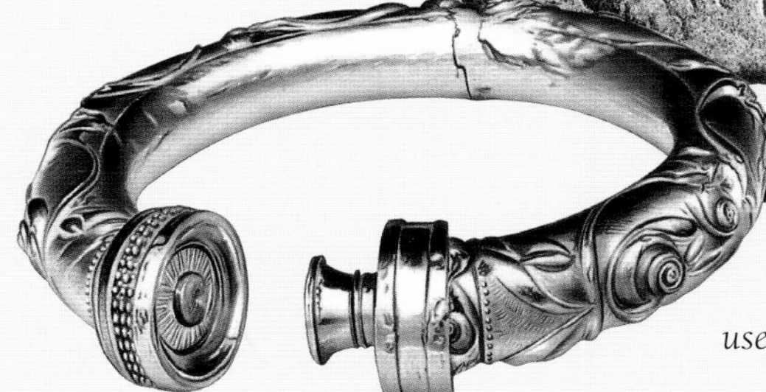

This tubular gold torque, an ornament worn around the neck, was found in Ireland and dates back to c. 100 BCE.

Britain and Ireland

Before the Romans' arrival, Celtic-speaking people occupied most of Britain and Ireland. Western Scotland was inhabited by another group of non-Celtic people called Picts. Britain was a famed center of Druidism, the Celtic religion. After the conquest, Celtic languages survived in Wales and Scotland. Ireland was never conquered by the Romans.

Celtic Society

The Celtic hillforts of the Iron Age developed in later times into fortified settlements the Romans called *oppida*. Here lived the tribal chiefs, elected for life by the nobles who formed the next social layer. Leading warriors and priests called Druids also ranked high. Below them were well-off farmers and artisans, with laborers, serfs, and slaves at the bottom of the heap.

A statue of a Gaulish warrior of the late 1st century BCE wearing an iron mail shirt, cloak and a torque around his neck.

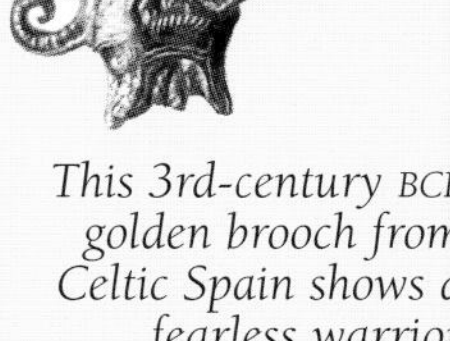

This 3rd-century BCE golden brooch from Celtic Spain shows a fearless warrior confronting a lion.

Warrior Culture

Fighting was a way of life for the Celts. Neighboring tribes frequently raided one another's lands to steal cattle, and the raids easily escalated into open war. No quality was more highly regarded than bravery in battle, which was celebrated by bards in songs and poems. Chiefs fought in chariots, other ranks on foot, and leading warriors often challenged one another to single combat.

CELTIC RISE AND DECLINE

390 BCE
Celtic warriors sack Rome.

279 BCE
Celts attack Greece, before settling in Asia Minor (modern-day Turkey).

192 BCE
Romans defeat the Celts settled in northern Italy.

181 BCE
Romans conquer the Celts of Cisalpine Gaul.

118 BCE
Romans establish Narbo Martius, a colony in southern Gaul.

58 BCE
Julius Caesar invades and conquers northern Gaul.

55 BCE
Julius Caesar raids England, returning in 54 BCE.

52 BCE
Julius Caesar completes conquest of Gaul.

21 CE
Tiberius (reigned 14–37 CE) suppresses a rebellion in Gaul.

43 CE
The Romans conquer southern England.

Defeat by Rome

For all the Celts' courage in battle, their armies were at best loosely organized and in the long run proved no match for the highly disciplined Roman legions. Celtic disunity also played a part; the tribes never managed to come together in a single, combined army. As a result Gaul fell to the Romans by 52 BCE and much of Britain in the 1st century CE.

Warring Neighbors

The Germanic peoples who confronted the Roman Empire across the Rhine River were made up of a confusing mosaic of tribes. The lands they inhabited stretched from Scandinavia through Germany itself into southern Russia. They lived by farming and herding, and were organized in clans that from time to time allied against the Romans.

Tombstone of a Roman legionary who served and died on Rome's Germanic frontier.

This iron spearhead, found on a sacred site on the Danish island of Funen, is decorated with a pattern of circular inlays of silver and brass.

Invasions

The Romans first fought Germanic warriors in the late 1st century BCE, when the Cimbri invaded northern Italy. Julius Caesar tried to pin the tribes behind the Rhine River, but from time to time they broke out. From the 3rd century on, Rome was on the defensive. Eventually the barrier broke, and Goths, Franks and Saxons swept across western Europe (see pages 156–7).

Germanic tribesmen attack soldiers defending Rome's frontier on the Rhine River.

GERMANIC PEOPLES IN EUROPE

Tribal Migration
The Germanic lands had no natural frontiers to the east, where they bordered on the vast plains inhabited by the nomadic steppe peoples. Whenever there was a major population movement westward among these horsemen, it had a knock-on effect on the Germanic tribes, pressing them west and south toward the Roman Empire's borders. This tendency reached a climax in the 4th century CE, when Asiatic Huns swept into the German lands, fatally increasing the pressure on Rome.

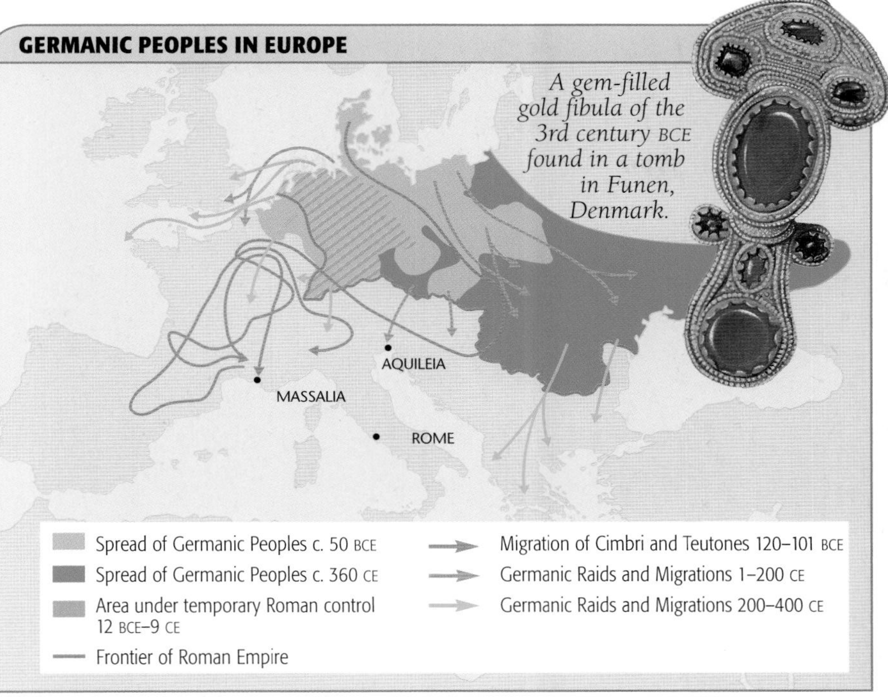

A gem-filled gold fibula of the 3rd century BCE found in a tomb in Funen, Denmark.

GERMANIC PEOPLES

105 BCE
Germanic Cimbri defeat Romans at Arausio.

58 BCE
Julius Caesar defeats the Suebi, setting Rhine River as Rome's frontier.

12–9 BCE
Roman general Drusus Germanicus (38–9 BCE) occupies German territory between the Rhine and Elbe rivers.

4 CE
The future Emperor Tiberius (reigned 14–37 CE) launches a fresh campaign.

9 CE
Germanic leader Hermann (d. 21 CE) destroys three Roman legions in the Teutoburg Forest.

16 CE
Emperor Tiberius recalls his general Germanicus Caesar (15 BCE–19 CE), bringing Germanic wars to a temporary end.

98 CE
Roman historian Tacitus writes Germania, *a treatise on the origins of the Germanic tribes.*

177 CE
Marcomanni invade across River Danube, to be driven back by Emperor Marcus Aurelius.

254–256 CE
Emperor Gallienus' (reigned 253–268 CE) victories over the Germanic peoples are commemorated on coins.

269 CE
The Alamanni invade Italy.

277–278 CE
Emperor Probus (reigned 276–282) restores the frontier on Rhine and Upper Danube.

Rituals and Burials

The northern Germanic peoples worshiped the Norse gods Thor, Odin, and Freya. According to the Roman historian Tacitus (c. 56–120 CE), they performed rituals in the open air in forest groves. Archeologists have found the remains of people who died violent deaths thrown into bogs, perhaps as human sacrifices.

Body of a man found in Tollund Fen, Denmark. He had been strangled, perhaps as a sacrifice.

Decorated cup from a tomb uncovered in Denmark. The decorative motifs imitate the Roman style.

The Germanic Style

While the Germanic peoples imported many luxury goods, their craftsmen had a long tradition of their own, working mainly in wood and metals. Germanic taste tended to intricate patterns.

Trade

There was an active trade in metals and amber across the Germanic lands from Bronze Age times. During the Roman era, the flow of goods increased, particularly in border areas along the Rhine and Danube rivers. Clan chiefs gradually developed a taste for luxury goods, including Roman gold and silverware. By the time of the great invasions, the tribes were at least partly Romanized.

Roman cup from a Danish tomb. Trade carried luxury goods around Europe.

The Roman Empire

The Roman Empire was built up over many centuries. First Rome conquered the Italian peninsula, then the western Mediterranean following victory over Carthage in the Punic Wars. The conquest of Greece and Asia Minor took place in the 2nd century BCE. The imperial age proper got under way when the Roman Republic gave way to the rule of the emperors, from the time of Emperor Augustus on. For a century after the death of Augustus the empire continued to grow, reaching its greatest extent under Emperor Trajan in the early 2nd century CE.

Hadrian's Wall

When Emperor Hadrian decided that the empire should expand no further in Britain, he settled on a line roughly equivalent to the modern border between England and Scotland at its northern limit. To keep in check the northern tribes, which had never been fully conquered, he ordered the building of a wall that stretched along the frontier from sea to sea. Hadrian's Wall served for border control rather than as an impenetrable barrier. It remained in use to the end of the Roman occupation of Britain.

The Porta Nigra at Trier, an imperial city in present-day Germany.

Roman sentries on guard duty along the wall searched people and wagons for smuggled goods or concealed weapons.

THE EXTENT OF THE EMPIRE

Extent of the Roman Empire 117 CE
Hadrian's Wall

BRITANNIA
GALLIA
DACIA
HISPANIA
ITALIA
ROME
ASIA
MESOPOTAMIA
MAURETANIA
PALAESTINA
AFRICA
LIBYA

Roman Expansion

Stretching from the Scottish border in the north to the Sahara Desert in the south, and from the Atlantic Ocean to the Persian Gulf, the Roman Empire at its greatest extent early in the 2nd century CE was the largest the western world had ever seen. Its central focus was the Mediterranean Sea, but additional provinces were added to the north, south, and east in a never-ending quest to conquer as much as possible. In the long run the empire over-reached itself: the task of defending the long land borders proved more than Rome could manage.

A GROWING EMPIRE

12 BCE
The empire's frontier is extended north to the Danube River under the emperor Augustus.

6 CE
Judaea becomes a Roman province.

9 CE
Rome's attempt to conquer northern Germany ends in defeat at Teutoburg Forest.

42 CE
Mauretania becomes a Roman province, completing the Empire's grip on the Mediterranean coast.

43 CE
Emperor Claudius conquers England. Lycia, in southwest Asia Minor, becomes a province.

106 CE
Arabia is annexed. The empire is at its fullest extent under the emperor Trajan.

113 CE
Armenia is conquered.

116 CE
Emperor Trajan conquers Mesopotamia.

The Provinces

An important cultural divide separated the empire's eastern and western provinces. The eastern part of the empire was Greek-speaking and made up of regions with a long history of urban civilization. In contrast, western provinces like Gaul and Britain were formed in what the Romans considered "barbarian" lands, with no previous tradition of city living. The split lay at the root of the empire's eventual division into eastern and western halves (see page 154).

Stone relief showing tax payment from Neumagen, Germany.

Relief from Leptis Magna, in the North African province of Tripolitania (present-day Libya).

The Pax Romana

The Roman Empire was mostly created by force, but once peace had been established it brought real benefits to its subjects. Under the Pax Romana ("Roman peace"), which was guaranteed by the legions, people could travel throughout a war-free empire. The result was an upsurge in trade and general prosperity.

Relief of the goddess Roma, divine personification of the strength and benevolent power of the empire.

Paying Taxes

The provinces had to bear the costs of running the empire, which grew as the size of the army and the bureaucracy increased. Under the emperors the amount individuals paid was settled by regular censuses of people's property. From the 3rd century on, taxes became so high that they stifled business activity, seriously weakening the empire.

Religious Beliefs

The Romans believed in many different gods and goddesses. Some were their own—gods of agriculture and nature that their farming ancestors had worshiped. Others came from outside, from the Etruscans or the Greeks. There was an official state religion that involved sacrificing animals and repeating set ceremonies in the temples. It was every Roman's patriotic duty to follow these rites, but few found them spiritually satisfying. Instead they chose to worship their own household gods or else to follow foreign religions brought to Rome from the East.

The Imperial Cult

Roman gods acted like powerful humans, so in time it seemed natural to treat Rome's own greatest rulers as gods. Julius Caesar was the first Roman to be deified —pronounced a god after his death. Later, some of the best emperors were also declared gods by the Senate, but always after their death; while alive they were only human. All Romans were expected to worship the divine emperors.

Statue of the Emperor Claudius portrayed as the god Jupiter.

Janus depicted on a coin. The cult of Janus was quite popular among the Romans.

ROMAN GODS

Jupiter
Greatest and best of the gods, associated with the sky and with thunder and lightning.

Juno
Jupiter's wife. Goddess of marriage and childbirth.

Mars
God of war, also worshiped by farmers. The second most important of the Roman gods.

Venus
Partner of Mars, and goddess of love and beauty.

Janus
Two-faced god who guarded gates and doorways, and also new beginnings. The month of January is named after him.

Vulcan
God of fire, worshiped by blacksmiths.

Minerva
Goddess of wisdom; also a patroness of crafts and trades.

Mercury
The messenger of the gods, shown with hat, winged shoes and a staff with snakes entwined around it. Also the god of trade and merchants.

Vesta
Goddess of hearth and home, whose sacred fire was tended by the Vestal Virgins.

Saturn
God of agriculture and vegetation whose annual festival each December, the Saturnalia, was the Roman equivalent of Christmas.

A 1st-century BCE relief showing animals being brought to an altar for ritual sacrifice.

Household Worship

For the Romans religion began at home. Each house had its hearth sacred to Vesta, and also its lares and penates. The lares were the spirits of dead ancestors, while the penates looked after the store cupboard, making sure the family had food to eat. Each day the head of the household would pray to the gods and would leave food offerings before the shrine where their images were kept.

A lar, or household god, as shown in a detail from a 1st-century CE Pompeiian shrine.

Vestal Virgins tend the sacred flame at their temple in the Roman Forum. Romans believed that disaster would strike the state if the fire went out, and any Vestal who allowed it to happen was whipped.

The Vestal Virgins

Vesta was the Roman goddess of the hearth, and a fire burned in every home in her honor. The state decided that it too should have its own sacred flame, which burned in a temple in the Roman Forum in Vesta's honor. Four (later six) girls of noble birth were selected to guard it. They held the job for 30 years, during which they had to remain unmarried.

Christianity

Christianity reached Rome soon after the death of Jesus Christ. At first officials regarded it as just a troublesome sect, but as the faith spread, rulers feared that it was anti-Roman and launched major persecutions. Everything changed in the 4th century CE, when the Emperor Constantine became more tolerant of Christianity.

A Christian image of Jesus Christ portrayed as the good shepherd from the catacombs, underground burial places used by early Christians.

Foreign Religions

Christianity had rivals in the shape of other religions from the East. The first such cult to reach Rome was that of Cybele, the Great Mother, which came from Asia Minor. Then there was Mithraism, a Persian religion that was only open to men and was popular in the legions. In contrast, the worship of the Egyptian goddess Isis spread widely among women.

A sistrum, or rattle, used by priests of Isis in religious ceremonies and processions.

Altar of the Matronae Aufaniae, a triad of mother goddesses from Roman Germany.

BUILDING ACCOMPLISHMENTS

Concrete
First used in the 3rd century BCE. Made of sand from volcanic rocks mixed with lime, rubble, and water. Without it the great Roman monuments could not have been built.

Arches
Used to carry great weights and to build vaulted roofs and domes. Vaults and arches were supported by a timber framework that was removed when the concrete set.

Hoists
To lift heavy masonry, Roman engineers devised special hoists, powered by huge wheels turned by slaves. Pulleys operated by the wheel hauled heavy stone blocks high into the air.

Roads
Roman roads were built in layers on a base of levelled sand, topped with a foundation of large stones overlaid with pebbles and gravel. The top layer was made of cobbles or large paving stones or gravel set in concrete.

Basilicas
Long buildings with a central aisle flanked by columns separating off side aisles. The Romans used them for law courts and other official buildings, but the design was later copied for churches.

Triumphal Arches
Huge freestanding gateways covered in sculptures and inscriptions designed to celebrate military victories. A very Roman type of building. (See the arch of Constantine on page 155.)

Emperor Hadrian, a great builder who reconstructed the Pantheon in its present form.

Roman Building Technology

Rome's genius was a practical one, and its civilization excelled in building roads, bridges, and aqueducts. If Greece was famous for her philosophers and poets, Rome's glory was her engineers. Using concrete—a Roman invention—they constructed towns and highways across the empire, many of which survive today. Their greatest triumph was the city of Rome itself, the center of the road network and the site of the empire's finest buildings.

Building an Empire

The empire provided great opportunities for building. The building of towns involved the construction of temples, public buildings, and defensive walls. Aqueducts were cut through the countryside to bring water for the citizens. Officials wanted out-of-town villas and retirement colonies were needed to house old soldiers.

An Impressive Water System

Engineers went to great lengths to bring fresh water to the cities. The water was carried underground where possible, but sometimes aqueducts had to be built to carry it over river valleys. Water carried over to towns by the aqueducts was piped to homes, baths and street fountains.

Detail from Trajan's Column in Rome showing legionaries building a military camp.

Architects of Rome

The credit for the empire's great buildings went more to the emperors who ordered them than the architects who designed them. Few names of Roman architects have survived, although Vitruvius (active 1st century BCE), the author of a book on the subject, is still remembered. Many of the big construction projects were in fact carried out by engineers employed by the army.

The Pantheon

A temple to all the gods, the Pantheon was first built in 25 BCE but totally reconstructed under Emperor Hadrian. The main part of the building was a circular hall topped by the largest dome built in the ancient world. At its summit was a round hole that let in sunlight. The Pantheon became a church when the empire turned Christian, and is still standing today.

Cutaway diagram of the Pantheon, showing its revolutionary circular design and domed roof.

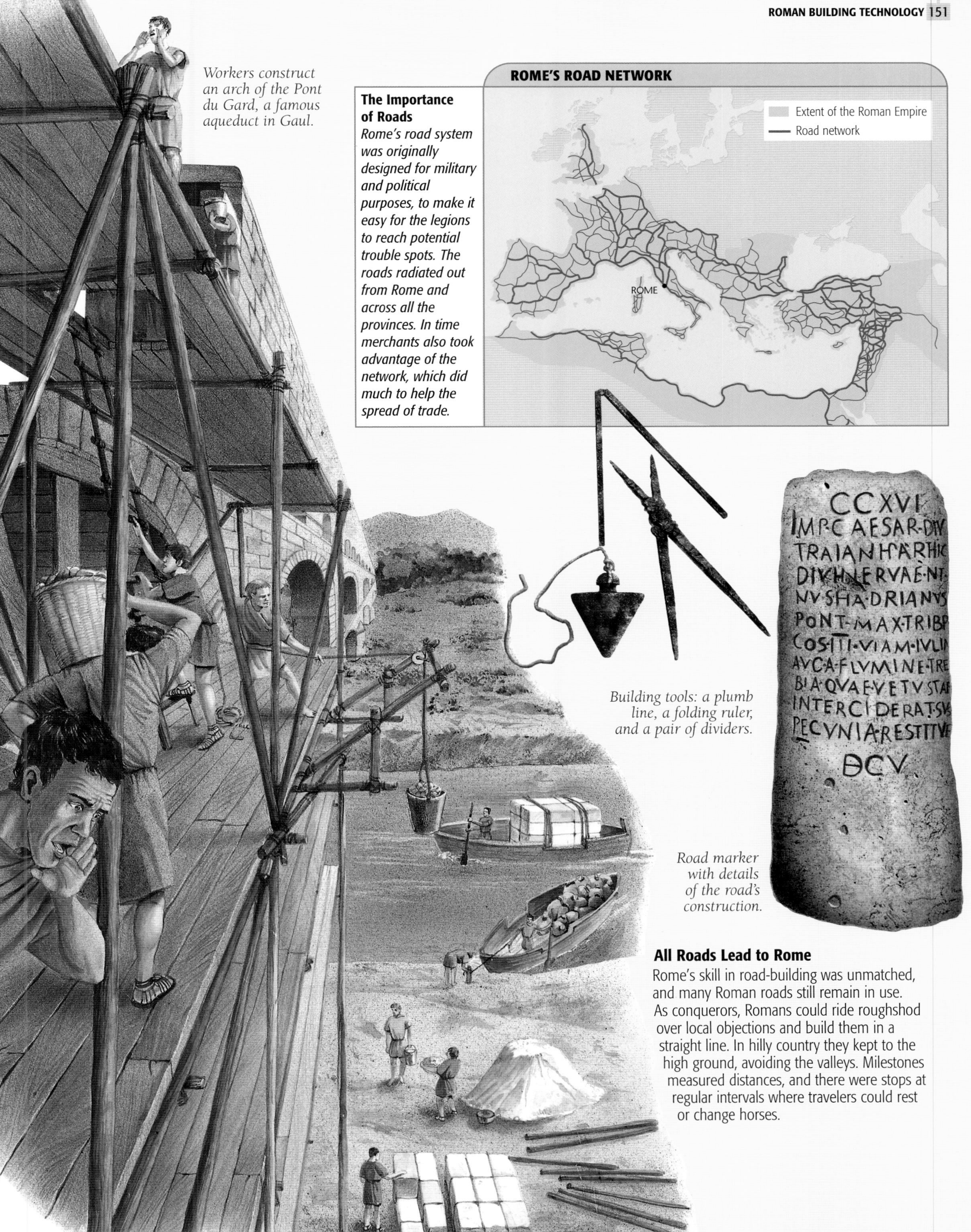

Workers construct an arch of the Pont du Gard, a famous aqueduct in Gaul.

The Importance of Roads

Rome's road system was originally designed for military and political purposes, to make it easy for the legions to reach potential trouble spots. The roads radiated out from Rome and across all the provinces. In time merchants also took advantage of the network, which did much to help the spread of trade.

Building tools: a plumb line, a folding ruler, and a pair of dividers.

Road marker with details of the road's construction.

All Roads Lead to Rome

Rome's skill in road-building was unmatched, and many Roman roads still remain in use. As conquerors, Romans could ride roughshod over local objections and build them in a straight line. In hilly country they kept to the high ground, avoiding the valleys. Milestones measured distances, and there were stops at regular intervals where travelers could rest or change horses.

The City of Rome

The Rome of the emperors was the greatest city the world had ever known. More than a million people thronged its streets, which were adorned with fine monuments built with the wealth of conquered lands. Talented people from around the empire flocked to live there, and its citizens benefited from free bread and entertainments provided by the emperors to keep them happy. Yet there was another side to the city. The poorer districts were noisy and foul-smelling, crime was rife, and about a third of its inhabitants were slaves.

MONUMENTS OF ROME

1 Theater of Marcellus
2 Forum Holitorium (produce market)
3 Forum Boarium (cattle market)
4 Temple of Jupiter Capitolinus
5 Arch of Janus
6 Temple of Juno Moneta
7 Circus Maximus
8 Tabularium
9 Temple of the Divine Trajan
10 Temple of Concord
11 Arch of Septimius Severus
12 Basilica Julia
13 Forum of Trajan
14 Forum of Caesar
15 Curia
16 Basilica Aemilia
17 Temple of Castor and Pollux
18 Temple of Cybele
19 Markets of Trajan
20 Temple of Apollo
21 Forum of Augustus
22 Temple of the Divine Julius
23 Forum of Vespasian
24 Basilica of Maxentius
25 Imperial Palace
26 Domus Augustana
27 Domus Flavia
28 Temple of Venus and Rome
29 Temple of the Caesars
30 Palace of Septimius Severus
31 Septizonium
32 Aqua Claudia
33 Arch of Constantine
34 Colossus of Nero
35 Colosseum
36 School of the gladiators
37 Temple of the Divine Claudius
38 Aqua Marcia

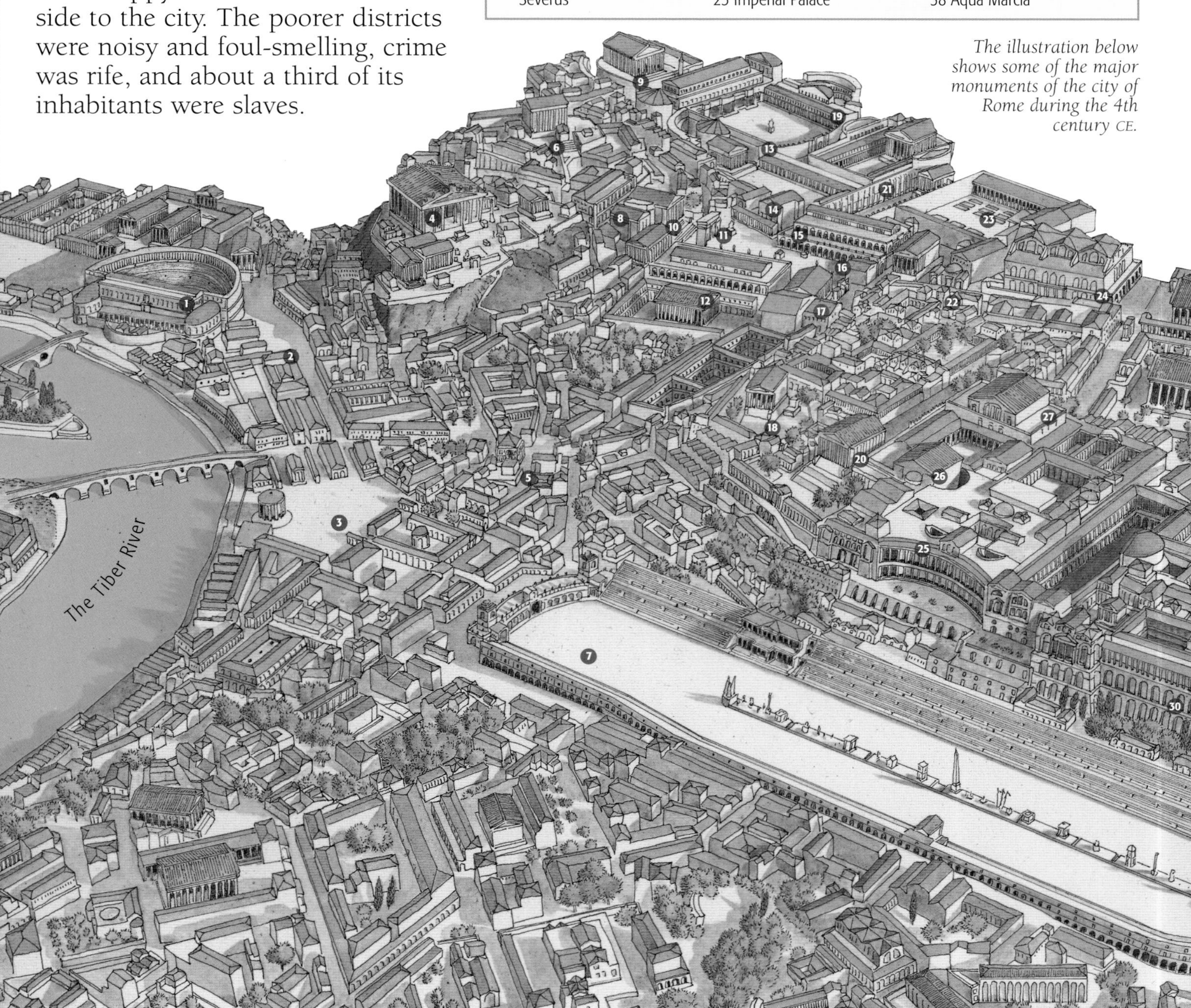

The illustration below shows some of the major monuments of the city of Rome during the 4th century CE.

Hazards in the City

Fire was a constant hazard in Rome's cheap and crowded tenements, which sometimes also collapsed because of their poor construction. In 64 CE, the Great Fire of Rome completely razed three of the city's 14 districts and partially destroyed seven more, leaving only four untouched. Other everyday hazards included being hit by litter thrown from upstairs windows.

Romans blamed Nero for starting the Great Fire of 64 CE to clear space for his palace.

Markets

The Roman Forum was the city's original shopping center, but by late republican times it was filled with public buildings, and the tradesmen, except for gold- and silversmiths, had moved on. New shopping areas were provided—the biggest, Trajan's Market, had room for 150 shops. The main fruit and vegetable markets were near the Tiber River. Shops also lined the streets; most consisted of a single room opening onto the road, with a flat above the premises where the shopkeeper lived.

Stone relief plaque showing a cloth merchant's shop, with fabrics and cushions hanging from a ceiling rack.

Columns decorated with rams of defeated ships were erected to celebrate naval victories.

The Forum

Most Roman towns had a central forum that served as a gathering-place and market. The Forum in Rome grew up in just such a way, but was later dignified with temples and public buildings, including the Curia where the Senate met. In imperial times different emperors added forums of their own to adjoin the original one.

Monuments to Victory

Rome's streets were full of monuments proudly celebrating military victories. The biggest were the triumphal arches built for the victory parades of emperors returning from battle. Tall sculpted columns were also popular—the best-known, Trajan's Column, rose 125 feet (38 m) high.

Water Supply

Rome's earliest aqueduct was completed in 312 BCE. By early imperial times there were eight of them, supplying about 47 gallons (180 liters) of water each day for every inhabitant of the city. Wealthy people had water piped to their homes, but the rest collected it from public fountains.

Stone fountains like this one were the main water source for ordinary Romans.

The Late Empire

In the 3rd century CE the empire's problems multiplied. A strong new enemy arose in the East in the shape of Sassanian Persia; in 260, Persian forces defeated and captured the Emperor Valerian (reigned 253–260). Many other emperors came and went, some murdered by their own men. Inflation soared as spending on the army increased, making money almost worthless. Order was finally restored by Emperor Diocletian, a strong ruler who decided to divide imperial authority to lessen the burden of command.

The Tetrarchy
When Emperor Diocletian decided to divide imperial authority, he took control of the Eastern lands and gave command of the West to an old friend, Maximian. Seven years later he extended the idea of joint rule by appointing two lesser co-emperors, Constantius I (reigned 305–306) and Galerius (reigned –). The four-man system of government was known as the Tetrarchy, from a Greek word meaning "four."

Marble statue of Diocletian, Maxentius and the two lesser co-emperors, called Caesars.

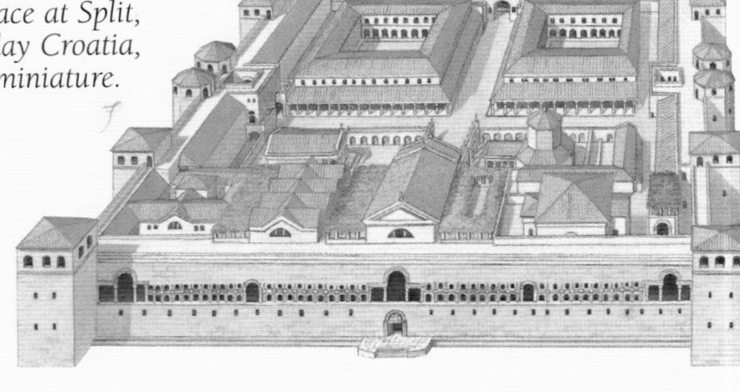

Emperor Diocletian's Palace at Split, in present-day Croatia, was a city in miniature.

THE EMPIRE DIVIDED

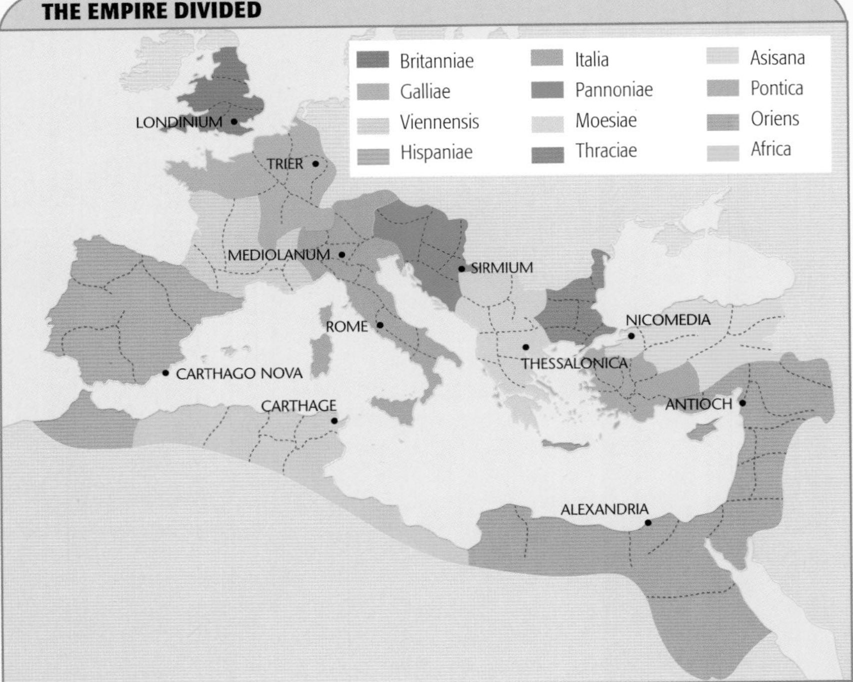

Division of Power
Each of the four tetrarchs controlled his own geographic area from four new capitals. Emperors Diocletian and Galerius controlled the East from Thessalonica and Nicomedia while emperors Maxentius and Constantius I ruled in the West from Mediolanum (present-day Milan) and Trier. As a result of Emperor Diocletian's reorganization, provinces were arranged into 12 dioceses, or administrative regimes, each ruled by a vicar. To prevent any single provincial governor or vicar from gaining too much power, governors and vicars were not given military authority. Instead, the army was controlled by a separate system independent of provincial boundaries.

The Battle of the Milvian Bridge outside Rome, where Constantine's forces defeated Maxentius in 312 CE.

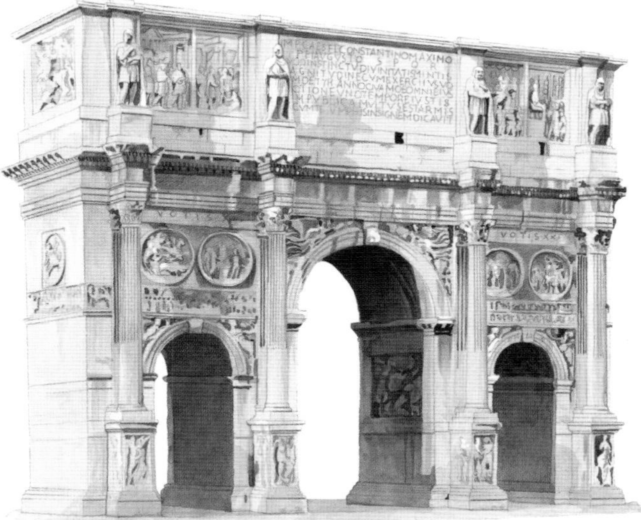

The Arch of Constantine in Rome, built to commemorate the emperor's victory over his rival Maxentius.

Constantine's Victory

The weakness of the Tetrarchy was that it only worked when all four rulers agreed to co-operate. After Emperor Diocletian's reign the system broke down and rival emperors in the East and West vied for power. The man who reunited the empire was Emperor Constantine. First he overcame three rivals to become emperor in the West. He then defeated the Eastern emperor, Maximian, to become sole ruler in 324 CE. Emperor Constantine built his capital, Constantinople, on the site of the ancient city of Byzantium (present-day Istanbul).

Christianity Recognized

Emperor Constantine was won over to Christianity by a vision of the cross of Jesus Christ before his victory at the Milvian Bridge. The faith had spread widely by his day, but had been fiercely persecuted, particularly by Emperor Diocletian. Now Constantine not merely tolerated but actively encouraged Christianity, building many churches. According to some, he himself was baptised a Christian on his deathbed.

THE DECLINE

248
The 1000th anniversary of the founding of the city of Rome is celebrated with shows and games.

260–274
Postumus (reigned 260–269), governor of Lower Germany, is proclaimed emperor by the Rhine legions. A separate state, known as the Gallic Empire, survives for almost 15 years.

274
Emperor Aurelian's (reigned 270–275) attempt to increase the value of imperial currency ends in revolt.

286
Emperor Diocletian divides imperial authority.

312
Constantine defeats his rival Maxentius to become emperor.

313
Emperor Constantine ends persecution of Christians.

324
Constantinople is founded as the chief city of the Eastern Empire.

361
Emperor Julian seeks to revive paganism.

363
Pagan revival ends with death of Emperor Julian.

391
Emperor Theodosius I makes Christianity the official religion of the empire.

392
Emperor Theodosius I briefly reunites the Eastern and Western halves of the Empire.

395
The Empire is divided permanently.

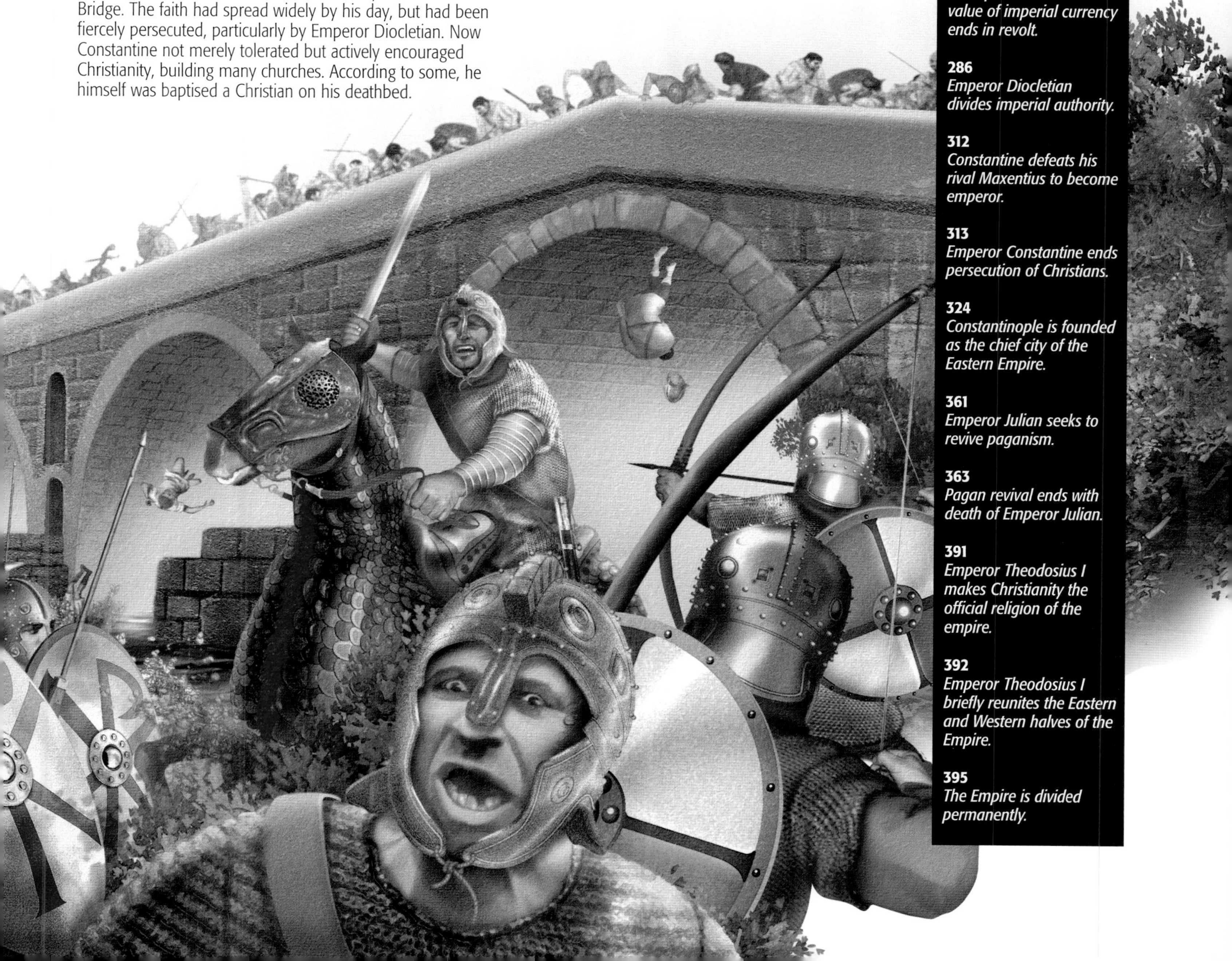

Crisis in the West

In the 5th century CE, the Western Empire collapsed, although Rome's eastern provinces went on to survive as the Christian Byzantine Empire. Rome was fatally weakened when it lost control of the frontiers on the Rhine and Danube rivers that it had held for over four centuries. A wave of Germanic peoples swept into Gaul and other western provinces and also into Italy—even, on two occasions, into Rome itself. Yet all was not completely lost. These "barbarian" invaders themselves adopted some features of the Roman civilization they displaced.

THE FALL OF THE WESTERN EMPIRE

370 CE
Huns invade Germanic lands.

372
Huns defeat the Ostrogoths.

376
Visigoths settle within the frontiers of the Eastern Empire.

378
Visigoth settlers rebel, killing the eastern Emperor Valens (reigned 364–378).

404
Ravenna replaces Rome as the capital of the Western Empire.

406 CE
Germanic invaders cross the Rhine.

410
Negotiations with Emperor Honorius break down. The Visigoths sack Rome and occupy the city for three days.

439
Vandals seize North Africa.

445
Attila kills his brother and becomes sole leader of the Huns.

455
Vandals sack Rome.

476
The last western emperor is deposed.

Foreign Invaders in Rome
Visigoths invaded northern Italy in 401 and 403, only to be turned back by Flavius Stilicho (c. 365–408), commander of the Roman forces. He was killed in 408, and no-one else proved able to stop the invaders, who sacked Rome itself in 410–the first time it had fallen to an enemy army since 390 BCE. Forty-five years later it was the turn of the Vandals, who stayed in the city for two weeks to plunder its treasures.

Stilicho, half-Vandal and half-Roman, was imprisoned and killed after rumors that he wanted to put his son on the Eastern throne.

Ravenna
After the Visigothic invasions of northern Italy in 401 and 403 CE, Emperor Honorius (reigned 395–423 CE), son of Emperor Theodosius I (reigned 379–395 CE), decided that Rome was no longer safe from attack. Instead he moved his court to Ravenna in northeastern Italy, which was protected by lagoons. Ravenna remained the capital of the Western Empire until its fall.

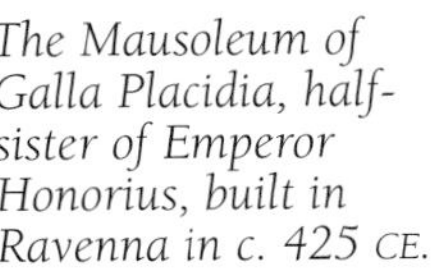

The Mausoleum of Galla Placidia, half-sister of Emperor Honorius, built in Ravenna in c. 425 CE.

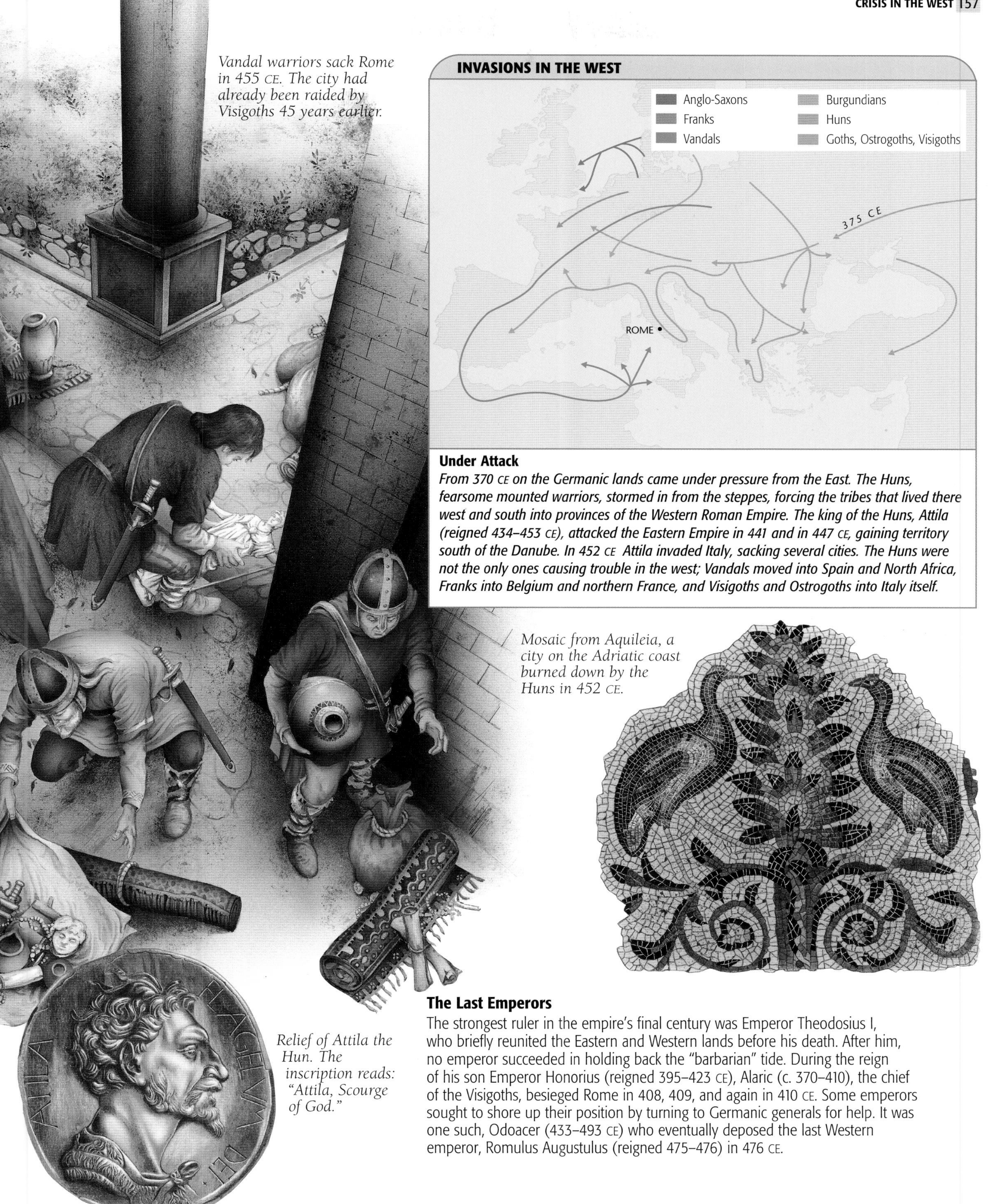

Vandal warriors sack Rome in 455 CE. The city had already been raided by Visigoths 45 years earlier.

Under Attack

From 370 CE on the Germanic lands came under pressure from the East. The Huns, fearsome mounted warriors, stormed in from the steppes, forcing the tribes that lived there west and south into provinces of the Western Roman Empire. The king of the Huns, Attila (reigned 434–453 CE), attacked the Eastern Empire in 441 and in 447 CE, gaining territory south of the Danube. In 452 CE Attila invaded Italy, sacking several cities. The Huns were not the only ones causing trouble in the west; Vandals moved into Spain and North Africa, Franks into Belgium and northern France, and Visigoths and Ostrogoths into Italy itself.

Mosaic from Aquileia, a city on the Adriatic coast burned down by the Huns in 452 CE.

Relief of Attila the Hun. The inscription reads: "Attila, Scourge of God."

The Last Emperors

The strongest ruler in the empire's final century was Emperor Theodosius I, who briefly reunited the Eastern and Western lands before his death. After him, no emperor succeeded in holding back the "barbarian" tide. During the reign of his son Emperor Honorius (reigned 395–423 CE), Alaric (c. 370–410), the chief of the Visigoths, besieged Rome in 408, 409, and again in 410 CE. Some emperors sought to shore up their position by turning to Germanic generals for help. It was one such, Odoacer (433–493 CE) who eventually deposed the last Western emperor, Romulus Augustulus (reigned 475–476) in 476 CE.

After the descendants of nomadic hunter-gatherers started growing their own crops many thousands of years ago, farming villages grew up in different parts of Asia. Simple settlements developed into important civilizations in great river valleys, such as the Indus Valley in present-day Pakistan and the Yellow and Yangzi rivers in modern China.

Rulers founded dynasties, and some small city-states turned into great empires. Wars were fought and rulers rose and fell, but at the same time great progress was made in art and technology. This was also true in Korea, Japan, and Southeast Asia, where Chinese influence was great. Our look at early Asian civilization ends around 1,500 years ago, when a variety of cultures were flourishing throughout the continent.

Kongfuzi (c. 551–479 BCE), known as Confucius, was a great teacher and philosopher. His ideas have had enormous influence throughout Chinese society as a guide to morality and good government.

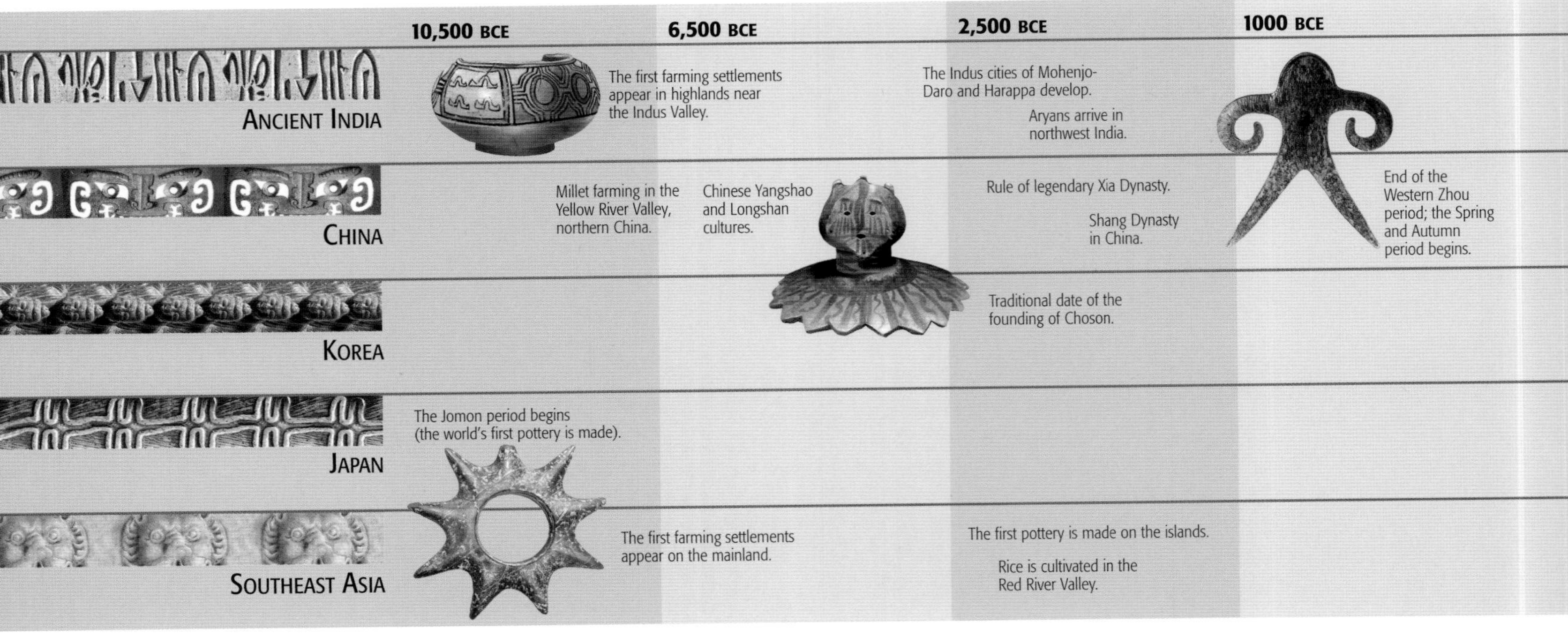

	10,500 BCE	6,500 BCE	2,500 BCE	1000 BCE
ANCIENT INDIA	The first farming settlements appear in highlands near the Indus Valley.		The Indus cities of Mohenjo-Daro and Harappa develop. Aryans arrive in northwest India.	
CHINA	Millet farming in the Yellow River Valley, northern China.	Chinese Yangshao and Longshan cultures.	Rule of legendary Xia Dynasty. Shang Dynasty in China.	End of the Western Zhou period; the Spring and Autumn period begins.
KOREA			Traditional date of the founding of Choson.	
JAPAN	The Jomon period begins (the world's first pottery is made).			
SOUTHEAST ASIA	The first farming settlements appear on the mainland.		The first pottery is made on the islands. Rice is cultivated in the Red River Valley.	

Asian Civilizations

Marble panel with Buddhist figures from Gandhara, in the ancient Kushan Empire (present-day Pakistan) dating from the 2nd century CE.

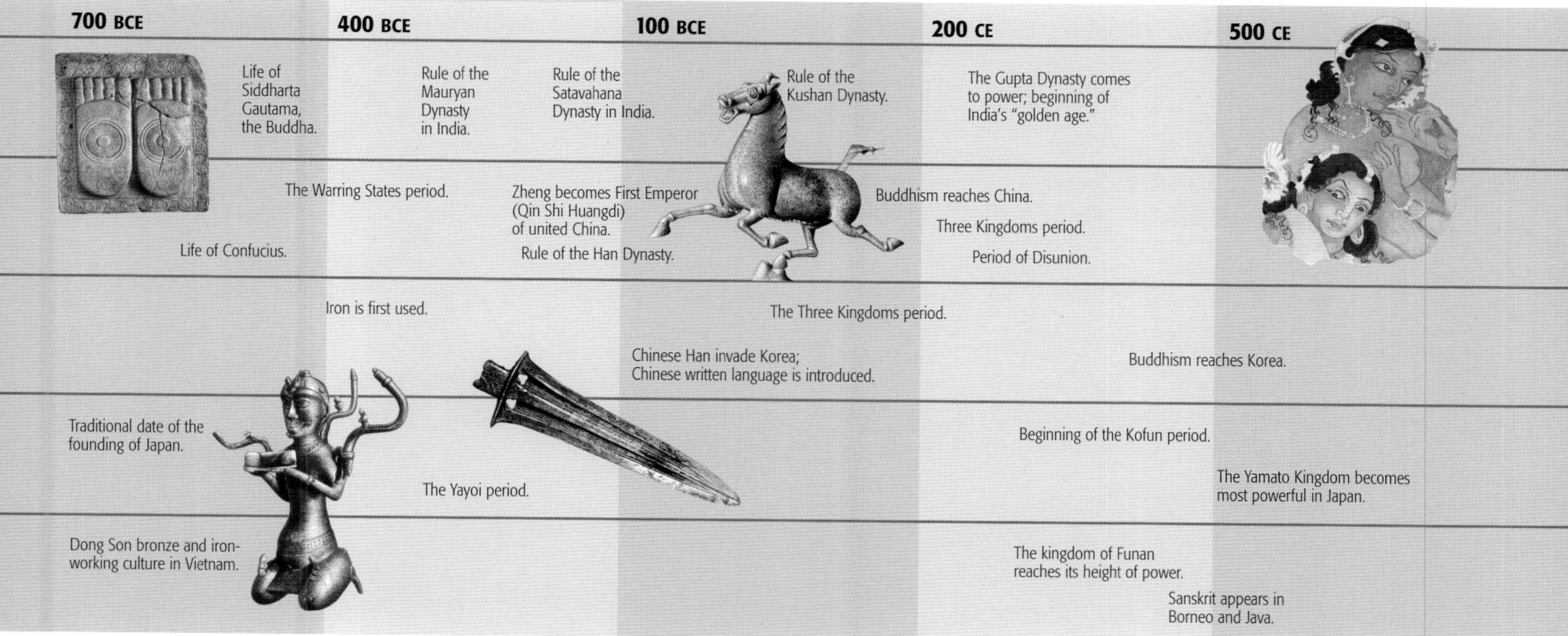

Origins of Indus Civilization

Around 7000 BCE the descendants of Stone Age hunter-gatherers were settled in the hills to the west of the Indus River. There they began to grow cereal crops and domesticate animals. By 6000 BCE people were farming on the plain that was watered by the great river and its tributaries, where the soil was enriched by the annual flood. Farming settlements grew into villages and towns, and two large cities developed and flourished for many hundreds of years.

ANCIENT INDUS CIVILIZATION

Early Cities

The cities of Harappa and Mohenjo-Daro are sometimes referred to as the northern and southern capitals of the Indus civilization. This covered a wide region of present-day Pakistan, making it the largest of the Bronze Age civilizations. The area marked on the map above shows the area of Indus Civilization and the major sites.

Pottery and Jewelry

The earliest Indus art included terra-cotta figurines, mainly of young women wearing jewelry but also of bearded men. Potters made massive storage jars, water pitchers, and smaller decorated vases, which were all fired in large kilns. Craftworkers made intricate jewelry, especially necklaces and other items of small soapstone beads. They also used gold, silver, and gemstones imported from surrounding regions.

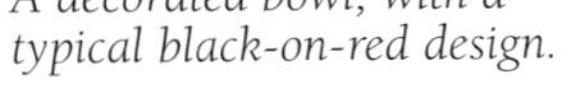

A decorated bowl, with a typical black-on-red design.

A metal balance scale and set of weights from the Indus Valley.

Weights and Measures

Indus traders used stone weights carved into cubes. These were standard throughout the region. The basic unit was 16, and weights varied from tiny cubes used for measuring spices to large blocks for weighing metals.

This necklace was found among other grave goods in Mehrgarh.

This terra-cotta amulet shows an Indus boat.

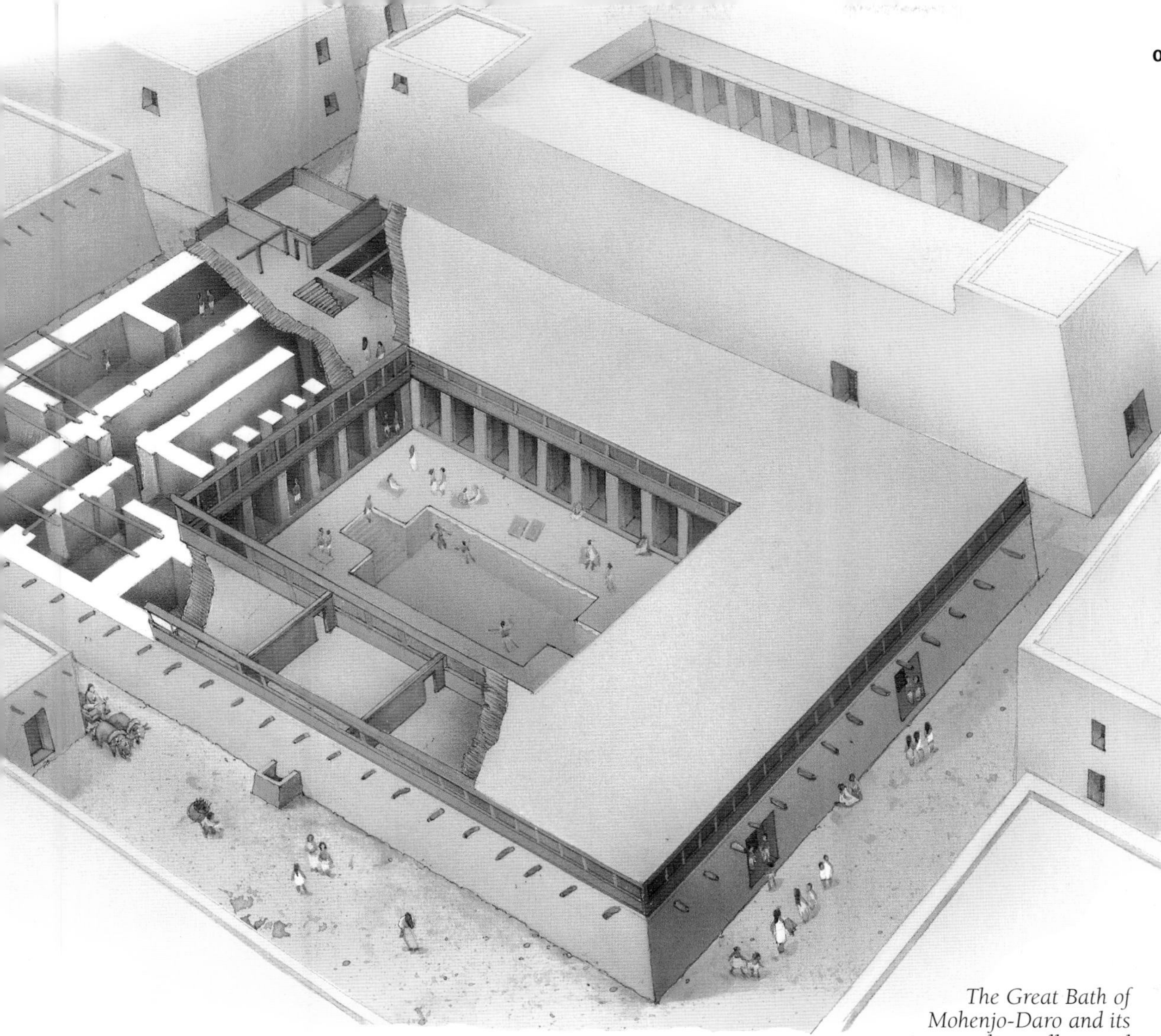

The Great Bath of Mohenjo-Daro and its surrounding gallery and rooms were made of baked mud bricks. The bathing pool measured about 39 x 23 feet (12 x 7 m) and was more than 8 feet (2 m) deep.

INDUS CIVILIZATION

7000 BCE
Farming begins in the highlands to the west of the Indus Valley.

6000 BCE
People begin to farm on the Indus floodplain; earliest pottery and use of copper.

3500 BCE
Development of small towns; craftworkers start using the potter's wheel.

2600 BCE
The plow is used in the Indus Valley; the cities of Mohenjo-Daro and Harappa develop.

2500 BCE
Cotton cloth is woven at Mohenjo-Daro. Development of Harappan script. Bronze is used to make weapons and tools.

2400–2000 BCE
Height of the Indus civilization.

2350 BCE
Trade with Mesopotamia.

2300 BCE
Harappa and Mohenjo-Daro grow to a population of up to 35,000 each.

1900 BCE
Indus civilization undergoes a great transformation. Cities are abandoned and people return to a simpler lifestyle.

Mohenjo-Daro

At the city of Mohenjo-Daro there was a Great Bath symbolically elevated on a mound and surrounded by a colonnaded gallery and important buildings. Historians believe that the bath was used for ritual bathing, perhaps before worship in a nearby temple. The city had a network of wells, and most houses in the residential district had washrooms and lavatories which were connected to drains running beneath the streets.

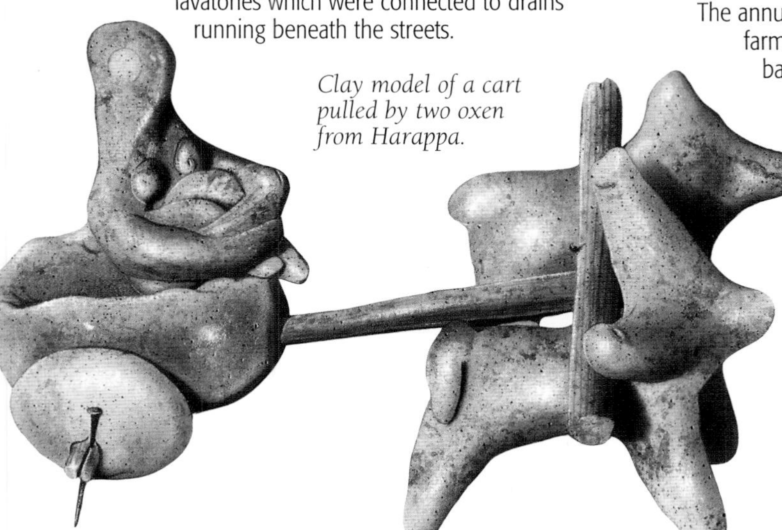

Clay model of a cart pulled by two oxen from Harappa.

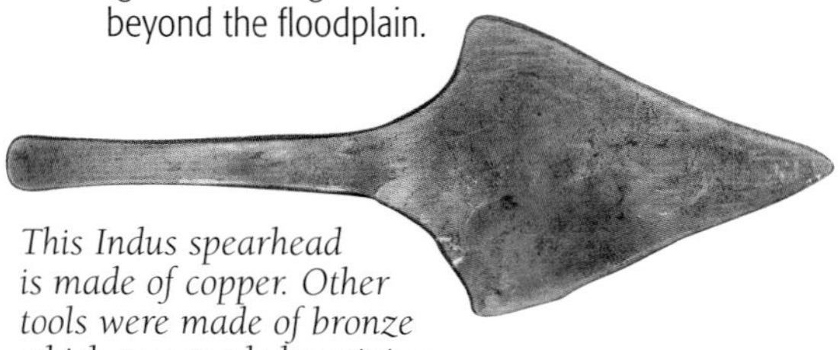

Indus Agriculture

The annual Indus flood created good conditions for farming. The main food crops were wheat and barley, and some farmers also grew rice and cotton. There were domesticated cattle, sheep, goats, pigs, asses, and fowl, and hunters may have chased deer and other game on the grasslands beyond the floodplain.

This Indus spearhead is made of copper. Other tools were made of bronze which was made by mixing copper and tin.

Life in the Indus Valley

From finds at Mohenjo-Daro and other sites, we know how Indus Valley cities were laid out. We also know something of how people lived in the Indus civilization. But we still have much to learn about their social and political organization. The cities had buildings that may have had a religious or ceremonial purpose, and historians believe there was an important class of priests. But no palaces have been found.

City Planning

Mohenjo-Daro was a well-planned city, with streets laid out in a grid pattern. It was made up of two sections: a mound, where there were important public buildings, and a lower district of ordinary residential houses. Though close together, the houses were quite separate, with an entrance off a quiet back lane rather than the busy street.

Cutaway reconstruction of a two-storey mud-brick house at Mohenjo-Daro. It was built around a central courtyard, and people probably spent a lot of time at roof level, where there was plenty of light and air.

Religious Beliefs

We know little about Indus religion, but figurines have been found that are thought to represent a mother-goddess. She may have been accompanied by a male "great god," and both were probably worshiped at home or in small, local shrines. No large temples have been found in the cities, but experts believe that busts of bearded men may represent priests or kings.

This limestone head of a bearded man may represent an Indus Valley priest-king.

Writing

The people of the Indus Valley had their own writing system, which was made up of pictographs. This was used by traders on the thousands of stone seals that have been found. The seals were probably used to identify goods, but experts have not yet been able to decipher the script.

Carved soapstone seal from Mohenjo-Daro, used to mark clay tags for goods. Unfortunately we do not know what the short inscription means.

BRONZE STATUETTES

As well as terracotta figurines, artists produced excellent cast-bronze statuettes. These represented carts and animals, as well as dancing girls. The bronze girl shown here wears only a necklace and bangles on her arms. The girl's posture suggests a dance, which was later to become an important part of Indian temple ceremony.

This bronze statuette is just 5.5 inches (14 cm) tall.

Trade

The Indus people traded near and far. Local merchants went from city to city, bartering the goods that they carried overland by pack animal or along the river by barge. Those that ventured further afield obtained metals such as gold, copper, and lead from the surrounding highlands, and gemstones such as lapis lazuli and turquoise from Persia. The port of Lothal, on the Gulf of Cambay, was used for sea trade with Ur and other Mesopotamian city-states. Cotton textiles were one of the most important Indus exports.

Terra-cotta mother-goddess figurines from Mohenjo-Daro.

Reconstruction of a busy street in Mohenjo-Daro, where farmers brought their wheat and barley to the city granary at harvest time.

The Aryans

Around 1500 BCE a new group of people arrived in the Indus Valley region. They came from central Asia and called themselves Aryans. By that time the Indus civilization had declined, and the Aryans established themselves amidst the local people of ancient India. The Aryans brought with them the Sanskrit language, and their traditions, hymns, and beliefs gradually developed into the Hindu religion.

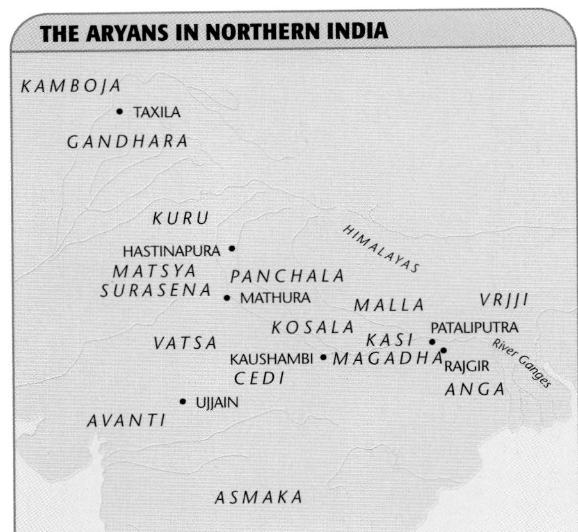

Territories
The Aryans came to the subcontinent across the passes of the Hindu Kush mountains. They called the first region they came to, near the Indus, the "land of seven rivers." Each Aryan clan or family group was headed by a warrior-chief. Some groups continued south toward the plains of the Ganges River, where the annual flood was more predictable. This map shows the 16 "great realms" that had developed in northern India by 600 BCE.

This copper harpoon blade may have been for ceremonial use only.

The Aryans

The Aryans brought with them herds of cattle, sheep, and goats. They also brought horses, which were used to pull chariots, and dogs. Their animals provided them with meat and milk, and the Aryans measured their wealth in cattle and horses. They probably subdued and overawed many of the people whose territories they moved into.

This pottery bowl is in a style called painted grey ware, which was produced in northern India from 900 BCE.

Much of what we know about the way the Aryans lived comes from a collection of Sanskrit hymns called The Vedas. They mention chariot races, games, and dancing. However, historians do not know for sure what the Aryans looked like.

Religious Poems

The Aryans composed a series of poetic hymns, prayers, and rituals dedicated to the proper conduct of ritual sacrifice, called the *Rig Veda*. The teachings in this and three other *Vedas* were passed down the generations by word of mouth, until they were finally written down in Sanskrit as more than a thousand hymns. The prayers were addressed to deities called *devas*, or "shining ones," whom the Aryans worshiped under the open sky.

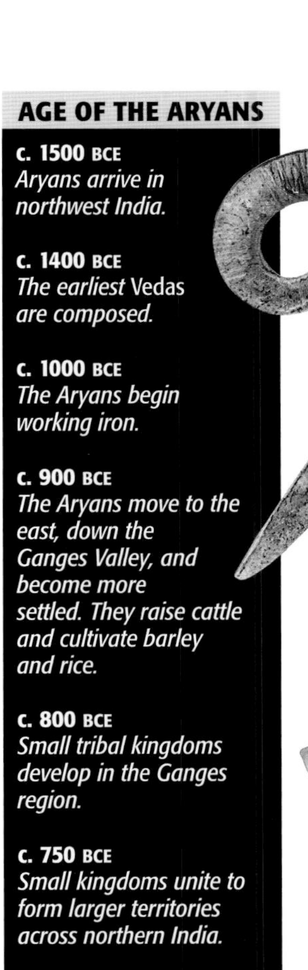

AGE OF THE ARYANS

c. 1500 BCE
Aryans arrive in northwest India.

c. 1400 BCE
The earliest Vedas *are composed.*

c. 1000 BCE
The Aryans begin working iron.

c. 900 BCE
The Aryans move to the east, down the Ganges Valley, and become more settled. They raise cattle and cultivate barley and rice.

c. 800 BCE
Small tribal kingdoms develop in the Ganges region.

c. 750 BCE
Small kingdoms unite to form larger territories across northern India.

c. 700 BCE
The Hindu sacred writings called Upanishads *appear.*

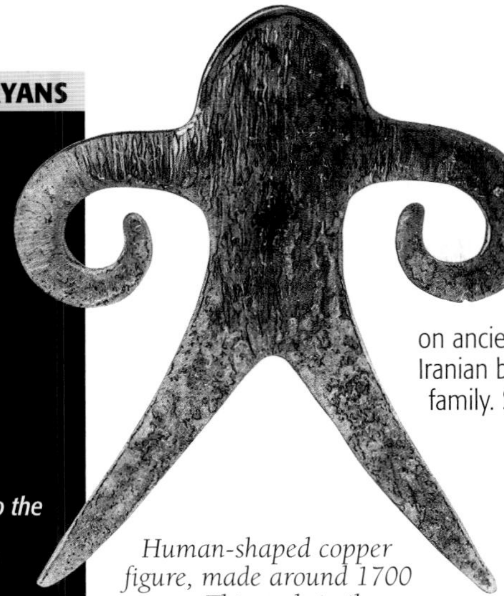

Human-shaped copper figure, made around 1700 BCE. This and similar objects may have been dedicated to the gods.

Sanskrit

This complex language was spoken long before it was ever written down. It is written in a script called Devanagari, which has 48 letters and is written from left to right. Modern Indian languages such as Bengali, Gujarati, and Hindi are based on ancient Sanskrit, which belongs to the Indo-Iranian branch of the Indo-European language family. Sanskrit is still used as a sacred language.

The Aryans believed that every year Indra, the god of rainstorms and war, used a thunderbolt to slay the serpent of drought. For this he was greatly praised and worshiped.

Fourth-century CE Brahmi inscriptions from southern India. The Devanagari alphabet, which was originally developed in the 11th century CE to write Sanksrit, derived from the Brahmi script. Some scholars believe that Brahmi developed from the script that was used in the Indus Valley until about 2000 BCE.

Hinduism

The great world religion of Hinduism developed at this time from the faiths and philosophies expressed in the *Vedas* of the Aryans. Hinduism teaches that the human soul never dies, but is reborn in a continuous process of reincarnation.

The First Dynasties of India

EARLY DYNASTIES

c. 599–527 BCE
Life of Vardhamana Mahavira, founder of the Jain religion.

c. 525 BCE
The founding of Buddhism.

326 BCE
Alexander the Great conquers the northwestern region of India.

c. 321–185 BCE
Rule of the Mauryan Dynasty.

c. 305 BCE
Chandragupta Maurya defeats Seleucus I (died 280), general of Alexander the Great and king of Syria, and gains parts of modern Afghanistan.

c. 260 BCE
Ashoka makes Buddhism the state religion.

250 BCE
Buddhism reaches the very south of the Indian subcontinent.

c. 230 BCE – 230 CE
Rule of the Satavahana Dynasty in central India.

185 BCE – 72 CE
Rule of the Shunga Dynasty.

75 BCE – 28 CE
Rule of the Kanva Dynasty.

c. 50–250 CE
Rule of the Kushan Dynasty.

c. 80–100 CE
Height of the Kushan Empire.

Following the Aryan invasion, many small Hindu kingdoms developed across the Ganges plain and challenged each other for power. During the 6th century BCE two new religions were founded—Jainism and Buddhism—and these spread rapidly throughout the region. Two hundred years later, Alexander the Great, king of Macedonia, led his army to a tributary of the Indus River, but his troops refused to go any further. This allowed a young local warrior to take power and found the great Mauryan Empire.

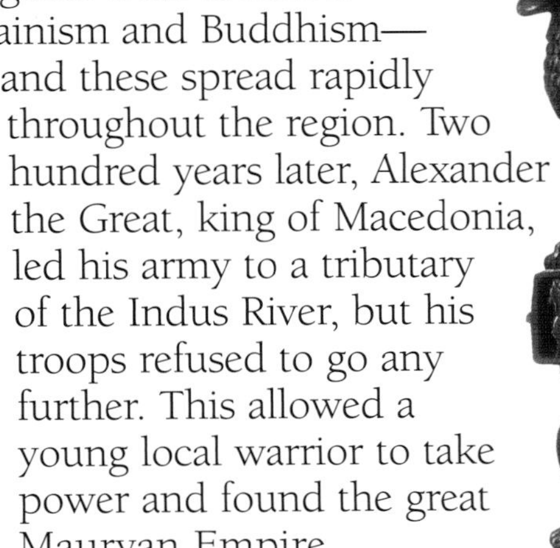

Carved limestone panel of the Buddha's feet, each inscribed with the Buddhist wheel of law.

Buddhism

The Buddhist religion developed from the teachings of Siddhartha Gautama (c. 563–c. 483 BCE), the son of the ruler of a small Himalayan kingdom in present-day Nepal. After the prince left his father's palace, he set out to discover how ordinary people's suffering could be stopped. He became enlightened when he understood the truth about life, and was known as the Buddha (meaning "enlightened one").

Mauryan Empire

Five years after fighting against Alexander the Great (reigned 336–323 BCE), the young military commander Chandragupta Maurya (reigned c. 321–c. 293 BCE) conquered the kingdom of Magadha in the fertile Ganges Valley. He founded an empire that covered much of present-day northern India, Pakistan, Bangladesh, and Afghanistan. The Mauryan Empire reached its height under the founder's grandson, Ashoka (reigned 273–232 BCE), who expanded into much of southern India. He converted to Buddhism and made it the state religion. After his reign the empire declined. The last Mauryan ruler was assassinated in 185 BCE and the Shunga Dynasty was established.

The lion-headed capital (above), with the wheel of law, stood on one of the many pillars put up by Ashoka throughout his empire. It became the emblem of the modern state of India.

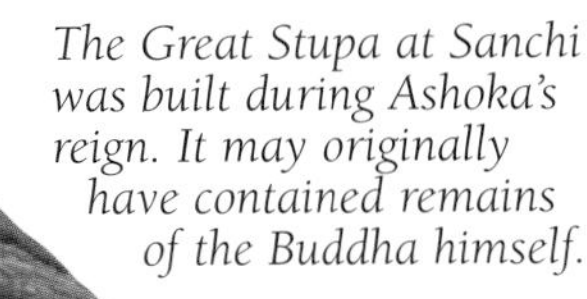

The Great Stupa at Sanchi was built during Ashoka's reign. It may originally have contained remains of the Buddha himself.

Growth of Trade

The Mauryan capital was at Pataliputra (modern Patna), on the Ganges, and the large empire was divided into provinces. There were good roads between them, and this led to an improvement in trading networks. Craftworkers made items of wood, cloth, and gold, and the empire traded with Mesopotamia, Persia, and Greece.

This Kushan gold relic-container dates from about 50 CE.

Right: Ivory plaque made by Andhra artisans showing two yakshis, or earth spirits, from about 50 CE.

Satavahana Dynasty

Toward the end of Mauryan rule, a tribal people known as the Andhras came to power in central India. They may have been local officials who gradually became independent rulers, and their ruling family was called Satavahana. The Satavahana defeated the Kanva Dynasty, who had taken over lands of the Shunga Dynasty. The Satavahana, with their capital at Amaravati, became the dominate power in central India.

This Kushan gold pendant of the Greek goddess Aphrodite was found with the remains of a young woman in a Bactrian grave. Showing Greek and Indian influences, the pendant is about 2,000 years old.

The Kushans

The Kushans were a group of nomadic tribes from central Asia. They first conquered the kingdom of Bactria (in modern Afghanistan), before invading northwest India and advancing to the Ganges plain. Their great ruler Kanishka (reigned c. 80–100 CE) became a Buddhist, but the Kushans showed great respect for other religions. They traded extensively throughout Asia, including with the Chinese along the Silk Road, and with the Roman Empire.

Kanishka is shown on this gold coin conducting a fire ritual.

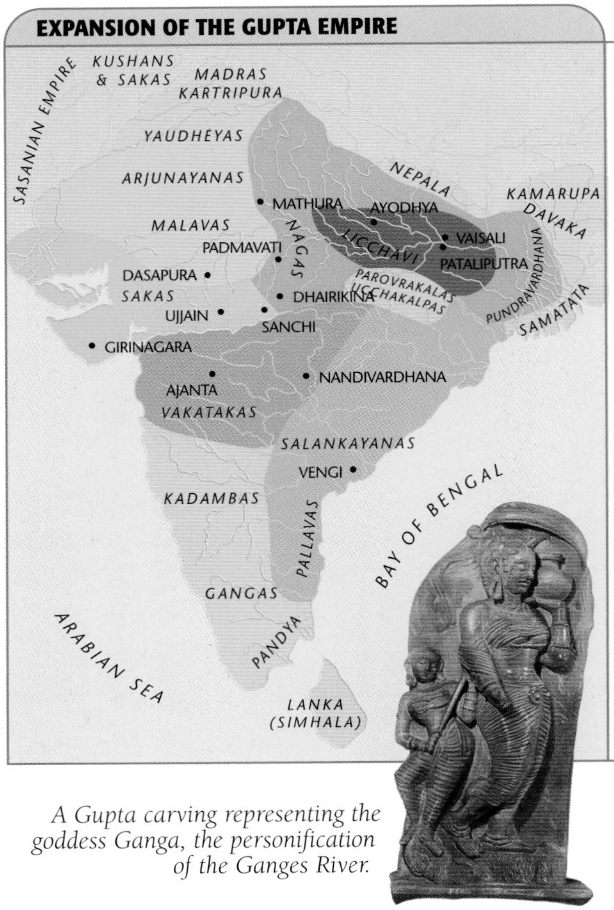

EXPANSION OF THE GUPTA EMPIRE

India Under the Guptas

By the beginning of the 5th century, the Gupta Empire covered the whole of the north and much of the eastern region of the subcontinent. Chandra Gupta I's son, Samudra Gupta (reigned 335–375 CE), made many conquests and adopted the title "Exterminator of Kings;" his southern campaign brought 13 kings and princes under Gupta rule. Later, Chandra Gupta II (reigned 375–415 CE), known as the "Sun of Power," gained more territory in the Ganges and Indus valleys.

- Empire of Chandra Gupta I
- Added by Samudra Gupta
- Temporary tributary to Samudra Gupta
- Added by Chandra Gupta II
- Tributary tribes and states
- Under Gupta influence c. 380–410 CE

A Gupta carving representing the goddess Ganga, the personification of the Ganges River.

This scene, based on a wall painting at Ajanta, shows a raja, a Hindu prince, at his court.

Gupta Origins

We do not know for certain where the Gupta family originated. Many historians believe that the family's homeland was in the region of the Ganges Valley, where they became landowners. From about 240 CE the head of the family was known as a *maharaja*, or prince, and in 305 CE Chandra Gupta I married a princess of the important Lichchavi family, who ruled the kingdom of Magahda.

The Gupta Empire

Detail from an Ajanta wall painting.

The Gupta dynasty of rulers came to power in the northeastern Ganges region, expanding their influence by both marriage and conquest. By 400 CE they controlled a large empire, though the regions furthest from their homeland were allowed considerable independence. The Guptas were followers of Hinduism, and their rulers revived many rituals of the Brahmans, or Hindu priests. But they were also happy to encourage Buddhist beliefs and ways of life.

Wall Paintings

Between the 2nd century BCE and the 6th century CE, Buddhist sanctuaries and monasteries were cut into the cliffs of a narrow gorge at Ajanta, near the southern boundary of the Gupta Empire. The walls of the caves were decorated with wonderful paintings of palaces, forests, and scenes from the Buddha's life.

The entrance to one of the Ajanta sanctuaries shows relief sculptures of the Buddha.

Religious Tolerance

Most Gupta rulers were Hindus, and many were followers of the Hindu god Vishnu (the Preserver). They respected all the other Hindu cults, and people throughout the Gupta Empire worshiped images of Hindu gods and goddesses. Buddhism and Jainism also flourished, however, and the Gupta emperors showed great religious tolerance.

Fifth-century sandstone head of a bodhisattva. According to Buddhist belief, a bodhisattva is a person who has reached enlightenment but stays in the human world to help others.

THE GUPTAS

240–280 CE
Sri Gupta heads the Gupta family as a maharaja in the Ganges Valley.

280–319 CE
Ghatotkacha heads the Gupta family.

c. 320 CE
Sri's grandson, Chandra Gupta (reigned c. 320–335), becomes the first great ruler and founder of the Gupta Empire.

c. 330 CE
Chandra Gupta I names his son, Samudra Gupta (reigned 335–375), successor to the throne. Since Chandra Gupta I had many other older sons who claimed the throne, Samudra Gupta spent the first years of his reign putting down revolts.

401–410 CE
A Chinese pilgrim, Fa-hsien (active 399–414 CE), visits India in search of sacred Buddhists texts.

415–455 CE
Reign of Kumara Gupta, who favors religious tolerance and keeps the empire intact.

455–467 CE
Reign of Skanda Gupta, who defeats Hun invaders and resists internal revolts.

467–473 CE
Reign of Skanda's brother, Puru Gupta. The empire starts to decline.

473–476 CE
Reign of Puru's grandson Kumara Gupta II.

477–497 CE
Budha Gupta becomes king. After his death in 497, Gupta lands are divided into many independent kingdoms.

EARLY CHINESE CULTURE

c. 7000 BCE
Millet farming in the Yellow River Valley, north China.

c. 6500 BCE
Rice farming in the Yangzi Valley, south China.

c. 5000–3200 BCE
Yangshao culture.

c. 5000 BCE
Millet is cultivated around the village of Banpo, near present-day Xian.

c. 4000 BCE
Jade is used to make ornaments and weapons.

c. 3200–1800 BCE
Longshan culture.

c. 3000 BCE
The potter's wheel is introduced in China; evidence of plows being used.

2700 BCE
Possible first weaving of silk.

c. 2500–2000 BCE
First casting of bronze ornaments and tools.

2207–1766 BCE
Traditional dates of the legendary Xia Dynasty.

1766 BCE
Traditional date of the founding of the Shang Dynasty.

c. 1600 BCE
Possible origins of pictographic writing.

Reconstruction of a kiln from Banpo c. 4500 BCE. Pots were placed in a separate chamber above the fire.

Lid of a pottery vessel, dating from about 2500 BCE. It shows a human head, possibly that of a shaman.

Early Potters

At Banpo, there was a pottery-making area beyond the ditch surrounding the village. The pots were shaped by hand, until the potter's wheel was developed around 3000 BCE. The potters' area included six simple kilns, where the clay pots were fired. Heat from the firing chamber baked the pots hard, and their red surface was painted with black designs after firing. Some designs were of animals, others were geometrical patterns.

This bulging terra-cotta pot, dating from about 2200 BCE, was painted with a toad-like design.

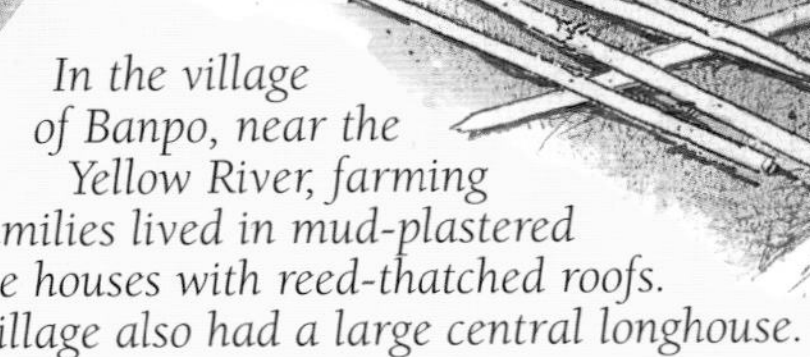

In the village of Banpo, near the Yellow River, farming families lived in mud-plastered pole houses with reed-thatched roofs. The village also had a large central longhouse.

Early China

Chinese agriculture and civilization developed around two great rivers. The Yellow River (or Huang He) was named for the color of its mud and clay, which made dry, fertile land for growing millet. Further south, the even longer Yangzi River (or Chang Jiang) flowed through a wetter landscape that was ideal for cultivating rice. Successful farming villages gradually grew into towns, the population increased, and by 2000 BCE a large region was being governed by powerful dynasties.

YANSHAO AND LONGSHAN CULTURES

Fertile Lands

The Yangshao culture developed on the fertile banks of the Yellow River and its tributaries. Farming villages were surrounded by fields of millet, and the villagers also kept pigs. Later, the Longshan culture developed in the same region and covered more territory to the south and east, where the wetter conditions allowed farmers to grow rice as well as millet. As the map shows, rice cultivation developed to the south, especially around the River Yangzi.

Xia and Shang Dynasties

There is no historic record of the Xia Dynasty of rulers, which has become mixed up with ancient myths and legends. Some tell of a heroic ruler called Yu the Great, who supposedly restored the course of the Yellow River after flooding. Certainly we know that the river constantly changed course in ancient times. The first documented dynasty—the Shang—was founded by a ruler named Tang in or around 1766 BCE.

Tortoise shells such as this, as well as animal bones, were used by Shang priests to foretell the future. Questions and answers were inscribed on the shell.

Early Writing

The earliest Chinese writing was produced during the Shang period, but the exact date is not known. Picture symbols were used to represent objects, but many of the pictographs were written on wood or silk, which have not survived. By about 1450 BCE they were being inscribed on oracle bones (and shells) and bronze vessels.

Some examples of early Shang pictographs.

Shang Society

The region ruled over by the Shang Dynasty centered on the middle reaches of the Yellow River. Historians believe that there were about 30 successive kings and that their capital moved several times. Royal ancestors were worshiped, and they in turn were thought to mediate on behalf of the living king with the supreme, divine ancestor Shang Di, the "Lord on High." On his death, a king went to heaven to join his great ancestor. The precise year in which the Shang Dynasty came to an end is disputed, but usually quoted as c.1050 BCE.

THE SHANG ERA

1766 BCE
Traditional date when founder Tang overthrows the last Xia king, Chieh.

c. 1700 BCE
Production of bronze vessels.

c. 1557 BCE
Zhengzhou becomes Shang capital.

c. 1400 BCE
The Shang capital moves to Anyang.

c. 1350 BCE
War and hunting chariots come into use.

c. 1200 BCE
The Shang king proclaims himself human counterpart of the supreme deity.

c. 1050 BCE
Shang king, Di Xin (reigned c. 1068 – c. 1050 BCE), is overthrown by the Zhou king Wu (died c. 1056 BCE).

The Bronze Age

People of the Shang period were great workers in bronze (an alloy of copper and tin). Craftworkers melted the metal in a pottery crucible and then made casts by pouring the molten metal into clay molds. They used bronze, which is harder than copper, for ritual vessels, weapons and armor. Skillful Shang craftsmen also used jade for utensils and jewelry.

Spearhead with a jade blade attached to inlaid bronze.

Hunting

The Shang rulers acted as military leaders, and they and their nobles probably spent a great deal of time hunting. This was a useful way of practising and improving their skills in horsemanship and war. The Shang cavalry was drawn from the ranks of the nobles, who in battle wore bronze helmets and armor made from rhinoceros and buffalo hides. Their preferred weapon was the halberd.

Bronze wine vessel in the shape of a rhinoceros, from the late Shang period.

Hunters may have ambushed rhinoceros in narrow valleys and then used spears and halberds, as well as bows and arrows, to bring the animals down.

Ritual Burial

Later kings of the Shang Dynasty were buried in a large rectangular pit with ramps on each side. The royal coffin was surrounded by the bodies of men and women who were intended to accompany the dead king to the other world. The large tomb was surrounded by smaller pits with dead soldiers, horses, and war chariots. There were also rich grave goods, though the tombs were robbed in ancient times.

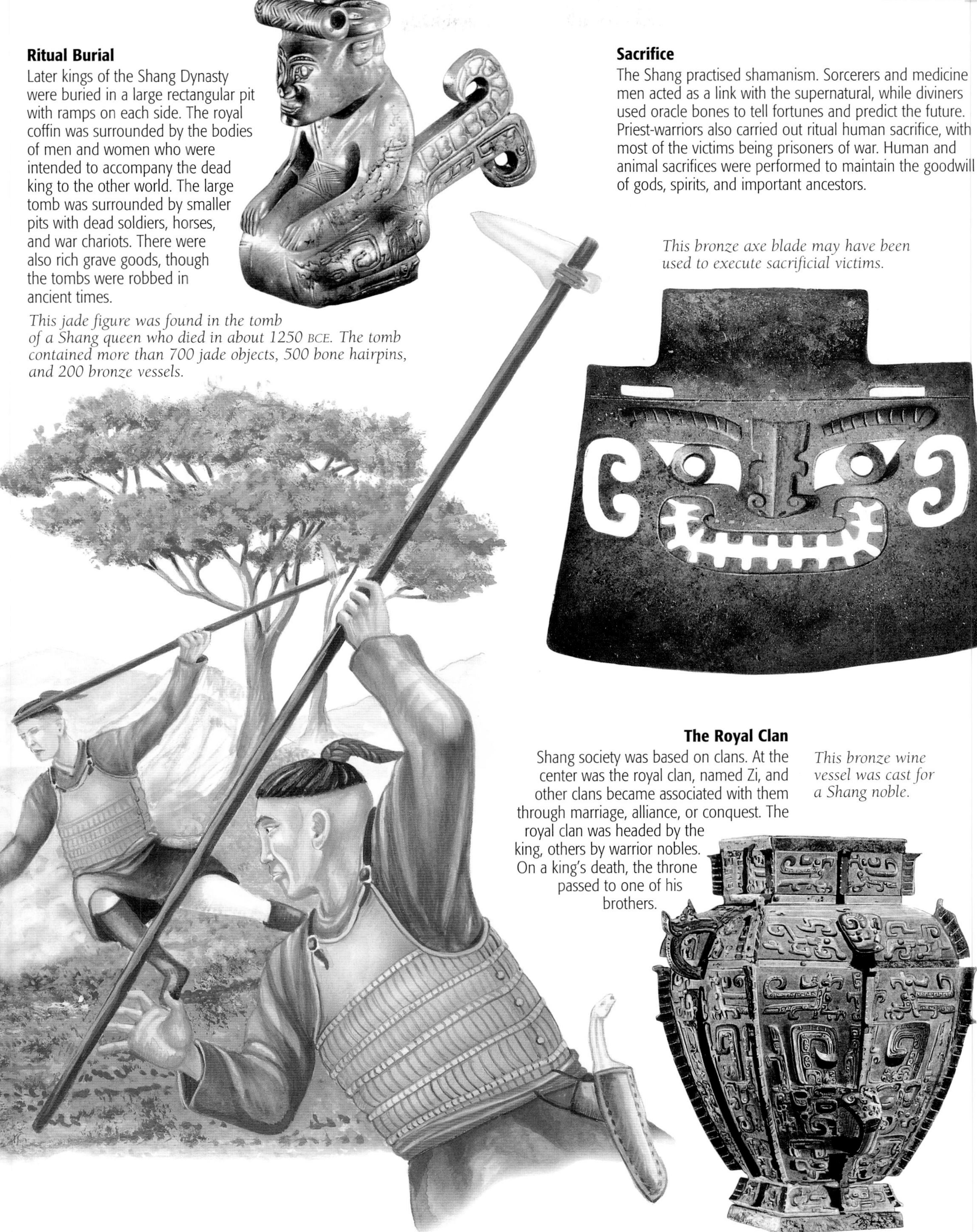

This jade figure was found in the tomb of a Shang queen who died in about 1250 BCE. The tomb contained more than 700 jade objects, 500 bone hairpins, and 200 bronze vessels.

Sacrifice

The Shang practised shamanism. Sorcerers and medicine men acted as a link with the supernatural, while diviners used oracle bones to tell fortunes and predict the future. Priest-warriors also carried out ritual human sacrifice, with most of the victims being prisoners of war. Human and animal sacrifices were performed to maintain the goodwill of gods, spirits, and important ancestors.

This bronze axe blade may have been used to execute sacrificial victims.

The Royal Clan

Shang society was based on clans. At the center was the royal clan, named Zi, and other clans became associated with them through marriage, alliance, or conquest. The royal clan was headed by the king, others by warrior nobles. On a king's death, the throne passed to one of his brothers.

This bronze wine vessel was cast for a Shang noble.

THE ZHOU PERIOD

c. 1050 BCE
Beginning of the Western Zhou period.

841 BCE
Nobles expel a tyrant at the Zhou court.

841–828 BCE
Dukes Zhou of Lu and Shao of Yan rule until the crown prince is old enough to become king.

827–782 BCE
Reign of King Xuanwang.

c. 800 BCE
The earliest Chinese poetry is written as the Shijing *(Book of Songs), and is sung at court.*

781–770 BCE
Reign of King Youwang.

c. 770 BCE
End of Western Zhou period; capital moves to Luoyang.

Rise of the Zhou

The satellite state of the Zhou overthrew their Shang rulers in the 11th century BCE. The early centuries of the new rule are known as the Western Zhou period because the capital, Hao, was in the west. The Zhou kings ruled wisely, giving authority in their scattered vassal states to junior family members and nobles. This period was looked on by later Chinese philosophers as a golden age of good government and culture.

The Last Shang Capital

After moving their capital, the Shang ended their rule at Anyang. Like the previous capital Zhengzhou, the city was built on a rammed-earth platform, on which there were royal palace buildings. This was surrounded by less important buildings and workshops, as well as a large residential area. In recent years, archeologists have uncovered the foundations of buildings and important tombs beneath the modern city of Anyang.

This bronze wine vessel from the late Shang period shows a tiger protecting a man, who may represent a shaman.

Reconstruction of the royal palace at Anyang, which measured 567 feet (173 m) long and 295 feet (90 m) wide. Remains of burned walls and floors suggest that the palace burned to the ground.

Feudal Network

The Zhou king ruled directly over the royal domain around the western capital of Hao. The rest of the kingdom was divided into feudal states, which were controlled by dukes chosen from among the king's relatives. Each state was run from a fortified city, and the people of neighboring states formed close ties through marriage and shared culture.

This bronze vessel was made to celebrate a royal marriage.

Fragment of a silk manuscript of the Yijing *(Book of Changes), a collection of symbolic figures used to predict the future. They were probably collected early in the Zhou period.*

Zhou Origins

The Zhou people, who may have descended from those of the legendary Xia state, came originally from south of the Yellow River. They migrated north, perhaps coming in contact with people of the northern steppes before settling in the valley of the Wei, a tributary of the Yellow River. They gradually expanded eastward toward Shang territory and became one of their satellite states.

Portrait of King Wu, represented with a statesman's hat and a scholar's robe. According to tradition, King Wu was a hero because he overthrew the last Shang ruler who was an evil tyrant.

Rule and Authority

Zhou rule was based on the powerful authority of the king, who was seen as the "Son of Heaven." This gave him the right to rule over the whole world, so long as he did so justly and with proper concern for his people. The first ruling king after the overthrow of the Shang, Wu, was greatly respected by his people but died shortly after the conquest.

The Revolt of King Wu

The Shang kingdom was made up of provinces and vassal states. One of the vassal kings, Wu, from the state of Zhou, formed an alliance with other surrounding states. Meanwhile, the Shang army was becoming weaker and weaker due to wars and expeditions in foreign lands. Taking advantage of this situation, Wu's army was able to overthrow the Shang emperor and establish the longest-lasting dynasty in Chinese history.

The Zhou made weapons and armour from bronze. This is an early helmet.

The Eastern Zhou Period

The Eastern Zhou period was one of a great struggle for supremacy among many small states, after the central power of the dynasty declined. Towns and cities increased in size and number throughout the various regions, and constant warfare meant that important settlements had to be well defended. By the time of the so-called Warring States period, a small number of regions dominated the scene, and all were eventually taken over by the Qin state.

THE EASTERN ZHOU

c. 770–476 BCE
The Spring and Autumn period.

685–643 BCE
Huan rules the state of Qi and adopts the title of "overlord" of the Zhou states.

636–628 BCE
Wen rules the state of Qin and further develops the position of overlord.

c. 600 BCE
Iron comes into use (and is later cast for tools and weapons).

551–479 BCE
Life of Confucius.

c. 500 BCE
Bronze coins come into use.

475–221 BCE
The Warring States period.

361–338 BCE
Rule of Xiao over the state of Qin.

c. 350 BCE
Invention of the crossbow; Qin becomes the leading state.

246 BCE
Zheng (259–210 BCE) becomes king of Qin.

230–221 BCE
Qin conquers Han, Zhao, Wei, Chu, Yan and Qi in turn.

The Spring and Autumn Period

The Spring and Autumn period is named after a chronicle of the early Eastern Zhou Dynasty. The capital had moved east from Hao to Luoyang because of "barbarian" attacks. Three centuries of growing disorder followed as central authority and the power of the Zhou dynasty declined. The nobles effectively became the rulers of small independent states, which vied with each other for supremacy. In the 7th century BCE the ruler of the state of Qi took on the title of "overlord."

Above: Bronze statue of a Mongolian girl holding two jade birds. Mongolian nomads were a threat to the northern states.

The Warring States Period

By the 5th century BCE, seven important states had become dominant. The southern Chu and western Qin took over much of the former Western Zhou domain, while the northern Jin and eastern Qi absorbed many people who had been outside Zhou influence. But as the states continued to battle with each other, Jin was broken up into three states, the others were taken over by new rulers, and none paid much attention to what was left of the Zhou royal court.

The first coins were miniature implements, such as this bronze knife from the state of Qi.

Chariots were important symbols of power in the Warring States period. These bronze chariot fittings are inlaid with gold.

QIN TERRITORY

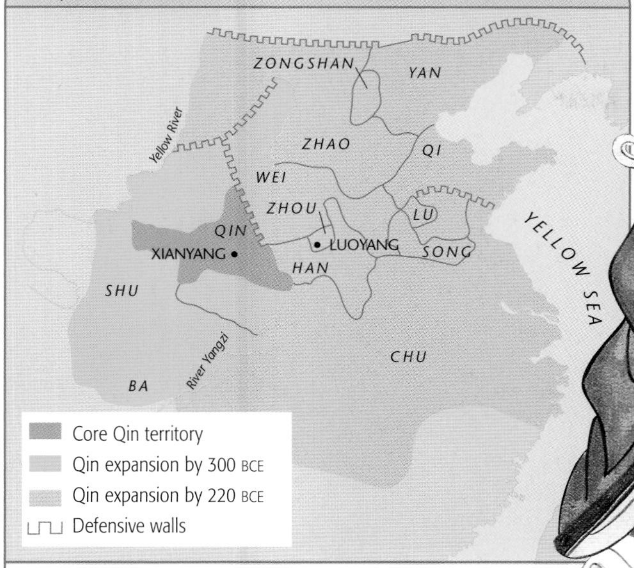

ZONGSHAN
YAN
Yellow River
ZHAO
QI
WEI
ZHOU
LU
YELLOW SEA
QIN
XIANYANG
LUOYANG
SONG
HAN
SHU
River Yangzi
CHU
BA

Core Qin territory
Qin expansion by 300 BCE
Qin expansion by 220 BCE
Defensive walls

Qin Dominance

By about 350 BCE Qin had become the most powerful state, and its rulers soon adopted the title of king. Qin continued to wage war against the other states, showing great ferocity and military discipline. The Qin ruler, King Zheng, began a series of successful lightning campaigns against neighboring states in 230 BCE.

The Teachings of Confucius

Kongfuzi (c. 551–479 BCE), known as Confucius (a Latin name), was born in the eastern state of Lu. He became a great teacher and philosopher, who committed himself to living in harmony with others and inspiring people to do good. He respected the family as the most important part of society. His ideas—Confucianism—have had enormous influence throughout Chinese society as a guide to morality and good government.

The beliefs of Taoism are based on the teachings of Laozi (c. 570–490 BCE), shown here sitting on a water buffalo. The followers of Confucius saw him as a great philosopher, while others venerated him as a god.

The teachings of Confucius were spread by his disciples, who collected his sayings.

Zhou Music

Music played an important part in Zhou court life, and poems such as those in the *Shijing* (*Book of Songs*) were set to music and performed on ritual occasions. The ancient Chinese believed that music could be a positive, moral force, helping to bring people into harmony. Musical instruments included stone chimes, bronze drums, and bamboo flutes.

This 65-piece set of bronze bells was found in the tomb of a nobleman from the state of Zheng, who died about 433 BCE. The bells were suspended from a lacquered wooden frame and struck with a stick.

The First Empire

By 221 BCE King Zheng of Qin had defeated all the other rival states, and he was able to declare himself Qin Shi Huangdi—the First Sovereign Emperor of Qin. This made him the first ruler of a unified empire; our name for China comes originally from Qin (pronounced "chin"). Qin Shi Huangdi's reign as First Emperor lasted for 11 years, during which time his harsh leadership achieved much. But after his death the Qin Dynasty lost control of the empire in just four years.

Military generals were each given half a token, such as this bronze tiger. An imperial order was only to be obeyed if its messenger carried the other half of the tiger.

THE QIN DYNASTY

221 BCE
The state of Qi is conquered by Qin, which now controls a large empire; Zheng becomes the First Emperor.

219 BCE
Qin Shi Huangdi makes a first tour of inspection of his empire.

218 BCE
Failed assassination attempt on the emperor.

215 BCE
General Meng Tian (died 209 BCE) leads 300,000 men against Xiongnu nomads.

214 BCE
Large construction work on the Great Wall.

213 BCE
The Emperor orders the burning of Confucian and other books that do not agree with his policies.

212 BCE
Construction of the imperial Afang Palace.

210 BCE
Qin Shi Huangdi dies on his fifth tour of inspection.

209 BCE
The emperor's second son, Hu Hai (230–207 BCE), becomes Er Shi (Second Emperor).

207 BCE
Er Shi's nephew Ziying becomes Qin ruler. Ziying, who reigns for only 46 days, is forced to surrender to a minor Qin official, Liu Bang (247–195 BCE).

206 BCE
The Qin imperial family is killed and rebels take the capital Xianyang.

Qin Shi Huangdi's Rule

The First Emperor broke up the old Zhou feudal system and replaced it with a centralized government. He divided the empire into 36 administrative units ruled by governors, and forced former rival chiefs to move to his capital, Xianyang. This all-powerful control led Qin Shi Huangdi to prophesy that his empire would last for 10,000 generations. Yet he was deeply superstitious and had a terrible fear of death.

Standardization

In order to make communication quicker and easier, and to improve central control, the Qin Empire was standardized. Weights and measures were unified, along with coinage, and the pictographic writing system was simplified. Qin Shi Huangdi ordered the construction of roads and canals, and even the width of cart and chariot axles was made standard.

Strict Laws

Qin Shi Huangdi believed in so-called legalist government. This was based on the idea that people are basically undisciplined or even evil. They therefore needed to be kept in order by a combination of strict laws and harsh punishments. The emperor tried to control all knowledge, burning books that disagreed with his system. Scholars who resisted were buried alive, while ordinary citizens were forced into occupations such as farming or the army.

A woodcut of Qin Shi Huangdi.

This bronze model of a horse-drawn chariot was buried near Qin Shi Huangdi's tomb.

The Imperial Guard

After several attempts on his life, Qin Shi Huangdi took steps to protect himself. Each night he slept in a different place, and he and his guards always traveled with more than one carriage. He had a huge tomb complex built, so that he would be protected even after his death. Hundreds of thousands of workers and craftsmen were needed for the complex, which included a model army.

The First Emperor's "terra-cotta army" was made up of more than 7,000 life-sized clay soldiers, along with clay horses and wooden chariots.

Gold buckle of the Xiongnu people, nomads who threatened the new Chinese empire.

The Great Wall

More than 300,000 men were conscripted to join and extend a series of earlier walls that had been built by the conquered states. In this way the emperor wanted to make a continuous barrier against the nomadic northern tribes. The wall was made of pounded earth, and there were garrison stations and signal towers at regular intervals. This was a huge undertaking, and later dynasties maintained and rebuilt the Great Wall in the form that it can still be seen today.

The simple pounded earth wall was rebuilt and restructured by later dynasties. Building the Great Wall—across land that was scorching hot in summer and freezing cold in winter— was desperately hard work.

WESTERN HAN

206 BCE–8 CE
Western (or Former) Han period.

206 BCE
Liu Bang becomes king of Han.

202–195 BCE
Reign of Liu Bang as Emperor Gaodi ("High Emperor") of the Han Dynasty.

196 BCE
Exams for entry to official posts are introduced, developing the civil service.

166 BCE
Up to 140,000 Xiongnu horsemen raid deep into China.

141–87 BCE
Long reign of Wudi, great-grandson of Gaodi.

133 BCE
Emperor Wudi sends 300,000 troops into Xiongnu territory.

119–117 BCE
Iron and salt become state monopolies.

117–115 BCE
Han conquer the western Gansu corridor and build a new wall to protect it.

104–102 BCE
Chinese army crosses the Pamir Mountains and defeats Ferghana.

c. 100 BCE
Sima Qian (145–c. 85 BCE) writes the Shiji, a historical record of China.

2 CE
A census counts 59.6 million people in the empire.

7–9 CE
Reign of Ruzi, aged two when he succeeds to the imperial title.

The Western Han Dynasty

When the Qin official, Liu Bang, defeated his rivals and declared himself Emperor Gaodi in 202 BCE, he took the dynastic title of Han. The name came from the old kingdom that had been conquered by the Qin 28 years earlier. The new Han capital, Changan (modern-day Xian), was on the banks of the Wei River near Xianyang. The so-called Western Han Dynasty ruled uninterrupted for more than 200 years, and during this time the Chinese took up contact with the west, along the famous Silk Road.

Royal Burial

The Han people saw the soul as having two aspects. When a person died, the lighter aspect would go up to the clouds and perhaps join the immortals, while the heavier aspect stayed in the earthly grave. From about 140 BCE, the Han began building tombs in the style of dwellings, often digging them out of cliffs. High-ranking deceased were surrounded by pieces of jade, which were believed to help the soul live forever.

Liu Sheng, son of Emperor Jingdi (reigned 157–141 BCE), and his consort were buried about 113 BCE in suits made from jade plates fastened with gold wire. Their rock-cut tomb included stables, storerooms, and a bathroom.

Han soldiers had to defend their empire against attacks by groups of Xiongnu warriors from the steppes of central Asia and Mongolia. In this scene, Xiongnu horsemen mount a surprise attack on the Great Wall.

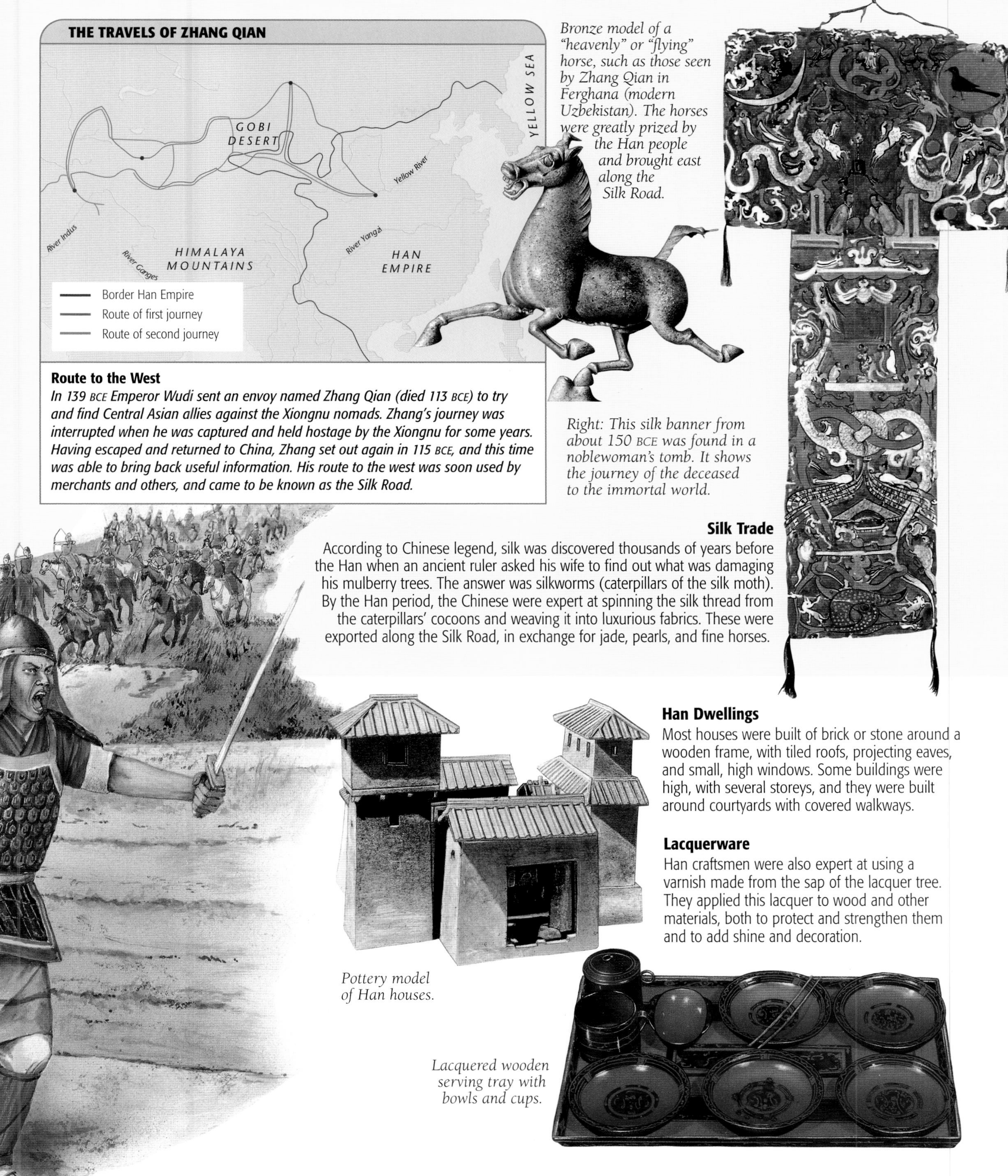

Route to the West

In 139 BCE Emperor Wudi sent an envoy named Zhang Qian (died 113 BCE) to try and find Central Asian allies against the Xiongnu nomads. Zhang's journey was interrupted when he was captured and held hostage by the Xiongnu for some years. Having escaped and returned to China, Zhang set out again in 115 BCE, and this time was able to bring back useful information. His route to the west was soon used by merchants and others, and came to be known as the Silk Road.

Bronze model of a "heavenly" or "flying" horse, such as those seen by Zhang Qian in Ferghana (modern Uzbekistan). The horses were greatly prized by the Han people and brought east along the Silk Road.

Right: This silk banner from about 150 BCE was found in a noblewoman's tomb. It shows the journey of the deceased to the immortal world.

Silk Trade

According to Chinese legend, silk was discovered thousands of years before the Han when an ancient ruler asked his wife to find out what was damaging his mulberry trees. The answer was silkworms (caterpillars of the silk moth). By the Han period, the Chinese were expert at spinning the silk thread from the caterpillars' cocoons and weaving it into luxurious fabrics. These were exported along the Silk Road, in exchange for jade, pearls, and fine horses.

Han Dwellings

Most houses were built of brick or stone around a wooden frame, with tiled roofs, projecting eaves, and small, high windows. Some buildings were high, with several storeys, and they were built around courtyards with covered walkways.

Lacquerware

Han craftsmen were also expert at using a varnish made from the sap of the lacquer tree. They applied this lacquer to wood and other materials, both to protect and strengthen them and to add shine and decoration.

Pottery model of Han houses.

Lacquered wooden serving tray with bowls and cups.

Wang Mang

In 9 CE a distant relative of the imperial Liu family took over from the 4-year-old Ruzi and declared himself emperor. Wang Mang named his dynasty Xin (meaning "New"), but the founder was to be the only Xin emperor. During his reign he attacked the privileges of wealthy landowners and tried to abolish private slave-ownership, but met with great opposition.

Rebellion

Rebel groups rose up against the rule of Wang Mang, and the emperor received no help from the wealthy classes. In 23 CE there was fighting in the streets of Changan, and rebels broke through to the imperial palace. Wang Mang and his attendants were killed.

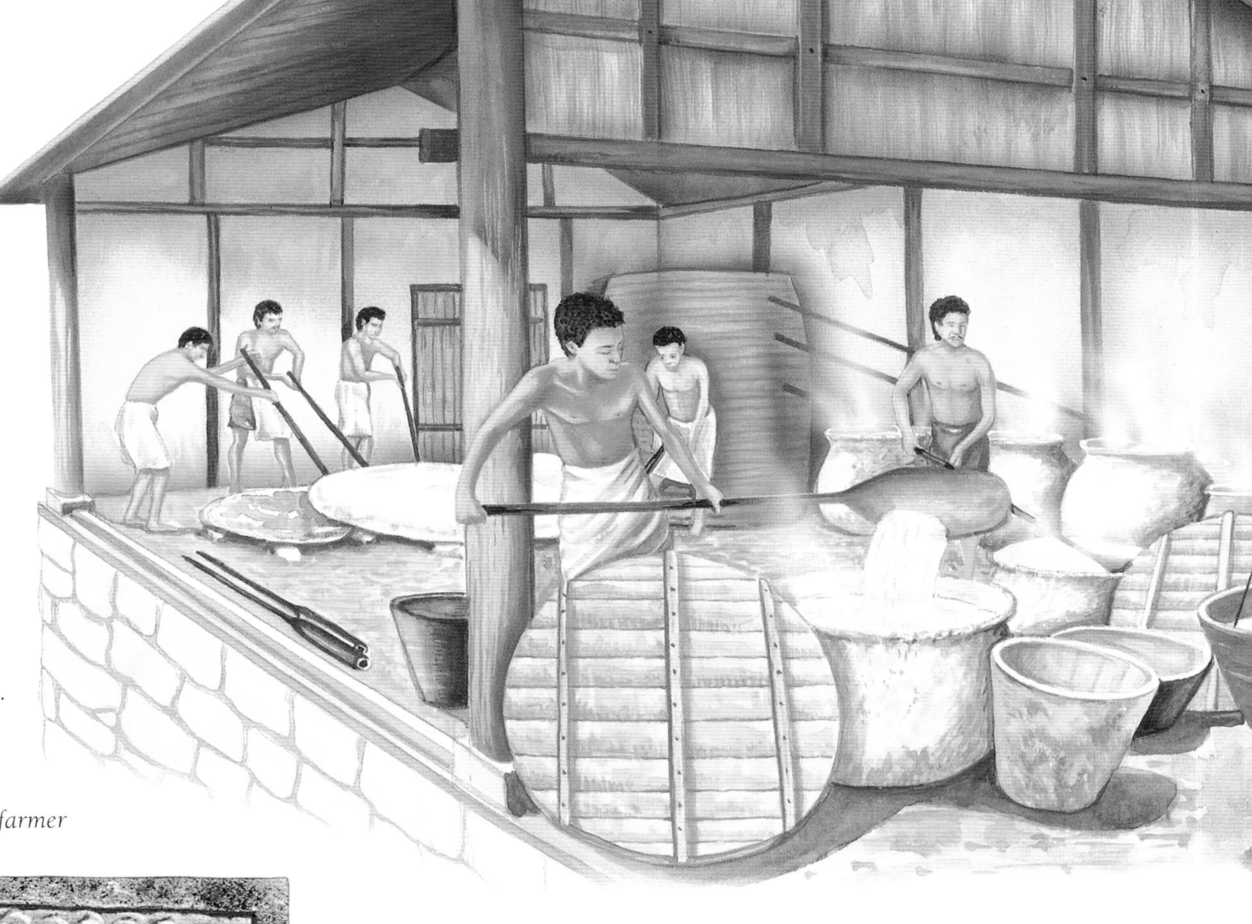

Stone relief showing a Han farmer using an ox-drawn plow.

The Eastern Han Dynasty

For a period of 16 years after 9 CE, the rule of the Han Dynasty was interrupted by rebellion, civil war, and the reign of Xin emperor Wang Mang. When Han power had been regained, 12 emperors of the so-called Eastern Han Dynasty ruled for almost 200 years. During this period government was less centralized, as farming methods improved, trade flourished, and merchants and landowners grew rich and powerful. Power struggles at court eventually weakened the empire.

Xin dynasty tortoise-topped seal and its imprint.

Salt Wells

Salt was important for preserving meat and fish, and in Han times people developed new methods of obtaining it. Around the area of Zigong, north of the Yangzi, workers sank wells using percussion drills—pointed tools that were dropped or hammered down bamboo tubes—to recover brine. The liquid was boiled in large vats, leaving behind high-quality salt.

At the salt well, tall wooden derricks were put up as a framework to support the drill. Natural gas was burned to boil the brine.

Moving East and South

The city of Changan was ruined during the rebellion and civil war that followed, and Han emperor Guang Wudi moved the capital east to Luoyang in the lower Yellow River Valley. Luoyang was much smaller than Changan and soon became very crowded. Though imperial power was in the east during this period, there was also a great movement of the population towards the south. In the Yangzi Valley, irrigation schemes meant that rice production increased dramatically.

This bronze standard measure, introduced by Wang Mang, has five separate measuring parts.

EASTERN HAN

9–25 CE
Reign of Wang Mang, who founds the Xin ("new") dynasty.

11 CE
Yellow River changes course and causes disastrous floods.

25–57 CE
Reign of Liu Xiu, a descendant of earlier Han emperor Jingdi, as Guang Wudi ("Shining Martial Emperor").

25–220 CE
Eastern (or Later) Han period; capital moved to the east (Luoyang).

c. 100 CE
First Chinese dictionary is compiled, explaining more than 9,000 characters.

c. 105 CE
Paper comes into use.

126 CE
Peasant revolts against landowners.

150 CE
Buddhism reaches China.

184 CE
Uprising by the Taoist Yellow Turban rebel group.

189–220 CE
Reign of the last Han emperor, Xiandi.

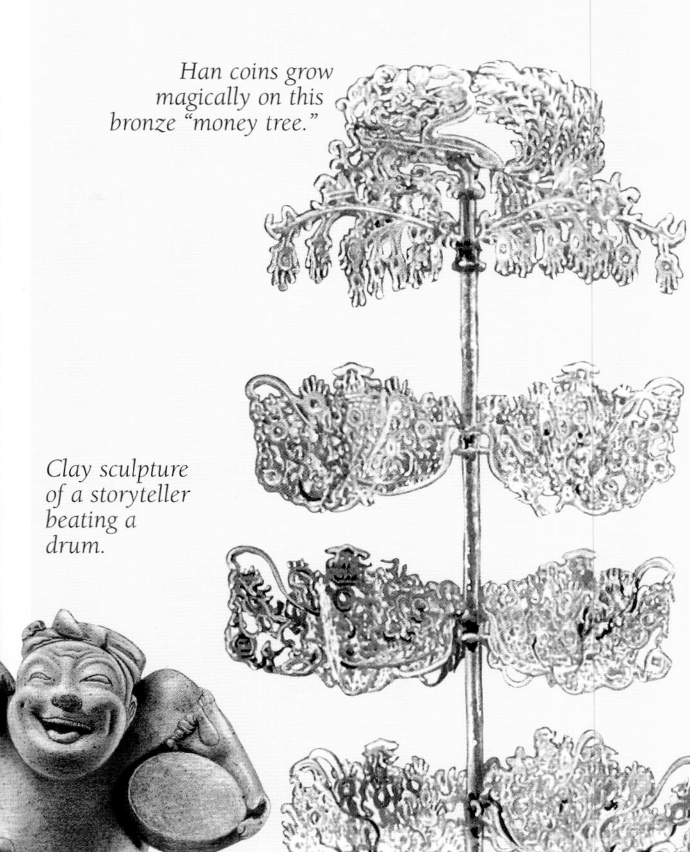

Han coins grow magically on this bronze "money tree."

Clay sculpture of a storyteller beating a drum.

Decline of the Han

During the reign of Huandi (146–168), there were many natural disasters—floods, earthquakes, plagues of locusts, drought, and resulting famine. Over the next 50 years the Han Dynasty lost power, as their administration became corrupt. Provincial officials gained power, rivalry between imperial relatives and the court's eunuchs led to violence, and eventually regional warlords had more authority than the emperor. In 220 CE the last Han emperor handed over power.

Chinese Civilization

Ancient Chinese rulers were seen as passing on the "mandate of heaven," or divine authority, through their sons to their descendants and future dynasties. The empire's subjects were divided into orderly classes according to Confucian tradition, with the majority working on the land, and a new element was added with the introduction of Buddhist culture. Despite the many battles, civil wars and periods of disunity, the resulting Chinese civilization was highly successful, producing great scientists, scholars, craftsmen, and artists.

Agriculture

The ancient Chinese economy was based on agriculture. Farming families had high status in theory, because they were so important to the empire, but they had very hard lives. Peasants paid a large part of their earnings to rich landowners or to the state in taxes. In the dry north, where the land was difficult to work, there were smaller farms and families looked after themselves. In the more fertile south, families worked for others on larger farming estates.

These hard-working men and women are shown bringing in the rice harvest.

Confucian Society

According to the Confucian view of the world that ruled after the 5th century BCE, society could be divided into four main groups. At the top were educated scholars, nobles and landowners; next came hard-working peasants; third were skilled workers and craftsmen; and at the bottom of the social scale were merchants. This scale was based on the importance of individuals to the whole population.

Confucius taught the importance of respect for parents and the family. This wicker basket of the Eastern Han period is painted with scenes of men showing respect for their parents.

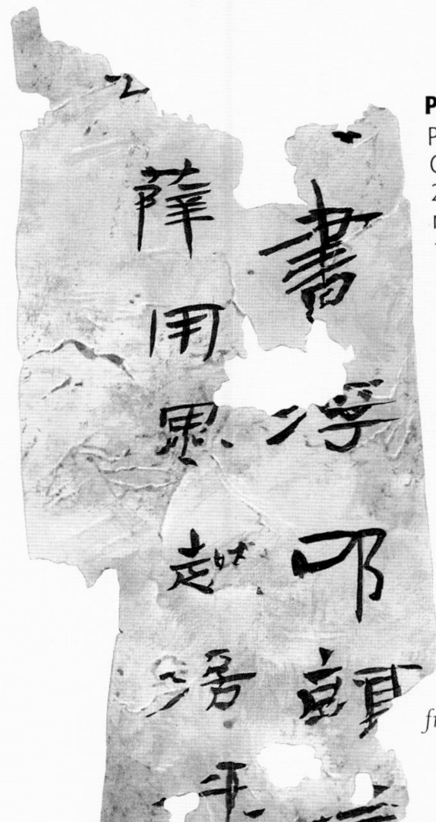

Papermaking

Paper was invented in ancient China, probably during the 2nd century BCE, when it was made from hemp and other fibres. Before that texts were written on strips of wood or bamboo, and also on silk. In 105 CE the invention of paper was officially reported to the emperor, and after that date papermakers used the bark of certain plants to make paper that was stronger and finer. The Chinese kept the art of papermaking a secret for several centuries.

A fragment of paper from the 2nd century CE.

Board used to play liubo, *an entertaining game which was sometimes played to predict the future.*

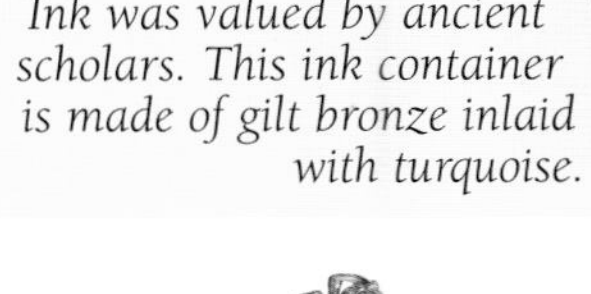

Ink was valued by ancient scholars. This ink container is made of gilt bronze inlaid with turquoise.

Trade

Though they were supposedly at the bottom of the social scale, merchants were successful and became rich. They used a growing network of roads and canals to move goods within the empire. To the west, the desert routes of the Silk Road linked oases and trading settlements all the way to central Asia and beyond. Individual merchants did not accompany their caravans the whole way, but simply took their goods to the next stage, where they sold or exchanged them.

Science and Technology

Astronomy was an early science in China, and ancient astronomers carved a detailed star chart of the heavens on a stone mound in about 3000 BCE. Later scholars studied mathematics and medicine, including forms of acupuncture that are still used today. Scientists also made many practical inventions, such as the wheelbarrow in the 2nd century CE.

This seismoscope, invented by a Chinese astronomer in 132 CE, warned of earthquakes and their location. An Earth tremor would cause a dragon to drop a bronze ball into a waiting toad's mouth.

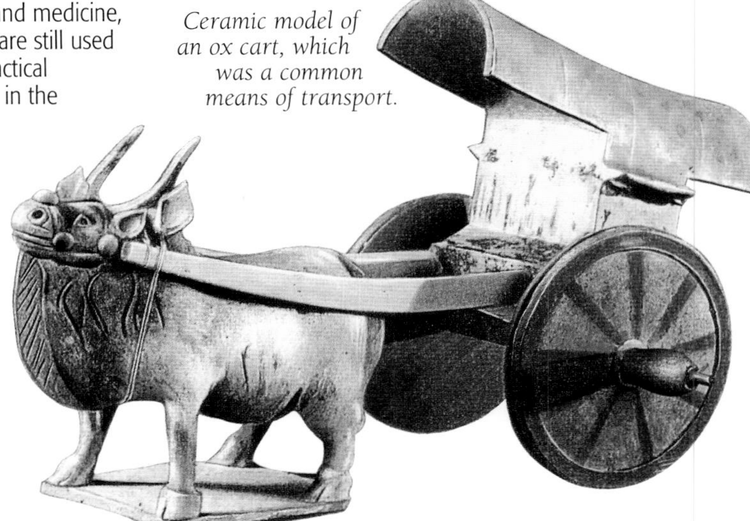

Ceramic model of an ox cart, which was a common means of transport.

PERIOD OF DISUNION

220–280 CE
The Three Kingdoms period (220–265 Wei, 221–263 Shu, 222–280 Wu).

265–589 CE
The Period of Disunion.

265–316 CE
Reign of the Western Jin Dynasty.

c. 280 CE
Wudi (reigned 265–289) collects an imperial library of more than 30,000 volumes in Luoyang.

310 CE
An army of Huns sweeps across the north-east and kills more than 100,000 Chinese.

317–419 CE
Reign of the Eastern Jin Dynasty.

365–427 CE
Life of great poet Tao Yuanming.

381 CE
Eastern Jin emperor Xiao Wudi (reigned 373–396) becomes a Buddhist and fills his palace with monks.

386–581 CE
Period of the Northern Dynasties (Northern Wei, Qi and Xhou).

420–589 CE
Period of the Southern Dynasties (Liu Song, Qi, Liang and Chen), with capital at Jiankang (present-day Nanjing).

494 CE
Northern Wei capital moves from Pingcheng to Luoyang.

589 CE
China is reunified by Wendi (reigned 581–604), first emperor of the Sui Dynasty.

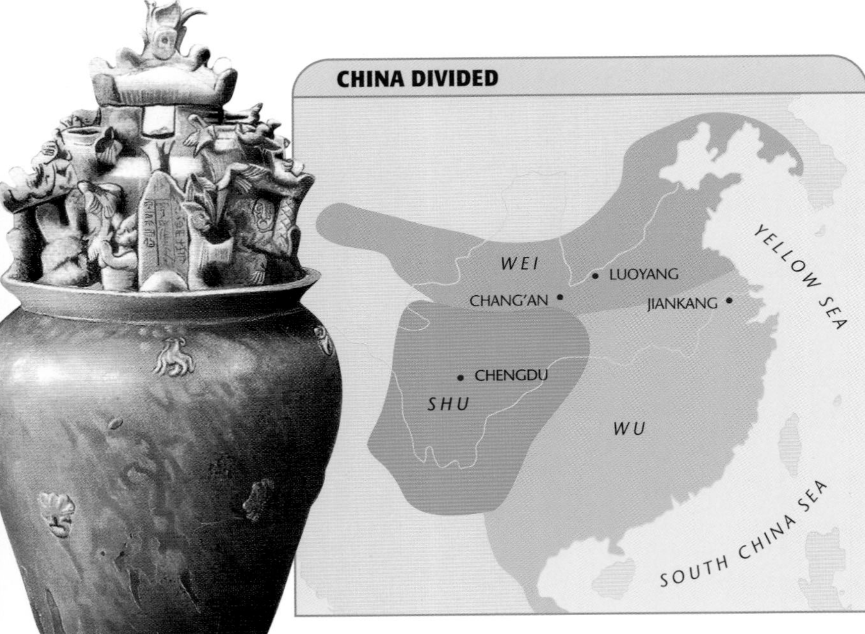

This pottery spirit jar has a miniature shrine on its lid in honor of clan ancestors.

The Three Kingdoms
The most powerful kingdom was Wei, which lay around the Yellow River Valley. Its first emperor was Wei Wendi (reigned 220–226), the son of the warlord Cao Cao (155–220 CE), protector of the last Han emperor. The western Shu Kingdom was the first to fall, when its capital, Chengdu, was captured by the Wei. The rulers of the large Wu Kingdom, to the south, had no historic links to the Han clan. Chinese historians generally regard the Wei as the official imperial line.

The Period of Disunion

After the collapse of the Eastern Han Dynasty, China was first divided into three kingdoms. Threats from steppe nomads continued in the north, and they eventually united under northern dynasties, though these are not recognised by Chinese historians. In the south, a series of dynasties reigned over a region where calligraphy, painting and literature flourished. China was finally reunited in 589 CE under another new dynasty, the Sui.

The Jin Dynasties

In 265 CE the Wei throne was taken by one of the kingdom's generals, Wudi (reigned 265–289 CE), who founded the Western Jin Dynasty. Fifteen years later, the Wu Kingdom was also defeated and the Western Jin emperor, Wudi, briefly reunited China. After conflicts within the imperial family and many attacks by northern steppe tribes, including the sacking of Luoyang and Changan, Jin leaders fled south-east. In 317 CE Yuandi (reigned 317–322 CE) established the Eastern Jin Dynasty, with its court at Jiankang.

Spread of Buddhism

Buddhist beliefs and practices spread throughout the Chinese region during this period. People paid less attention to traditional Confucian views of society, and by the 4th century CE Buddhism was the dominant religion. Buddhist missionaries and merchants from India also brought ideas about sculpture and painting that had a great impact on Chinese artists.

Lion-shaped pottery lamp-holder from the Western Jin period.

This Chinese gilt-bronze Buddha, dating from 338 CE, was based on a formal Indian style.

Young ladies of the court were guided by an instructress who dictated the correct rules of behavior.

Life at Court

During the time of the Eastern Jin, there was a great flowering of the arts, especially around the capital Jiankang. At court and elsewhere, women were expected to behave with great decorum. As well as enjoying the company of the empress and secondary wives, the emperor surrounded himself with young women who were given the titles "honorable lady," "beautiful lady" or "chosen lady."

A court official wears the cylindrical hat of a noble courtier.

A 5th-century CE dragon-shaped jade pendant from southern China. Since the north was threatened by invasion of foreigners, the cultural center of China moved to the south.

North and South

In the late 4th century CE nomadic people of Turkic origin took over the entire northern region. Their rule has come to be known as the Northern Dynasties period. In the south, the first of the so-called Southern Dynasties—the Liu Song—took over from the Jin and continued the Han tradition. By the end of the 5th century CE, the non-Han northern rulers had taken up much of traditional Chinese culture.

KOREA

c. 7000 BCE
The earliest known Korean pottery is made.

c. 5000 BCE
Introduction of comb-pattern pottery.

2333 BCE
Traditional date of the founding of Choson by legendary Tangun.

c. 1500–1000 BCE
Rice cultivation is introduced, probably from China; millet and barley are also cultivated.

c. 1000 BCE
Bronze technology reaches Korea from China.

c. 900 BCE
More elaborate burial practices, including dolmens.

c. 400 BCE
Iron comes into use.

108 BCE
Han invasion; Chinese written language is introduced to Korea through Lelang.

57 BCE–668 CE
Traditional dates of the Three Kingdoms period.

57 BCE
Traditional date of founding of Silla by Pak Hyokkose.

37 BCE
Traditional date of founding of Koguryo by Chu-mong.

18 BCE
Traditional date of founding of Paekche by Onjo.

313 CE
Koguryo conquers Chinese Lelang and takes control of northern Korea.

372 CE
Buddhism is introduced to Koguryo by a Chinese monk.

The Founding Legend

According to legend, the first Korean ruler was Tangun, who became king of Choson in 2333 BCE. Grandson of the creator god Hwanin, he was the son of divine King Hwanung and a she-bear that had magically turned into a woman. There are several different versions of the legend, which is important to many Koreans because it links their state with a heavenly origin.

This table-type dolmen stands about 8 feet (2.5 m) high.

Dolmens

As in other parts of the world, simple stone structures were placed over many burials in ancient Korea. These tomb structures, called dolmens, were of different types. In the north, many were of the table type, with a large capstone raised high off the ground. In the south, the capstone often rested on smaller stones at ground level. The dolmens may have been seen as status symbols.

An illustration of one version of the legend of Tangun, which includes a tiger with the bear.

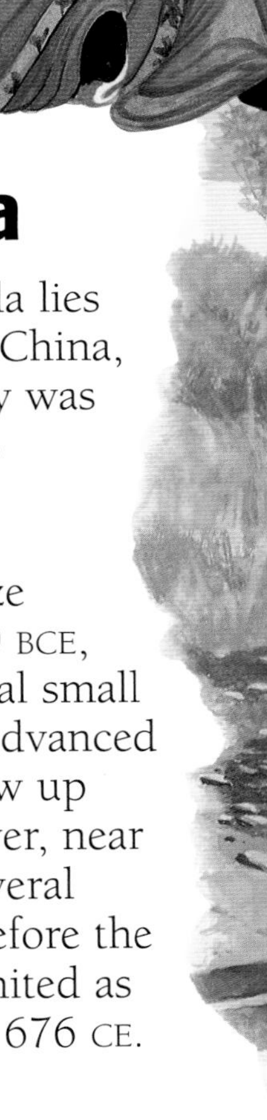

Ancient Korea

The Korean peninsula lies to the northeast of China, and its early history was greatly influenced by its Chinese neighbors. In ancient times, and especially after its Bronze Age began around 1000 BCE, the peninsula had several small tribal states. The most advanced was Choson, which grew up around the Taedong River, near modern Pyongyang. Several other states emerged, before the peninsula was finally united as the Kingdom of Silla in 676 CE.

Comb-Pattern Pottery

Around 7,000 years ago, the region's potters were putting together coils of clay to make wide-mouthed storage and cooking vessels with a pointed or round base. Before firing the pots, they decorated the damp clay with patterns of diagonal lines. They may have used a comb-like tool to achieve this.

This large comb-pattern pot, dating from about 3500 BCE, was found near the River Han in modern-day Seoul.

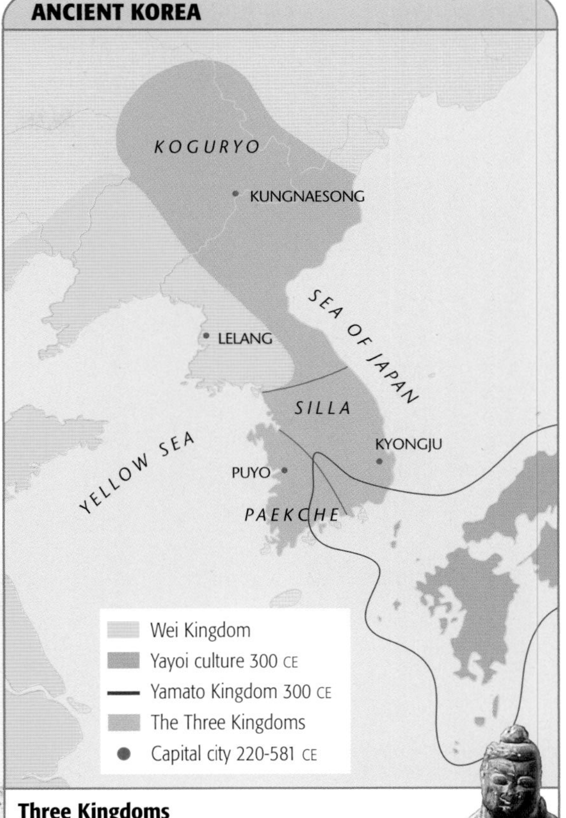

Underfloor Heating

In ancient times (perhaps as early as the 4th century BCE), the Koreans began heating their wooden houses with an ingenious underfloor system. This was called *ondol*, meaning "warm stone." It worked by directing hot air and smoke from a wood-burning stove through pipes beneath the floor, before releasing them through outdoor chimneys. Today, the Korean *ondol* system works by pumping hot water through underfloor pipes.

Three Kingdoms

Beginning in the 1st century CE (though the traditional dates are much earlier), Korean tribes came together to form the kingdoms of Koguryo, Paekche, and Silla. This period in Korean history is known as the Three Kingdoms. The northern kingdom of Koguryo was the largest, and its king built a strong army, which eventually drove the Chinese from Lelang. All three kingdoms developed advanced cultures.

Soft stone Buddha from Paekche. Buddhism was introduced to the Three Kingdoms during the 4th century CE.

Han Invasion

In 108 BCE, during the reign of the Han emperor Wudi (see pages 180–182), the Chinese invaded and conquered much of the Korean peninsula. The Chinese organized their new territory into four military districts. Korean tribesmen succeeded in winning back three of these districts by 75 BCE, but the fourth Chinese colony, called Lelang (or Luolang), lasted for over 400 years.

Reconstruction of ironworking in Korea after the Han invasion. With a longer tradition of ironworking, the Chinese helped improve Korean technology.

Early Japan

The ancient Japanese are credited with making the world's first pottery, more than 12,000 years ago. A hunter-gatherer culture, called Jomon after its style of pottery, developed near the coast. This flourished for thousands of years, until the skills of rice-growing and ironworking were introduced from the Asian mainland and changed ways of life. People of the Yayoi culture lived in settled farming villages, which in time came to be controlled by local chieftains.

EARLY JAPAN

c. 10,500 BCE
The first pottery is made in Japan (earliest in the world).

c. 10,500–400 BCE
The Jomon period.

c. 2000 BCE
Peak of the Jomon culture.

660 BCE
Traditional date for the founding of Japan by the legendary first emperor, Jimmu Tennō.

c. 500 BCE
Wet-rice agriculture is introduced.

c. 300 BCE–300 CE
Yayoi period; pottery is less decorated and more practical.

c. 300 BCE
Bronze and iron weapons are introduced.

57 CE
Japanese messengers travel to the Han court in China.

300 CE
Spread of wet-rice agriculture throughout Japan.

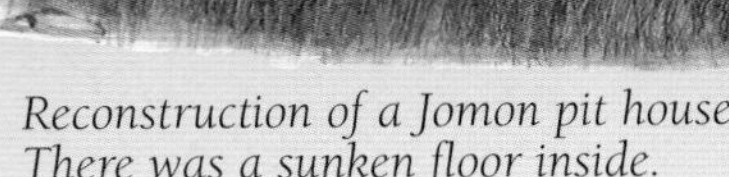

Reconstruction of a Jomon pit house. There was a sunken floor inside.

Early Settlements

People of the early Jomon culture lived in pit houses clustered together in groups, probably in a circle. Early settlements may have been made up of about 50 people. The floor of each dwelling was dug into the ground, and a wooden framework supported walls and roof. People lived by hunting and gathering, especially by fishing and shellfish-collecting near the coast.

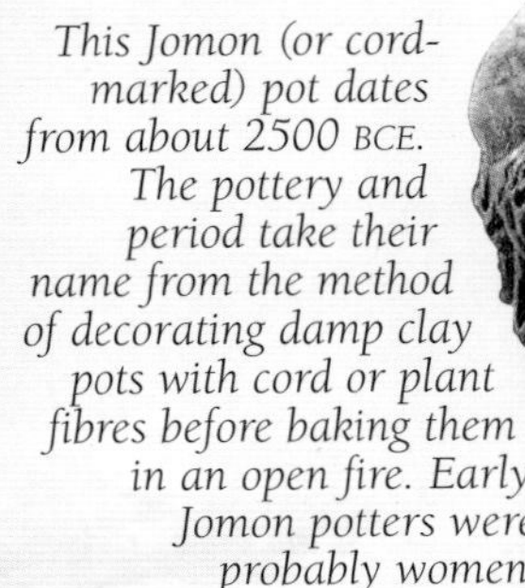

This Jomon (or cord-marked) pot dates from about 2500 BCE. The pottery and period take their name from the method of decorating damp clay pots with cord or plant fibres before baking them in an open fire. Early Jomon potters were probably women.

Shinto

People of the Jomon culture lived close to nature and had great respect for natural forms and forces. Their beliefs contributed to the ancient Japanese religion of Shinto, which means the "way of the gods." These gods were the spirits of nature, such as the forces present in animals, plants, mountains, seas, storms, and earthquakes. Shinto had no founder or scriptures. Its followers saw the legendary first emperor, Jimmu Tennō, as a descendant of the sun goddess Amaterasu.

Mount Fuji, a dormant volcano and the highest mountain in Japan, has always been sacred to the followers of Shinto.

Burial Jars

During the Yayoi period, clay jars were used for burials. Children were usually placed in a single jar, while adults were buried in large paired jars that were sealed together with clay. Graves were marked by mounds of earth or stone slabs, and many were placed close together in large cemeteries. Precious objects were placed in or near some jar burials.

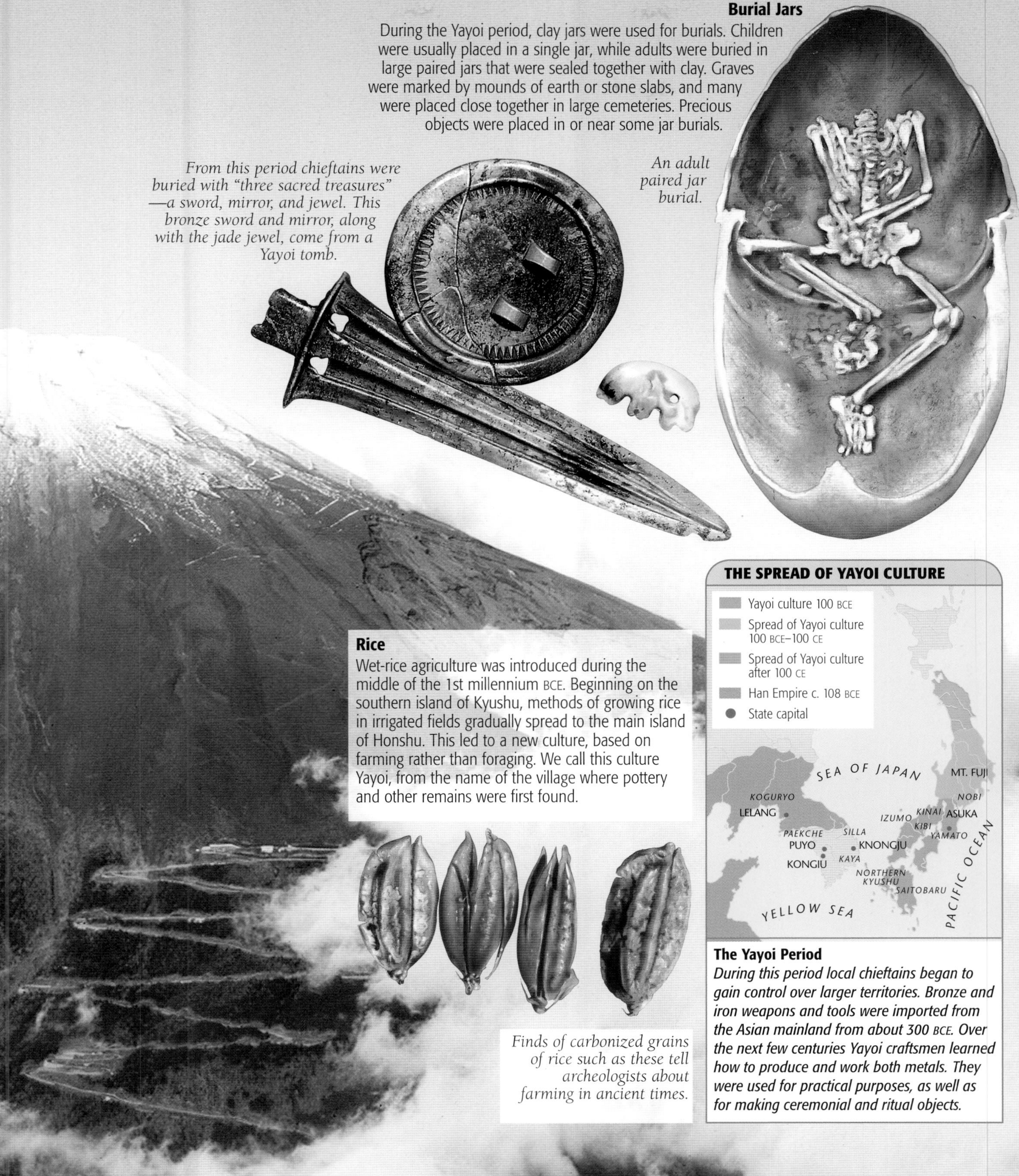

From this period chieftains were buried with "three sacred treasures" —a sword, mirror, and jewel. This bronze sword and mirror, along with the jade jewel, come from a Yayoi tomb.

An adult paired jar burial.

Rice

Wet-rice agriculture was introduced during the middle of the 1st millennium BCE. Beginning on the southern island of Kyushu, methods of growing rice in irrigated fields gradually spread to the main island of Honshu. This led to a new culture, based on farming rather than foraging. We call this culture Yayoi, from the name of the village where pottery and other remains were first found.

Finds of carbonized grains of rice such as these tell archeologists about farming in ancient times.

The Yayoi Period

During this period local chieftains began to gain control over larger territories. Bronze and iron weapons and tools were imported from the Asian mainland from about 300 BCE. Over the next few centuries Yayoi craftsmen learned how to produce and work both metals. They were used for practical purposes, as well as for making ceremonial and ritual objects.

The Daisen burial mound in the city of Sakai. This keyhole-shaped mound is 1,594 feet (486 m) long.

Later version of a page from the Kojiki or "Record of Ancient Matters." This was originally written in 712 CE using Chinese characters with added Japanese kana symbols.

This haniwa takes the form of a young soldier kneeling in respect. These pottery figures may have been seen as military guardians for the deceased.

Burial Mounds

Mound-covered tombs became more elaborate during this period. By the 5th century CE the largest had a keyhole-shaped mound, surrounded by rows of small pottery objects (called *haniwa*) and one or more moats. Beneath the mound was a stone-lined burial chamber with a stone sarcophagus, as well as swords and other grave goods.

Chinese Influence

Early in the 5th century CE, the Chinese system of pictographic writing was brought to Japan from Korea. The Japanese adopted the Chinese system, which they called *kanji* and which was used by courtiers and other educated people. A few centuries later, a system of Japanese pronunciation symbols was added, called *kana*.

The Kofun Period

The period of Japanese history from the 4th to the 6th century CE is known as the Kofun period. The name comes from the distinctive large burial mounds (*kofun*, or "old tombs," in Japanese). During this period, powerful clans began to dominate others and form states or kingdoms. The Yamato Kingdom, named after a region on the Nara plain of Honshu, became the most powerful and wealthy state. The dominant Yamato clan took control over a large area and founded the imperial line of Japan.

THE KOFUN PERIOD

c. 250 CE
The earliest burial mounds are built.

c. 300 CE
Beginning of the Kofun period; formation of the Yamato state.

c. 400 CE
Chinese system of writing arrives in Japan; high-fired grey pottery is introduced from Korea.

c. 500 CE
The Yamato Kingdom becomes most powerful and dominates all others.

552 CE
Buddhist missionaries arrive from Korea.

Ruling Clans

Kofun society was based on clans. Every family belonged to its own clan, which was further broken down into smaller groups who specialized in various occupations. Some groups were farmers or hunters, others were potters or metalworkers, and the most important groups worked for and protected the clan rulers.

This decorative vessel, with its own pottery stand, was found at a Kofun burial mound. It may have been used in rituals conducted in front of the tomb.

Introduction of Buddhism

In 552 CE, the ruler of the Korean kingdom of Paekche sent Buddhist missionaries to the court of the Yamato ruler as a gesture of friendship. Buddhism had reached Korea 180 years earlier. Buddhist beliefs, customs, and art styles quickly spread, despite some opposition from followers of traditional Shinto.

This group of bronze Buddhist statues was made near Nara in the early 7th century CE.

Warfare

Chinese documents of the period tell of many chieftains and warfare among them in Japan. There is also evidence that horse-riding warriors invaded from Korea in the 4th century CE. The local rulers of the Kofun period were certainly powerful in military terms, with armored warriors who carried swords and other iron weapons.

Warriors on the charge. Armies such as this helped clan rulers extend their control over neighboring groups, and their horses were a valued possession.

EARLY SOUTHEAST ASIA

c. 6000 BCE
The first farming settlements; the first pottery on the mainland.

c. 2500 BCE
The first pottery and domesticated animals on the islands.

c. 2000 BCE
Use of bronze in Thailand; Phung Nyugen culture with rice cultivation in the Red River Valley, Vietnam.

1500–1000 BCE
Dong Dau bronze-working culture in Vietnam.

1000–500 BCE
Go Mun bronze-working culture in Vietnam.

c. 700 BCE
The first use of iron in the region.

700 BCE
Beginnings of Dong Son bronze and iron-working culture in Vietnam.

c. 300 BCE
Early form of writing, based on Sanskrit from India, is used in Cambodia.

250 BCE
The first walled settlements (in Vietnam).

c. 200 BCE
Water buffalo used as a draught animal.

SOUTHEAST ASIA IN PREHISTORY

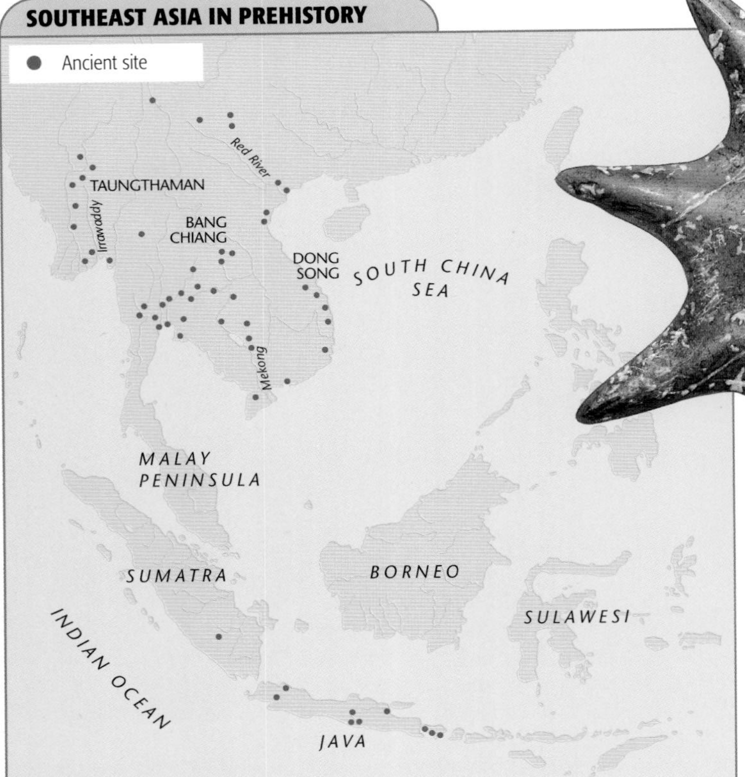

Archeological Sites
In prehistoric times there were large movements of people throughout the region, as increasing populations looked for fresh sources of food. This map shows some of the important archeological sites of Southeast Asia. Most of the interesting discoveries on the mainland of Myanmar, Thailand, and Vietnam (at Taungthaman, Bang Chang, and Dong Song) were first made during the 20th century.

Stone bracelet from a burial site at Taungthaman, beside the River Irrawaddy.

Stone Age Migration
We believe that the first farmers of the region came from tribal groups that migrated south from China down great rivers such as the Irrawaddy. Some of these groups may have carried on their nomadic hunting and gathering way of life, while others settled in the river valleys of present-day Myanmar and developed methods of cultivating rice. In the settlements they made elaborate stone tools and built a strong farming culture.

Red spiral patterns decorate this pot from Ban Chiang, which dates from around 300 BCE.

Civilizations of Southeast Asia

As in other parts of the world, the early people of the Southeast Asian mainland and islands used stone to make increasingly sophisticated tools and weapons. Some of those who settled in the fertile river valleys began making bronze, and its use spread throughout the region. Early bronze drums have been found on the islands of Sumatra and Borneo, as well as in the modern mainland countries and southern China. Pottery was another early development.

Ban Chiang
Decorative pottery, bronze objects, and elaborate burial offerings have been found at the settlement of Ban Chiang, in the northeast of present-day Thailand. The settlement was beside a tributary of the Mekong River, where people were smelting and casting bronze from about 2000 BCE. Many historians believe that this technology developed separately in the region rather than being introduced from elsewhere.

A carved megalith found on an island off Sumatra, Indonesia.

This bronze Dong Son model drum dates from some time after 300 BCE. It represents larger bronze drums that may have been played at religious ceremonies, to rally men for battle, or even to encourage rain.

This hollowed-log coffin dates from the Dong Son period. The deceased was buried with a spear, axe heads, a bamboo ladle, and pottery vessel at his feet, all for use in the afterlife.

Bronze Dong Son lamp-holder in the form of a kneeling man with a bowl.

Dong Son Culture

The settlement of Dong Son, on the plain south of the Red River Valley (and present-day Hanoi) in northern Vietnam, has given its name to a culture of the late Bronze Age and early Iron Age. Most of the tools and weapons found at the site and in the surrounding region were made of bronze. Burial places contained ritual and personal objects such as ceremonial daggers, buckles, musical instruments, and drums.

Trade with India

Iron appeared in the region around 700 BCE, and many experts believe that it was worked locally. However, there is evidence that items such as beads of glass, agate, and carnelian were acquired by trade from India, which leads some historians to think that the earliest iron objects appeared in the same way.

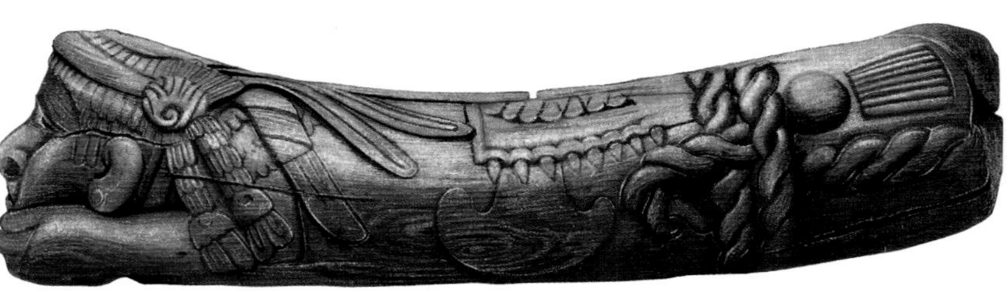

Aztec ceremonies included dancing and music. This drum, carved from a hollow log, depicts a person in ornamental costume, including a tassled headdress adorned with feathers.

The first people reached North America about 18,000 years ago, crossing the Bering land bridge which connected the continent to Asia. Over the centuries various cultures developed throughout the continent. Native Americans in the north were hunters and gatherers, and some groups, living in more hospitable lands, became farmers. Groups continued to migrate, and by 3600 BCE hunter-gatherers began cultivating crops in Central America. Here the Olmecs, Zapotecs, and Maya flourished, and the Mixtecs, Toltecs, and Aztecs built cities. In South America the Chavin, Nasca, and Moche cultures paved the way for the great Inca civilization in the Andes Mountains.

In Southeast Asia there were large migrations. Seafaring peoples reached the Australian continent and the western Pacific islands about 40,000 years ago. The Aborigines, the native people of Australia, developed into diverse cultural groups, as did the peoples of the Pacific Islands. In about 1200 CE, New Zealand was settled by the Maori, who were farmers and fierce warriors. All these cultures were destined to change when the first European navigators reached these lands.

	60,000 years ago	**40,000 years ago**	**8000 BCE**	**6000 BCE**
NATIVE AMERICANS OF THE NORTH		The Bering land bridge connects North America to the Siberian landmass.	Dogs are used as pack animals to pull sleds in the Arctic. Archaic cultures are established in the Northwest Coast.	Chumash culture develops in California.
OLMECS, ZAPOTECS, AND MAYA				
MIXTECS, TOLTECS, AND AZTECS				
NASCA AND MOCHE CULTURE AND INCA				
ABORIGINES		People migrating from Asia become the first settlers of Australia.		
PEOPLES OF THE PACIFIC AND THE MAORI	The first people sail from Southeast Asia to the landmass of New Guinea.	Sailors from northern New Guinea settle in the Solomon Islands.		

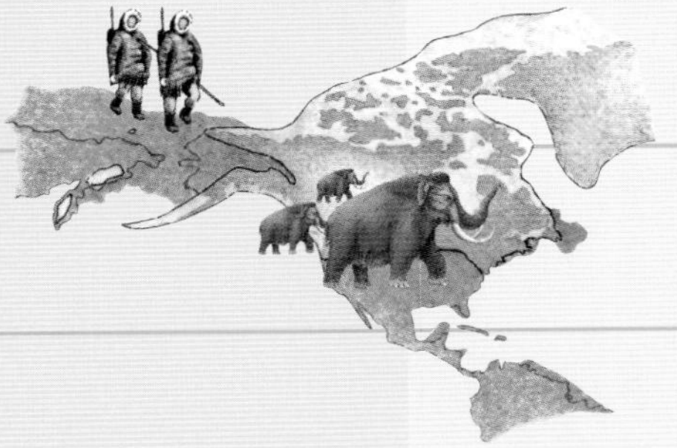

The Americas and the Pacific

Native Americans of the Northwest Coast carved totem poles from tall trees. They were erected to serve as clan symbols, with carvings of animals such as birds and sea creatures.

4000 BCE	2000 BCE	1 CE	600 CE	1200 CE
Haida culture develops in present-day Canada. Bison hunting begins on the Great Plains.	The Inuit become fishermen and hunt caribou. Small villages appear in the Southeast.		Pueblo people build villages in the Southwest.	Farmers on the Great Plains live in villages. Spanish explorers bring horses. Europeans arrive.
Maize is first cultivated in Meso-America.	Olmecs build Tres Zapotes. The Maya settle in the Yucatan Peninsula. The Zapotecs develop writing.	Tikal becomes the most powerful Maya center.		
		Pyramids are built at Teotihuacan.	The Veracruz culture is at its peak. The Mixtecs dominate southern Mexico. The Toltecs build their capital at Tula.	Aztecs build their capital, Tenochtitlan.
The first permanent settlements emerge in the Andean region.	Chavin culture emerges.	The Moche control the northern coastal region of Peru.		The Chimu civilization develops into an empire. Inca culture develops in the Valley of Cuzco. The Inca conquer the Chimu.
	The Aborigines acquire domesticated dogs from Indonesia and begin to use smaller stone tools.			
			People from Tahiti, the Marquesas Islands and other eastern Polynesian islands settle the Hawaiian Islands.	The Maori settle in New Zealand. The first European travels through Oceania.

Inhabitants of the North

THE ARCTIC AND THE SUB-ARCTIC

25,000 years ago
The Bering land bridge, connects mainland North America to the Siberian landmass.

18,000 years ago
Hunters from Siberia settle in North America.

8000 BCE
Dogs are used as pack animals to pull sleds.

c. 2000 BCE
The Inuit become fishermen and hunt caribou.

c. 800 BCE
Simple pottery is made in the Arctic.

c. 450 BCE
People make special wooden utensils.

c. 1500 CE
Europeans begin to explore Canada.

Native Americans in the north inhabited the forbidding land of the Arctic and Sub-Arctic regions, adapting to cold, prolonged darkness, and lack of vegetation. Using the few materials available to them, such as animal furs and ice, they developed the kayak, harpoon, igloo, and dog-sleds more than 2,500 years ago. The hunters of the Sub-Arctic region used wood, bone, and antlers to produce tools and weapons, and canoes and toboggans to transport people and goods across a landscape of forests, plains, rivers, and lakes.

Asian hunters pursued game such as mammoths into North America, crossing Beringia (where the Bering Strait now separates the two continents). From there they followed ice-free valleys south and east into the continent.

Settling North America

For much of the past two million years, the Bering Strait has been dry. Sea levels during the Ice Age were almost 300 feet (91 m) below those of today. About 25,000 years ago, a low-lying area called Beringia, or the Bering land bridge, emerged. This land bridge allowed Asian people to migrate into North America. The Bering land bridge remained passable for 11,000 years, at the end of which rising temperatures caused sea levels to rise, covering the land bridge once more.

Many igloos included a series of domes, with separate storage areas linked to living quarters by narrow passages. A pair of experienced builders could make an entire dome in less than two hours.

A Home of Snow

The Inuit of the central Arctic region developed ice and snow houses known as igloos. These were temporary houses built during the winter seal-hunting season. Men would cut blocks of ice and arrange them in a spiral fashion until a complete dome was made. Women and children filled in cracks inside and out. Alaskan Inuit built karmaks, dome-shaped houses with frames of driftwood or whalebone, covering them with sod. These homes were partly underground, providing extra insulation from the cold.

Lands of the Arctic and the Sub-arctic

The Arctic region, generally made up of flat, low-lying treeless land, is the northernmost region of the Earth. It includes modern-day northern Canada, the coast of Alaska, parts of Russia, Iceland, and Greenland. There is no real boundary between the Arctic and the Sub-arctic regions, but most agree that the northernmost tree line, of the Northern Forests, or the Sub-arctic, divides the two regions. The Sub-arctic region, which is characterized by many lakes, rivers, marshes, and forests, occupies most of modern-day Canada and Alaska.

The husky, a breed of dog that thrives in cold conditions, was the only animal domesticated by the Inuit. The dogs' keen sense of smell also helped Inuit hunters locate seals.

Dog Power

The Inuit of the Arctic region began building dog-sleds about 2,500 years ago. The best—and most lightweight—sleds had frames of driftwood, but local populations often had to use whalebones instead. Rolled and frozen seal-skin sometimes served as runners if wood and bones were in short supply. Depending on the size and weight of the sled, teams of between 6 and 16 huskies would pull it across the snow and ice.

Inuit women spent hours making and repairing clothing. A parka—lightweight, warm, and waterproof—was the ideal outer wear for seal-hunting populations.

Surviving in the North

Basic survival was a constant concern through the long Arctic winters with temperatures often averaging only -25° F (-32° C). The Inuit developed clothing that was both warm and waterproof. The basic outer garment was the parka (anorak), often made from strips of seal intestines. Seal-skins and caribou hides were also valuable materials for making trousers, mittens, and up to four layers of footwear.

This Yupik mask was made for use in dancing rituals. It represents the many spirit beings that can affect human lives.

The Spirit World

The barren lands of the Arctic and Sub-arctic regions were—to their inhabitants—full of spirits and demons. To deal with these supernatural forces, the Inuit developed a complex system of rituals and taboos. Inuit turned to shamans for advice and help in their struggle with the natural and spirit worlds. Shamans also helped people construct masks that depicted animals, spirits, or events.

THE NORTHWEST COAST AND THE PLATEAU

Northwest Coast
The Plateau
PACIFIC OCEAN
ROCKY MOUNTAINS
River Fraser
River Columbia
CASCADE RANGE
COAST MOUNTAINS

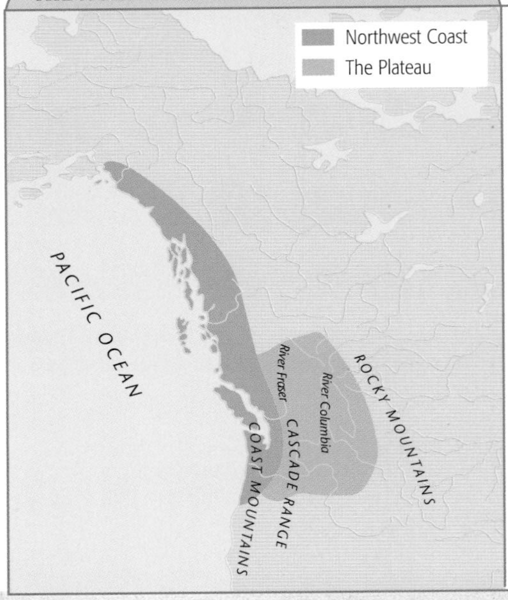

Lands of the Northwest Coast and the Plateau
The Northwest Coast is a long, narrow strip of land running down along the Pacific Ocean. It has many bays and inlets. The region has a mild, damp climate and frequent rain nourishes the abundant plant life. The Plateau is bordered by the Rocky Mountains to the east and the Cascade Range to the west. Two great rivers, the Columbia and the Fraser, run through the region which includes mountain forests, deep valleys, and large, open stretches of land.

Story-Telling

Storytellers recited tales relating to an enormously complicated mythology. Animals and fish, such as the salmon, figured heavily in these tales, which were often told during ceremonies. Listeners would be familiar with the Raven, a trickster who could either free human beings or bring about chaos. Tellers often wore masks relating to one of the characters. No two masks were the same and no storyteller ever told the whole story relating to the mask.

A wooden mask of the winter ceremonies representing the spirit of the Sun, made by the Bella Coola people of coastal British Columbia.

Potlatch guests arrive in a Haida canoe. Carved from a single cedar tree, a large canoe could hold up to 60 people. Such canoes were the mark of real wealth and power.

The Northwest Coast and the Plateau

Rich natural resources made hunting and fishing easy on the Northwest Coast bordering the Pacific Ocean and many peoples inhabited the region. People had time to build elaborate social systems. Craftsmen perfected the skills of working wood, while boatmen went in search of fish and even whales. But the preoccupation with wealth and social standing led to bitter rivalries and violent disputes among neighboring communities. The people of the Plateau, like those of the Northwest Coast, had plentiful sources of food, including great rivers and streams with an abundance of fish. The river systems of the Plateau facilitated trade and made cultural exchange with tribes of other regions possible.

Luxury Goods

The people of the Northwest Coast spent a lot of time making handicrafts. These goods were prized possessions and lay at the heart of a bustling trade. Many such goods were the result of long hours of manufacture. A Tlingit blanket, made from goat's wool and cedar-bark fiber, might take as long as six months to make.

A dancing shirt, woven from cedar-bark fiber and goat's wool, was one of the most prized goods a Tlingit could own. Designs depicted animal clan symbols.

A Display of Wealth

The woodcarvers of the Northwest Coast produced elaborately carved pieces that were either put to practical use or prized as decorative possessions. The wealthy and powerful accumulated many such goods, but they strengthened their social standing by giving them away or even destroying them. An important event such as a wedding was celebrated with a feast called *potlatch*. The host would give his prized goods to the assembled guests, ensuring his strong social position in the process.

The horn of a bighorn sheep, hunted by the Plateau peoples in the mountain forests, was used to make this decorative bowl.

A storage bag, made from hemp and maize husk, decorated with traditional geometric designs.

NORTHWEST COAST AND PLATEAU

c. 7700 BCE
Archaic cultures are established on the Northwest Coast.

c. 3500 BCE
Haida culture develops in present-day Canada.

c. 500 CE
Population increases on the Northwest Coast; elaborate ceremonies are developed.

1200–1300 CE
Permanent winter villages are established in the Plateau region.

Salmon were plentiful on the Northwest Coast, and they were important for both economic and religious reasons. People honored immortal men who had turned themselves into fish in order to feed humans.

Plateau Fishermen and Traders

Like the peoples of the Northwest Coast, the inhabitants of the Plateau were skilled fishermen. During the fishing season, from May to November, people lived beside the Columbia and Fraser rivers. They built weirs along the rivers where salmon swam upstream. Peoples of the Plateau also became great traders, taking advantage of the region's river systems to transport goods. They traded deer skins, bitterroot, hemp for making ropes, mats, and baskets.

California and the Southwest

California, a land rich with natural resources, plants, and animals, was home to many peoples who, although they spoke a great variety of languages and dialects, had much in common. They were skilled basket-weavers, using a variety of materials available from the land. The desert-like landscape of the Southwest can seem as inhospitable as the Arctic, yet this region saw many developments, including the rise of agriculture. There were many different cultures, from the Navajo farmers to the nomadic Apache, who were hunters and raiders.

CALIFORNIA AND THE SOUTHWEST

c. 5000 BCE
Cochise people in the Southwest cultivate vegetable crops. Chumash culture develops in California.

c. 3500 BCE
Craftsmen begin making animal figurines from twigs for ritual use.

c. 1000 BCE
Farmers in the Southwest begin to cultivate the staple crops–maize, beans, and squash.

c. 100 CE
Anasazi culture appears in the Southwest.

c. 200 CE
Cotton plant is cultivated.

c. 700 CE
Pueblo people build villages in the Southwest.

c. 1275 CE
Drought forces peoples in the Southwest to abandon villages.

c. 1600 CE
European missionaries establish themselves in Hopi areas.

CALIFORNIA AND THE SOUTHWEST

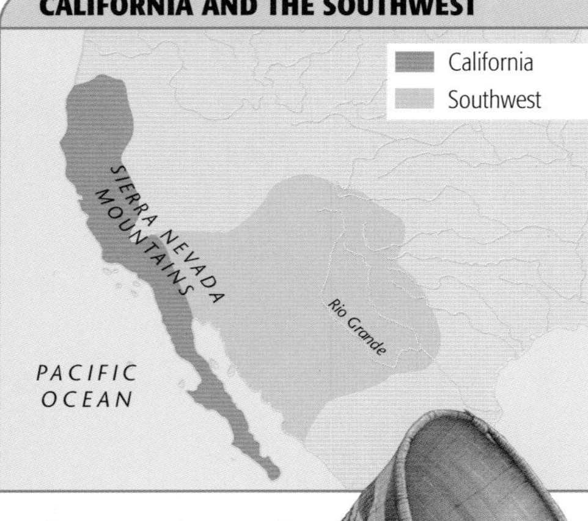

Peoples of California and the Southwest

The peoples of California were hunters and gatherers. The rich and varied land of the region, running along the Pacific coast, provided a huge variety of foods. Acorns, collected from oak trees, were the staple food for many peoples. The Sierra Nevada Mountains formed the eastern border, isolating the central Californians. The arid plateaus and desert lands of the Southwest were inhabited by a surprising number of peoples who made the change from hunting and gathering to farming. The Southwest also included fertile river valleys, like that of the Rio Grande, and vast grasslands.

Baskets were decorated with geometric designs. Large ones were used for gathering and carrying seeds.

Pomo Basketmakers

A group of small tribes, called Pomo, lived near the coast of northern California. Women of the Pomo tribes made fine baskets from a number of materials such as willow shoots, sedge roots, redbud bark, and bulrushes. Baskets were used for gathering and storing food, carrying water, and even cooking.

The Kiva

The Anasazi people lived in pithouses dug into the desert and covered with thatch roofs. From about 700 CE, their descendants, the Pueblo people, began to use adobe (sun-dried mud) and stone to build above-ground living structures. Sunken chambers, called *kivas* (meaning "world below"), remained a feature of their communities. They were used as sanctuaries for spiritual rites and as a place for men to weave.

Acorns were gathered and ground into flour or meal.

Kachina dolls, representing supernatural beings, were important parts of Kiva ceremonies.

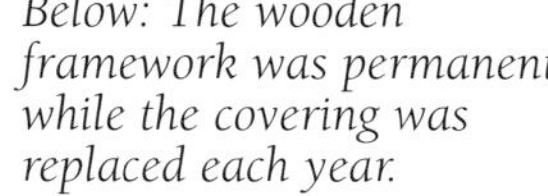

Below: The wooden framework was permanent while the covering was replaced each year.

Californian Homes

The native peoples of California built many different kinds of homes. The Maidu tribe in the south had one of the most unique types. They lived in dwellings that were dug into the ground and covered with mud roofs. Other tribes built dome-shaped huts with a wooden framework covered with earth, brush, bark, or reeds.

Desert Farming

Farming was not easy in the Southwest. Using complex irrigation systems, farmers were able to water the desert soil to grow maize as well as beans, squash, pumpkins, and avocados. Ceremonies were held to bring rain to the dry region and to assure a good harvest. They was plenty of work to be done throughout the year. Public ceremonies for planting, sifting, and grinding maize brought farmers together.

The Bow and Arrow

The bow and arrow was the principal weapon for hunting and warfare. Skilled hunters could pick off mountain goats, squirrels, and jackrabbits. The nomadic Apache, whose name means "enemy" in Athabascan languages, gained a reputation as fierce warriors. They used their bows and arrows to attack neighboring communities when hunting was poor or to rob them of essential supplies.

Village women of the Southwest were responsible for pottery-making, which was usually done on a roof exposed to the Sun.

Wood was scarce, so hunters needed to aim well to preserve their supply of arrows.

Stone-walled homes, called pueblos, were found in Southwest villages. These were often surrounded by farmlands, where farmers worked the dry soil with stone hoes.

The Great Plains and the Great Basin

People of the Great Plains were primarily hunters who relied on the buffalo for survival. The village was the heart of their society, acting as a center for celebrations, religious ceremonies, and trade. Women handled most of the daily chores while men went out to hunt or to gather food. The peoples of the barren desert region of the Great Basin were surrounded by little vegetation and wildlife. They foraged for edible seeds, nuts, roots, and berries. They also hunted game and caught fish.

Red stone pipe with lead inlays. Carved stems of wood were smoked as acts of friendship; these are known as "peace pipes."

Sacred Tobacco

The Great Plains people believed that tobacco had special powers—to make war or peace, to heal the sick or to ensure a successful hunt. Each man had his own long-stemmed pipe, which was his most valued and sacred possession. No fighting was allowed at quarries where men went to find stone for their pipes. The most highly prized red stone, called catlinite, came from a quarry in present-day Minnesota.

The Valuable Buffalo

The people of the Great Plains relied on the buffalo (or bison) for food, clothing, tools, and even religious ceremonies. Evidence from nearly 11,000 years ago suggests that hunters (probably disguised with buffalo hides) drove herds over cliffs or into narrow canyons. The buffalo was central to religious rites, such as the Mandan Buffalo Bull Dances, which appealed to the buffalo spirit.

The Mandan Buffalo Bull Dance combined special songs and dances in a ceremony calling for success in the buffalo hunt.

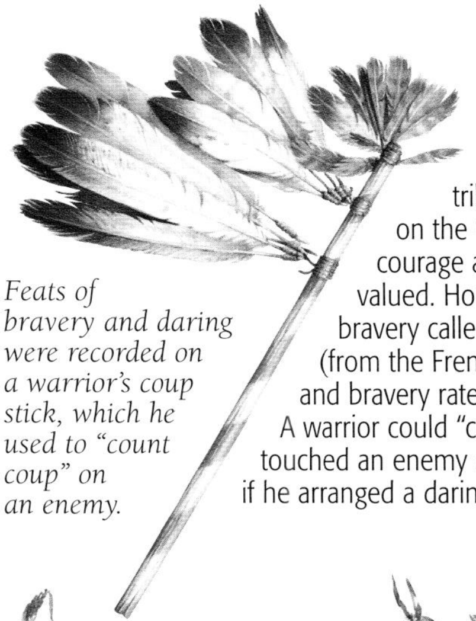

Honor Through War

All-out war between tribes was uncommon on the Great Plains, but courage and daring were highly valued. Honor came from feats of bravery called "counting coup" (from the French word for "hit"), and bravery rated higher than killing. A warrior could "count coup" if he touched an enemy during combat or if he arranged a daring escape.

Feats of bravery and daring were recorded on a warrior's coup stick, which he used to "count coup" on an enemy.

Living in the Great Basin

People living in the Great Basin had to make the best of what was available. Besides foraging for seeds, nuts, roots, and berries, tribes of the Great Basin hunted antelope, rabbits, birds and lizards. They searched for food year-round, and each season brought its own food. When men were not busy searching for food they spent time in the sweat lodge, for it was believed that sweating purified the body and spirit.

Pine nuts were gathered in September from small pine trees on the hillsides of the Great Basin.

Heat and steam were created inside the sweat lodge by pouring water over hot stones.

GREAT PLAINS AND GREAT BASIN

c. 9200–8900 BCE
Hunters and gatherers begin making stone tools.

c. 7500 BCE
The world's first cemetery is made in present-day Arkansas.

c. 3500 BCE
Bison hunting begins on the Great Plains.

c. 1500 BCE
Duck hunters in the Great Basin use duck decoys to catch their prey. Bone fish hooks are also used.

c. 700 CE
Sledges and hammerstones are used to mine salt.

c. 1250 CE
Farmers on the Great Plains live in villages.

c. 1750 CE
Spanish explorers bring horses, which are quickly adopted by the peoples of the Great Plains.

Tipi Village

The tipi was the ideal type of house for a people that was always on the move. It was easy to carry and quickly assembled. The tipi itself had spiritual meaning: its round shape echoed the sacred life circle while the floor represented the Earth where people live and the sides pointed upwards to the sky.

The opening of the tipi always faced east, away from the prevailing west winds that swept across the Great Plains.

THE GREAT PLAINS AND THE GREAT BASIN

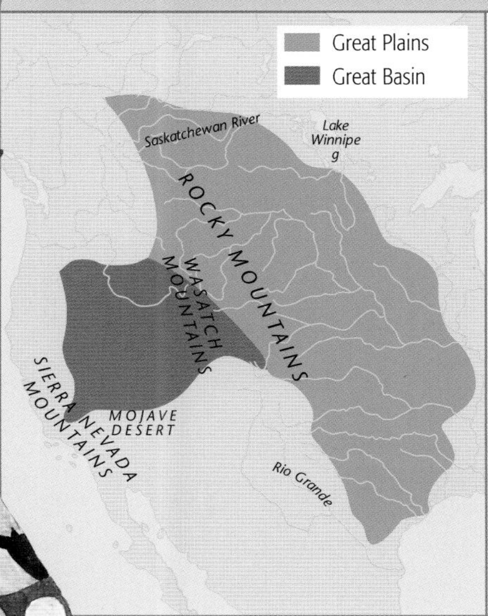

Lands of the Great Plains and the Great Basin

The huge area of land of the Great Plains, also known as the "Great American Desert," stretches from the Rio Grande in the south to the Saskatchewan River in the north. The Rocky Mountains form the western border while a long mountain-side cliff extends to form the eastern border. The Great Plains area is a vast plateau of semi-arid grasslands. The Great Basin lies between the Sierra Nevada Mountains and the Wasatch Mountains, just north of the Mojave Desert. The region is made up of wide valleys of mostly desert land.

Peoples of the East

The eastern half of North America has borne the mark of human life for at least 12,000 years. The many peoples living among the lakes and forests of the Northeast had a profound respect for their natural surroundings. But warlike people, especially the Iroquois, would often menace their neighbors. In the warmer Southeast, Native Americans developed permanent settlements, which were larger than any others north of Mexico. These people became skilled farmers and created delicate carvings and pottery goods. In the heart of the region were the mound-builders, whose mysterious works still puzzle observers.

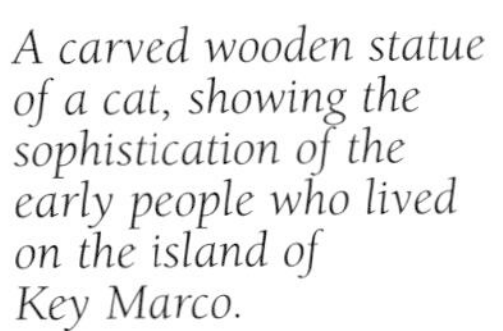

A carved wooden statue of a cat, showing the sophistication of the early people who lived on the island of Key Marco.

Mysterious Early Culture

Key Marco lies just off the west coast of Florida. Here archeologists have uncovered traces of the early—but advanced—Calusa culture. Its inhabitants developed technology to deal with their island environment. Using tools made from shells, they built seawalls and drainage basins. Carvings, executed with sharks' teeth, show a link with cultures in the Mississippi area.

Life in the Longhouse Village

The Iroquois peoples of present-day New York State were fierce warriors who had an advanced social and political system. They lived in longhouses, built with wooden frames and covered with elm-bark. These houses, which could measure as long as 66 feet (20 m), were inhabited by large family groups. Women were at the heart of village society, owning both the longhouses and all their tools and other possessions. Men moved into their wives' longhouse when they married.

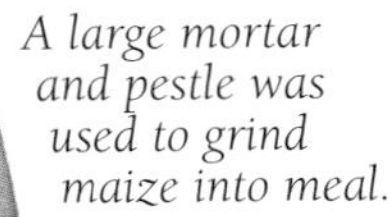

A large mortar and pestle was used to grind maize into meal.

THE EAST

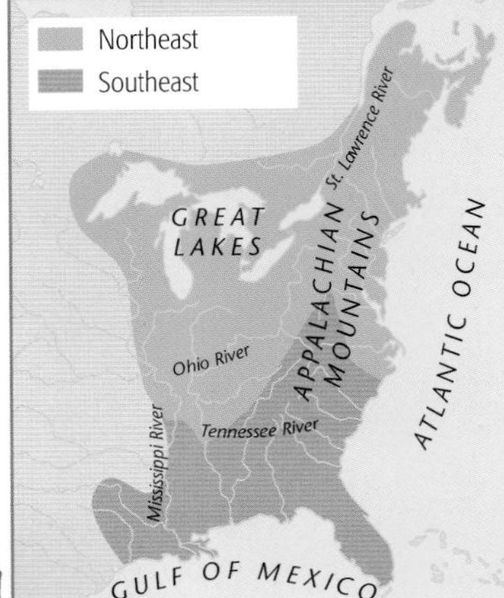

Lands of the East

The wooded lands east of the Mississippi River were the home to many peoples. The Northeast is composed of fertile woodlands and prairies and encompasses the area of the Great Lakes, reaching to the St. Lawrence River in the north. The Southeast extends westward from the Atlantic cost to the lower Mississippi and southward to the Gulf of Mexico. The Appalachian Mountains run along the northern border of the region. Mild winters and abundant rainfall make the climate of the Southeast ideal for farming. Its forests, rivers, and streams also provided an abundant food supply.

The Cherokees, one of the largest tribes of the Southeast, built their capital city along the Tennessee River.

The basic equipment for the game of lacrosse has changed little since the sport was developed by the native peoples of Canada.

THE EAST

c. 2000 BCE
Copper, found in natural deposits, is used to make spearheads in the Great Lakes region.

c. 1500 BCE
Pottery appears in the Southeast.

c. 1800 BCE
Sunflowers are cultivated.

c. 1800 BCE
Axes are used to clear land and cut down trees.

c. 1500 BCE
Small villages appear in the south; circular houses are made of wooden poles and thatched coverings.

c. 700 BCE
Farmers begin to cultivate crops and build villages.

c. 200 BCE
The Hopewell people, the great mound builders, establish widespread trade contacts.

c. 900 CE
Rise of Copena civilization.

c. 1150 CE
End of Hopewell civilization.

c. 1450 BCE
Calusha peoples of the Southeast control Cushing, a site at Key Marco.

1620 BCE
European pilgrims arrive in the Mayflower.

Lacrosse

The Algonquian peoples of Canada developed a stick-and-ball game called baggataway to train young men to become warriors. Villages competed against each other in warlike matches. French-Canadians later called the game "lacrosse" because the netted stick resembles a bishop's cross.

Effigy Mounds

For thousands of years, the people of the Ohio and Mississippi valleys built huge earthwork mounds along ridges and high ground. The purpose and shape of these mounds differed—some had buried artifacts, others were used as burial sites. Later examples, known as effigy mounds, were built in the shape of people, birds, panthers, and snakes.

The meaning of Ohio's Great Serpent Mound—built by the Adena people and stretching nearly 1,760 feet (400 m)—remains a mystery.

Green Maize Rite

The Creek, Shawnees, Cherokees, and other Southeastern farmers prized maize as a crop. In late summer, as the last of the maize was ripening, they held the Green Maize Rite. Spread over several days during the full Moon, this ceremony gave thanks for the harvest and ushered in a new year. The rituals and dancing ended with a feast featuring maize prepared in many forms.

The most sacred part of the Green Maize Rite was the dance around a ceremonial fire. Coals from the fire were used to light village hearths, signalling the beginning of a new year.

Ancient Meso-America

Evidence suggests that the first human inhabitants of Meso-America were descendants of Asian peoples who crossed the Bering land bridge. Fanning out southward and eastward, they arrived in present-day Mexico many thousands of years ago. These first settlers were hunters and gatherers, but eventually they developed settled communities based on cultivation of crops such as maize. The Olmecs and the Zapotecs were two of the first cultures to develop in this region.

MESO-AMERICA

3600 BCE
Maize is first cultivated in Meso-America, signaling the permanent change from hunter-gathering culture to farming.

2300 BCE
The first permanent farming communities develop in southern Mexico. Pottery is first developed at about the same time.

1400 BCE
The Olmecs begin to cultivate maize.

1200 BCE
The first Olmec ceremonial center is built at Tres Zapotes near the coast of the Gulf of Mexico.

1000 BCE
The Maya people begin to settle in the Yucatan Peninsula of southern Mexico.

c. 800 BCE
The Zapotecs develop Meso-America's first writing.

500 BCE
The Zapotecs build the mountain-city of Monte Albán as political states develop in the Oaxaca Valley of southern Mexico.

MESO-AMERICA

GULF OF MEXICO
CHICHEN ITZA
YUCATAN PENINSULA
TRES ZAPOTES
LA VENTA
SAN LORENZO
OAXACA VALLEY
MONTE ALBÁN
SANTA CRUZ
PACIFIC OCEAN

- Area of Olmec influence
- Area of Maya influence c. 1000 BCE
- Area of Maya influence c. 800 BCE
- Area of Zapotec influence
- Sites settled by, or influenced by the Olmecs

Meso-American Cultures

Few settlements developed in the towering mountain ranges that run the length of Meso-America, but civilizations took root in some of the more welcoming landscapes in the region. The Olmec and Zapotec cultures developed in the south, near the coast of the Gulf of Mexico. Jutting northeast from that area is the Yucatan Peninsula, the tropical home of the Maya civilization (see map on page 211). The fertile Valley of Mexico, high on a plateau, was the cradle of other Meso-American civilizations–including the Aztecs (see page 218–21).

Early Writing

The Zapotecs were the first in Meso-America to develop a writing system. (It would be expanded by the later Maya civilization). By about 800 BCE, the Zapotecs were using a system of hieroglyphs. Recognizable images and patterns of images clearly spelled out important details of Zapotec warfare, business, religion, and culture.

A giant Olmec head, found at La Venta. It was carved from a single piece of basalt that was dragged to the site.

The Olmecs

Olmec culture developed in about 1100 BCE in southern Mexico, an area of prime maize-growing country which provided the Olmecs with an ample supply of food and, ultimately, time to devote to other pursuits. The Olmecs created some enduring works of art, many of them featuring remarkable depictions of humans and animals. Some were modelled from clay; others were carved from stone and precious minerals. Huge, brooding stone statues of human heads were probably created to commemorate noted Olmec chieftains and hereditary leaders.

Stone slab with Zapotec carving and writing depicting a bride and groom at their wedding (top) and a female and male ancestor (lower level). Running around these images is a border of hieroglyphs that include the names of 13 relatives of the newlyweds.

The Wonders of Maize

The transition from hunting and gathering to farming came between 7000 and 2000 BCE as the Meso-American climate became drier. Settlements became more stable as flood plains dried out enough to become cultivated. People began cultivating avocados, squash, pumpkins, beans, and maize. By about 1500 BCE, about 40 percent of the Meso-American diet was made up of maize. Ample rainfall and constant heat allowed up to four crops of this nutritious grain each year.

Maize became (and remains) the staple grain of farming communities in Central America. It can be eaten fresh or dried and ground into flour for baking.

The Zapotecs at Monte Albán

Some of the most extensive Meso-American buildings are found at the site known as Monte Albán, the Spanish name for a mountain-city in the southern highlands of Mexico. Monte Albán was the center of the Zapotec culture, which flourished in the Oaxaca Valley from 500 BCE to about 750 CE. More than 30,000 people lived in this administrative and cultural center. About 2,000 stone-carved houses surrounded a vast main plaza. Huge staircases led from the plaza to temples and a ceremonial ball-playing court. Throughout the city, warriors and deities were commemorated in stone wall carvings.

Stylised Zapotec jewelry showed an intricacy and imaginative eye in keeping with a culture that had developed an elaborate system of cultural and religious beliefs.

The massive city of Monte Albán stood on the top of a flattened mountain. The scale of the city and its central plaza is huge. The plaza alone measures 984 x 492 feet (300 x 150 m).

Maya Society

The most sophisticated of the Pre-Columbian civilizations of Meso-America was developed by the Maya. They had settled the humid tropical lowlands of the Yucatan Peninsula by about 1000 BCE. Within a few centuries they began draining swamp land, making it into arable farming land. Initially absorbing the advances of the neighboring Zapotecs, they went on to develop a network of prosperous communities. Maya civilization became noted for its works of art and architecture. Extensive trading networks linked communities throughout their region, although these same communities often engaged in bitter warfare.

THE MAYA

c. 1000 BCE
The first Maya people begin to settle in the Yucatan Peninsula. Their origins are mysterious; some believe they were Olmecs who fled eastward.

500 BCE
The Maya begin to establish notions of monarchy and nobility.

c. 350 BCE
City-states begin to develop in the Maya region. They are independent, but share aspects of culture and language.

150 BCE
El Mirador emerges as the largest center of early Maya civilization.

c. 200 BCE
Volcanic eruption of Mount Ilopango destroys much of the southern Maya civilization.

411 CE
Tikal becomes the most powerful Maya center in what archeologists describe as the "Classic Period" of Maya history.

The Maya had no metal tools. Artists carved stone using stone tools. The figure depicted in this jade mask is wearing typical Maya ceremonial headgear, including heavy earplugs.

Maya Artists

The Maya developed a distinctive artistic style using many different materials, including wood and stone sculpture, murals and pottery. Most of the wooden sculpture has decayed, but limestone carvings and bas-reliefs are full of ornamentation and intricate carving. Murals depicted religious and historical themes while colorful examples of pottery have been found as ornaments in many Maya graves.

Trade

Although the Yucatan Peninsula does not have a rich supply of natural resources, the Maya still managed to develop lucrative trading links based on their local goods. Salt was one of the few natural resources that the Maya traded. Along with chocolate, colorful feathers, and slaves, the Maya traded salt for essential items such as copper tools. The dense tropical forest made passage difficult, so much of this trade was carried out by boat—either by river or along the coast.

This chocolate container dates from around 500 CE. The Maya ground cacao beans into a paste, which they then mixed with hot water to make drinking chocolate.

This Maya mural depicts a group of merchants, guarded by their patron god "The Black Scorpion" (the dark figure in the center). He was also the guardian of cacao, a prized trading good.

Expert Farmers

The lands of the Yucatan Peninsula are not ideal for farming, but the Maya adapted to them successfully with a number of intensive farming techniques. Swamps were drained to open up farmland while areas of thick jungle were cut down with stone axes. The felled trees were burned, depositing soil-enriching ash on the cleared land. Maya farmers also created terraces on sloping terrain to gain more growing space.

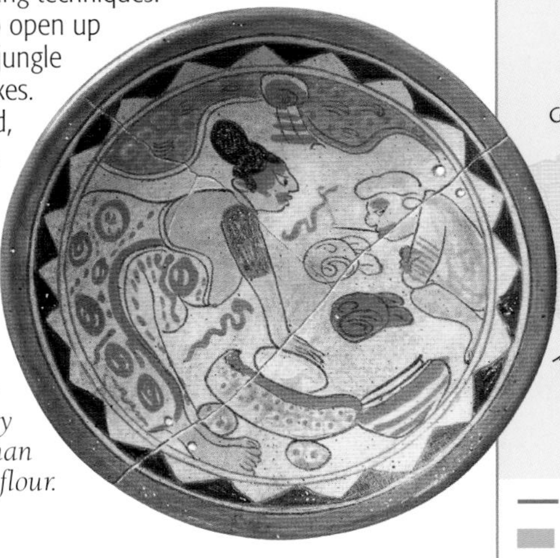

This elaborately decorated Maya pottery bowl shows a woman grinding maize into flour.

Warfare

Maya civilization was not centralized under one acknowledged leader. Instead, independent city-states shared a culture and trading links and often went to war with each other. The purpose of these conflicts was not to gain territory so much as to capture soldiers. Captives either became slaves (who could be traded) or were sacrificed to the gods.

THE LAND OF THE MAYA

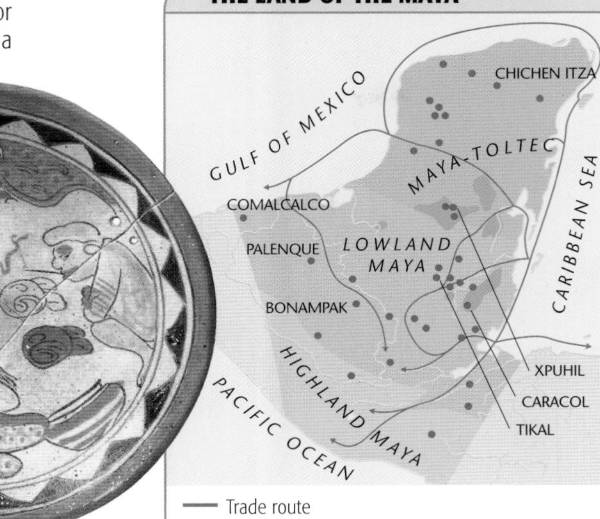

Maya Civilization
The area covered by the Maya civilization extended across the Yucatan Peninsula in present-day southern Mexico and Belize, and as far as Guatemala, Honduras, and parts of El Salvador. Most of the region is low-lying, except for the gentle highlands of the region where Mexico meets Guatemala. A number of tribes speaking similar languages settled there. The Maya, the largest tribe, has given its name to both the language group and the civilization of the region.

In 1946, archeologists discovered a vivid mural covering several walls of a ceremonial building at Bonampak, in southern Mexico. The colorful images depict battle scenes during a Maya dynastic struggle of 792 CE.

Maya Achievements

The Maya created one of the most advanced civilizations in Meso-America—and in the ancient world. They used some existing knowledge, such as the Zapotec hieroglyphic writing system, as a springboard for their far more intensive investigation and recording of the world around them. Many of their most notable advances came in the fields of technology, astronomy, arithmetic, and architecture. They developed a complex calendar which was linked to heavenly motion. Maya temples represented the peak of their scientific and technological skills. These buildings show remarkable adaptability in using available building materials, often in remote locations.

A series of intricately carved Maya hieroglyphs.

The Maya Alphabet

The Maya developed a written alphabet that was based on hieroglyph principles. By about 100 CE, the system was in common use throughout the region. Overall, about 1,000 different signs were used to represent gods, animals, and other features of the observable world. This writing system remained a mystery until archeologists realised that the signs were of two types—either pictorial representations of the things themselves or symbols for spoken words.

Recorded Knowledge

Much of what the Maya wrote—often on bark, which rots away over time—has been lost. However, four codices have survived along with the many detailed stone carvings on walls and monuments. A fuller picture of Maya life is emerging as it becomes apparent that scribes recorded not just history, astronomy, and prophecies, but many details of how political life operated in Maya society.

A decorative bowl showing a Maya scribe at work. Apart from the scribes themselves, only priests and noblemen could understand the Maya script.

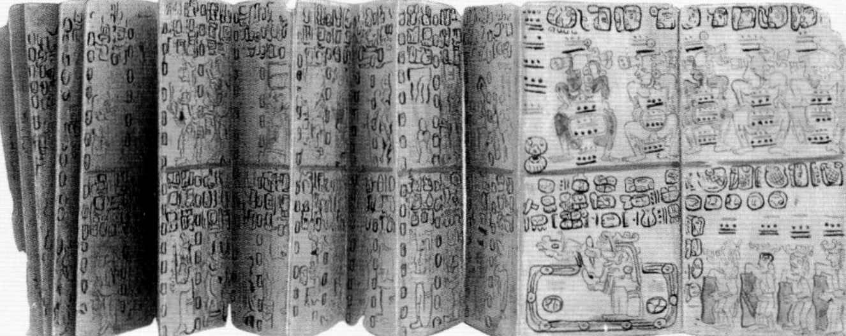

A codex was written on thin strips of fig tree bark and folded into an accordion shape to create pages. The glyphs were read from top to bottom and left to right.

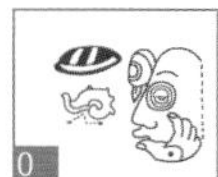

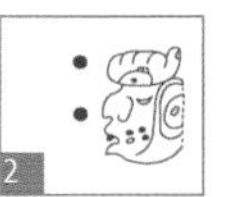

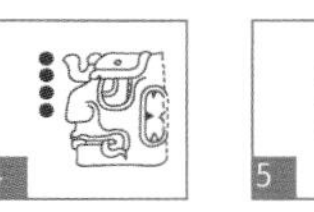
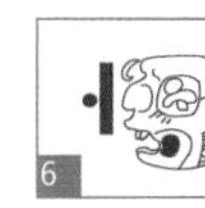
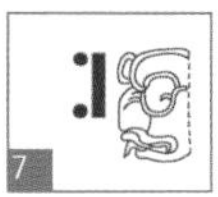

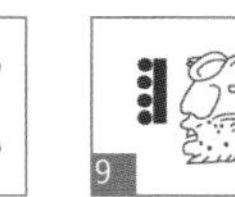
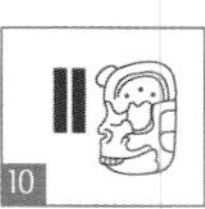
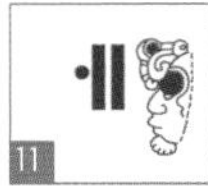

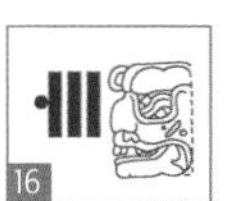

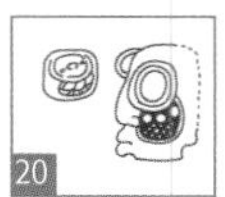

Maya symbols representing the numbers. A dot represented the number one and a bar stood for five.

Counting Innovation

The Maya were brilliant mathematicians, and as in so many other developments, arithmetic was linked to other fields of knowledge such as astronomy and the calendar. Numbers were recorded in a pattern of dots, dashes, and a stylized shell. Maya mathematicians understood the concept of zero, allowing them to represent (and understand) huge numbers with relatively few symbols.

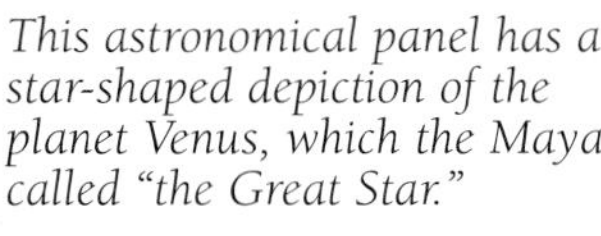

This astronomical panel has a star-shaped depiction of the planet Venus, which the Maya called "the Great Star."

Watching the Stars

The passage of the Moon, planets, and stars was important to the Maya, who combined astronomical observation with astrological beliefs. Their advanced calendar allowed them to predict eclipses and other heavenly occurrences with great accuracy. Priests almost certainly doubled as astronomers, making their observations from the tops of temples high above the surrounding trees.

The Maya Calendar

The Maya were able to record time with amazing accuracy, using their mathematical and astronomical skills to produce a calendar as sophisticated as most in use today. They represented their calendar on two types of wheel, each indicating 20-day months. One wheel had 13 months; the other had 18 (with eight "unlucky" days added to make a solar year of 365 days). Each day within a 20-day cycle had special significance, carrying with it traditions of good or bad luck.

This ceremonial urn is covered with hieroglyphs representing the Maya calendar.

Building Technology

Maya architects used local building materials to produce impressive results. Limestone was cut into blocks, which fit together neatly. The builders laid some of these blocks in a staircase-like pattern—each side jutting out to meet over a passage—to create corbelled vaults. Lime-based plaster coated walls, staircases, and even the base of plazas to create a smooth finish. Many temples and palaces were decorated with reliefs.

The graceful temples of Palenque, in the modern Mexican state of Chiapas. Inside the Temple of Inscriptions (shown here in a cutaway view) archeologists found the sarcophagus of a Maya king, K'inich Janaab' Pakal I (reigned 615–683 CE).

Maya Beliefs and Rituals

Religion played an important—and often terrifying—part in the everyday life of the Maya. The blood of royal people and outright human sacrifices were regular features of religious ceremonies that were dictated by the seemingly infallible Maya calendar. The arrival of solar and lunar eclipses, as predicted by the priests' calendar, served to reinforce belief among the people at large. A vast number of gods and goddesses represented the forces that had the greatest impact on the lives of the people. Most of these were gods of rain, sunshine, and other natural forces. Others included an array of deities associated with the animals native to the tropical Yucatan environment.

The Maya Pantheon
Archeologists are still puzzled by the vast number of Maya deities. Some of the confusion arises because many of the deities were considered to be up to four different individuals, and sometimes a deity had a male and a female aspect.

A ceremonial incense burner depicts Itzamna as an old man with a crooked nose. The Maya believed that Itzamna named all the Maya villages and cities.

MAYA DEITIES

Itzamna
The most important deity and creator of the Universe. He is credited with inventing writing and is the patron of science and learning.

Ix Chel
Rainbow deity and wife of Itzamna. The Maya believed that Ix Chel and Itzamna were the parents of all the other deities. She is also the deity of weaving, medicine, and childbirth.

Chac
The benevolent rain deity, whose intervention was often sought by Maya farmers.

Yum Kaax
Deity of maize and patron of husbandry.

Yum Cimil
A death deity. He had many forms, one of which presided over the nine underworlds.

Buluc Chabtan
A war deity, associated with violent death and human sacrifice.

The Role of Priests
Maya priests all came from the noble class, and their sons usually succeeded them in office after a long period of training. Priests were charged with linking the complicated network of religious rites and ceremonies with the intricate Maya calendar. In this regard, they were also responsible for recording and predicting the astronomical events that intrigued the Maya. Like other shamans, Maya priests regularly used substances to achieve an altered state of being.

By using substances which changed their state of being, Maya priests believed that they could get in touch with supernatural forces. The Maya used alcoholic beverages made from maize, honey, tree bark, and other plant materials. They interpreted their experiences to predict future events.

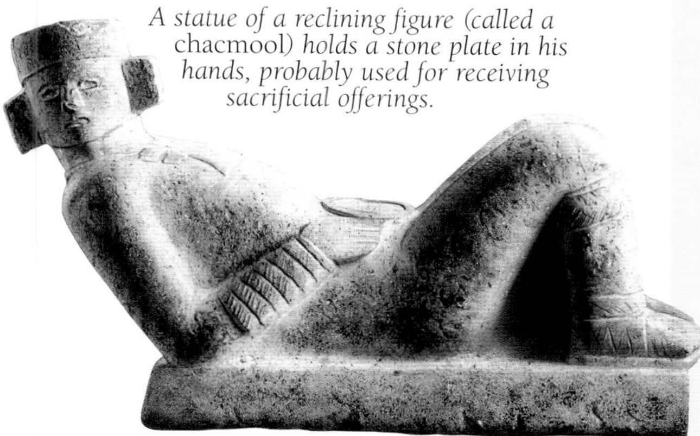

A statue of a reclining figure (called a chacmool) holds a stone plate in his hands, probably used for receiving sacrificial offerings.

Royal Blood

Since royal people, according to Maya belief, were descended from one or more of the gods, royal blood was considered especially important in religious ceremonies. Blood-letting rites, taking blood from a city-state's own ruler, were carried out on special occasions. Blood was spattered on thin bark or passed down hollow tubes into special vessels. Captured nobles and royals were also sacrificed, with their hearts placed in special statuary bowls.

A carved relief shows a ruler holding a torch while his wife passes a thorn-studded rope through her tongue to extract blood.

Human Sacrifices

The Maya deities demanded regular sacrifices to ensure peace and prosperity. Archaeologists believe that the earliest Maya societies sacrificed only plants and animals, but over time the practice of human sacrifice became widespread. The usual victims were captives or slaves, but sometimes illegitimate children were sacrificed in religious ceremonies. The sacrifice of royal blood was believed to be especially effective. Priests would hold down the victim's arms and legs while another would open up the chest above the heart.

Royal Maya women clad in white garments perform the blood-letting ritual in this detail from a wall painting at Bonampak, Mexico. They are gathered round a throne and are attended by a male servant holding a sharp object.

Below: A vase depicting a Maya priest conducting a religious ceremony. The priest is wearing parts of a slaughtered jaguar as leggings (including the tail) and mittens.

Animal Powers

Animals played a large part in everyday Maya life, both for their practical contribution and for their religious significance. Effigies of dogs have been found in Maya burial sites, signaling their importance in the journey to the afterlife. Other animals had more mystical significance. The armadillo, for example, was associated with the Maya underworld. The jaguar, also associated with the underworld, was admired for its stealth, cunning, and deadly power.

A stylized statue of a jaguar, the jungle creature that the Maya admired and feared the most.

MEXICO

1500 BCE
Pilgrims begin to travel to sacred shrines at what would become Teotihuacan.

c. 100 CE
The first great temples and pyramids built are at Teotihuacan.

c. 500 CE
Chichen Itza built around sacred wells in the Yucatan Peninsula.

c. 600–800 CE
The Veracruz culture is at its peak.

c. 650 CE
Teotihuacan begins to come under repeated attack.

c. 750 CE
Teotihuacan is abandoned.

c. 800 CE
Mixtec culture dominates southern Mexico.

c. 900 CE
The Toltecs build their capital, Tula, in the Valley of Mexico.

c. 1200 CE
Toltec invaders capture Chichen Itza.

Mexican Empires

Elsewhere in Meso-America other cultures achieved a high degree of development. They borrowed ideas from each other and from the people they conquered. To the north of the Maya region lay the city-state of Teotihuacan, built around a vast city that supported a population of perhaps 200,000. Veracruz culture developed along the Gulf of Mexico and in southern Mexico the Mixtecs took over the site of Monte Albán. The Toltecs, warriors from northern Mexico, migrated south to the Valley of Mexico.

Teotihuacan attracted craftsmen from a wide region. This unusual chicken-shaped ceramic container is decorated with jade and colorful shells.

A broad thoroughfare called the Avenue of the Dead ran between the ceremonial buildings of Teotihuacan. Temples dedicated to different deities were built on the flat tops of the pyramids.

The Largest City in America

Teotihuacan developed in the first century CE, with massive temples forming its core. The Pyramid of the Sun—the third-largest pyramid in the world—stood 200 feet (60 m) high and was aligned with the rising and setting Sun on the summer solstice. Teotihuacan flourished for five centuries as an important regional center and one of the largest cities in the world. From 650 CE it was attacked repeatedly, and by about 750 CE, Teotihuacan was largely destroyed and abandoned.

MESO-AMERICAN CULTURES

EL TEUL
TAMUIN
TOLLANTZINCO
TULA
EL TAJIN
CHAPULTEPEC
CULHUACAN
TEHUACAN
TEOTITLAN
MONTE ALBÁN
SAN LORENZO
PACIFIC OCEAN

Teotihuacan
Spread of Teotihuacan culture
Veracruz
Spread of Veracruz culture
Monte Albán
Spread of Monte Albán culture
Toltec area
Toltec capital

Mexican Empires

Meso-America can be divided into two main areas: the Maya and the Mexican. Cultures in each group had similar languages, religious beliefs, writing systems, and artistic styles. Although independent city-states were the hallmark of the Maya (eastern) region, large empires developed in the Mexican (western) region, where Teotihuacan and the Toltec capital of Tula developed in the Valley of Mexico. Monte Albán (center of Zapotec and Mixtec culture) was in the southern highlands, near the Pacific coast. The Veracruz culture flourished on the Gulf coast, east of the Valley of Mexico.

Chichen Itza

Chichen Itza, built around sacred wells in the northern Yucatan Peninsula, began as a Maya center around 500 CE. Pilgrims came to make offerings to the rain deity. By the late 600s it was abandoned by the Maya, but around 300 years later it was rebuilt by the Itza tribe (after whom it is named). Toltec invaders from neighboring Tula conquered it around 1200 CE, adding to it over the next two centuries.

Chichen Itza means "mouth of the wells of the Itza." Pilgrims from all over the region came to the Sacred Well of Sacrifice to make offerings, like this intricate carving, to the deity of rain.

Veracruz Culture

El Tajin was the centre of the Veracruz culture. Within the city, several courts were designed for the ceremonial ball game developed by the Maya and popular throughout Meso-America. Carvings represent the protective equipment worn by the players. Pottery from the Veracruz lowlands shows a distinctive style called Remojadas, in which objects are depicted realistically but embellished with geometric designs.

This stone carving represents a protective yoke worn by players around the waist in the ceremonial ball game at El Tajin and elsewhere in Meso-America.

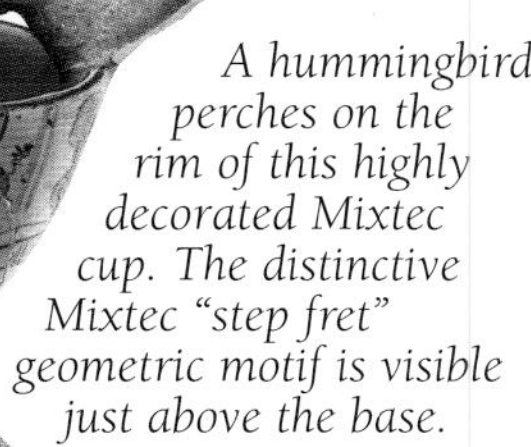

A hummingbird perches on the rim of this highly decorated Mixtec cup. The distinctive Mixtec "step fret" geometric motif is visible just above the base.

The Mixtecs of Monte Albán

The Mixtecs of southern Mexico became known as the best craftsmen in the region. They used diplomacy and arranged marriages with conquered rivals to secure a homeland, with the former Zapotec city of Monte Albán as one of its centres. The Mixtecs recorded their military and political history in colourful pictographs. They were also noted for their metalwork, stonework, mosaics, pottery, embroidery and weaving.

Warriors of Tula

The warlike Toltecs migrated south to the Valley of Mexico after the decline of Teotihuacan in the 8th century CE. They built a new capital, Tula, and controlled the first military empire in the region. The Toltec civilization declined in the 12th century as other peoples invaded and sacked Tula. Some of the Toltecs moved further south and were absorbed by the Maya.

Toltec craftsmen celebrated their culture's warlike reputation. This ornament represents a coyote warrior, whose face peers out from the open jaws of a coyote mask.

THE AZTECS

c. 1150 CE
Nomadic hunters known as the Aztecs (or Mexica) move south into the Valley of Mexico. The leaders of several existing city-states employ them as mercenaries.

c. 1325
Aztec priests spot an eagle devouring a snake on a rock by Lake Texcoco, fulfiling a prophecy that they would build a civilization there. Work begins on draining land and building the capital, Tenochtitlan, on islands in the lake.

c. 1350 CE
Using Tenochtitlan as a base, the Aztecs begin to conquer most of their neighbors in the Valley of Mexico, extracting tribute as they build an empire based on military might.

c. 1500
The Aztecs overcome the two other powers—the Texcoco and Tlaleloco—with whom they had shared control of the empire. The Aztec-ruled territory extended from today's central Mexico to the Guatemalan border.

A farmer poles his flat-bottomed boat along a canal running between cultivated areas. The chinampas, which had begun as rafts, were eventually anchored to the shallow lake bottom.

A carved calendar stone reflects the circular passage of time in the Aztec calendar.

Stone Carving

Stoneworking was important to the Aztecs. Their huge capital city, Tenochtitlan, was built from stone that was quarried and cut into massive blocks. Stone carvings served religious and historical purposes. The complex Aztec creation myth stated that the Earth had undergone a series of destructions and reconstructions. These were plotted and recorded on stone carvings representing the Aztec calendar.

Aztec Origins

Waves of newcomers flooded into the fertile Valley of Mexico after the fall of the Toltec civilization in the 12th century CE. The nomadic Aztecs—among the last to arrive—were forced to establish themselves on the swampy western shore of Lake Texcoco. However, the Aztecs would turn this hardship into a real advantage, reclaiming land for farming and for their capital, Tenochtitlan. With this easily defended city as their base, the warlike Aztecs proceeded to conquer their neighbors and to establish a powerful empire that still held sway when the Spaniards arrived in the early 1500s.

A legend told that the Aztecs would build a great civilization when they saw a cactus growing out of a rock and an eagle perched upon it. Aztec priests claimed to have seen this vision on the shores of Lake Texcoco.

Agricultural Innovations

Despite their justified reputation as fierce warriors, the Aztecs were also excellent farmers. They reclaimed low-lying marshland by the shore of the lake for farming. Networks of canals drained excess water, gaining more arable land. Seeds of corn and other crops were sown in raised fields called *chinampas* (meaning "rafts"), which ran between rows of trees. The rich soil between the rows of trees came from sediment and mud extracted from a neighboring canal.

Aztec Religion

The Aztecs had a complex religion that absorbed many beliefs of the peoples they conquered. Aztec myths number at least 1,600 different deities, and these deities could assume many forms. One of the most important gods was Huitzlipochtli, the god of war and the Sun, who guided the Aztecs on their journey to the Valley of Mexico. His name comes from the Aztec word for "hummingbird," reflecting the Aztec belief that warriors were reborn as hummingbirds.

This Aztec mask of Tezcatlipoca, the deity of destruction, was made by laying precious stones over a human skull.

Aztec warriors wore uniforms that indicated their military rank. Those who had captured many enemy warriors were entitled to use highly adorned shields like this one, made of jaguar skin and feathers.

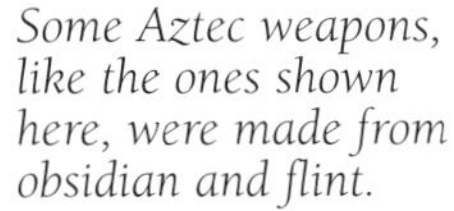

Some Aztec weapons, like the ones shown here, were made from obsidian and flint.

Aztec Warriors

The Aztecs prized bravery and military success among their warriors. Aztec wars were fought for many reasons–to gain military control, new farming land, or to find captives to be used as slaves or sacrificial victims. Exceptional bravery allowed soldiers to join one of two highest military orders, the otomies or the "shorn ones." Members of these orders had special privileges, which included being able to drink *pulque*, a beer-like beverage, in public.

AZTECS IN THE VALLEY OF MEXICO

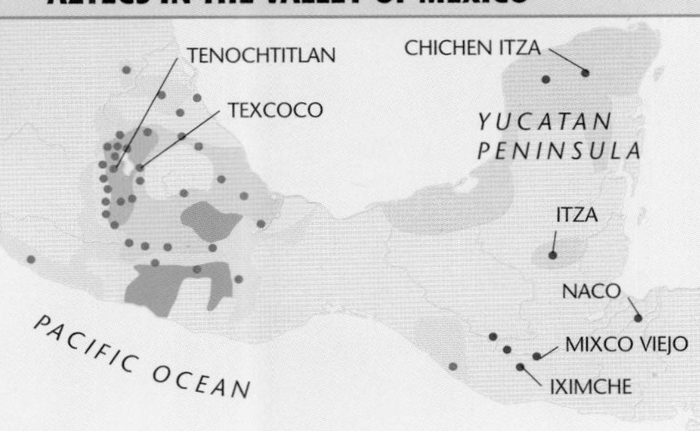

- Aztec empire under Itzcoatl 1427–1440 CE
- Aztec empire under Moteuczoma Ilhuicamina 1440–1468 CE
- Aztec empire under Axayacatl 1469–1481 CE
- Aztec empire under Ahuitzotl 1486–1502 CE
- Aztec empire under Moteuczoma Xocoyotl 1502–1520 CE
- Aztec province
- Independent Maya states
- Major Maya center

Aztec Origins

Aztec civilization developed at a troubled time in Meso-American history. Other peoples had taken over the cities and farming lands of the declining Toltec and Maya civilizations. The Aztecs, who numbered only a few hundred at first, settled on inferior land and initially acted as mercenaries for the Tepanec, a neighboring people. As they gained in power and confidence, they turned on the Tepanecs and went on to conquer other Mexican peoples as they built up an empire of their own.

Aztec Society

Tenochtitlan was a thriving metropolis that supported a population of locally born people as well as slaves and traders from the more remote areas under Aztec control. Although the Aztecs had no knowledge of the wheel, the 300,000 people living in the city found a constant supply of new goods at the markets. These markets drew thousands of people, including many who had walked long distances from outlying cities. Running through the heart of Aztec society at the same time, though, was a profound awareness of religion, with its ceremonies, rituals, and taboos.

A page from the Codex Mendoza, a 16th-century Spanish manuscript recording Aztec customs, shows girls being taught cooking and weaving skills.

Class System

Aztec society was divided into three well-defined classes. People of a certain class could be identified by their clothing, housing, and even the foods they ate. At the top were the nobles and members of the royal family. Only they could wear elaborate feathered outfits. Below them —making up the majority of the population— were commoners. Within this group there were further subdivisions based on profession or military success. At the bottom were serfs who worked for others.

The headdress of Emperor Moctezuma II (reigned 1502–1520 CE) was 4 feet (1.2 m) tall and made of bright green quetzal feathers. Gold disks and blue plumes added a further note of status.

Children and Family

Family life was important to the Aztecs, and several families would live together in a single household. The arrival of a new child was a joyous occasion. The Aztec baptismal ceremony welcomed the child into society, laying out tools appropriate to the sex of the child—weapons for a boy, weaving and cooking tools for a girl. Older children were given household chores such as carrying loads or helping to prepare food. Punishments for misbehavior included spanking, pinching, or even being held over a fire of roasting chili peppers.

A stone carving of an Aztec mother holding two children. Mothers were highly respected, and immediately after childbirth they would be applauded as warriors who had "captured" a child.

Aztec Ceremonies

Religion was an essential part of everyday Aztec life. Sacrificial ceremonies were conducted to placate the gods. Death and blood-letting played an important part in the Aztec belief that the gods had shed their blood in creating the world. Offerings of blood were a way of repaying the gods for their sacrifice. The Aztecs also performed elaborate sacrifices to the deity Huitzlipochtli (see page 219) to ensure that the Sun would return each morning. Fertility deities, as well, played an important part in Aztec rituals since terrible droughts often threatened Aztec life.

Victims to the gods were stretched out across a special stone and their hearts were torn out with a sacrificial stone knife like this one.

Aztec Markets

Trade was a vital component in the success of the Aztec empire. Crops, precious jewels and feathers, artwork, and even slaves, were transported great distances to Tenochtitlan and other Aztec centers. Canoes laden with market goods crowded the canals running through the island capital. People came to buy and sell, but also to exchange information about events occurring far from the heart of the Aztec domain.

The distinctive orange and black Aztec pottery has been found throughout Mexico, giving evidence of the extensive Aztec trading links.

As many as 60,000 people crowded into some markets on a main market day.

Chavin stone carving of the Staff God, showing the intricate detail that is a feature of all Chavin artwork.

Chavin Culture

Chavin culture was widespread across the Andean region, reaching its peak about 900–200 BCE. Its highly developed artwork indicates a religion based on the worship of animals such as eagles, jaguars, and snakes. Like the Olmec culture in Meso-America (see page 208), Chavin culture initiated many of the beliefs and cultural traditions that later Andean civilizations preserved and developed. Temples and stone carvings discovered across northern Peru give an idea of the extent of Chavin influence.

This whale ivory statue shows the Nasca practice of tying boards to an infant's skull to produce a slanted forehead.

This Paracas-style garment, from the southern coast of Peru, was found in a tomb. It shows a highly developed artistic sense coupled with exquisite workmanship.

Peoples of the Andes

Like other peoples of the Americas, the settlers in the South American Andes were descendants of Asian hunters and gatherers who had crossed the Bering land bridge (see page 198). By about 3500 BCE, some of these settlers had begun to establish permanent farming settlements. These early farmers defied the harsh, high-altitude conditions to cultivate native plants such as potatoes, beans, peppers, and maize. Many settlements grew into cities, some numbering thousands of inhabitants, in the high Andean valleys and along the coast. The ruins of these cities offer some information about these ancient cultures, but much still remains to be learned. Pottery and other artifacts—many found at burial sites—have shed some light on these mysterious early cultures.

Nasca Culture

The Nasca culture flourished along the southern coast of Peru from about 200 BCE to 600 CE. Faced with a forbidding land, the Nasca people built aqueducts to irrigate their desert farmland. Their large settlements—some probably with populations of 8,000 or more—have been described as South America's first cities. They created monumental architecture as well as highly decorated pottery. The Nasca also left behind huge geoglyphs. Some of these are zigzags, spirals, and other geometric patterns; others take shape of animals.

Many of the mysterious Nasca lines, drawn across the desert floor, can only be deciphered from above.

Gold and turquoise figures, such as the one shown here, formed the handles of Chimu ceremonial knives.

THE ANDES

c. 3500 BCE
The first permanent settlements, based on farming begin to emerge in the Andean region.

c. 900 BCE
The Chavin culture, which influenced most later Andean civilizations, begins to emerge and lasts for about 700 years.

c. 200 BCE
The Nasca civilization begins to flourish along the southern coast of Peru.

c. 100 CE
The Moche people begin to control the northern coastal region of Peru after the decline of the Chavin culture.

c. 850 CE
Work begins on Chan Chan, which becomes the capital of the Chimu civilization.

c. 1200 CE
The Chimu civilization develops into an empire.

1470 CE
The Chimu empire is conquered by the Inca.

Moche Warriors

The Moche civilization emerged as a power around 100 CE, after the decline of the Chavin culture in the same region of Peru. Like the Nasca to the south, the Moche people constructed large irrigation systems. They were also fierce warriors. Painting, pottery, and ceramic sculpture show Moche myths as well as their devotion to fighting. Some of the most dramatic images show prisoners of war being sacrificed.

This ceramic Moche sculpture vividly depicts a prisoner of war bound to a stake and waiting sacrifice.

Chimu Gold

The Chimu developed the dominant Andean culture around 900 CE, reaching a peak in the 14th and 15th centuries. The Chimu kingdom extended across much of coastal Peru. The Chimu developed extensive irrigation works to create a flourishing agricultural economy in the semi-arid landscape. The ruins of the Chimu capital, Chan Chan, are among the largest archeological sites in South America. The Chimu were eventually defeated by the Inca (see page 224) around 1470 CE.

This ornate pair of sculpted golden arms shows the artistry and metalworking skills of Chimu craftsmen.

The Rise of the Inca

By about 1200 CE, a new group of people had emerged as the dominant power in the Andes. These people spoke a language called *Quechua*. The term "Inca" is used to refer to both these people and their emperor. From their capital of Cuzco, high in the Andean valleys, the Inca extended their influence along much of western South America. They were skilled farmers, producing enough food to support a large population. Inca farmers cultivated the dizzyingly steep mountain slopes, building terraces to make use of every available area of farming land.

THE INCA EMPIRE

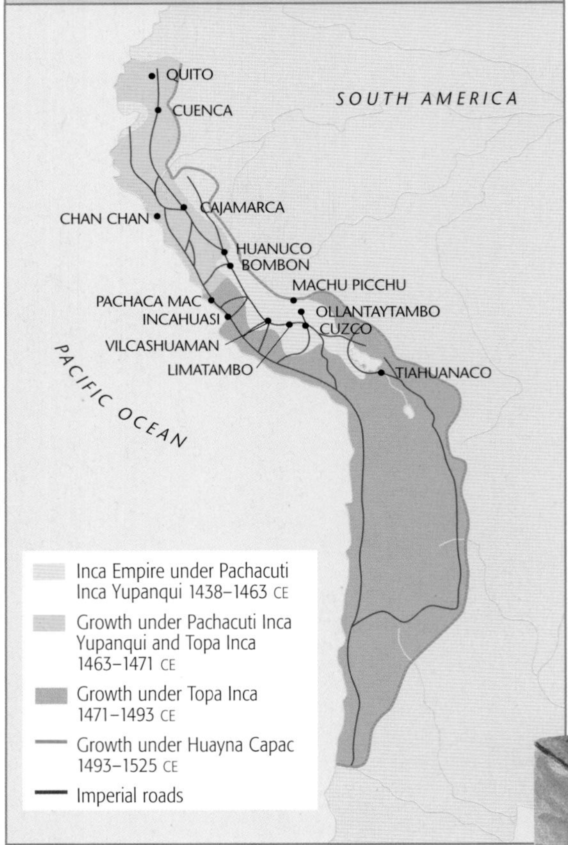

The Inca Empire

The Inca Empire had reached its greatest extent at about the time of the Spanish conquest in the early 16th century. It was the largest Native American empire, extending more than 2,500 miles (4,000 km) north-south along the Andean valleys, and about 500 miles (800 km) east-west. Some 12 million or more people lived within the empire. Conquered peoples paid tribute to the Inca and were ruled from the Inca capital Cuzco, which was built in the shape of a puma.

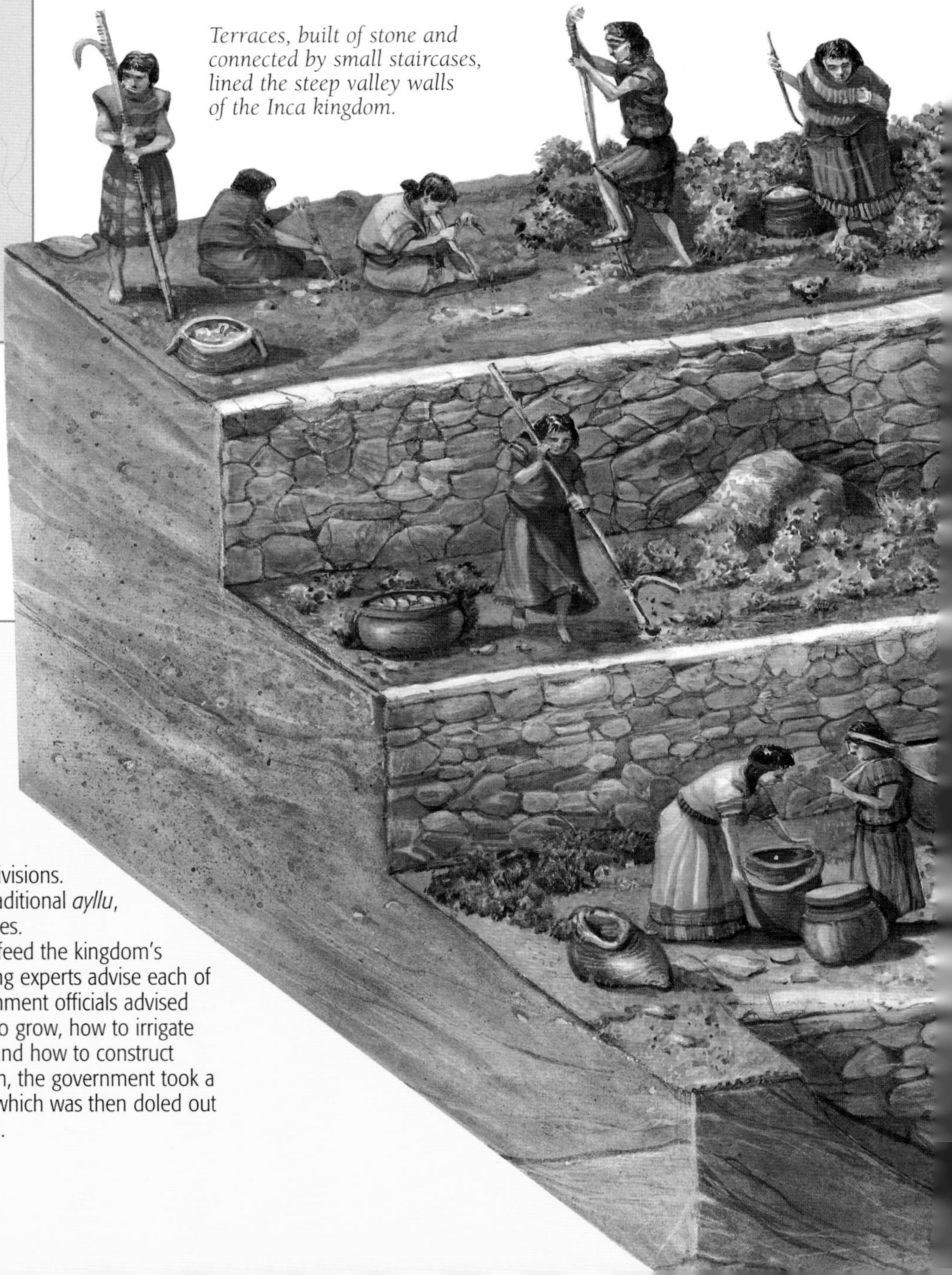

Terraces, built of stone and connected by small staircases, lined the steep valley walls of the Inca kingdom.

A pitchfork used to work the land. A plentiful harvest required lots of hard work. All members of the family shared the chores on the family plot.

High-Altitude Farming

Inca society had many subdivisions. An important one was the traditional *ayllu*, composed of groups of families. The government needed to feed the kingdom's population, so it had farming experts advise each of these subdivisions. Government officials advised farmers on which crops to grow, how to irrigate and fertilise their land, and how to construct stone terraces. In return, the government took a share of the harvest, which was then doled out where it was needed.

Mountain Animals

Alpacas, llamas, vicunas, and guanacos—all members of the camel family—were domesticated by the Andean people as early as 4500 BCE. These sure-footed mountain animals were ideal for carrying loads along steep and narrow mountain paths. They also provided a source of food and their wool was used to make clothing. Few other animals were domesticated, although the Inca and other Andean peoples ate guinea pigs as a source of protein.

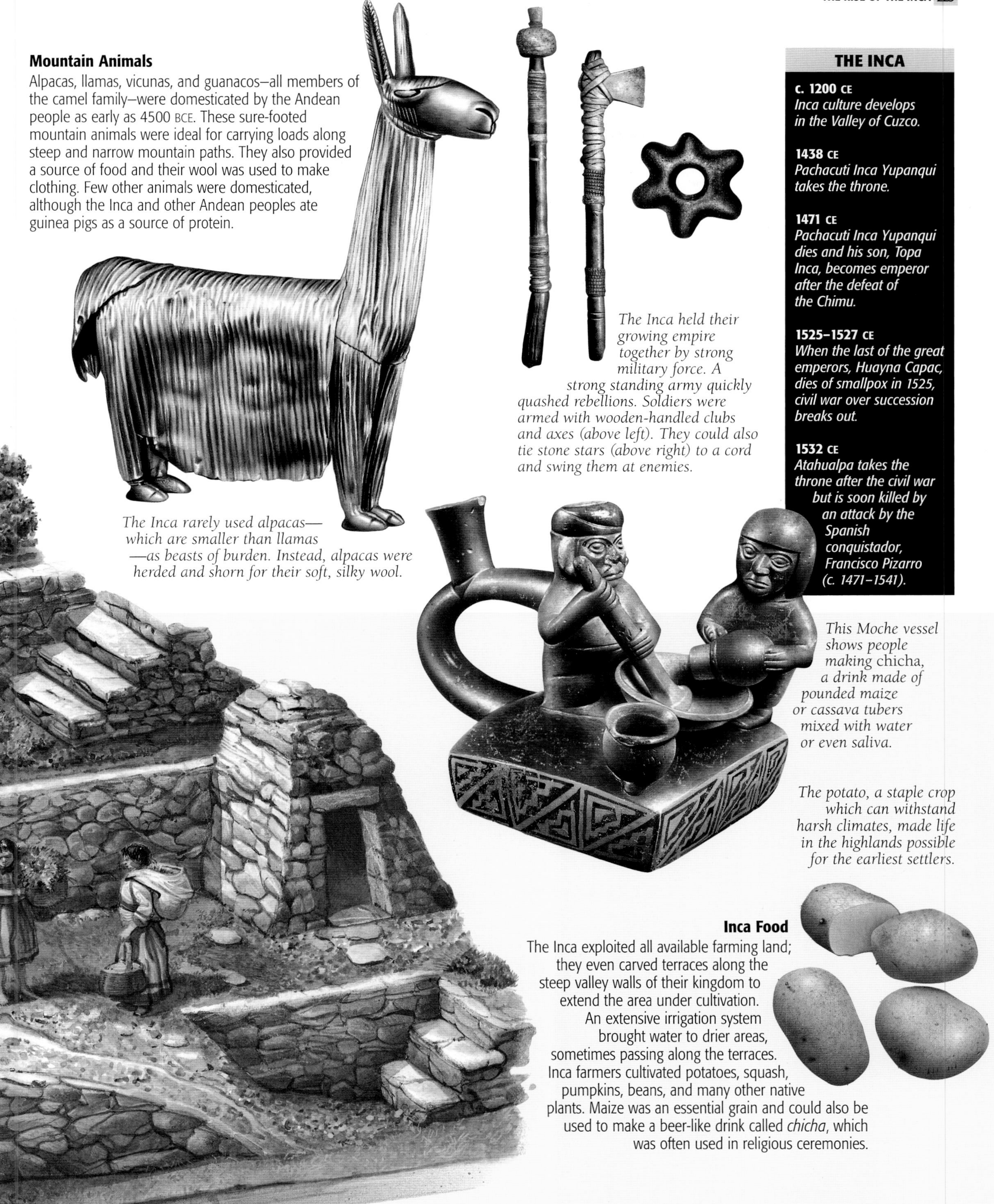

The Inca rarely used alpacas—which are smaller than llamas—as beasts of burden. Instead, alpacas were herded and shorn for their soft, silky wool.

The Inca held their growing empire together by strong military force. A strong standing army quickly quashed rebellions. Soldiers were armed with wooden-handled clubs and axes (above left). They could also tie stone stars (above right) to a cord and swing them at enemies.

THE INCA

c. 1200 CE
Inca culture develops in the Valley of Cuzco.

1438 CE
Pachacuti Inca Yupanqui takes the throne.

1471 CE
Pachacuti Inca Yupanqui dies and his son, Topa Inca, becomes emperor after the defeat of the Chimu.

1525–1527 CE
When the last of the great emperors, Huayna Capac, dies of smallpox in 1525, civil war over succession breaks out.

1532 CE
Atahualpa takes the throne after the civil war but is soon killed by an attack by the Spanish conquistador, Francisco Pizarro (c. 1471–1541).

This Moche vessel shows people making chicha, a drink made of pounded maize or cassava tubers mixed with water or even saliva.

The potato, a staple crop which can withstand harsh climates, made life in the highlands possible for the earliest settlers.

Inca Food

The Inca exploited all available farming land; they even carved terraces along the steep valley walls of their kingdom to extend the area under cultivation. An extensive irrigation system brought water to drier areas, sometimes passing along the terraces. Inca farmers cultivated potatoes, squash, pumpkins, beans, and many other native plants. Maize was an essential grain and could also be used to make a beer-like drink called *chicha*, which was often used in religious ceremonies.

Accounting System

Despite running the largest Pre-Columbian empire in the Americas, the Inca had no system of writing. Nevertheless, they were able to keep accurate accounts of government business with a system of knotted and colored strings called *quipus*. Using these *quipus*, government officials could keep track of population, gold production, harvests, and the labor tribute paid by the people of the kingdom. The Inca also painted accounting information on to beans or wove them into patterns on textiles.

The many knotted and colored strands of a quipu *conveyed detailed and accurate information about the business of the Inca Empire. Government messengers passed these* quipus *from remote districts back to the capital.*

Serving the State

The Inca—men and women alike—had to contribute to the government, usually in the form of labor that served as a form of tax. Men were called on to fight or to work on large building projects. Women worked as weavers or brewers. The Inca ruler rewarded workers with gifts of cloth produced at state workshops. He also provided food (gained as a farming tax) in times of shortage.

The finest fabric, cumbi, *was made by professional weavers as tax payment. It could only be used by Inca rulers. The checkerboard and triangle design on this tunic symbolizes bravery and high military rank.*

The Wealth of the Inca

Tales of abundant Inca gold attracted the Spanish to the Andes in the early 16th century. When the Inca ruler Atahualpa (reigned 1532–1533 CE) was held by the Spanish, the Inca easily filled a palace room with gold in a vain attempt to use it as the king's ransom. The Inca economy however valued labor over gold, which had a mainly spiritual, religious purpose. Most Inca gold was shipped to Europe after the Spanish conquest.

This gold figurine of a woman, which was found in a tomb, may have been made as a religious offering.

Inca Society and Religion

Governing a kingdom as large as that of the Inca required enormous political skills. Without a strong central government, conquered peoples would have been able to cut themselves off in remote Andean valleys and mount rebellions against Inca rule. To prevent this—and to ensure effective government—the Inca state was all-encompassing. Backed by the military might that had helped the Inca gain power, the government made sure that Inca society was highly structured. From the royal family downward, every person had a responsibility to the state, either through farming, government service, or in the army. The Inca kingdom had four main regions, which were further subdivided into local units. Government administrators operated at every level. Underpinning Inca society was a strong tradition of ancestor worship. Religion was highly formalized and the Sun was deified as the source of all life.

Mummification

The practice of mummification—helped by the dry air of the Andes—was already employed in the region for thousands of years before the Inca came to power. The Inca used this technique to preserve the bodies of their leaders, believing that their ancestors should be venerated. The mummified body of an emperor was treated with great respect, as though the emperor were still alive. It was kept in the royal palace and attended to by the emperor's descendants.

The Power of the Sun

Inca priests presided over a religion that had many rites and ceremonies, including human sacrifice. Inca beliefs stressed the importance of the Sun. Inti, the sun god, was the most important of the Inca deities, responsible for giving life and warmth to the land. The Inca believed that their rulers were descendants of Inti. The most important religious temple, located in the heart of the capital Cuzco, was dedicated to Inti.

This exquisite figurine was found near the body of a boy who was probably sacrificed to Inti.

The women depicted on this vase may represent priestesses who served as ceremonial brides of Inti and other gods.

During festivals the royal mummy, which was covered with fine garments and adorned with gold jewelry, would be taken out and carried in procession.

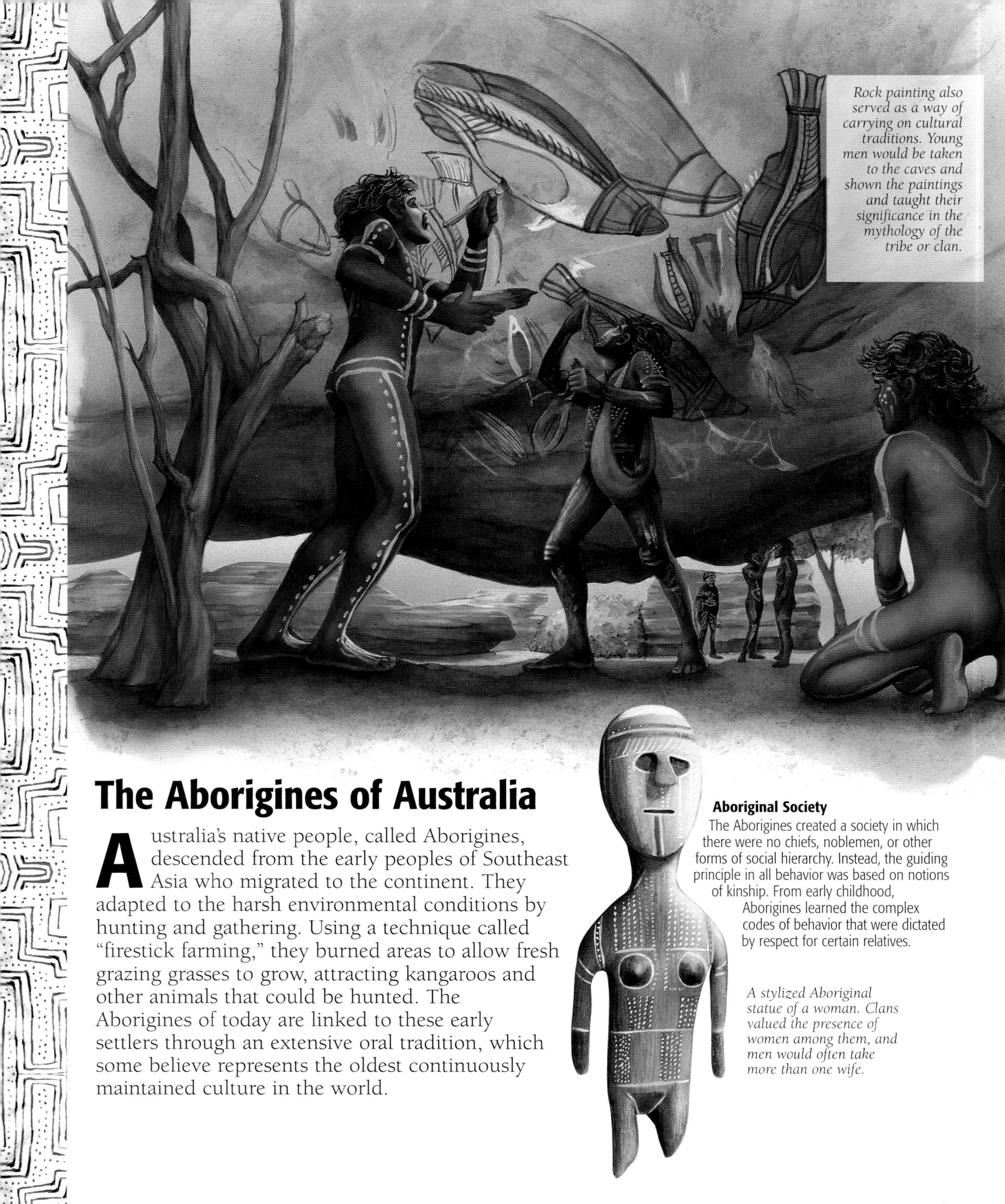

Rock painting also served as a way of carrying on cultural traditions. Young men would be taken to the caves and shown the paintings and taught their significance in the mythology of the tribe or clan.

The Aborigines of Australia

Australia's native people, called Aborigines, descended from the early peoples of Southeast Asia who migrated to the continent. They adapted to the harsh environmental conditions by hunting and gathering. Using a technique called "firestick farming," they burned areas to allow fresh grazing grasses to grow, attracting kangaroos and other animals that could be hunted. The Aborigines of today are linked to these early settlers through an extensive oral tradition, which some believe represents the oldest continuously maintained culture in the world.

Aboriginal Society

The Aborigines created a society in which there were no chiefs, noblemen, or other forms of social hierarchy. Instead, the guiding principle in all behavior was based on notions of kinship. From early childhood, Aborigines learned the complex codes of behavior that were dictated by respect for certain relatives.

A stylized Aboriginal statue of a woman. Clans valued the presence of women among them, and men would often take more than one wife.

Rock Painters

The Aborigines used natural pigments to create painted images on rock walls, usually in caves or rocky overhangs where they took shelter. The walls were sometimes decorated with engravings. These images were tied to the Dreamtime myths and combined realistic portrayals of hunters and prey with more abstract, geometric designs. The less realistic aspects of these rock paintings is believed to be linked to magical qualities inherent in the spirit creatures, qualities that can bestow luck on hunting or other human activities.

The nomadic Aborigines enjoyed the chance to trade goods, such as this mother-of-pearl pendant, with other groups when they met on social occasions.

Bark painting was one of the most common forms of Aboriginal artistic expression. Like other art forms, such as music and dance, painting had a spiritual dimension. This painting stresses the spirit of the hunted emus rather than their physical appearance.

Aboriginal Festivals

When food was plentiful, groups of hundreds of Aborigines would join together for social gatherings called *corroborees*. Singing and dancing were the main features of these gatherings, with men from different groups or clans showing off their dancing skills to the beat of clapping, singing, or the music of the didgeridoo.

The didgeridoo, made from a hollow log, was widely played in gatherings in northern Australia. It was also associated with ceremonial music.

Boomerangs designed to return to the thrower were lighter than the hunting versions. Aborigines used them for amusement or to frighten birds into nets laid as traps.

Hunting and Weapons

Hunting and gathering were the source of food for Aborigines. Men were skilled at tracking prey such as kangaroos, wallabies, and emus over long distances. They would kill the animal by throwing clubs, woomeras, or boomerangs. Aborigines also built fish traps in rivers and lakes. Women did most of the food gathering, using stone axes to reach small mammals, birds' eggs, and bees' nests in hollow trees. People also gathered nuts, berries, and other fruit.

THE ABORIGINES

c. 40,000 years ago
People migrating from Asia become the first settlers of Australia.

c. 30,000 years ago
Most parts of Australia are settled by the Aborigines.

c. 25,000 years ago
Harsh climatic conditions cause Aborigines to abandon the arid interior of Australia, reoccupying it 10,000 years later when conditions improved.

c. 13,500–8,000 years ago
Rising sea levels cause Tasmania to become an island, isolating the Aboriginal population from the mainland.

c. 2000 BCE
The Aborigines introduce the dingo, or domesticated dog, to Australia. At the same time, they begin to use small, flaked stone tools.

1788 CE
At the time of the first European settlement, Aboriginal culture had diversified, with more than 200 languages spoken.

MIGRATIONS TO AUSTRALIA

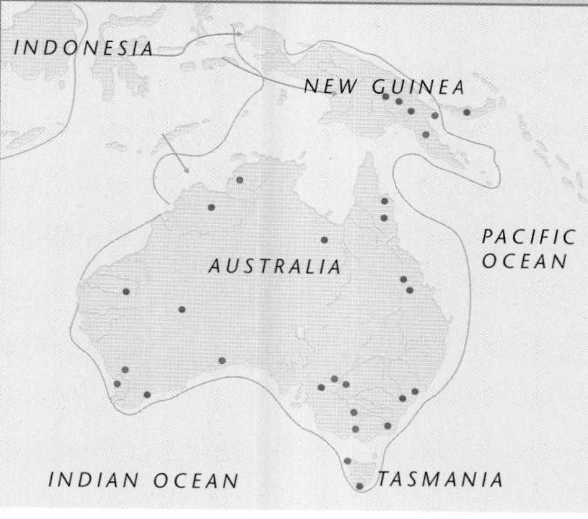

Maximum extent of Sunda Landmass c. 20,000 BCE
Maximum extent of Sahul Landmass c. 20,000 BCE
Probable migration routes
Human presence before 20,000 BCE
Human presence after 20,000 BCE

Populating the Continent
Asian settlers were the first human inhabitants of Australia, arriving around 40,000 years ago, although some evidence suggests that they arrived long before –perhaps as early as 60,000 years ago. Lower sea levels at that time shortened the sea crossing distance between the Sunda landmass (Asia) and the Sahul landmass (Australia and New Guinea).

The Dreamtime

Aboriginal religious belief centers on the idea of Dreamtime, a complex view of the world that combines the past, present, and future. They believe that mythic creatures created the Earth and all life, leaving behind a set of rules on how to preserve this legacy. Aboriginal religion and art carries on the traditions and ceremonial duties associated with Dreamtime.

This bark painting depicts a Wandjina, an ancestral being associated with the Dreamtime and believed to control rainfall and the fertility of animals.

THE PACIFIC

c. 40,000–60,000 years ago
The first people sail from Southeast Asia to Australia and New Guinea.

c. 28,000 years ago
Sailors from northern New Guinea voyage east and settle in the Solomon Islands.

c. 3,500 years ago
Settlers from Southeast Asia settle the group of islands in the Bismarck Sea and then move eastward to settle Fiji, Tonga, and Samoa in central Polynesia.

c. 600 BCE
The Society Islands, the group containing Tahiti, in eastern Polynesia, are settled.

c. 600–1250 CE
Polynesians from Tahiti, Marquesas, and other eastern islands sail more than 2,000 miles (3,200 km) to settle the Hawaiian Islands.

1521 CE
Portuguese explorer Ferdinand Magellan (c. 1480–1521), on his round-the-world voyage, becomes the first European to travel through Oceania.

Pigs were an important commodity and were only killed on special occasions. They were slaughtered with special hammers like this one from Vanuatu (in Melanesia), carved with two ancestral faces—one facing down at the pig and the other facing up at the holder.

THE PACIFIC

The Divisions of Oceania
The Pacific, largest of the Earth's oceans, covers more than a third of the surface of the planet. Oceania is subdivided into three main areas. Melanesia includes the large island of New Guinea and other islands in the western Pacific south of the Equator. Micronesia lies in the northwest of Oceania as far north as the Tropic of Cancer. Polynesia covers the vast southern and southeastern area of Oceania. It makes up a huge triangle, with New Zealand, Hawaii, and Easter Island considered to be the three points. Most of Oceania has a tropical climate, with regular heavy rain, although the northeast is drier but prone to sporadic fierce storms.

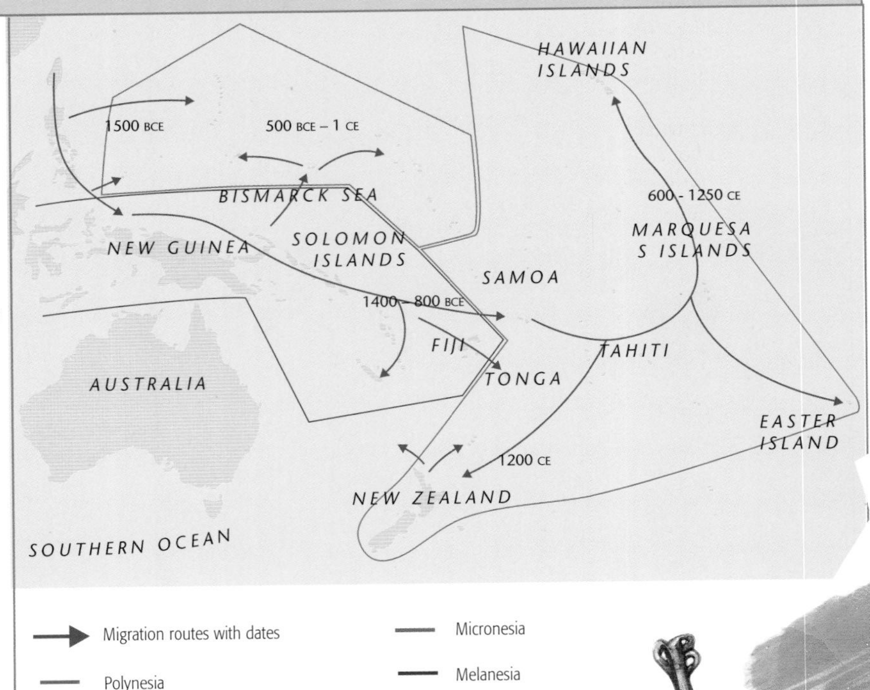

Ancestor Worship
Despite being dispersed across a vast region, the inhabitants of Polynesia had a number of cultural similarities. Chief among these was ancestor worship. This formed the core of religious beliefs and practices on the islands. People believed that the spirits of the dead were spiritual beings that could still play a part in everyday life. They would keep reminders of dead relatives to consult on important matters.

The Pacific Islands

Volcanic activity produced—and continues to shape—many of the islands of the Pacific Ocean. There are more than 30,000 islands, most of them small or of moderate size. Together, these islands are known as Oceania. Some islands, such as Tahiti and the Hawaiian Islands, are actually the tips of huge mountains that rise up from the sea floor. Others, called atolls, are ring-shaped coral reefs which once surrounded a mountain that has sunk back into the sea. The far western islands (near New Guinea) of this vast collection of scattered islands were the first to be settled between 40,000 and 60,000 years ago.

The people of New Guinea believed that a dead person's skull provided a link between that person's spirit and the present. Skulls were ritually washed and adorned with feathers and colorful shells.

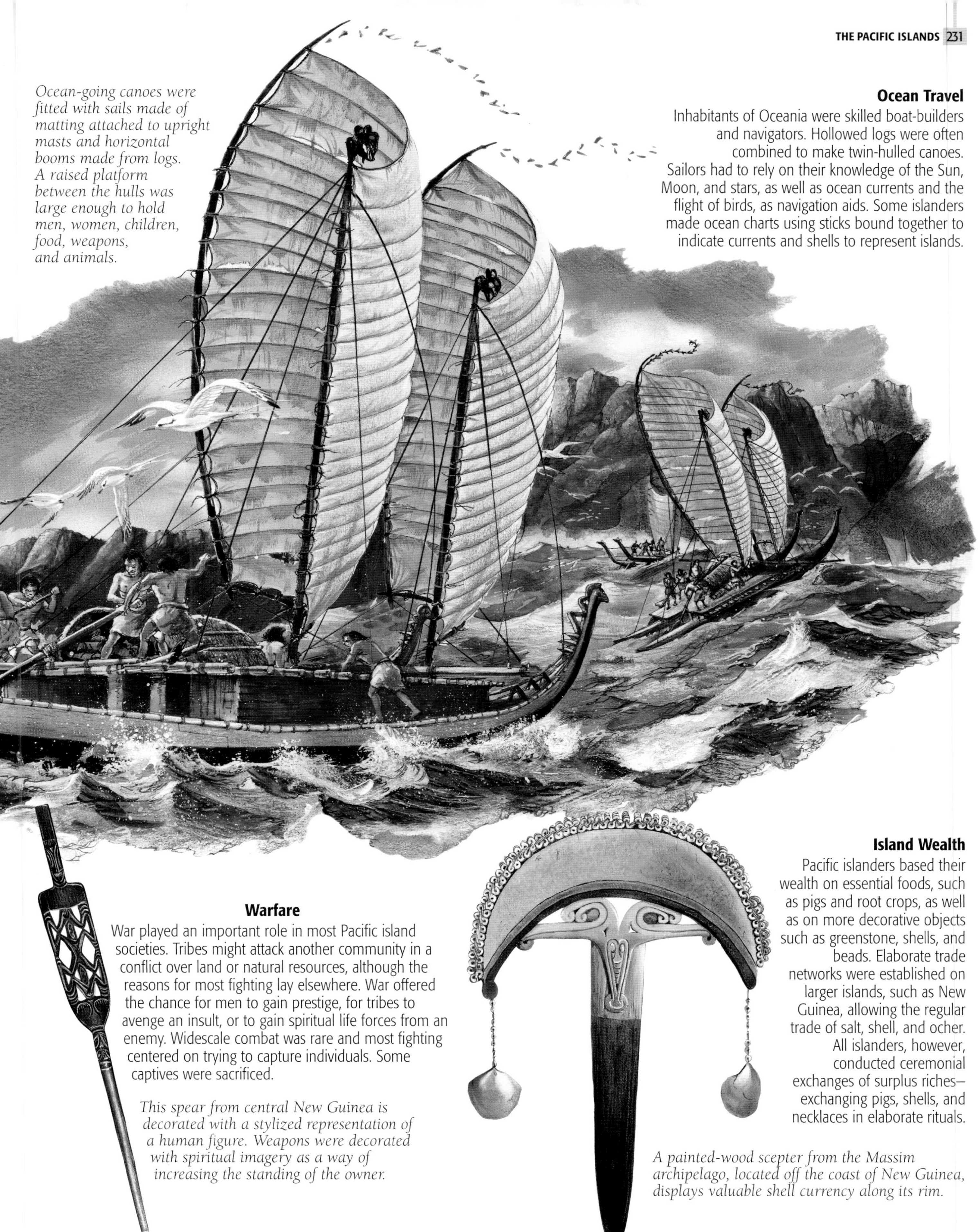

Ocean-going canoes were fitted with sails made of matting attached to upright masts and horizontal booms made from logs. A raised platform between the hulls was large enough to hold men, women, children, food, weapons, and animals.

Ocean Travel

Inhabitants of Oceania were skilled boat-builders and navigators. Hollowed logs were often combined to make twin-hulled canoes. Sailors had to rely on their knowledge of the Sun, Moon, and stars, as well as ocean currents and the flight of birds, as navigation aids. Some islanders made ocean charts using sticks bound together to indicate currents and shells to represent islands.

Warfare

War played an important role in most Pacific island societies. Tribes might attack another community in a conflict over land or natural resources, although the reasons for most fighting lay elsewhere. War offered the chance for men to gain prestige, for tribes to avenge an insult, or to gain spiritual life forces from an enemy. Widescale combat was rare and most fighting centered on trying to capture individuals. Some captives were sacrificed.

This spear from central New Guinea is decorated with a stylized representation of a human figure. Weapons were decorated with spiritual imagery as a way of increasing the standing of the owner.

Island Wealth

Pacific islanders based their wealth on essential foods, such as pigs and root crops, as well as on more decorative objects such as greenstone, shells, and beads. Elaborate trade networks were established on larger islands, such as New Guinea, allowing the regular trade of salt, shell, and ocher. All islanders, however, conducted ceremonial exchanges of surplus riches—exchanging pigs, shells, and necklaces in elaborate rituals.

A painted-wood scepter from the Massim archipelago, located off the coast of New Guinea, displays valuable shell currency along its rim.

The Maori of New Zealand

The native inhabitants of New Zealand—the Maori—arrived around 800 years ago. The Maori brought with them the domesticated Polynesian dog along with important food plants such as the kumara (sweet potato), taro, and yam. As well as cultivating these staple crops, the Maori adapted to their new surroundings by hunting and fishing. Their culture was warlike, with an emphasis on pride and honor. Insults, often arising from long-standing feuds, were avenged violently. All men were warriors, who prepared for battle with the ceremonial *haka* dance. As a result, the Maori fortified their towns against attack.

The Maori built large baskets to trap fish along the coast and in rivers.

The wooden stern piece of a Maori canoe. The Maori valued their canoes highly and decorated them with traditional circular motifs.

The Maori Arrive in New Zealand

Archeology indicates that New Zealand was settled by the Maori in about 1200 CE. They arrived from central Polynesia, perhaps the Cook or Society Islands. Several canoes might have been involved in the early voyages.

Maori Villages

With warfare so common, the Maori tribes would build a stockaded defensive area called a *pa*, where villagers could congregate during fighting. Ditches and banks added to the defensive strength of a *pa*. Residential houses were built in the more open village, called a *kainga*. Houses in the *kainga* all surrounded a public plaza. Villages also had a *pataka*, or storehouse for preserved foods and weapons. Carvings on the *pataka* honored village ancestors and celebrated the status of the chief.

EARLY SETTLEMENT OF NEW ZEALAND

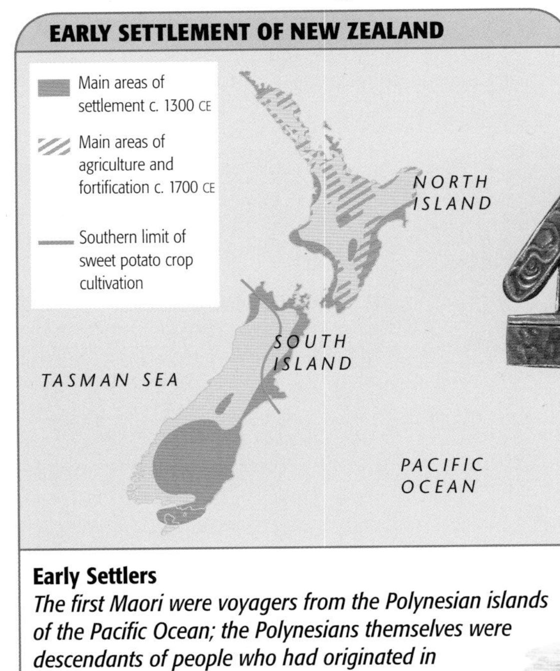

Early Settlers

The first Maori were voyagers from the Polynesian islands of the Pacific Ocean; the Polynesians themselves were descendants of people who had originated in Southeast Asia.

The village pataka stood on raised piles, several feet off the ground, and was located in the central plaza, or marae. The pataka had special significance for the Maori, who rated it second only to war canoes in terms of social status.

THE MAORI

c. 1200 CE
The first permanent settlers, Polynesian navigators from the Pacific region, arrive in New Zealand and establish the Maori culture. They arrive in large, ocean-going canoes and establish coastal settlements, especially along the temperate east coast.

c. 1500 CE
The Maori construct over 5,000 earthwork pa *in the North Island and northern South Island. Many of these still survive today.*

c. 1350 CE
Maori tradition cites this time as the date of the "great fleet" of canoes bringing large numbers of new immigrants from Polynesia.

Late 18th and early 19th centuries
European whalers and missionaries establish the first white settlements in New Zealand. They are opposed–often fiercely–by neighboring Maori.

The Maori hunted moas, New Zealand's flightless birds, to extinction.

Maori Hunters

When the early peoples settled in New Zealand, large, flightless birds similar to ostriches, called moas, inhabited the land. Some of the largest moas were up to 6.6 feet (2 m) high. The moas were hunted by the Maori settlers who were probably armed with spears and hunting dogs. Moas provided not only a good source of food, but their bones were used to make weapons, tools, and jewelry.

Facial Decoration

Men of high social standing often had tattoos on their thighs and faces. The circular designs of head tattoos, unique to New Zealand, had symbolic significance. Tattoo artists were highly respected, and were considered *tapu*, or sacred. They used bone chisels to dig patterns in the skin and then rubbed in soot to make the designs permanent.

A carved wooden head displays the distinctive circular facial decorations of the Maori.

Artwork

Wood carving was subject to *tapu*, the spiritual rules placing restrictions on aspects of Maori life. Felling trees was considered to be cutting down a descendant of the god of forests and humanity; even woodchips falling from carving could not be burned or discarded. The lizard was the principal feature in Maori carving. Craftsmen also shaped greenstone from the South Island for use as tools, war clubs, and pendants.

Distinctive Maori hei tiki *pendants were carved from greenstone. The human-like figure was considered to have great power.*

Glossary

Acupuncture A method of treating disease and easing pain by inserting needles in certain parts of the body.

Aeon (also spelt eon) A unit of time too long to measure. A unit of time in the history of the world which is broken down into smaller units called eras.

Alloy A mixture of two or more different metals, usually to make a new or stronger metal. Bronze, which is made by mixing, or alloying, copper and tin, is stronger and easier to work than copper.

Amphitheater An open-air building, usually round or oval, with seating built for the viewing of sports or other events taking place in the center of the structure. The Colosseum in Rome is an example of an amphitheater.

Amulet An object or charm that is worn by a person because it is believed to keep away bad luck or evil.

Aqueduct A system of channels, pipes, bridges, and canals which carries water to a town or city.

Archeology The science which studies the remains of ancient peoples, such as tools, weapons, pots, and buildings, to learn more about cultures of the distant past.

Astronomy The scientific study of the Sun, Moon, and stars and other heavenly bodies.

Bacteria Small forms of life composed of a single cell that can be seen only with a microscope, usually found in decaying matter.

Barbarian Term used in a negative way, meaning rude or uncivilized, to describe any foreigners or people who do not share a similar culture.

Barrow A mound of earth built over a burial site.

Bipedal Term used to describe animals that walk on their hind limbs.

Bronze Age The period in human development following the Stone Age in which people used bronze to make weapons and tools.

Citadel A fortress or an armed, commanding city built to act as a place of safety and defence.

Clan A group of people belonging to the same tribe who are related or share a common ancestor.

Codex (plural codices) A handwritten book or set of manuscripts from ancient times.

Colony An area or region controlled and settled by a group of people from a distant country.

Commodity A valuable item usually traded for other goods or sold for profit.

Confederation A group of states united for political reasons.

Cremation The act of burning a corpse to ashes.

Crop A plant or its product, such as grain, fruit or vegetables, grown by farmers.

Delta A triangle-shaped area of land near a river where the waters flow into the sea.

Democracy A form of government where ruling representatives are elected by the people.

Dictatorship A form of government in which one person exercises arbitrary authority.

Diviner A person believed to have the ability to tell the future.

Dolmen A simple structure made of upright stones which support a large stone slab.

Domesticate To tame and bring animals and plants under control so that they can live with and be of use to people.

Dyke A thick wall built to hold back the flow of water.

Dynasty A line of rulers coming from the same family, or a period during which they reign.

Effigy A representation of a person or spirit used for ritual purpose.

Embankment A mound of earth or stone built to hold back the flow of water.

Envoy A messenger sent by a government on a special mission and who acts as a representative of the government or state.

Epic A long poem which tells the story of gods and heroes or the history of a nation or people.

Epoch A unit of time in the history of the Earth during which specific events or development occurs. Two or more epochs make up a period.

Era A set of years or a unit of time in the history of the Earth beginning and ending at specific point in time, usually characterized by particular circumstances or events. An era is made up of two or more periods.

Extinct Term used to describe species of animals or plants that have died out.

Faience Glossy, hard blue or green substance made by heating a mixture of quartz sand with salts and copper powder.

Feudal system A social organization in which people held and worked the land owned by a lord who demanded military service in return.

Fibula A clasp or buckle used to fasten clothing worn in ancient times, often ornamented.

Forage To search for and collect food.

Fossil The remains or trace of an organism of the distant past, such as a hardened part or an imprint, embedded in the Earth's crust.

Geological Term used to describe anything of or pertaining to the Earth's history.

Geometric Term used to describe something decorated with or having the form of simple shapes such as squares, triangles and circles.

Griffin A mythological creature with the head and wings of an eagle and the body of a lion.

Halberd A combined spear and battleaxe.

Herbivore An animal that eats only plants.

Hereditary Something that is passed on from parent to child.

Hierarchy A classification system in which people or things are given higher and lower rank or importance.

Hieroglyph A symbol used to represent a word or idea.

Hippodrome A stadium with an oval track where horse and chariot races are held.

Hominid A human-like primate which walks on two legs. The only hominid species alive today is Homo sapiens, the species to which modern humans belong.

Ice Age A period of Earth's history in which huge sheets of ice cover a vast part of the Earth's surface.

Iron Age The period in human development following the Bronze Age in which people used iron to make weapons and tools.

Irrigation The process of bringing water to fields.

Kiln An oven used for baking, hardening, or drying materials such as grain, clay, or ceramics.

Krater A wide bowl with handles used by Greeks and Romans for mixing wine and water.

Labyrinth A structure of many confusing passages made in such a way so that it is difficult for a person to find his or her way out.

Mace A short heavy stick used as a weapon in ancient times.

Megalith A huge stone, usually standing, used in the construction of prehistoric monuments.

Mercenary A paid professional soldier who fights for a foreign country.

Metal Ages The periods in human development following the Stone Age in which people used metals, namely copper, bronze, and iron, to make weapons and tools. (See also Bronze Age and Iron Age).

Missionary One who is sent on a mission to a foreign land to educate or convert people to a particular religion.

Moat A deep wide ditch, usually filled with water, dug around a castle or fortress as protection from outside invasion.

Molten Melted, or in a liquid state under a very high temperature.

Mummification The process of preserving a dead body to prevent it from decaying.

Neolithic Term meaning "new stone" which is used to describe objects of or pertaining to the later part of the Stone Age.

Nomad A member of a tribe that travels from place to place in search of pastures for animals. A person who wanders and does not settle down in any particular place.

Omen A message or an event believed to be a sign of a future event.

Oracle A sacred place where questions about the future are answered. A person, such as a priest or a priestess, who speaks for a god, answering questions about future events, usually in riddles.

Orator A person who makes public speeches.

Ore Rock or earth from which a precious or useful metal can be obtained.

Phalanx A group of foot soldiers who march very close together so that their spears overlap and their shields join to form a protective barrier.

Pictograph A picture representing a word or idea.

Pigment Any colored substance used to make paint or a colored mixture. A natural substance which gives color to plants and animals.

Plain A vast or large, flat, area of land, usually without trees.

Pre-Columbian Word used to describe culture, peoples, or society in the Americas before the arrival of Christopher Columbus (1451–1506).

Primate A highly developed placental mammal with flexible hands and feet and a large brain.

Province One of many divisions of a state made by a government to have better control over the territory.

Pyramid A large, four-sided triangular stone building constructed in ancient times.

Relic An object that has survived from the past and is kept for its spiritual or historical significance. A sacred object, such as a part of the body or an object, that once belonged to a holy person.

Sarcophagus A container made to store dead bodies, usually made of stone.

Sceptre A short stick or cane carried by a king or ruler on ceremonial occasions as a symbol of his or her power and authority.

Scribe In ancient times, a person who wrote down or recorded important events. A person who copied important documents---.

Shaman A priest who is believed to be able to contact the spirit world and who practices magic to heal, predict the future, and control natural events.

Smelting The process of melting down earth (or an ore) in order to separate and extract its metallic parts.

Soothsayer A person believed to have the ability to predict future events.

Species A group of related organisms which share important characteristics and are given a common name. An organism belonging to such a group.

Sphinx A mythological creature, sometimes winged, with the body of a lion and the head of a human.

Stele A stone slab or piece of stone, generally carved with an inscription or design.

Steppe One of the large areas of flat, tree-less land of southeastern Europe and Siberia.

Stone Age The early period in human development before the Metal Ages when people used only stone to make weapons and tools.

Stupa A dome-shaped monument built to store Buddhist relics.

Tactician A clever person, usually a military officer, who knows how to lead army or naval forces to get desired results.

Treaty An agreement made between two or more states to make peace or settle a dispute. The actual document upon which the agreement is recorded.

Trident A long fork-like weapon with three sharp pointed prongs.

Vizier A chief minister of ancient Egypt or a high government officer in a Muslim country.

Wadi A river which sometimes runs dry.

Ziggurat An ancient Mesopotamian stepped pyramid-like structure with a temple on top.

Index

PICTURE CREDITS

All efforts have been made to obtain and provide compensation for the copyright to the photos and illustrations in this book in accordance with legal provisions. Persons who may nevertheless still have claims are requested to contact the copyright owners.

MAIN ILLUSTRATIONS: Alessandro Baldanzi p. 224–225; Emmanuelle Etienne pp. 130–131, 142–143; Valeria Ferretti pp. 18–19, 26–27, 38–39; Giacinto Gaudenzi pp. 100–101, 126, 144–145, 187, 188–189, 218–219; Paolo Ghirardi pp. 94–95; MM comunicazione (Manuela Cappon, Monica Favilli) pp. 40–41, 48–49, 50–51, 52–53, 55, 69, 72–73, 76–77, 90–91, 103, 108–109, 110–111, 113, 134–135, 150–151, 198–199, 204–205, 216–217, 227; Alessandro Menchi pp. 80–81, 104–105, 156–156, 192–193; Leonardo Meschini pp. 98–99, 172–173, 182–183; Francesca D'Ottavi pp. 42–43, 44, 154–155; Luisa della Porta pp. 146; Antonella Pastorelli p. 21, 62–63, 66–67, 78–79, 86–87; Paola Ravaglia pp. 36–37, 106–107, 117, 133, 148–149, 168–169, 208–209; Claudia Saraceni pp. 60–61, 74–75, 120–121, 160–161, 200–201, 212–213, 228, 233; Sergio pp. 22–23, 24–25, 30–31, 34–35, 56–57, 92–93, 170–171; Studio Stalio (Ivan Stalio, Alessandro Cantucci, Fabiano Fabbrucci, Margherita Salvadori) pp. 9, 10–11, 12–13, 14–15, 16–17

SMALLER ILLUSTRATIONS: Studio Stalio (Alessandro Cantucci, Fabiano Fabbrucci, Margherita Salvadori)

MAPS: Paola Baldanzi

PHOTOS: Bridgeman Art Library, London/Farabola Foto, Milan p.30t, 89; Corbis/Contrasto, Milan pp. 59t, 70–71b, 83b, 114b, 124–125b ©Adam Woolfitt, 166b ©Richard A. Cooke, 176–177b ©Asian Art & Archaeology Inc, 190–191 ©Charles E. Rotkin, 211b ©Charles & Josette Lenars, 223t ©Yann Arthus-Bertrand; Frank Teichmann, Stuttgart p. 90tr; Foto Scala, Florence pp. 118–119b, 138r, 140–14; Werner Forman/Art Resource, NY pp. 184b